JUSTICE and PEACE

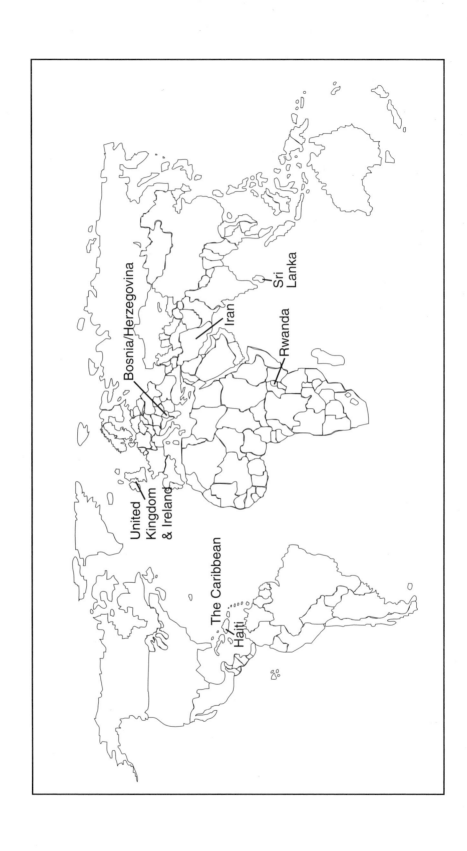

JUSTICE and PEACE

A Christian Primer

J. Milburn Thompson

ORBIS BOOKS

Maryknoll, New York 10545

Fifth Printing, September 2000

The Catholic Foreign Mission Society of America (Maryknoll) recruits and trains people for overseas missionary service. Through Orbis Books, Maryknoll aims to foster the international dialogue that is essential to mission. The books published, however, reflect the opinions of their authors and are not meant to represent the official position of the society.

Published by Orbis Books, Maryknoll, NY 10545-0308
Manufactured in the United States of America

Library of Congress Cataloging-in-Publication Data

Thompson, Joseph Milburn, 1947–
    Justice and peace : a Christian primer / J. Milburn Thompson.
        p.   cm.
    Includes bibliographical references.
    ISBN 1-57075-141-2 (pbk.)
    1. Christianity and justice. 2. Social justice. 3. Peace—Religious aspects—Christianity. I. Title.
    BR115. JBT46 1997
    261.8—dc21   97-35485
                                                                              CIP

To my parents, Joe and Dorothy Thompson

Contents

Permissions

Excerpt from *The Great Ascent: The Struggle for Economic Development in Our Time* by Robert L. Heilbroner, copyright © 1963, reprinted with permission of HarperCollins Publishers.

From *The Fate of the Earth* by Jonathan Schell, copyright © 1982, by Jonathan Schell. Reprinted by permission of Alfred A. Knopf, Inc. and Jonathan Cape (U.K.). Originally appeared in "The New Yorker."

Figure 4.1 from "Moral Claims, Human Rights, and Population Policies," by the Yale Task Force on Population Ethics, copyright ©1974, reprinted with permission of *Theological Studies*.

Table on "America's Political/Economic Choices," from *Peace and Change* in a review by Seymour Melman, copyright © 1993, reprinted with permission of Blackwell Publications Company.

Data in the tables in the Appendix from *World Resources 1996–97* database diskettes, copyright © 1996, reprinted with permission of the World Resources Institute.

Data in the tables in the Appendix from *Human Development Report 1996*, copyright © 1996 by the United Nations Development Programme, reprinted with permission of Oxford University Press.

Introduction

"Peace is both a gift of God and a human work. It must be constructed on the basis of central human values: truth, justice, freedom, and love."[1]

"The life and words of Jesus and the teaching of his Church call us to serve those in need and to work actively for social and economic justice. As a community of believers, we know that our faith is tested by the quality of justice among us, that we can best measure our life together by how the poor and the vulnerable are treated."[2]

The world changed dramatically at the beginning of the 1990s. With the collapse of communism in Europe, symbolized by the fall of the Berlin Wall in 1989, we entered the post-Cold War world. This has meant that humanity is faced with different problems, rather than fewer problems.

Because of the dramatic change in global politics, now is a good time to study international relations and foreign policy. Indeed, this new situation calls for fresh faces and innovative thinking to replace the outmoded perspectives developed during the Cold War (1945–1991).

OBJECTIVES AND AUDIENCE

This is a starter book, a primer. It is written for college students, thoughtful Christians, and anyone who is concerned about global issues and wants to learn more. It is intended for budding scholars, not established experts. It strives to be scholarly in the sense of being well-researched, accurate, and balanced in seeking the truth. Its scope precludes any pretense of making major contributions to the understanding or the solution of the myriad problems it reviews. It hopes to inform citizens well enough that they can be active participants in public policy debates and catalysts for constructive change in the contemporary world. Participation and transformation are the responsibilities of citizens in a democracy, and certainly of Christian citizens.

This is therefore a getting-started book as well.[3] Information, understanding, and rigorous critical analysis are necessary first steps for creating a more just and peaceful world. Analysis, however, is not sufficient; society needs to be changed.

Public policy primarily reflects values and interests. For example, should the alleviation of global hunger be a goal of foreign policy or is national self-interest its only objective? Should a particular piece of legislation serve the basic needs of the poor or the welfare of corporations? These are fundamentally questions about values and interests. Once one decides which values public policy should serve, it remains complex and often controversial to translate those values into appropriate policies. Citizens, however, can and should participate in the discussion and in the development of policies and systems. When citizens "leave it to the experts," they simply ensure that the expert's values and interests become policy.

Any analysis of American foreign policy and of the global situation must be undertaken from some perspective. Every analyst, whether located in the Pentagon, a university, or the local café, brings assumptions, values, goals, and objectives to debates about international relations. This book brings a Christian perspective to bear on the world situation.

A Christian perspective is grounded in the conviction that God is sovereign and that God's rule is loving and just. In creating human beings in God's own image, God has bestowed upon each and every person an intrinsic dignity and an infinite value. This human dignity is nourished and developed in community. Humanity is God's people—a family—called to love and care for one another and for the Earth. As co-creators with God, human beings are responsible for creating a just community conducive to the flowering of each person's potential.

Such a perspective means that an analysis of the contemporary global situation is important. Christians are called to care for brothers and sisters, near and far. Christians should be concerned about what public policies do for and to people. There should be no gulf between faith (the relationship with God) and everyday life.[4] Christians are called to live their faith in the world, and this means that politics, economics, and social policy are significant.

This study will operate on three interrelated levels. The first level focuses on the reality of the situation. The first step is to ask what ethicist Daniel Maguire calls "reality revealing questions."[5] What is going on? Who is doing what to whom? The goal here is to seek information and gather the facts.

The second level involves analysis and evaluation. Here the task is interpretation. One's perspective is brought to bear on the facts, seeking insight and surfacing possible solutions. What are the causes of this problem? What are the objectives and consequences of various solutions? Analysis is complex, and there will be differences of opinion. Often disagreements are rooted in the values and interests that are brought to the analysis. For example, nearly everyone agrees that there is a need for national welfare reform. The differences in the proposals for welfare reform are rooted both in different values and goals—to enable poor children to reach their full potential versus to balance the budget, for example—and in different analyses as to the causes of the problem and the consequences of various solutions.

The third level moves to commitment and action. Reasonable solutions must be sought and implemented; strategies for change need to be devised and deployed. This, too, is complex, difficult, and often frustrating. Sometimes creative solutions fail to be realized. Other times solutions fall short of resolving the problem or bring with them new problems. There are times, too, when remedies work, and real change can be celebrated. Obviously this process of reflection and action is ongoing, as Christians move in faith and hope toward the Kingdom God has promised.

There is a spiritual dimension that corresponds to this conceptual and ethical framework. Peace activist Ammon Hennacy once wrote:

> Love without courage and wisdom is sentimentality, as with the ordinary church member. Courage without love and wisdom is foolhardiness, as with the ordinary soldier. Wisdom without love and courage is cowardice, as with the ordinary intellectual. Therefore one with love, courage, and wisdom is one in a million, who moves the world, as with Jesus, Buddha, and Gandhi.[6]

The Eastern Christian tradition repeats the Jesus Prayer, "Lord Jesus Christ, Son of the living God, have mercy on me, a sinner," as a sort of centering mantra. A substitute, based on the quote from Ammon Hennacy, might be, "God, my mother, teach me the compassion, the wisdom, and the courage of your heart."

These three virtues correspond helpfully to the three levels of social analysis. A compassionate heart is essential for seeing those who are poor and suffering in our midst. Without compassion a statistic such as "one in every four American children is poor" elicits only indifference and apathy. Compassion is essential, yet unless we pause to seek wisdom—to gather information and interpret it carefully—we may do more harm than good. And without the courage to raise our voices and to get our hands dirty in the struggle to change society, compassion lapses into mere sentimentality, and wisdom is academic in the worst sense. Compassion, wisdom, and courage give a spiritual dimension to the seeing, judging, and acting[7] that are essential for social analysis.

This book, then, is an introduction to the obstacles to justice and peace posed by the post-Cold War world.[8] It seeks to inform the reader through a critical analysis of the pressing problems facing humanity at the dawn of the twenty-first century, and to transform both the reader and the world.

The book begins by tracing the major trends in the development of the post-Cold War world—colonialism, the industrial/technological revolution, and the Cold War and its end. Succeeding chapters focus on the obstacles to a more just and peaceful world: the gap between the rich and the poor, the population explosion and environmental destruction, violations of human rights, ethno-nationalist conflict, weapons of mass destruction and the trade in arms, and an inadequate theory of international relations as well as an unclear foreign policy. The final chapter of the book reflects directly on the Christian perspective and on the meaning of Christian citizenship. Resources for action on behalf of justice and peace and for further study are provided. Although the book focuses on global issues and foreign policy, it also attends to related domestic issues.

This organization of the book makes sense, but the chapters could easily be organized differently. The final chapter on the Christian perspective could come first or second. While it makes sense to read the historical chapter before the chapters on issues, the latter could be rearranged in many different ways. Although those chapters are somewhat interconnected, each could stand on its own, and the reader (or teacher) might want to impose his or her own order on these topics. Not only is humanity interdependent, but the issues facing humanity are deeply interrelated. Each of the issues addressed here, for example, is a genuine "security" issue, a threat to peace. The words of Pope Paul VI point to the interrelated themes of the book, "If you want peace, work for justice."

The study questions after each chapter aim to stimulate further discussion of the issues raised in the text rather than test comprehension of the material. The "For Reflection" sidebars in the text are also to provoke reflection and discussion.

ACKNOWLEDGMENTS

Teaching and learning is a communal activity. I have presented this material in the classroom for over twenty years. The responses of students have refined these ideas and transformed me again and again. I extend my thanks to all those students, and to those who presented this material to me, my teachers, and colleagues in a more formal sense. I hope this book will be as good a teacher as those books and articles I have read in researching it. I look forward to the responses of colleagues and students, to continuing the dialogue.

I want to thank Saint Joseph College for the incentive to write this book, and, more importantly, for giving me time to write it. I received a sabbatical leave during the fall semester 1996, in part through the generosity of my colleague Dorothy Keller, making it possible to complete this project. My friends in the Religious Studies Department—John J. Stack, Ann Marie Caron, and Joan M. Kelly—have supported and encouraged me. Fr. John Stack, in particular, has been a mentor to me.

Two political scientists, John Kikoski and Kenneth J. Long, have read and commented on virtually the entire text, and this is a much better book because of their suggestions. Others have commented on various chapters: Rosemarie Gorman, Jean M. Graustein, Michael Hovey, Peter Markow, Harold T. McKone, Shyamala Raman, Ruth Rosenbaum, John J. Stack, and Kathryn Wrinn. Each of them has contributed significantly to the clarity and accuracy of the text, and I appreciate their time and ideas. My editor at Orbis Books, Susan Perry, has been wonderful. She was receptive to the idea of this book, confident that I could actually write it, and painstaking in her critique and corrections. My wife, Mary Ann, who is also on the faculty at Saint Joseph College, is the first to read and critique the drafts of my writing. She is at once a tough critic and a strong advocate. In some instances I have stubbornly resisted the wise counsel of these many colleagues. Probably, the next time I will know better.

Various members of the staff at Saint Joseph College have assisted in finding research materials or in generating the graphics in the book: Deborah Ahl, Donald Gustafson, Kathleen Kelley, Bonnie Merk-Birman, Dorothy

O'Dwyer, and Patricia Senich, as well as my friend, Paul Doherty. Their assistance is much appreciated.

Finally, I dedicate this book to my parents, Joe and Dorothy Thompson. I have been fortunate to have loving parents and a functional family, and I am grateful.

CHAPTER ONE

The Post-Cold War World:
How Did We Get Here?

". . . The most fundamental task is for our community of faith to understand and act on two fundamental ideas. The first is drawn from the Beatitudes: 'Blessed are the peacemakers, they will be called children of God.' The second is the familiar call of Pope Paul VI: 'If you want peace, work for justice.' These two deceptively simple statements outline the key elements of our mission: To be Christian is to be a peacemaker and to pursue peace is to work for justice."[1]

World politics changed dramatically at the beginning of the last decade of the twentieth century with the virtual collapse of communism. This positive political development, however, had little practical effect on realities such as global economic inequality, population pressures, or environmental destruction. While poverty has bedeviled humanity from its origins, modern economic systems, the global economy, and ecological concerns are relatively new. The aim of this chapter is to trace the three major trends or historical movements that set up the current economic, political, and environmental situations.

Obviously, this is a look at the big picture. Understanding these historical megatrends is very important if humanity is to overcome the obstacles to a more just and peaceful world. Trying to remedy a problem without addressing its history is like trying to rid a yard of dandelions without pulling up their roots. It doesn't work.

The three historical movements that have produced the contemporary world are colonialism, the industrial/technological revolution, and the Cold War and its aftermath. Each will be examined in turn.

COLONIALISM

Commemorating Columbus

In 1992 the peoples of the Americas commemorated the 500th anniversary of Columbus landing in what we now call the Caribbean. There was much controversy about this anniversary. While earlier generations in the United States might have unabashedly danced in the streets in honor of this cinquecentennial, and some wished to do so, many people were too aware of the ambiguities for a wholehearted celebration. This paragraph's first sentence was carefully crafted to attend to some of the politically sensitive issues raised by this anniversary, and dissecting that sentence can introduce those issues.

"The peoples of the Americas": Contrary to the assumptions of some Americans, Columbus did not find the United States, but the Americas—North, South, Central, et al. He first landed in what is today the Dominican Republic, and he explored the Caribbean on subsequent journeys. Columbus thought he was in India, so he called the people who were here "Indians."

"Landing, not discovery": As the comedian and social commentator Dick Gregory used to say, "How do you 'discover' a land that is already occupied?" Yet in elementary school I learned that Columbus discovered America in 1492. There is a good deal of hubris and more than a touch of racism in the notion that until Europeans set foot in a place, it does not really exist. The Americas were a "New World" for the Europeans, but these lands were already home for the indigenous people.

"Caribbean": The Carib people were found on many of the islands in the sea named after them when Columbus arrived. The Carib people are now extinct. They were wiped out by the diseases and the swords brought over by the Europeans. When whites arrived in the Americas there were about 100 million aborigines in the hemispheres. Within about a century that number was reduced by nearly 90 percent. This "demographic disaster has no equal in history, not even the Black Death."[2]

"Commemorate": It is, in part, because we are acutely aware of the fate of native peoples, resulting from Europeans coming to the Americas, that we remembered, rather than celebrated, this anniversary. The European "settlement" of the Americas was a mixed tragedy. From the perspective of the aboriginal peoples the settlement was a conquest that led to the exploitation of their labor and resources, the loss of their land and freedom, and their death.

The next chapter in the story is the enslavement of Africans to work on the plantations in the Caribbean and North and South America. This is surely one of the most tragic stories of exploitation and oppression in all of human history. There were, of course, winners and losers in this sad saga. Europe and some Europeans benefited immensely from the exploitation of the resources of the Americas, and there was a mutual enrichment that developed from the mingling of these cultures and peoples. But despite benefits that may have accrued for the overall good of humanity from colonialism, the central story line is one of inhumanity and injustice. Basically white people from Europe exploited the people, lands, and resources of black, brown, red, and yellow people all over the globe. That is the story and the legacy of colonialism.

Thus far, the tale of colonialism has been introduced through the prism of the commemoration of the 500th anniversary of Columbus landing in the Americas. It is beyond the scope of this book to explore colonialism in detail, but it is important to communicate the breadth of European colonialism and a sense of what it meant to those who were colonized.

Europe Colonizes the World

The colonial period began around 1500 and lingers into the present, although nearly all colonies have now gained political (but not economic) independence. (See the Appendix for a list of former colonial powers and dates of independence.) During this period only a handful of countries escaped direct colonization, most notably China, Japan, and Turkey.[3] No country, however, escaped the impact of European military and economic power. Indeed, these exceptions avoided direct colonization principally because of the balance of power among contending European colonizers.

In the case of China, for example, the European powers and the United States agreed on an Open Door policy after the British navy defeated China in the Opium Wars of 1839–1842. This agreement was designed to block Russia and Japan from actually annexing Chinese territory, thereby keeping the wealth, technology, and resources of China open to the exploitation of all. Through its victory, Britain won the "right" to profitably export deadly opium *into* China.[4]

Another set of figures indicates the extent of European colonial control. "In the year 1800, Europe, its colonies, and its former colonies already covered 55 percent of the world's land surface. By 1914, that figure reached an astonishing 84 percent of the land surface."[5] Given the indirect colonial control of countries like China and Turkey, virtually every people on earth has experienced the domination or influence of Europeans.

Phase One—1500–1815

The colonial period of European expansion can be divided into two phases.[6] The first phase, from 1500–1815, was characterized by exploration and trade. Spain and Portugal, and later the Netherlands, were the dominant powers during this period.

As Marco Polo learned, the crafts and goods of the Orient were at first superior to those of Europe. By the sixteenth century, Europe was beginning to trade on a more equal basis with the East. European goals regarding the East were to establish trading posts and trade routes, and to compete favorably with each other for the goods of the Orient. The Europeans found Africa to be inhospitable for settlement because of disease, climate, and terrain. Thus, they tended to establish heavily armed forts in African ports for the sake of trade.

In Central and South America, however, Spain and Portugal established colonies. Here the environment was amenable and the natives were easily conquered because the Europeans had swords, guns, and horses. The Europeans came in and took control. Mexico provides a good example of what happened in this first phase of colonization.

Mexico. When Hernán Cortéz landed on the coast of Mexico in 1519 with perhaps 600 soldiers, he encountered the Aztec empire which had swallowed

Mexico during the seventy-year rule (1427–1496) of its great leader Tlacaelel. The Aztecs were themselves foreign conquerors of the various peoples in Mexico. They had demanded onerous tribute from the indigenous people, and sacrificed tens of thousands of them to their gods. The Aztec empire was no Garden of Eden.

The Aztec capital, Tenochtitlan, on the site of today's Mexico City, with its streets of water and huge market, was superior to the stinking burgs of medieval Europe. "It could boast archives of bark books, a magnificent calendar, and priests versed in math and astronomy. All Aztec children went to school."[7]

The sophistication of the Aztec civilization, however, did not include metals, horses, or the wheel. When Cortéz brandished his sword, fired his blunderbuss and cannons, ran his horses, and declared himself a god, he found a willing reception among the oppressed indigenous people and a woefully ill-armed opponent in the Aztecs. Cortéz conquered the capital and melted down the exquisite jewelry in the Aztec treasury into gold bars. The Spanish soldiers raped the women, took the land, and enslaved the people. Angered by human sacrifice, the Spanish killed the Aztec priests and scribes, and burned their bark books, reducing this pre-Columbian culture to smoke. In their single-minded search for wealth and their sadistic cruelty, the Spaniards managed to make the Aztec tyranny pale in comparison.

The Indians dropped from overwork in the mines and on the plantations, despaired because of the destruction of their culture, and died from the diseases brought by the Europeans—smallpox, malaria, influenza, measles, typhoid, dysentery, etc.—to which they had no resistance. "The net result of this ruthless exploitation was that the native population declined from seventeen million in 1522 to a mere one million by 1608. Here, surely, is a piece of genocide that rivals any in history!"[8]

By the seventeenth century, Spain had set up a system of "trade" with its colonies that was enshrined in law. The colony sent gold and silver, sugar and tobacco to Spain, and the "mother" country sent back consumer goods. "Bales of tobacco leaves floated to Seville; the Spanish worked these into cigarettes and returned them to Mexico City."[9] Manufacturing was a monopoly of Spain and strictly forbidden to the colonies. All trade was required to use Spanish ships. Thus did colonization cripple the economies of the colonies with economic dependency.

Spain set up two systems within its colonies that have left a lasting legacy throughout Latin America—the hacienda and a three-tiered caste structure. The hacienda was a large, nearly self-sufficient plantation growing sugar, cotton, or, later, coffee (an import from Africa, via the Middle East, to the New World). The hacienda was owned by a landlord and worked by indebted peasants under the supervision of a foreman. This pattern of a landed elite and impoverished landless peasants still endures throughout Latin America and in much of the Two-Thirds World. A 1975 World Bank survey of eighty-three former colonies found that, typically, only 3 percent of landowners controlled 79 percent of farmland.[10]

Intermarriage between the Spanish and the Indians created a three-tiered caste system in most of Latin America. At the top were the "pure" Europeans, often well-educated and wealthy, called creoles. Next were the mestizos, or mixed bloods, who occupied a middle role. At the bottom were the Indians or indigenous peoples, who continue to be the poorest people in the lowliest positions. In some countries, such as Brazil, Cuba, and Puerto Rico, the slave trade added Africans to this mix. Caste, color, and class continue to present problems of justice in much of Latin America.

Along with the sword came the cross. In Mexico, at least, the first Franciscan and Dominican missionaries tried to convert the Indians and to protect them from the murderous and greedy soldiers. Bartolomé de las Casas, for example, boldly denounced the inhumane treatment of the Indians to some temporary effect. After Juan Diego's vision of the dark Virgin of Guadalupe in 1531, Indians flocked to the Church. By the beginning of the seventeenth century, however, the early missionaries had moved on to other parts of Central America and California. They were replaced by bishops, appointed by the King of Spain, and secular priests who were often aristocrats seeking their fortune in Mexico. Now the Church became a direct agent of Spanish imperialism and itself a large landowner in the hacienda system. The religious message to the peasants was that the Lord would reward their humble obedience in the next life. Through the power of the Church, Spain was able to rule for almost three centuries with barely an army present.[11]

The sixteenth through the eighteenth centuries established the global dominance of Europe and the economic patterns that endure to the present. The basic pattern was that Europe got richer and the colonies were impoverished. This happened because the colonizers established the rules of the game to benefit themselves. The colonial relationship was lopsidedly exploitative. Europe stole the rich resources of their colonies and then used the colonies as a market for European goods. This plundered wealth strengthened Europe for even greater plunder. Within the colonies a similar system prevailed. The wealthy elite, who now possessed the land, became richer through the labor of the peasants under their control. Whether one's perspective is global or domestic, the rich became richer and more powerful because they developed a system that exploited others for their benefit. Here lie the roots of injustice in the contemporary world.

Phase Two—1815–1945

The nineteenth century witnessed the zenith of the British Empire. In 1815 Great Britain defeated Napoleon. With France subdued and Spain in decline, Britain ruled the seas. "By 1914, fully one-quarter of all humanity was under the rule of this relatively tiny island state, and it was literally true that the sun never set on the British Empire."[12]

The wealth garnered from the colonial system fueled the Industrial Revolution, which in turn strengthened the power of the colonial system. "It was in part the cash of Liverpool, centre of the triangular trade in slaves, cotton and rum between West Africa, the West Indies and Britain, that financed the mills of South Lancashire, the cradle of the industrial revolution."[13] The British plunder of the Bengal region of India in the mid-eighteenth century provided London with enough capital to be midwife to the birth of the Industrial Revolution. In turn the Industrial Revolution gave the European states, and especially Britain, a considerable technological advantage. This commercial and military advantage quickly converted mutual trade relations with the East into the lopsided exploitation which characterized the colonial system. In other words, the colonial powers *caused* the underdevelopment of the colonies. British economic policy in India provides one example.

India. Before Britain arrived in India, there was a thriving textile industry based in small shops. When this inexpensive cloth began to compete with the developing textile mills in England, Britain imposed export restrictions (such as a 75 percent tariff) on Indian goods. This diminished cotton exports to Britain in the period of 1815–1832 by a factor of thirteen. In Bengal, the British went so far as to deliberately break the little fingers of thousands of Indian weavers so they could no longer practice their craft. This ruthless policy resulted in massive unemployment.

> The net effect of this policy of enforced complementarity of the British and Indian economies was that the non-agricultural population decreased from 45 percent of the whole in early 1800 to only 26 percent by 1940. Simply put, India had been well on its way toward becoming an industrial, diversified economy. This was reversed by the British.[14]

Through such practices, Britain underdeveloped India.

British trade policy toward its colonies worked as follows. The colony could only export to or import from Britain, using only British ships. The manufacture of certain goods that might compete with those produced in Britain was forbidden, and the whole protectionist system was buttressed by tariffs.[15] It was such policies that eventually caused British subjects who had relocated to the North American colonies to revolt. For example, at one time, no wool or cloth could be produced in the colonies except for local use, and steel furnaces and rolling mills were forbidden. Goods often had to be shipped to England even if their destination was the colony next door. And, of course, there were the taxes and tariffs that burdened the colonists. In North America there was a successful revolt. In Asia and Africa these policies stood.[16]

Africa. Although Britain was the dominant power in the nineteenth century, it was not without rivals. In Africa, competition became so sharp that the European powers gathered at the Congress of Berlin in 1884 and carved up the map of Africa into zones of control. The countries created at Berlin bore no resemblance to the natural frontiers or the historical boundaries of various tribes and peoples. Traditional enemies were often lumped together in one state, while in other instances, single tribes were divided into two or three different countries. The casual arrogance of the Congress of Berlin continues to reap a bitter harvest of ethno-nationalist conflict and political chaos in contemporary Africa.[17]

The Congress of Berlin acknowledged Great Britain's control of Uganda and Kenya. Britain was interested in East Africa, and especially Kenya, in part, to protect its trade routes to Asia through the Suez Canal. The colonial administrators decided that Kenya, with its fertile highlands, should produce corn, coffee, wheat, and sisal for export to England. To that end, it created plantations for white settlers by moving the Masai and Kikuyu tribes from their lands and into reservations.

Providing cheap labor for the white settlers, however, turned out to be a problem. The Kikuyu and Masai peoples were self-sufficient and saw no need to work for money. Thus, to meet the need of white settlers from Britain and South Africa for cheap labor, the colonial administration had to adopt measures to undermine native economic independence and to force the local people to depend on a paid labor market for their needs.

First the colonials instituted a hut tax that had to be paid in cash. Thus the natives would have to earn money to stay out of jail. Next officials reduced the size of the reservations so that there was not enough land to meet the needs of the tribe. They also taxed the few commodities used by Africans which raised prices. Finally they instituted a passbook system and required tribal leaders to produce a quota of workers or be replaced. While the few thousand whites in Kenya received full government services and assistance, the four million blacks were neglected.

Not surprisingly the black population decreased from 4 million to 2.4 million in the first two decades of the twentieth century. Indeed, many whites expected that the blacks would simply die off. "As Kenya's colonial commissioner commented in 1904, after he had pushed the Masai and many other tribes further back into preserves, 'There can be no doubt that the Masai and many other tribes must go under. It is a prospect which I view with equanimity and a clear conscience.'"[18] Thus did the colonial plantation system come to Africa.

In dozens of other ways the colonial system skewed the development of the colonies. For example, the capital cities in colonies often were not established in the best place to administer the country, but in the spot which gave easiest access to the outside world. Thus, twenty-eight African capitals are in port cities, while those in Chad, Niger, and Mali are all in the extreme south-west corner of these vast countries.[19] The plantations produced cash crops for export—sugar in the Caribbean, coffee in Brazil, tea in Sri Lanka—instead of subsistence crops for local consumption—corn, beans, or rice. The frequent result was a local economy skewed to cash export that was dependent upon the "mother" country and vulnerable to the fluctuations of the international market, while local people often went hungry.[20] Economic dependency and underdevelopment are two of the legacies of colonialism. It can be said that the colonial powers created the Third World.

The Church, by now Protestant and Catholic, continued to play an ambivalent role in the process of colonization. Missionaries were certainly sincere in their belief that they were bringing a saving truth to peoples who had not heard the gospel, that they were saving souls.[21] The idea that Europeans were bringing Christianity and civilization to primitive cultures and heathen peoples was used to justify European expansion and colonial domination. In hindsight, this appears to be a smokescreen for a pattern of exploitation that runs directly contrary to the gospel. But there were surely many people who sincerely thought they were doing good and right. Anglican Archbishop Desmond Tutu, who won the Nobel Peace Prize for his nonviolent resistance to apartheid in South Africa, reflects on the connection between Christianity and colonization from the African perspective: "They used to say that the missionaries came to Africa and they had the Bible and we had the land. And then they said, 'Let us pray.' And when we opened our eyes, we had the Bible and they had the land!"[22] Although having the Bible may be a good thing, using the Bible to steal the land and dominate the people is diametrically opposed to the Bible's teaching.

Education soon became a primary activity of the missionaries, but this too was ambivalent, if not insidious. "The colonial education system was geared to building a class of unimaginative but obedient administrators and concentrated on Westernizing the most able of the indigenous people."[23] Education communicated the so-called superior values of the colonial masters to the elite among the indigenous people and created a cadre of dutiful bureaucrats to carry out the ruler's orders.[24] This fostered a "colonial mentality," that is, a cultural inferiority complex that becomes a self-fulfilling prophecy. An exploited people begin to internalize the stereotypical characteristics born of the prejudices of their exploiters. The result is a dependence that is rooted not only in economic and social structures but in a psychic sense of inferiority. It is no wonder, then, that when Mahatma Gandhi, aware of events like the British maiming of Bengali weavers and the massacre at Jallianwalla Bagh,[25] was asked by a British reporter what he thought of Western civilization, he replied, "I think it would be a good idea." The deleterious effects of colonialism were not only economic and social, but also cultural and psychological. Colonialism was an assault on human dignity, perpetuated by Western Christians. Colonial peoples have experienced this and generally understand this history, but colonial powers often manage to deny or rationalize or forget what happened.

The importance of the history of colonialism for relations among people today was driven home to me by an Irishman I once met on a ferry from France to Ireland. He told me that in his worldwide travels people often mistook his accent to be British, as had I. He said that once he set them straight, people welcomed him with generous hospitality. He could tell that his anecdote had puzzled this naive American, so he explained: "The British have oppressed people all over the globe, but the Irish have never had an empire.

Lots of people dislike the British, but they love the Irish, because we have a lot in common with them." I now know the difference between a British and an Irish accent, and the difference it can make.

Phase Three—The United States Emerges as a Neo-Colonial
Power in the Twentieth Century

As the power of Portugal and Spain declined in the nineteenth century, their colonies in Latin America won their political independence. In the twentieth century the remaining European powers and the emerging powers in Asia spent themselves in two world wars and in efforts to maintain their empires against colonial rebellions. During the twentieth century, and especially in the period after World War II, most colonies in Asia, Africa, and the Caribbean gained their political independence. The economic structures established during colonial rule, however, have allowed the North to continue to exploit the South. This pattern of economic domination, in the absence of direct political rule, is called neo-colonialism. The United States emerged as the pre-eminent neo-colonial power in the twentieth century.

Because the United States freed itself from colonial rule, one might think it would be in sympathy with anti-colonial sentiment, and in solidarity with those trying to shake the shackles of a colonial past. Indeed, in the 1950s, Ho Chi Minh, having read the U.S. Declaration of Independence, wrote to the U.S. President asking for assistance in Vietnam's struggle for independence from French colonial rule. But by the beginning of the twentieth century, as the European powers declined, the United States was ready to step in to fill their boots, militarily and economically—as Ho Chi Minh discovered. The United States first supported France, then took France's place on the battlefield in Vietnam in the 1960s.

In 1898, the United States occupied Cuba, Puerto Rico, and the Philippines as part of the spoils from the Spanish-American War. Puerto Rico, some would argue, remains a colony of the United States. In the Philippines, the United States inherited the Filipino rebellion against Spanish colonial rule and crushed it.[26] American textbooks tend to call this episode the Philippine Insurrection. Filipino historians refer to it as the Philippine-American War.

President William McKinley captured the American mindset toward the world at the beginning of the twentieth century in a personal revelation to a group of Protestant missionaries who were visiting him at the White House. McKinley told the visitors how he had agonized and prayed about what to do with the Philippines. Then late one night it came to him:

(1) That we could not give them back to Spain—that would be cowardly and dishonorable; (2) that we could not turn them over to France or Germany—our commercial rivals in the Orient—that would be bad business and discreditable; (3) that we could not leave them to themselves—they were unfit for self-government—and they would soon have anarchy and misrule over there worse than Spain's was; and (4) that

there was nothing left for us to do but to take them all, and to educate the Filipinos, and uplift and civilize and Christianize them, and by God's grace do the very best we could by them, as our fellow-men for whom Christ also died.[27]

First, of course, the United States had to subdue the Filipinos, already a deeply Catholic people, who were fighting for the very self-government that McKinley thought they were incapable of achieving.

Americans thought of themselves as benevolent colonizers, trying to remake the Philippines in our image through education and a market economy.

But the U.S. performance in the Philippines was flawed. The Americans coddled the elite while disregarding the appalling plight of the peasants, thus perpetuating a feudal oligarchy [imposed by Spanish colonial rule] that widened the gap between the rich and the poor. They imposed trade patterns that retarded the economic growth of the islands, condemning them to reliance on the United States long after independence. The American monopoly on imports into the Philippines also dampened the development of a native industry. At the same time the unlimited entry of Philippine exports to the United States bound the Archipelago inextricably to the American market. Economically at least, the Filipinos were doomed to remain "little brown brothers" for years—though many, despite their nationalist rhetoric, found security in the role.[28]

Despite American pretensions of a more relaxed attitude and benevolent intentions, American colonialism seems indistinguishable from European colonialism.

With the exception of these three countries that were the spoils of the Spanish-American War, the United States did not have direct colonial relationships. Instead of imposing political control, the United States usurped economic influence and control over former colonies as the power of European countries declined and as its own power rose during the twentieth century. This economic influence was backed up by military power. The Philippines illustrates this very clearly, though it is hardly a singular case.

Since the Spanish-American War, the United States has intervened militarily in the Caribbean and Central America over twenty times. Early in the twentieth century the United States created the country of Panama so we could build our canal. The most recent U.S. intervention in Panama was in 1989. The United States occupied Haiti from 1915–1934, the Dominican Republic from 1916–1924, and Nicaragua from 1926–1933. It intervened in the Dominican Republic in 1965 to prevent a constitutionally elected president, who had been overthrown, from returning to power, and in Haiti in 1994 to return an elected president to power (a better idea). The United States sponsored a rebellion in Nicaragua throughout the 1980s. It has supported brutal despots in Haiti, Nicaragua, Guatemala, the Dominican Republic, and Panama.[29]

The rationale for this intervention has been a mixture of economic and strategic interests. The Caribbean, after all, is perceived by America to be its "backyard," as president after president has repeatedly proclaimed in justifying these interventions.[30] The United States brought to these adventures the same condescending domination that characterized its relationship with the Philippines. Americans have been surprised to find that even if we start schools and build roads, people deeply resent being controlled by, or dependent on, others.

America's backyard, according to the Monroe Doctrine, extends well beyond the Caribbean into South America. In the early years of 1970, Chile, a stable and relatively prosperous democracy, elected a socialist president, Salvador Allende, who won a plurality of votes in a three-way contest. When Allende began to nationalize the copper industry, depriving American companies of their lucrative profits, he was overthrown and killed in a CIA-aided coup that resulted in a military dictatorship under General Augusto Pinochet.[31]

United States influence in Latin America, however, has generally been economic, rather than overtly military. The perpetuation of the economic domination of the Third World by the First World after the colonies achieved political independence is simply a new form of colonialism—neo-colonialism. The domestic and global structures of injustice usually did not change when

Europe ceded or lost direct political control of the colonies. Theologically this systematic injustice is social sin. The global economic inequity, that is, the widening gap between the rich and the poor (the topic of chapter 2), is rooted in the patterns and structures established under colonialism.

THE INDUSTRIAL REVOLUTION

The interplay between colonialism and the Industrial Revolution has already been noted. The wealth amassed from colonialism fueled the Industrial Revolution which, in turn, further consolidated the power of Europe over the colonies. The point of this section is to try to communicate a sense of how technology has shaped the modern world and of what that means in terms of justice and peace.

When Britain Was the World's Workshop

The Industrial Revolution is a phenomenon of the nineteenth century. It began in Britain. By the end of the century, it had spread to Europe and the United States. The development of science and the scientific method during the Enlightenment (eighteenth century) prepared the way. Science seeks to understand the way things work; technology applies science to practical problems. The last three centuries have produced an explosion of scientific knowledge and technological advances. Since we are at the crest of this historical wave, we forget how far and how fast the industrialized nations have come. It is important to appreciate the amount and the rate of change that has occurred.

The impact of the Industrial Revolution is dramatized at the Welch Folk Museum near Cardiff, Wales. The museum has reproduced replicas of the same family cottage, furnished in a typical fashion for a working class family, at 50 year intervals from 1650 through 1950. Thus, there were seven identical houses in a row. The inside of the house hardly changed from 1650 through 1850. A wooden table and chairs stood on a rough hewn wooden floor. The family had few and simple possessions. Suddenly in 1850 there was a dramatic change. There appeared curtains and rugs, table settings, a stove for heat and cooking, even knickknacks decorating the room. Life was becoming progressively more refined and more cluttered. By 1950 the house itself hardly seemed adequate for a family. Where does one put the bathroom? refrigerator? Bedrooms?[32]

> **For Reflection**
> William Manchester titled his bestselling book on the Middle Ages and the Renaissance *A World Lit Only by Fire* (Boston: Little, Brown & Co., 1992). No electricity, only candles. No steamships, only sailing ships. No engines, only horsepower. What a very different world that was.
>
> Yet, when traveling in remote areas in the Philippines, I encountered villages "lit only by fire." There are different worlds in our contemporary world.

Historians now talk of a First Industrial Revolution, primarily in Britain, from 1750–1871, and of a New or Second Industrial Revolution throughout the developed world from 1871 to 1960. The development of an industrial economy in nineteenth-century Britain was preceded by social and technological innovations in agriculture which dramatically increased the productivity of the land. A confluence of other social and technological changes seem to have erupted in the Industrial Revolution: the transition from a feudal to a market economy, developments in textile production, improvements in iron and steel manufacture, and the creation of the steam engine. All this led to the rapid transition from crafting by hand to producing by machine, thus multiplying the productivity of labor a hundredfold. In the nineteenth century the Gross National Product of Great Britain increased by an astounding 400 percent.

The Industrial Revolution increased other things as well: human misery, pollution, and population. An economy based on industry more than agriculture meant the movement of people from rural areas to overcrowded cities where they worked long hours for low wages in dangerous mills or mines. The industrialists increased their profits by exploiting the labor of children, women, and men. Unemployment was a constant worry in a rapidly changing economy. The cities were ill-prepared to handle the influx of so many people. It is the condition of working people that Dickens would dramatize, Marx would decry, and Pope Leo XIII would address in the first social encyclical, *Rerum Novarum (The Condition of Labor)* (1891).[33]

Industry produced more goods, but its byproducts fouled the air and polluted rivers and lakes, harming the health of humans and the habitats of animals. The increase in productivity and wealth came at a terrible cost to the environment.

In the late eighteenth century there was a surge in the population in Europe, and even in countries as far removed as the United States and China. The causes of this population boom are not clear. There were improvements in public health and in the food supply and diet, and women were marrying younger. Whatever the exact reasons, there were suddenly many more "have-nots" crowding into major cities and stuffed into rural hovels. This increasing labor force would fuel the Industrial Revolution as much as the coal and the steam it ran on, and the steel it produced.

At first, however, the Industrial Revolution produced the prospect of a mismatch between the number of people and the resources of a finite earth to sustain them. In 1798 Thomas Robert Malthus, an English country curate, expressed this concern in his now famous *Essay on Population*. Malthus noted that population increased geometrically, like interest on a savings account. If the annual population growth rate is 2 percent, then the population will double every 35 years. Britain's population was doubling every 25 years. Malthus thought it inconceivable that the productivity of the land could keep pace with this growth in population. He predicted that population would be kept in check only by widespread famine, disease, and/or war. Malthus' pessimism was out of step with the optimism of the intellectuals of his day who were anticipating the perfectibility of humanity and who engaged Malthus in critical debate.[34]

In the nineteenth century Malthus' dire predictions proved to be wrong. Three escape hatches prevented the Malthusian trap from closing on the British people. The first was emigration. Between 1815 and 1914 around 20 million Britons left the country and settled in the United States, Canada, Australia, and southern Africa. Nearly half of Britain's population emigrated. The second was the remarkable improvement in agricultural productivity. Not only did Britain itself produce considerably more food, it was also able to import food from the lands its subjects were settling. In the nineteenth century the power of the land was able to match the power of population. The third and most significant development was the Industrial Revolution with its leap forward in productivity and wealth. "During the nineteenth century as a whole, the British population grew *fourfold*, whereas the national product grew *fourteenfold*."[35] Human ingenuity, then, was key to avoiding the Malthusian trap.

> Thus, "the power of population" was answered, not so much by "the power in the earth" itself, but by the power of technology—the capacity of the human mind to find new ways of doing things, to invent new devices, to organize production in improved forms, to quicken the pace of moving goods and ideas from one place to another, to stimulate fresh approaches to old problems.[36]

Moreover, the Industrial Revolution led to social changes that decreased population growth. Thus, Britain went through a demographic transition that stabilized population over time.

It is important to note that not every country escaped the Malthusian trap in the nineteenth century. Ireland and India, two countries under British domination, experienced famine. These famines, however, like most famines, were caused more by oppressive political and economic policies, rather than by simple Malthusian scarcity. War, in the form of the social turbulence of the French Revolution and the attempt at imperial conquest under Napoleon Bonaparte, served to vent France's population pressures.[37]

As we approach the twenty-first century, Malthus' predictions pose an acute problem. The earth's population continues to explode—6 billion in 1998, around 8 billion by 2025—and the growth is happening primarily in the developing countries that lack the wealth and technology to cope with the increase. The escape hatches open to Britain are closing or are already closed today. In the next century Malthus may prove to be right after all. (Chapter 3 will further discuss this problem.)

Future Shock

Change, more and faster, has characterized the New Industrial Revolution in the twentieth century. Technology, now powered by coal, oil, and nuclear energy and converted into electricity rather than steam, has produced an astounding array of inventions which have dramatically altered patterns of human life and the arrangements of human society.

My maternal grandmother was born in 1900. A brief reflection on her life can serve to illustrate the amount and rapidity of change that humans have experienced in the twentieth century. Mamie Allen was born on a farm outside Louisville, Kentucky. She married a farmer and local sheriff, John Reinhardt, when she was sixteen. Her husband built the

> **For Reflection**
>
> Interview someone who is 75 or older about how much change they have experienced in their life and how they have coped with it.

house she would live in nearly all of her life. In that house she gave birth to two boys and a girl. When her daughter, Dorothy, married Joseph Thompson, the Reinhardts gave the couple a piece of land next to their home as a wedding present. Thus I grew up next door to my grandmother, my grandfather having died when I was very young.

It is instructive to think of all the changes that occurred as Grandma's life marked the progress of the century. Electricity was one of the first improvements. It had to be added to the house when the electric lines made their way into the environs of Louisville. With it would eventually come a multiplicity of appliances—refrigerators, stoves, washers, dryers, vacuum cleaners, fans, air conditioners—that would lighten the burdens of everyday life. I remember when the pipes for natural gas were laid in our neighborhood and the huge coal furnace in Grandma's rough basement was converted to gas. This meant that on cold winter mornings Grandma could simply adjust the thermostat rather than trudge down into the basement to start a fire.

Plumbing—running water and a bathroom—had been added to the house before I came along, but the old outhouse was still standing during my childhood. So was a stable where the horse used to be kept. Grandma never learned to drive. She never flew on a plane. In fact, she seldom traveled at all. Her grandson, on the other hand, has lived in Baltimore, New York City, and now near Hartford, and has traveled throughout Europe and the Philippines and to the Middle East and the Caribbean. Human beings have been to the moon and back, a feat Grandma refused to believe. Mobility was one change that Grandma decided to do without. The telephone, however, was a device she found exceedingly useful. Perched on a chair in her kitchen she would talk for hours with her family and friends. Every afternoon she could be found watching soap operas on the TV, another invention she enjoyed, along with the radio prior to that. She never went out to movies; she was in a nursing home when video cassettes came along. Her grandson has thus far stubbornly resisted the compact disc innovation in music. Photocopy machines, faxes, and computers are foreign even to Grandma's children, but the stuff of life for her grandchildren.

Although Grandma didn't own one, the automobile, as she always called it, radically changed her life by making suburbs possible. Eventually she sold the farm to a developer, and a subdivision was built around her house. This led to a small shopping center across the street and a McDonalds on the corner. The city had arrived. Henceforth our dogs would have to be tied up.

Grandma was married during World War I, her son and son-in-law fought in World War II, her grandsons are of the Vietnam generation, and her great-grandchildren were eligible for the Gulf War, Somalia, Haiti, and Bosnia. Given the development in destructive weaponry over her lifetime and the frequency of its use, she was lucky not to lose any of her progeny to war.

When the doctors decided she needed a pacemaker for her heart, she decided that "no one was going to cut her open," and none of us could persuade her otherwise. Amazingly that so-called weak heart sustained her through her eighty-ninth year. The modern health care system eventually prevailed upon her to have a different lifesaving operation at a later point in her life, but it could do little to stave off the diminishment she suffered from Alzheimer's disease.

Along with the technological changes came profound social change. Grandma was a traditional, even old-fashioned, woman whose life centered on home and family. Yet she was a very independent woman. She never grasped my sister's commitment to a career, yet the independent model that Grandma provided has surely been a part of my sister's success.

The depth of change that has characterized the twentieth century is captured by Kenneth Boulding, an eminent economist and imaginative social thinker: "The world of today . . . is as different from the world in which I was born as that world was from Julius Caesar's. I was born in the middle of human history, to date, roughly. Almost as much has happened since I was born as happened before."[38] Alvin Toffler, the author of *Future Shock*, suggests that if the last 50,000 years of human existence were divided into lifetimes of approximately 62 years each, there have been about 800 generations. The overwhelming majority of all the goods we use in daily life have been developed in this the 800th lifetime. If agriculture was the first wave of economic development and nineteenth-century industrialism was the second, then we have already moved into the third stage, the service or information economy. The high-tech economies of the developed world now depend on the developing countries for their manual labor.

Until the Industrial Revolution the speed of travel was limited to about twenty miles-per-hour, the speed of a horse-drawn coach or a sailing ship. Trains and steamships increased our speed dramatically, but in the 800th lifetime cars and planes have made everyday travel rapid and accessible while space shuttles and rockets travel much faster.

Now more books are produced *each day* than were produced in a year prior to the modern era. Most of what we know about science and technology has been discovered and developed in this 800th lifetime.[39]

People who move into another culture often experience culture shock. Familiar patterns and rituals do not work, and they are unfamiliar with the ones that do. This experience is the basis of Toffler's notion of future shock. The scope and speed of change can make it difficult for individuals and societies to cope or adjust. The skills a person has developed over a lifetime may suddenly be useless. Machines make it possible for women to take on new roles. The experience of successive generations can be so different as to make it difficult for parents and children and even siblings to understand each other and communicate. The pace of life tends to accelerate beyond endurance.

In the developed world, the blessings of technology have been real, but ambivalent. There is less drudgery in everyday life, and yet paradoxically less time to enjoy life. Geographical and social mobility are surely beneficial, yet mobility can fragment families and fracture communities. Answering machines may facilitate communication, but they reduce the number of real conversations. Miracles of healing take place in acute care hospitals, yet some children are not vaccinated against common diseases, and we seem to have forgotten how to die well. The energy that fuels the modern economy also pollutes the environment. Technology has given us nuclear energy and nuclear medicine, but also nuclear bombs. The Industrial Revolution has at once been a blessing and a curse.

A few years ago three people from rural Nicaragua were brought to Hartford on a speaking tour. Their hosts took them to Sturbridge Village, a tourist site in Massachusetts that re-creates life in eighteenth-century America. There the Nicaraguans discovered a lifestyle comparable to their own.

The Industrial/Technological Revolution characterizes the world and experience of people in the developed countries of the North. It is a basis of their wealth and power. By contrast, the experience of the majority of people in the less developed countries of the South seems that of another century, another age. The lack of technology is a basis of their poverty. This gap between the rich and the poor raises profound questions of justice.

A POST-COLD WAR WORLD

Colonialism and the Industrial Revolution help us understand the great divide between the North and the South and point to the historical sources of wealth and power in the contemporary world. If we are seeking justice and peace, it is also important to have a sense of more recent history as well. The Cold War dominated politics and international relations from the end of World War II in 1945, until around 1990, when it abruptly ended. It is also important to note the rise of democracy and the fall of tyranny in many places around the world since 1986. This is a time in history ripe with opportunity to create justice and make peace.

Great Powers and Empire

The Modern Era, from 1500 to the present, can be understood as a competition among Great Powers for empire. Indeed, imperialism is nearly synonymous with colonialism, and industrialization enabled a country to gain the economic and military power to join the competition for empire.

As we have seen, from the sixteenth through the nineteenth centuries, the Great Powers were all European. Each, in turn, tried to dominate the others.

Spain was the dominant power at the beginning of the seventeenth century. The Treaty of Westphalia in 1648 concluded the Thirty Years' War in Europe between the alliance of Spain and Austria versus most of the rest of Europe. Spain's defeat marked the decline of its hegemony and the rise of the power of the Netherlands. The Treaty of Westphalia confirmed the notion of sovereign states engaged in a balance of power relationship with each other. At the end of the eighteenth century France sought to dominate Europe, but Napoleon was ultimately defeated by an alliance led by Great Britain. The nineteenth was the century of the British Empire.

In the twentieth century two non-European powers entered the competition—the United States and Japan, and different countries in Europe began to jockey for power—Germany, Russia, and Italy. The First World War (1914–1918) was a horrific contest between European alliances led by Britain and Germany. Germany lost after the United States entered the war in 1917 on the side of Britain. Germany resented the punitive conditions imposed by the Treaty of Versailles in 1919. In Eastern Europe, the Russian Revolution of 1917 enabled Russia to incorporate its neighbors into the Union of Soviet Socialist Republics (U.S.S.R.) under Russian control. The Soviet Union represented the establishment of a Russian Empire.

In the 1930s, Japan, which had already occupied Taiwan and Korea, conquered China. In Europe, Germany, under the leadership of Hitler, was gaining ascendancy and gobbling up its neighbors. The German invasion of Poland in 1939 marked the beginning of World War II. Hitler signed a nonaggression pact with Stalin's Soviet Union which allowed him to quickly overrun France. Then he double-crossed Stalin and invaded the Soviet Union. After Japan destroyed much of the U.S. Pacific Fleet in a surprise attack on Pearl Harbor in late 1941, the United States entered the war, first against Japan, then against Germany. The Second World War brought the inhumanity of warfare to new lows through the attempted genocide of the Holocaust, the firebombing of enemy cities, and the introduction of nuclear weapons in the destruction of Hiroshima and Nagasaki.[40]

The Cold War

World War II decimated the great powers of Europe and Asia. The United States emerged relatively unscathed and with a robust economy. Of the 60 million deaths in World War II, by far the greatest share was suffered by the Soviet Union. Yet the Soviet army had repulsed the German invasion and by the end of the war controlled Eastern Europe and East Germany. When Churchill (U.K.), Roosevelt (U.S.), and Stalin (U.S.S.R.) met at Yalta in 1945, they agreed that Eastern Europe would remain under Soviet influence and that Germany would be split into four sectors, each controlled by one of the allies. Berlin, the German capital, deep within the eastern, Soviet sector, was also divided among the four allies—the United States, Britain, France, and the Soviet Union. Thus, what Winston Churchill called the Iron Curtain, dividing the West from the East, was established in Europe. In the early

1960s the Soviet Union turned Churchill's metaphor into a literal wall that divided West and East Germany and West and East Berlin. West Berlin became a capitalist and democratic island in the midst of communist East Germany.

The Second World War thus dissolved into the Cold War, a continuous, yet relatively stable, conflict between two superpowers—the United States (the West) versus the Soviet Union (the East)—and the ideological, political, and economic systems they represented—capitalist democracy versus socialist communism. Each developed a network of alliances—the North Atlantic Treaty Organization (NATO) led by the United States and the Warsaw Pact led by the Soviet Union—and struggled to retain Third World clients and to enlarge their spheres of influence. While this global struggle between West and East was fought on many fronts—Korea, Vietnam, the Caribbean and Central America, Africa, the Middle East, Afghanistan—the main fault line ran through Europe. The great fear of the West was that the Soviet Union would overrun Western Europe, thus consolidating the whole Eurasian landmass from Siberia to Ireland under the communist Russian Empire. The Soviet Union feared yet another European invasion from Western Europe.

The United States adopted a foreign policy of "containment" which sought to halt and oppose Soviet and communist expansion throughout the globe by whatever means possible—military, political, economic, ideological. The Soviet Union joined the fray. The two superpowers and their allies engaged in a massive arms race in both conventional and nuclear weapons in service of containment. Thus, anti-communism became the single, overriding goal of U.S. foreign policy during the Cold War. Anti-communism justified gargantuan defense budgets, a massive arsenal of doomsday weapons, wars, proxy wars, interventions, coups, counterinsurgency, foreign aid, and support of anti-communist dictators. While the Cold War led to several wars and civil wars throughout the Third World, it did not result in a direct confrontation between the two superpowers, in part, because they were deterred by the threat of "mutually assured destruction" by nuclear weapons.

It is not that these two superpowers and the systems they represent are of equal moral value. Communism is a totalitarian system that denies fundamental human rights and that deserves condemnation and committed opposition. Still, during the Cold War period, *both* sides too frequently practiced the dubious ethic of the end (winning the conflict) justifying the means, *any* means. The single-mindedness of the policy of containment may also have blinded U.S. policy-makers to the complexity of global situations and to the ambiguity of their own intentions and actions. Thus the Cold War led to many debates and divisions within the West about the ethics of foreign policy.

The End of the Cold War

After 45 years of conflict and tension, the Cold War ended with the collapse of communism in the West, first in Eastern Europe, then in the Soviet Union itself. In 1985 a reform-minded leader, Mikhail Gorbachev, rose to power in the Soviet Union. In 1989, when the Solidarity movement in Poland directly challenged the communist government, the Soviet Union sat back and allowed the government to fall. Soon refugees from Eastern Europe were pouring into Western Europe through gaping holes in the Iron Curtain. On November 12, 1989, Germans from East and West began chipping away the Berlin Wall with sledgehammers, wishing, as one of them quipped, that it had not been Germans who had built that wall. The fall of the Berlin Wall symbolized the collapse of communism in Eastern Europe. Within a year Germany had formally re-united and communist governments throughout Eastern Europe had been replaced by fledgling democracies. Except in Romania, this "velvet revolution" was accomplished nonviolently.

Gorbachev hoped that domestic reform would save the communist system within the Soviet Union, but he could not hold back the tide of change. By the end of 1991 democracy had swept aside communism in the Soviet Union itself, and the 15 republics of the U.S.S.R. were becoming independent. World maps were being revised to include new nations with unfamiliar names such as Belarus, Georgia, and Kazakhstan. It was a remarkable transformation.

Analysts differ on why the Cold War suddenly ended. Some argue that the Reagan arms build-up in the 1980s forced the Soviet Union into bankruptcy as it tried to keep pace. Others believe the Soviet system collapsed from economic stagnation and bureaucratic corruption. One thing is clear: Communism did not seem to work. In retrospect, Russia now is exposed as virtually a Third World economy with a genuinely frightening nuclear weapons capability, a respectable space program, and a large but ineffective military that has been unable to subdue the rebel province of Chechnya. Russia's transition to a market economy and a democratic polity remains halting and precarious.

A Wave of Democracy Sweeping the Globe

The democratization of Eastern Europe and the Soviet Union can be seen as part of a wave of democracy sweeping the globe.[41] Beginning in 1986 dictators throughout the world began to topple like dominoes. In the Philippines the "People Power Movement" swept Cory Aquino into power replacing the "conjugal dictatorship" of Ferdinand and Imelda Marcos.[42] On the heels of rapid economic growth, South Korea made the transition from a repressive government to a representative one. Baby Doc Duvalier was overthrown in Haiti, although the transition to democracy there has been a halting process. Nicaragua changed government by ballot. South Africa began the transition to majority rule, and several of the countries in southern Africa experienced positive political changes. By the end of the 1980s nearly every country in South America was, at least formally, a democracy. United Nations peacekeeping missions have supported positive change in Cambodia and El Salvador. The early years of the 1990s saw constructive developments in such seemingly intractable conflicts as those in the Middle East and in Northern Ireland, although progress in both of these cases remains precarious. In many ways, then, the global scene seems to be changing for the better.

Indeed, the end of the Cold War presents the global community with an opportune moment to create a world that is more just and that lives in peace. But there are many obstacles to justice and peace in the post-Cold War world. The gap between the rich and the poor continues to widen. Ethno-nationalist conflict has volcanically risen to the surface all over the globe in places such as Bosnia, Rwanda and Burundi, Sri Lanka, Chechnya, and Canada. Human rights are universally recognized, but widely violated. Nuclear weapons still hang over humanity's future like the sword of Damocles, and conventional weapons continue to spread like a plague. Environmental damage may threaten the entire planet and thus all of its inhabitants.

Now that we have a sense of how humanity arrived at this promising but precarious point in history, we are ready to address these issues.

STUDY QUESTIONS

1. How do you think Columbus Day should be commemorated?
2. The first phase of colonialism was dominated by Spain and the second phase by Great Britain. What similarities and differences do you see in the colonial rule of these two powers, and in the legacies and consequences of their colonial reigns?
3. There is no doubt that colonialism is exploitative and oppressive, yet it may also have some benefits. Do you think the European colonizers brought any benefits to their colonies? How did Europe benefit from the exchange with their colonies?
4. What injustices in the contemporary world are based in colonialism?
5. There have been other countries besides Europe that have colonized their neighbors or their region. The Incas, for example, had colonized Mexico by the time Cortéz arrived. China and Japan have tried to exercise hegemony in the Far East at various times, and various tribes (nations) in Africa have developed empires at one time or another. While colonialism is always exploitative, is it possible to rank some colonial regimes and their legacies as worse than others?
6. Is the United States an imperial power?
7. The condition of labor during the Industrial Revolution gave rise to the critique of Karl Marx and to the critique of Pope Leo XIII in his encyclical *On the Condition of Labor (Rerum Novarum)*. Compare and contrast these critiques. Is industrial capitalism inherently exploitative of labor? Why does there seem to be a decline in the Union Movement today? (For an historical perspective, see the film "Matewan" [1987] directed by John Sayles.)
8. Is the globalization of the economy a new phase of the Industrial Revolution? Who are the winners and losers in the Industrial Revolution? in the globalization of the economy?
9. What justice and peace issues in the contemporary world are based in the Industrial Revolution?

10. Why did communism in Eastern Europe and the Soviet Union collapse?
11. Does the collapse of communism mean that socialism is not a viable economic system? Is there any alternative to capitalism in the contemporary world? What problems are there with capitalism?
12. It would seem that the end of the Cold War presents the world community with an opportunity for peace. Do you think that is true? What are the obstacles to peace? How could the world take advantage of this historical moment?
13. Is some form of democracy (participative or representative government) necessary for a just society? Are most of the world's states becoming genuinely more democratic? How can the process of democratization be aided?

CHAPTER TWO

Poverty and Development

"Blessed are you who are poor, for the kingdom of God is yours. Blessed are you who are now hungry, for you will be satisfied. But woe to you who are rich, for you have received your consolation. Woe to you who are filled now, for you will be hungry." (Luke 6: 20–21, 24–25)

"Central to the biblical presentation of justice is that the justice of a community is measured by its treatment of the powerless in society. . . . The way society responds to the needs of the poor through its public policies is the litmus test of its justice or injustice."[1]

Poverty is the bane of humankind. It is not a new problem, but the gap between the rich and the poor is widening and worsening today. This is ironic, tragic, and unjust, because, perhaps for the first time in human history, there is enough wealth on Earth to meet the basic needs of every person. Until the misery and degradation of billions of brothers and sisters is alleviated there will be no justice, and there will be no peace.

This chapter explores the gap between the rich and the poor among nations, within nations, and within the United States. It begins by recounting personal experiences that have made me aware of the reality of global poverty and have stirred my compassion. Then it analyzes the economic gap between the North and South, examining the economic condition of various regions of the world, and focusing on key issues in the debate about economic development. The final section of the chapter explores two issues related to poverty in the United States.

THE HUMAN FACE OF POVERTY

In the Fall of 1990, I used a sabbatical leave to journey to the Philippines. I traveled widely throughout the islands, visiting small Christian communities in urban and rural settings. I was trying to understand and experience the problems faced by a developing country. It was a transforming experience.

In the United States there are pockets of poverty in the midst of wealth; most Americans never see the stark conditions in inner-cities or the hollows of Appalachia. In the Philippines there are isolated islands of wealth in a sea of poverty; human destitution is public, omnipresent, and pitiful. It is a different world.

Bishop Antonio Fortich of Bacolod, an advocate for the poor, called the

Philippine island of Negros a "social volcano."[2] Sugar cane covers the island in a coat of green; everywhere it is planted right up to the edge of the road. The land is owned by a few, but worked (when there is work to be had) by the many landless peasants. In the late 1980s not even the plantation owners were making a profit on sugar, and the poor were desperate. Some of them joined an underground resistance group, the New People's Army, to fight for a different society. The Philippine military struck back with even greater repression.

I visited a settlement of people on Negros who had been dislocated from their village by the military. Their rural village had been destroyed, and they were afraid to return. One of the women recounted how her son had been captured and beheaded by the military. Several other mothers told of sons who had "been disappeared." So these internal refugees had moved to this remote, uninhabited spot, and they were working to plant in this rocky ground and to build simple shelters. There was no electricity here. A nearby stream provided them with water. The Church in Bacolod was trying to supply them with rice until they could harvest their own. We had brought them supplies in the jeepney we hired for the visit. On our return to Bacolod some women with sick children came with us. As we bumped our way through the rocky field and then the rural roads, I meditated on the listless, pale children with brown, patchy hair nestled in the arms of their mothers. Mothers and children were all malnourished, and had little hope of finding adequate health care or better nourishment in the city. This is the sad human face of poverty. The plight of these children and their families haunts me.

There is a section of Manila called Smokey Mountain. It is the garbage dump, a mountain of refuse adjacent to Manila Bay. At the time of my visit, several thousand people inhabited Smokey Mountain, eking out a living by selling scraps from the dump. To a visitor the stench is overpowering. This is abject poverty, unknown to most Americans, but all too pervasive in the Two-Thirds World.

One out of every five persons on earth lives on less than a dollar a day. Out of every twelve children born, at least one dies before his or her first birthday.[3] "Every three seconds, somewhere in the world, a child dies as a result of malnutrition. That's over 1,000 every hour, 30,000 every day, 10 million every year."[4] It is as if every morning Camden Yards, the baseball stadium in Baltimore, were to be filled with children and by evening all were dead. What is wrong with the world that such suffering can exist?

By and large these are not the images we sometimes see on TV or in news magazines, children with distended stomachs and arms and legs like toothpicks, victims of *famine* in Ethiopia or Somalia. Some people do starve to death, but even famine, the extreme of hunger, is usually the result of war or social upheaval along with adverse weather conditions. Such was the case in both Ethiopia and Somalia. Most often, however, the poor die of disease after being weakened by *chronic malnutrition*. People are malnourished, not because there is not enough food, but because they cannot afford to buy food, because of poverty.

For Reflection

It is difficult for a middle-class American to walk in the sandals of a poor Kenyan or Pakistani or Guatemalan. Economist Robert Heilbroner suggests a thought experiment of transforming a typical suburban American family into a typical family in the Two-Thirds World to convey the point:

"We begin by invading the house of our imaginary American family to strip it of its furniture. Everything goes: beds, chairs, tables, television sets, stereos, lamps. We will leave the family with a few old blankets, a kitchen table, a wooden chair. Along with the bureaus go the clothes. Each member of the family may keep in his or her "wardrobe" the oldest suit or dress, one pair of jeans, a shirt or blouse. We will permit a pair of shoes for the parents, but none for the children.

We move to the kitchen. The appliances have already been taken away, so we turn to the cupboards. The box of matches may stay, a small bag of flour, some sugar and salt. A few moldy potatoes, already in the garbage can, must be hastily rescued, for they will provide much of tonight's meal. We will leave the family with a handful of onions, and a dish of dried beans. All the rest we take away: the meat, the fresh vegetables, the canned goods, frozen foods, the crackers, snacks, candy.

Now we have stripped the house: the bathroom has been dismantled, the running water shut off, the electric wires taken out. Next we take away the house. The family can move to the toolshed. [The cars, of course, exit with the garage.] . . .

Communications must go next. [No phone. No Internet.] No more newspapers, magazines, books—not that they are missed, since we must take away our family's literacy as well. Instead, in our shantytown we will allow one radio.

Now government services must go. No mail delivery. No garbage pick-up. No fire protection. No water. No sewers. There is a two-room school, three miles away. There are, of course, no hospitals or doctors nearby. The nearest clinic is ten miles away and is tended by a midwife. It can be reached by bicycle, provided the family has a bicycle, which is unlikely. Or one can go by bus—not always inside, but there is usually room on top.

[There are no banks, no ATMs, no credit cards.] We will allow our family a cash hoard of five dollars. . . ."

Robert Heilbroner, *The Great Ascent: The Struggle for Economic Development in Our Time* (New York: Harper & Row, 1963), pp. 33–35, slightly edited.

Poverty means that people are not able to meet their own basic needs. Poverty means being hungry and malnourished; drinking unsanitary water; having no access to even basic health care such as immunizations against childhood diseases; living in crowded, unsafe, inadequate or no shelter; having no shoes or shirt to wear; being illiterate. The poor are anxious and fearful, constantly struggling to survive. Poverty means breaking your back for twelve hours in the hot sugar cane fields only to go deeper in debt to the landowner, or sweating over a sewing machine for ten hours and still not being able to afford three simple meals a day. At least two out of every three people on Earth live in poverty. They represent the Two-Thirds World.

If poverty demeans human dignity and stunts human potential, its antidote is development. By *development* I mean changing the whole social system so that every person has the opportunity to fulfill his or her full human potential and live a dignified and productive human life. Development is more than an economic concept; it is a human concept. There are three core values included in the meaning of human development: *sustenance*—the ability to meet basic needs, including food, shelter, health, and protection; *self-esteem*—a sense of worth and self-respect; and *freedom*—the ability to participate in significant personal and social choices. Since poverty precludes the attainment of these values, development aims to establish economic conditions and structures conducive to the realization of human potential and dignity. Generally, economic development requires economic growth and the reduction of inequality. "Rising per capita incomes, the elimination of absolute poverty, greater employment opportunities, and lessening income inequalities therefore constitute the *necessary* but not the *sufficient* conditions for development."[5]

Before addressing some of the issues involved in economic development, it is important to understand the economic inequalities that characterize the contemporary world.

THE GAP BETWEEN THE NORTH AND THE SOUTH

Specialists in international relations often divide the Earth into nine regions:

1. North America (Canada and the United States)
2. Latin America (Mexico, Central America, the Caribbean, and South America)
3. Western Europe
4. Russia and Eastern Europe (Eastern Europe and the 15 republics of the former Soviet Union)
5. The Middle East and North Africa (The countries on the southern and eastern shores of the Mediterranean Sea and the Persian Gulf, often referred to as simply the Middle East)
6. Africa (Sub-Saharan Africa)
7. South Asia (from Afghanistan through Indonesia)
8. China
9. Japan and the Pacific (including Australia and New Zealand)

These designations will generally be used in this book, but it is important to note that other terms and other divisions are used, especially regarding Asia. East Asia usually refers to China, Korea, and Japan. Southeast Asia refers to the countries from Myanmar (Burma) through Indonesia and the Philippines. South Asia sometimes includes Southeast Asia, and sometimes it does not. The divisions are artificial, but they do reflect commonalities of politics, economics, culture, and religion among the countries in the different regions.

In terms of economics, the most important division is between the wealthy, technologically developed countries of the "North"—North America,

Western Europe, Russia and Eastern Europe, and Japan and the Pacific—and the poor, less technologically developed countries of the "South"—Latin America, Africa, most of the Middle East, and Asia.[6]

Dividing the world into North and South, the core and the periphery, is a helpful way to picture the current *economic* situation of humanity. "In 1992, the poorest half of the world's people accounted for less than 15 percent of the global GDP [Gross Domestic Product]. Conversely, the 15 percent with the highest incomes accounted for over 50 percent of the global GDP."[7] The North-South division does not, of course, tell the whole truth about a very complex situation.

The economically developed countries of the North generally belong to the Organization for Economic Co-operation and Development. Often these industrial democracies are referred to as the "First World." Among the OECD countries are the Group of 7 (G7)—the United States, Japan, Italy, Great Britain, Germany, France, and Canada—which exercise a dominant role in the global economy. Russia and the former Republics of the Soviet Union and Eastern Europe are not among the OECD countries, and, although they are industrialized, they are classified as middle income, rather than high income countries.[8] These are the countries formerly under communist domination, the so-called "Second World." They are making the transition from a socialist to a capitalist economy, and from a totalitarian to a democratic polity. The economies of all of these countries have declined significantly, causing much hardship and suffering. Their economic and political transition is difficult and precarious. Economically, they are teetering between the North and the South. Among these countries, only Poland seems to be moving up instead of sliding down.

Many of the Organization of Petroleum Exporting Countries (OPEC) of the Middle East, such as Saudi Arabia, Kuwait, Qatar, and the United Arab Emirates, are high-income countries because they possess a valuable resource and generally have small populations. They are not industrialized, and their wealth is not evenly distributed. Nor is oil enough to guarantee a high per capita GDP. Iran, Iraq, Venezuela, and Liberia are all OPEC countries, but Liberia is a low-income country, and the others are middle-income countries. They have much larger populations, have had to contend with external and/or internal conflict, and have suffered from bad government or poor management.[9]

The South has been labeled the "Third World," an unfortunate and outdated term. The term mixed apples and oranges, economics and politics. The difference between the First World and the Third World was economic—wealth vs. poverty, technological development and the lack thereof. The Second World, a term seldom used, referred to the communist countries, the East vs. the West, distinguished more by their politics than their economic development. Except for China, Cuba, and North Korea (politically worrisome exceptions to be sure), the Second World no longer exists. Nor is it easy to classify the economies of the formerly communist countries, most of which are industrialized, yet relatively poor and struggling through an economic transition.

Even before the end of the Cold War, the Third World was a problematic designation. It is a pejorative term. The First World are the winners, the Third World, the losers. The term refers only to economic and technological development, not to cultural or human development. India, for example, is one of the world's centers for spiritual development, and Filipinos may be among the world's most hospitable people. Nor does Third World capture the diversity of economic development found in the less industrialized countries. The economies of Niger, Nepal, and Haiti, which are among the poorest in the world, should not be lumped together with those of Algeria, Argentina, and Costa Rica which are much more economically developed. Moreover, the First and Third designations gloss over the history of colonialism and imperialism that is the background for the current situation, and there is more than a hint of racism lurking here.

It is, however, difficult to find more adequate language for highlighting the global reality that a minority of the countries of the world, with a minority of the world's population, enjoy a high standard of living, while most of the people on Earth must struggle to meet their most basic needs. The notion of the "Two-Thirds World" at least captures the idea that the poor greatly outnumber the rich, and the global North and South point to the reality of rich and poor countries in a helpful way.

OVERCOMING POVERTY

The meaning of poverty—its human reality and global prevalence—is almost beyond our comprehension. Certainly any compassionate and just person, when made aware that over a billion brothers and sisters on planet Earth are hungry, will care enough to want to right this wrong. The causes of global poverty, however, are complex and controversial, as are the solutions. Indeed, it is even hard to measure poverty.[10] In order to address the global issue of poverty, it is important to understand some economic terms.

The most common measure of poverty is *income analysis*, which is based on the annual *gross domestic product* (GDP)—the value of all goods and services produced within a country's borders—and/or *gross national product* (GNP)—GDP plus net income from abroad—divided by the number of people in the country to yield the *per capita* GDP or GNP. (See the Appendix for information on the GDP and GDP per capita of the various countries of the world.) While per capita GDP (or GNP) can give some sense of the economic well-being or standard of living of a country's average resident, it does not tell us anything about the distribution of income within the country. If a country has 10 people, for example, one of whom is enormously wealthy and the rest destitute, the per capita GDP may look fairly equitable even though most of the people are desperately poor. In countries with a rich elite and a multitude of poor, there is no average resident. The *Gini coefficient* is used to gauge the economic inequality of a nation. It ranges from 0 (exact equality) to 1 (one person owns everything). The higher the Gini coefficient the greater the inequality of wealth and income within a country.[11]

Until recently the comparative per capita GDP of various countries was based on the official exchange rates of the countries' currencies. These market exchange rates, however, may not reflect a currency's true purchasing power at home. Thus, since about 1992 some economists have begun making the comparison on the basis of *purchasing power parity* (PPP), that is, how much a common "market basket" of goods and services each currency can purchase locally. In general, PPP comparisons produce slightly lower per capita GDP figures in wealthy countries and higher ones in poorer nations.[12] (The table in the Appendix lists the per capita GDP based on exchange rates and on PPP for the various countries of the world for comparison.)

A different measure of poverty is a *basic needs approach* which yields the *human development index* (HDI). The HDI combines standard of living (real per capita GDP), life expectancy, and educational attainment in an effort to acknowledge that overall income is not the only measure of how well or ill a nation is doing in meeting the basic needs of its people. In 1993 the HDI ranking of 37 countries was more than 20 places higher or lower than their ranking by per capita income. Costa Rica, for example, ranks 31st on the HDI, but 54th in per capita GDP, while Kuwait is 51st in HDI and 5th in per capita GDP. Although Kuwait has nearly twice the per capita income, it does considerably worse than Costa Rica in meeting the basic needs of all of its people.[13] (See the Appendix for the HDI ranking and value and the gender development index [GDI], which measures the social and economic status and equality of women, for the countries of the world.)

No matter how poverty is measured, the gulf between the poor and rich in the world is becoming wider; the South and North are becoming polarized into two very different worlds. "The poorest 20% of the world's people saw their share of global income decline from 2.3% to 1.4% in the past 30 years. Meanwhile the share of the richest 20% rose from 70% to 85%. That doubled the ratio of the shares of the richest and the poorest—from 30:1 to 61:1."[14] "Of the $23 trillion global GDP in 1993, $18 trillion is in the industrial countries—only $5 trillion in the developing countries, even though they have nearly 80% of the world's people."[15]

There are bright spots and dark spots in this rather bleak picture. Since 1980 there has been a dramatic surge in economic growth in some 15 countries, mostly in Asia, bringing rapidly rising incomes to many of their 1.5 billion people. Yet, after experiencing 3 percent annual economic growth in the 1970s, per capita GDP decreased from 1981 to 1991 in the Middle East, Africa, and most of Latin America. Thus 1.6 billion people, about a quarter of the world's population, have suffered reduced incomes due to economic decline or stagnation since 1980.[16] The transitional economies of the former Soviet empire account for some of this decline, but the incomes of many of the world's poorest people are decreasing. This is especially so in Africa. If we examine the economic successes and failures in the developing world, we find that there is no simple or single way to economic development.

There can be no economic development without sustained economic growth, that is, unless the national economy registers a growth in GDP year after year.[17] Otherwise the population shares scarcity and is subject to lower levels of employment and income. In the first chapter we saw how the tremendous productivity of the Industrial Revolution (along with colonialism) allowed Britain (and then other countries) to attain remarkable economic growth.

A half dozen developing countries have achieved self-sustaining capital accumulation and impressive economic growth in recent times.[18] They are called the *newly industrializing countries* (NICs). The most successful NICs are the four tigers of East Asia—South Korea, Taiwan, Hong Kong, and Singapore. In part, at least, these Asian success stories are following in the footsteps of *the* Asian success, Japan.

South Korea has become competitive in steel and automobiles, Taiwan in electronics. Hong Kong's strength is banking and trade, and Singapore is well-situated to be a center of trade. The latter two are more city-states than nation-states, and Hong Kong reverted to Chinese sovereignty from British control in 1997. Taiwan was formerly a province of China, although it is not now under the control of China's communist government.

The NICs have used a capitalist model of development based on industrialization, export, and trade, fostered by authoritarian government, to achieve their impressive economic growth. By the end of the 1980s the authoritarian governments of South Korea and Taiwan were striding toward democracy.

Thailand, Malaysia, and Indonesia are trying to copy the NIC model for economic growth, but it is too soon to tell if they will succeed. This export-oriented model of development has become a mold that the international lending institutions—the World Bank and the International Monetary Fund (IMF)—impose on all developing countries which apply for loans (capital). This is problematic because (1) this mold does not match up with the diverse economic, social, and cultural situations in developing countries, (2) it often penalizes the poor for the past mismanagement or corruption of the ruling elite, and (3) it falsely assumes that economic growth will result in genuine development for the poor, overlooking the role of the distribution of income and wealth. This point will be further developed later in this chapter.

Since the late 1970s China, the world's most populous country, has achieved rapid economic growth and rising standards of living. After World War II, Mao Zedong and his communist revolutionaries seized control of China. Mao's socialist economic policy emphasized national self-sufficiency, central planning, and state ownership of property, farms, and industry.

Although a very poor country in terms of GDP, China was rather successful in meeting the basic needs of its people. By focusing first on agriculture, China eliminated the recurrent famines and starvation that had characterized its modern history; it basically succeeded in feeding its people. Wages were meager, but nearly everyone had a job. Everyone was assured of housing, education, and health care. Meeting the basic needs of its people was a remarkable feat for China.[19]

While China struggled to honor the economic rights of its people, it failed to recognize basic civil rights such as free speech, freedom of movement, participation in government, and fair trials. The repression suffered by the Chinese people during the Cultural Revolution from 1966–1976 was especially horrendous. Moreover, China's wealth and income were not increasing fast enough to continue to meet the basic needs of a population that was growing despite the Draconian one-child-per-family policy.

After Mao died in 1976, one of his lieutenants, Deng Xiaoping, instituted economic reforms based on capitalist principles, beginning in the southern coastal provinces. Foreign investment—from Taiwan, Japan, the United States, and Europe—flooded into China, hoping to get a foothold in the world's largest market. Economic growth has been rapid, but so have increases in class disparities, social problems, and a yearning for participation in government. When students and others filled Beijing's Tiananmen Square in 1989 to demonstrate nonviolently for a more representative government, they were crushed and silenced by the army. One wonders how long a free market in China can exist without a free government. At the moment China is stubbornly holding to its market communism.

India, the world's most populous democracy, has also developed a mixed economy, but its state-owned industries have been largely unprofitable, and government corruption and bureaucracy have discouraged foreign investment. Economic reforms in the early 1990s have resulted in modest economic growth in India, but it remains to be seen whether this can be sustained, increased, and fairly distributed.

With the exception of Japan and the four tigers, the countries of Asia are poor. Yet many of them show signs of genuine economic development. Even Bangladesh, a country with few natural resources, where flooding and hurricanes routinely ravage the land, has experienced modest economic growth and a democratic transfer of power in 1996.[20] In much of Asia, however, economic growth tends to get swallowed up by population growth or stolen through corruption.

Africa is a continent characterized by swelling populations, corrupt government, rampant disease, crushing poverty, ecological devastation, and brutal ethnic conflicts and civil wars. In the countries of Africa there is little economic growth to be swallowed or stolen.[21] A possible exception is South Africa which is moving, albeit unsteadily, toward a multi-ethnic, democratic society with a recovering capitalist economy that is trying to meet the basic needs of its black majority as well as its white minority. Some of the countries of southern Africa have at least resolved the conflicts (often fueled by Cold War tensions) that were tearing their societies apart, and Angola, Namibia, and Botswana have achieved per capita GDPs comparable to South Africa. Africa's overall development prognosis, however, is pessimistic.

The countries of Latin America illustrate two themes characteristic of the economic development debate—the debt crisis and the role of multi-national corporations (MNCs) in investment and trade.

THE DEBT CRISIS

Debt is a daunting obstacle to economic development for most countries in the Two-Thirds World. Brazil and Mexico, the largest developing countries in the Western hemisphere, have accumulated the largest debts. Brazil's external debt in 1992 was well over $100 billion and Mexico's was just under that amount. Nicaragua's $10 billion debt represents 112 percent of its annual GNP.[22]

In the late 1980s the world experienced a debt crisis when Brazil, Mexico, and other countries threatened to default on their loans. Had they done so, the international banking system might have collapsed.

The debt crisis began in the mid-1970s when the OPEC countries were awash in petrodollars, and banks were eager to lend billions. Developing countries borrowed billions at low, but adjustable or floating, interest rates.

Borrowing capital can be sensible, even advisable, when the money is invested in productive use, such as developing industry, because the profit can be used to repay the loan. Unfortunately, the ruling elites in many Two-Thirds World countries used the money for current consumption, not productive investment. Healthy chunks disappeared due to graft and corruption, as happened in the Philippines where Marcos and his cronies stole over $5 billion. Loans were used for showcase projects like the Cultural Center in Manila which has been a dismal failure in attracting profitable international events. Some of the debt was incurred to pay for oil which had become prohibitively expensive after 1973. In effect, the Arab sheiks had their petrodollars returned to them to be loaned again. Perhaps 20 percent of Third World debt went to purchase weapons.[23] Using a loan for unproductive or unprofitable purchases leaves the borrower with no way to repay the loans. Note that the poor did not benefit from these loans, nor did the poor participate in the decisions to borrow or how to spend the money.

Then in the 1980s interest rates floated upward dramatically. During the Reagan administration the United States lowered taxes and increased military spending by borrowing heavily, which sent international interest rates skyrocketing. A 1 percent increase on a $1 billion loan increases the interest payment by $10 million. Interest rates doubled and tripled, pushing the interest payment beyond the means of developing countries. At the same time prices for raw materials (commodities) plummeted, leaving poor countries with even less income to service their debt. Thus Brazil and Mexico considered defaulting on their loans, in effect declaring bankruptcy.

Commercial banks in conjunction with First World governments scrambled to re-negotiate the loans to prevent default. Several years of this process alleviated the debt crisis. The commercial banks, which were seriously overextended, have reduced their investment in developing countries and placed themselves on surer financial footing. Most First World banks are now sound and secure; Third World countries are not. They remain seriously indebted and less able to qualify for loans. Between 1982 and 1990 the poor nations of the Two-Thirds World transferred $418 billion into the coffers of the First World banks.[24]

No longer able to turn to commercial banks for capital, developing countries must turn to the World Bank or the International Monetary Fund (IMF). In order to insure that loans will be repaid the IMF imposes a program of *"structural adjustment"* on the borrower. This means that the government must cut spending in order to decrease its deficit and stabilize its currency, and it must convert its economy toward export production. Governments decrease spending by cutting social spending—education, health care, food subsidies, etc. For example, there were riots in the Middle Eastern country of Jordan in August, 1996 when King Hussein allowed the price of bread to more than double, from 13 cents to 28 cents a kilo, as part of an IMF structural adjustment program. Nearly one of three Jordanians live below the poverty level, and Jordan's national debt amounts to $2,700 for every Jordanian.[25] Export production often means growing more cash crops which are vulnerable to falling commodity prices. "Instead of penalizing the wealthy and the military, the burden of structural adjustment has fallen squarely on the poor and the middle class."[26]

Debt is a difficult hurdle to overcome. If a developing nation repudiates its debt, it risks retaliation and isolation. The various debt reduction plans, such as the 1989 Brady Plan, have helped somewhat, but they do not go far enough. The international banking system is no longer at risk. Thus the central concern now should be restoring economic growth and development to countries in the Two-Thirds World. These countries will not, because they cannot, ever repay their debt. Overall, the banks have been repaid with a handsome profit.

Perhaps it is time for the First World countries to take three steps in the interest of the economic development of the Two-Thirds World. First, heed the words of the "Our Father"—"And forgive us our debts, as we also have forgiven our debtors" (Mt. 6:12). It is at once generous, just, and realistic to forgive all or part of the debts of some developing countries, depending on their ability to pay. Many countries in Sub-Saharan Africa would benefit from being totally released from their debts, as would Nicaragua, for example. Other countries such as Brazil, Mexico, Venezuela and countries of Eastern Europe could perhaps afford to pay half of what they owe.[27]

Secondly the IMF needs to reassess its one-size-fits-all mold of structural adjustment. According to *Human Development Report 1996* there is a mutually reinforcing relationship between economic growth and human development (pp. 5–6). If that is so, then economic growth at the expense of the poor, which is the effect of structural adjustment, will not work. Genuine development depends on both growth and equity.

Thirdly, "The developed countries have a responsibility to create conditions whereby the poorer countries can interact more productively in international economic activities: their single most important contribution to this end might be in the area of reducing trade restrictions on the products of poorer countries."[28] Not only free trade, but preferential trade is key to the long term solution to poverty in the Two-Thirds World.

Developing countries have an essential responsibility here as well. In the debt crisis, the banks were greedy, but the governments of many poor countries were corrupt, self-aggrandizing, and inept. Developing countries have a responsibility to utilize funds effectively for productive goals. Lenders have a responsibility to foster that responsibility as well. The IMF is right to set conditions that endeavor to insure that loans are not poured into a sinkhole. The obscene personal profits of Marcos in the Philippines or Mobutu of Zaire should not be tolerated by the First World. In my observation, multi-million dollar projects in developing countries almost always serve primarily the elite and ignore or even harm the poor. Loans or grants in the tens of thousands of dollars range are generally much more likely to genuinely empower the poor. Such funds could ordinarily be channeled through community organizations, especially in situations where there is a corrupt government bureaucracy. For example, Oxfam is a private organization that implements this model in its development projects. (See the Resources section for information on Oxfam.)

MULTI-NATIONAL CORPORATIONS AND INVESTMENT

Latin American countries also illustrate the ambiguous role of MNCs in development. Multi-national corporations or trans-national corporations are centrally organized, but have no real home. Many of them, such as Exxon, Toyota, and Daimler-Benz, originate in OECD countries, but some are now appearing in the NICs, such as Samsung and Hyundai in South Korea, and even in some developing countries, like Pemex in Mexico. Whatever its national origin, a MNC seeks to maximize its own interests and those of its shareholders, rather than the interests of any country or of the poor. Although MNCs are not in the development business, their investment of capital, technology, and management skills, which can create jobs and foreign exchange for developing countries, can contribute to economic development. The question is: whose interests does this private foreign direct investment serve?

MNCs are central actors in the globalization of the world economy, that is, in the increasing integration of national economies into an international market. They are not the pawns of any state, rich or poor, but independent actors, influenced by a global market which they in large part create and manipulate, and from which they profit. The global economy has become fiercely competitive and unforgiving of inefficiency; it seems to transcend the control of even the most powerful governments or corporations.

In truth, however, the economy is a human reality, not one that transcends human control. The economy is a system set up by human choices, that should serve human needs, and that can be changed by human decisions.[29] It may be that some economic systems serve human needs better than others, and that an economic system can make it easier or harder for various actors in the economy to make ethical and just choices.

Table 2.1
100 Largest Economic Entities

COUNTRY/ CORPORATION	GNP/REVENUES ($ MILLIONS)	COUNTRY/ CORPORATION	GNP/REVENUES ($ MILLIONS)
1. United States	6,378,873	51. Israel	72,653
2. Japan	3,919,529	52. Daimler-Benz (Germany)	72,256
3. Germany	1,901,131	53. IBM (U.S.)	71,940
4. France	1,292,556	54. Matsushita Elec. Indus. (Japan)	70,398
5. Italy	1,133,287	55. General Electric (U.S.)	70,028
6. United Kingdom	1,045,994	56. Tomen (Japan)	67,755
7. Canada	574,786	57. Mobil (U.S.)	66,724
8. Spain	536,547	58. Nissan Motor (Japan)	62,568
9. Brazil	458,504	59. Volkswagen (Germany)	61,489
10. China (GDP)	425,611	60. Siemens (Germany)	60,673
11. Russian Federation	347,896	61. Malaysia	59,808
12. Korea, Rep	338,044	62. Venezuela	59,393
13. Mexico	324,997	63. Dai-Ichi Mut. Life Insur. (Japan)	58,052
14. Netherlands	320,120	64. British Petroleum (Britain)	56,981
15. Australia	307,967	65. Metro Holding (Switzerland)	56,459
16. India	269,460	66. Singapore	55,380
17. Switzerland	252,197	67. Philippines	55,080
18. Argentina	243,877	68. U.S. Postal Service (U.S.)	54,293
19. Belgium	217,537	69. Chrysler (U.S.)	53,195
20. Sweden	215,013	70. Philip Morris (U.S.)	53,139
21. Austria	184,829	71. Toshiba (Japan)	53,046
22. Mitsubishi (Japan)	184,365	72. Pakistan	52,805
23. Mitsui (Japan)	181,518	73. Tokyo Electric Power (Japan)	52,361
24. Turkey	177,003	74. Daewoo (South Korea)	51,215
25. Itochu (Japan)	169,164	75. Nichimen (Japan)	50,841
26. General Motors (U.S.)	168,828	76. Sumitomo Life Insurance (Japan)	50,710
27. Sumitomo (Japan)	167,530	77. Colombia	49,955
28. Maruben (Japan)	161,057	78. Kanematsu (Japan)	49,838
29. Indonesia	138,492	79. Unilever (Britain/Netherlands)	49,738
30. Denmark	138,049	80. Nestle (Switzerland)	47,780
31. Ford Motor (U.S.)	137,137	81. Sony (Japan)	47,581
32. Iran, Islamic Rep	134,174	82. Algeria	47,565
33. Saudi Arabia	133,275	83. Fiat (Italy)	46,467
34. Thailand	122,515	84. Veba Group (Germany)	46,279
35. South Africa	118,184	85. Deutsche Telekom (Germany)	46,148
36. Ukraine	113,928	86. Allianz Holding (Germany)	46,044
37. Norway	111,628	87. Ireland	45,928
38. Toyota Motor (Japan)	111,052	88. Nec (Japan)	45,557
39. Exxon (U.S.)	110,009	89. Honda Motor (Japan)	4,055
40. Royal Dutch/Shell Group (Brit./Neth.)	109,833	90. New Zealand	43,941
		91. Chile	43,816
41. Nissho Iwai (Japan)	97,886	92. Elf Aquitaine (France)	43,618
42. Finland	97,624	93. Electricité de France (France)	43,507
43. Wal-Mart Stores (U.S.)	93,627	94. Iraq	42,725
44. Portugal	89,848	95. Union des Assur. de Paris (France)	42,004
45. Poland, Rep	86,565	96. Iri (Italy)	41,903
46. Hitachi (Japan)	84,167	97. Prudential Ins. Co. of Amer. (U.S.)	41,330
47. Nippon Life Ins. (Japan)	83,206	98. State Farm Group (U.S.)	40,148
48. Nippon Tel & Tel (Japan)	81,937	99. Philips Electronics (Netherlands)	40,148
49. AT&T (U.S.)	79,609	100. Fujitsu (Japan)	38,976
50. Greece	76,599		

Sources: GNP 1993 from *World Resources 1996–97*. "Fortune's Global 500 — The World's Largest Corporations," *Fortune* 134 (Aug. 5, 1996), pp. F-1, F-2. Revenues are for 1995.

Corporations are also human realities. If their boards of directors and managers single-mindedly seek the maximization of profit without a thought for their workers, the environment, the communities in which they are located, then that is a choice, not the nature of a corporation. A corporation can also choose to seek a fair profit for its owners and to pay a fair wage to its workers, not harm the environment, and contribute constructively to the community. The tensions implied in these choices become particularly acute when powerful MNCs operate in poor countries.

One issue is the sheer wealth and power of MNCs in comparison with that of developing countries. As Table 2.1 indicates, in a ranking of countries and corporations according to the size of their annual product, over 40 percent of the top 100 consistently will be corporations. Thus, countries in the Two-Thirds World are often at a disadvantage in negotiating with a MNC for needed investment and jobs. This is especially so if the MNC is subcontracting with a foreign-owned factory in a free enterprise zone in a developing country. If, for example, the cost of labor rises in Indonesia, or if Indonesia raises taxes or strengthens regulations such as its minimum wage or environmental or safety laws, a company such as Nike can move its operations to Vietnam without having to move the factory. Nike simply terminates one contract, say with a Taiwanese-owned factory in Indonesia, and enters into another contract with a Korean-owned factory in Vietnam.[30] In this way, workers and communities are often at the mercy of MNCs.

Too often the end result of this global economic system of investment and trade is not the economic development of poor countries, but a net transfer of more wealth from the South to the North. Typically about $43 billion a year flows from the Two-Thirds World to the First World.[31]

MNCs argue that they invest large amounts of capital in developing countries and bring sophisticated technology and management skills there which create jobs, produce goods and services, and increase economic growth. Critics contend that the MNCs *control* capital and technology, introduce inappropriate technology (tractors instead of tillers), manipulate markets and crush cultures through advertising (infant formula instead of breast milk, Coca-Cola instead of fruit juice), and in the end take the profits home.[32] These critics interpret such MNC operations as neo-colonialism.

While MNCs are not always good for developing countries, in a global capitalist economic system (and at the moment there seems to be no serious available alternative to a market economy) investment, technology, and economic growth are essential (but not sufficient) for development. MNCs are not going to go away, and countries in the Two-Thirds World often need what they can bring. The challenge is to make sure MNC investment in the South results in genuine development, not exploitation.

International codes of conduct as well as reasonable national regulations such as minimum wage requirements that provide at least a subsistence wage for a family, safety standards, child labor prohibitions, environmental protections, the right to unionize, etc., can be helpful. In a competitive business environment a level playing field allows corporations to be at least minimally fair and ethical. If, for example, there is no minimum wage or no environmental restrictions, then the corporation that pays its workers well or controls its emissions is at a competitive disadvantage, at least in the short term. Obviously, independent monitoring and vigorous enforcement of corporate compliance is as important as the regulations themselves.

In the Spring of 1996 the responsibility of MNCs toward workers in developing countries was publicly debated. TV personality Kathy Lee Gifford, who was also the celebrity sponsor of a fashion line for Wal-Mart, was fingered by Charles Kernaghan of the National Labor Committee, at a Congressional hearing, for turning a blind eye to labor abuses in Honduras where the clothes were made. Ms. Gifford had been honored for giving $1 million of her clothing line's $9 million in annual profit to the Association to Benefit Children, which opened shelters for crack-addicted children and children with AIDS. Ms. Gifford was embarrassed and repentant, calling on Wal-Mart to monitor subcontractors in the Two-Thirds World regarding fair treatment of workers. When Michael Jordan, a $20 million a year spokesperson for Nike, was similarly criticized for Nike's treatment of workers in Indonesia, he dodged responsibility, passing the ball to Nike.[33]

As usual the issues here are complex and controversial. Critics of the MNCs contend that the *maquiladoras*, as the assembly factories in Central America are called, exploit poor workers to make exorbitant profits. Mexico's minimum wage varies from region to region, but in 1995 it was about $20.00 per week. The take home pay of a Zenith *maquiladora* worker in Reynosa, Mexico was $19.27 for the week of March 24, 1995, or 48 cents per hour. This worker was making Mexico's minimum wage, but his weekly check was not even a subsistence wage, much less a just or living wage, as called for in Catholic social teaching. A market basket survey in March 1995 showed that Mexicans need $6.66 a day to meet basic needs. This worker was receiving less than half that. If Juan wanted to purchase a Big Mac, Coke and fries at the local McDonalds it would take about a day's pay.[34] Similarly, the girls and young women who make Nike sneakers in factories in Vietnam make $1.60 a day, but three meals of rice and vegetables cost $2.10.[35]

In *maquiladoras* that produce clothes under contract for The Gap, J.C. Penneys, Sears, Eddie Bauer, etc., the cost of labor is often less than 1 percent of the retail purchase price of the finished product. For example, a Honduran woman is paid 16 cents to produce a shirt that The Gap sells for $20.00. A pair of Nike sneakers sells in the United States for more than a month's pay of the Indonesian workers who produce it.[36] It would seem that corporations could easily afford to pay workers better wages. Yet, in 1994, Allied Signal corporation paid Lawrence Bossidy, its Chief Executive Officer (CEO), $12.4 million, but it paid its entire Mexican workforce of 3,810 only an estimated $7.8 million.[37]

Philip Knight, the billionaire Chief Executive Officer (CEO) of Nike, argues that Nike subcontractors in Indonesia pay, on average, double the minimum wage there, plus provide free meals and subsidies for housing, health care, and transportation. MNCs bring desperately needed jobs to developing countries. If corporations do not seek the lowest possible wage they will not stay competitive and will go under. Then no one will have jobs. Mr. Knight points out that real wages have risen 55 percent in Indonesia since 1990.[38]

It is worth noting, however, that Nike posted a record $298 million profit in 1993, and that Nike's earnings had nearly tripled in five years. The average hourly wage paid in athletic footware factories in Indonesia was 18 cents. Less than 3 percent of the cost of a Nike sneaker goes for labor.[39]

When *New York Times* reporter Larry Rohter visited the free enterprise zone in Honduras—the site of the criticism of Ms. Gifford—he found that conditions in the apparel factories there varied widely. Some were unionized; some were union busting. Some were clean and air conditioned; others were hot and squalid. Some plants abused their workers, requiring overtime, imposing unreachable production quotas, and firing pregnant workers to avoid paying maternity benefits. But other plants respected worker rights, subsidized lunch, and provided free health care. Several of the Hondurans he interviewed considered their jobs in the *maquiladoras* a tremendous opportunity in comparison to the agricultural work they had been doing.[40]

Most of the factories were Taiwanese- or Korean-owned subcontractors with American MNCs. The subcontractors generally pledge to follow a code of conduct respecting worker's rights adopted by MNCs such as The Gap, but *monitoring* their compliance is the key. Indeed, consumer pressure, including a concerted effort by students at the College of Saint Catherine in St. Paul, Minnesota, resulted in The Gap agreeing to allow *independent* monitoring of the labor conditions in the *maquiladoras* in El Salvador and elsewhere.[41]

As incredible as it may seem, the question of child labor in developing countries is also controversial. Worldwide there are 250 million 5- to 14-year-olds working, half of them full-time. Slavery or child bondage is still practiced in parts of Asia and Africa. There are about a million child prostitutes in Asia and their number is increasing in Asia and Africa.[42] Who could support the practice of 10-year-olds working 10-hour days sewing soccer balls in Pakistan or rugs in India?[43] But what about a 14-year-old girl working six hours a day in an apparel factory in Honduras? Education for most Hondurans ends with the sixth grade. Honduran law allows 14-year-olds to work 6-hour days with their parent's permission. If teenagers are not allowed to work in the *maquiladoras* they will not be in school, but rather seeking more demanding work for even less pay in the fields.[44] Teen labor, however, is different from child labor. The first step, it would seem, is to monitor compliance with the laws already established in developing countries.

In response to this controversy over sweatshops, President Clinton established the White House Apparel Industry Partnership, a task force that included representatives of labor unions, human rights groups, and industry powerhouses, to develop a Workplace Code of Conduct. Not surprisingly, the task proved to be difficult and contentious. In April of 1997, the task force announced a tentative accord, more of a work-in-progress than a finished product. Apparel-makers who sign the Code of Conduct pledge to provide abuse-free factories, hire workers at least 15 years old, limit the workweek to 60 hours, pay at least the local minimum wage, and protect the right of workers to organize. Monitors of the code can be chosen by the companies as long as they are accredited by the overseeing association.

The accord did not resolve a dispute about whether violations should be made public or simply reported to the company. Because the local minimum wage is not even a subsistence wage in countries such as Indonesia and Haiti, labor and human rights representatives have argued that companies should commit themselves to pay a wage that could provide the basic needs for a family. Apparel companies and retailers insisted that a "living wage" could prove both too expensive and too hard to define. Companies that comply with the Code of Conduct will be able to declare that their products are not made in sweatshops, perhaps by attaching a "No Sweat" label. This accord seems to be a constructive first step. Its success depends on industry compliance, on rigorous enforcement, and on consumer support for companies which comply with the code.[45]

The exploitation of the worker has been a social justice issue since the beginning of the Industrial Revolution, and it continues to be a major concern as multi-national corporations routinely scan the earth in search of cheaper labor and higher profits.

FOREIGN AID

Another form of investment in developing countries comes from foreign aid from one government to another. Foreign aid has been unpopular among many Americans for some time because they think the United States should take care of its own poor and address its own social problems before helping others. This view is in tension with the theological notion that all humanity is the family of God, brothers and sisters to one another, each person with an unearned value from being created in the image and likeness of God. According to this perspective a hungry Chadian, Chinese, or Colombian child is of equal concern as a hungry American child. In justice, all of them deserve an opportunity to develop their full human potential. Indeed the greater need of brothers and sisters in the Two-Thirds World may invoke a greater responsibility from the more affluent in the human community. Moreover, as we have seen, there is at least an indirect connection between the wealth of the few and the poverty of the many on planet Earth. Our obligation to respond to the needs of the poor may be rooted in justice more than in charity.

This stinginess regarding foreign aid also goes contrary to the American perception of ourselves as a generous people. As the world's wealthiest country, surely we can afford to assist the neediest. And many Americans think, incorrectly, that the United States is generous toward the Two-Thirds World. There are some popular misconceptions regarding foreign aid, and there is certainly room for reform. But the reforms proposed by the Republican Congress in the Spring of 1995 played on the misperceptions and generally steered the country in the wrong direction.

In a national poll taken in January of 1995, 75 percent of Americans thought that the United States spent too much on foreign aid. When asked what percentage of the annual Federal budget is spent for this, the typical guess was 15 percent, and 41 percent of Americans thought that foreign aid was the largest single item in the budget.[46]

The truth is that foreign aid accounts for only 1 percent of the Federal budget, or about $15 billion, and only half of that goes for development assistance. Compared with other industrial countries, the United States gives the lowest percentage of its GNP, 0.15 percent, to foreign aid. With the world's largest economy, the United States used to give the largest gross amount to foreign aid, even though it was still the smallest percentage. No longer. In 1995 it fell to fourth place in amount of money contributed, behind Japan, France, and Germany, economies less than half the size of the United States.[47] The Scandinavian countries generally lead the list in percentage of GNP given for development assistance. By these numbers, it seems the United States should be increasing its foreign aid, not cutting it.

During the Cold War, there were some definite problems with the U.S. foreign aid program. Military aid and economic aid were lumped together (as they still are), and both tended to be used to fight communism and assist U.S. farmers and manufacturers, rather than assist in the development of the poor. Thus, if Georgia farmers had a surplus of peanuts (or, worse, tobacco), the United States would send peanut butter to the Philippines, not because they needed it, but because the Philippines was a strategically placed, anti-communist country. This helped Georgia farmers and Philippine dictators, but it might actually skew the Philippine market and hurt the poor.[48] Israel and Egypt, strategic allies in the Middle East, are still by far the largest beneficiaries of U.S. assistance, together receiving about a third of the total, and most of that in the form of military aid.[49] Although most foreign aid today is in grants, some of it is provided in loans, which contribute to the indebtedness of poor countries. Every college student knows the difference between a grant and a loan.

Bilateral foreign aid (directly from one country to another) is often conditioned on the recipient purchasing American products, such as Ford tractors. This ties a foreign market into American products and parts, but it might not be the best for the recipient. Competitive bidding might have resulted in getting less expensive tractors, if tractors are what the recipient needs in the first place. For example, in 1981 Norway, with the best of intentions, built a state-of-the-art fish freezing plant on the shore of Lake Turkana in tropical Kenya at a cost of over $20 million. This project was so culturally and technologically inappropriate as to be funny were it not so wasteful and disastrous. The cost of operating the freezers in tropical weather exceeded the income from the frozen fish fillets. The Turkana people were herders who disdained fishing. And periodic droughts shrunk the lake so that the plant was no longer on the shore.[50] Clearly a fish freezing plant was not the best use of Norway's aid funds.

As noted above, foreign aid has too often been lost to corruption or used for inappropriate, ostentatious, unwise, or even harmful projects. When the purpose of the aid was to support anti-communist dictators, the donor could turn a blind eye to corruption and waste. Enriching and arming dictators does create allies, but at the cost of moral principles and of greater suffering for the poor.

Thankfully, the end of the Cold War has eliminated the anti-communist rationale for foreign aid, and has corrected some of the abuses connected with that purpose. Yet the United States still uses foreign aid to serve its political and economic self-interest. It is perhaps unrealistic, and perhaps unwise, to think foreign aid should be blind to the interests of a nation's foreign policy, but its primary purpose should be humanitarian—to empower the poorest through assisting them in meeting their basic needs. Thus the primary criterion for receiving development assistance should be need, but other considerations, such as the human rights record of the government and even U.S. strategic interest could be considered. Development assistance should be separated from military aid. The former should increase; the latter decline. In general, development assistance should be channeled through multilateral institutions (such as the United Nations) in order to increase the effectiveness of the aid for the recipient, rather than for the donor. There should be grassroots participation of the recipients in the design and implementation of projects that empower the poor to realize their human potential. Small-scale projects may generally be much more likely to benefit the poor. In these ways foreign aid can become genuinely development assistance.[51]

TRADE AND NAFTA

Among those concerned for the economic development of poor countries there has been an energetic debate about trade policy. Some have argued for *inward-looking development policies* (called "import substitution") that attempt to build indigenous industries and technologies appropriate for a country's resources through high tariffs and import quotas that protect domestic production. Others have fostered *outward-looking development policies* (called "export promotion") that welcome foreign investment and encourage free trade in the large global marketplace. The latter strategy seems to have worked well for the East Asian NICs.[52]

The current consensus among development economists "leans toward an eclectic view that attempts to fit the relevant arguments of both free-trade and protectionist models to the specific economic, institutional, and political realities of diverse Third World nations at different stages of development. What works for one may not work for another."[53] Not only is it important to attend to the specific situation of a developing country, but fluctuations in the world economy can also have a decisive impact on the success of a particular development strategy. An expanding world economy, for example, can assist an export oriented policy, while a global recession can stifle it. Thus, the economic decisions taken by developed countries can have a devastating impact on developing economies.[54]

Four further insights can be garnered from reflection on the struggle for economic development during the past five decades:[55]

(1) An inegalitarian power structure can turn either an export oriented policy or an import substitution strategy toward more inequality. It is not only trade policy that is important, but whose interests the policy is intended to serve.

(2) Successful development seems to be linked to effective cooperation between the private and public sectors which have a shared commitment to a consistent and coherent development strategy. Consistent cooperation may be as important as the strategy itself.

(3) The expansion of trade among developing countries (South-South trade and regional trading blocs) may have important benefits for development not found in trade between developed and developing countries (North-South trade). South-South trade may foster greater collective self-reliance among developing countries and reduce some of the export instability found in the world economy.

(4) Trade barriers (tariffs, quotas, etc.) erected by developed countries against the exports of developing countries are a major obstacle to their efforts at diversification and trade expansion. Often these barriers were higher for processed products than for raw materials (higher for shirts than for cotton, for example), which adversely affected the terms of trade between developed and developing countries and hampered efforts at industrialization. The 1995 General Agreement on Tariffs and Trade (GATT) establishes freer trade between South and North, but it remains to be seen whether this more competitive free market will benefit the least developed countries. Perhaps the North needs to move beyond free trade with the South toward trade arrangements that give a preference to developing countries which need assistance in becoming more competitive and whose egalitarian domestic policies indicate that economic growth will likely mean genuine development for the poor.[56] Either free trade or preferential trade will require adjustment assistance programs for displaced workers in developed countries.

The North American Free Trade Agreement (NAFTA) has given some focus to this general discussion about the trade relationship between developed and developing countries. NAFTA was negotiated by the Bush and Clinton administrations and narrowly passed by Senate vote in 1994. It binds Canada, Mexico, and the United States together in a free trade arrangement that gradually reduces import/export tariffs between them. It was opposed by U.S. labor unions because of the fear of what third party presidential candidate Ross Perot called a "giant sucking sound" of jobs going South to Mexico. The Clinton administration claimed that NAFTA would actually create jobs in the United States.

It has been very difficult to assess the results of NAFTA because shortly after it went into effect, Mexico experienced an economic crisis that led to a dramatic devaluation of the peso and a hastily assembled U.S. emergency loan package to buoy up the Mexican economy and reduce the losses of investors. More recently, there have been revelations of economic corruption at the highest levels of the Mexican government.

There is no doubt that the economic crisis and corruption have hurt the poor in Mexico. The revolt of indigenous peasants in the province of Chiapas dramatized their anxiety that they would not be able to compete with U.S. farmers in the production of corn and their long-standing grievances over not benefiting from the rich resources of their region. Income disparity between the very rich and the very poor in Mexico has been steadily increasing for over a decade, and in the first year and a half after NAFTA the number of Mexicans living in extreme poverty increased by 5 million people to 22 million.[57] Although Mexico is currently enjoying hefty trade surpluses with the United States, Mexico has lost 1.6 million jobs in the process. The economic recovery stimulated by Mexico's surging exports is beginning to create new jobs to replace those lost, but often the new jobs pay lower wages. Still many analysts think Mexico would be in an even worse condition without NAFTA.[58]

There is also no doubt that some U.S. manufacturing jobs have been lost to *maquiladoras* in Mexico, but the resulting corporate efficiency has also created jobs in the United States, although not as many as the Clinton administration predicted.[59] Furthermore, many of the jobs moving to Mexico, some economists claim, would have moved somewhere because of the globalization of the economy. The U.S. economy is undergoing a structural transformation with or without NAFTA. Some argue that the challenge is not so much to protect outdated U.S. industry, but to educate a workforce for the high technology economy of the twenty-first century.[60] NAFTA, however, has not fulfilled the promise of its backers to create hundreds of thousands of jobs throughout North America, yet it does seem to have exerted downward pressure on wages.

The *citizens* of all three countries seem to view the treaty with suspicion. However, many economists and officials, recognizing that the Mexican crisis has skewed the early results, still support NAFTA as being in the best long term interests of all three countries. The debate about NAFTA is heating up again as North America ponders whether to bring Chile under the free-trade umbrella.[61] Free trade may stimulate economic growth, but the question remains: in whose interests?

DOMESTIC INEQUITY AND HUMAN DEVELOPMENT

Thus far this chapter has focused primarily on the gap between the North and South. The free market has a tendency to concentrate wealth. If the people in the Two-Thirds World are to meet their basic needs and have the opportunity to live a dignified human life, it is essential that they be the beneficiaries of their countries' economic growth. Achieving economic growth is not easy for developing countries in a competitive global economy. The system is stacked against them. Steps such as the reduction or forgiveness of debt, MNC's compliance with international codes of conduct, national social legislation, reformed development assistance, and free-trade agreements, can enable poor countries to accomplish economic growth. But economic growth, though essential, is only half the battle. Rising productivity and prosperity must be applied to *human* development as well. International or external economic reforms must be coupled with domestic or internal reforms if poverty is to be overcome. Indeed, without attention to human development or the equality of the distribution of goods and services, economic growth itself cannot be sustained.[62]

Within each country there is a gap between the rich and the poor, but economic inequity varies from country to country, and there are steps a government can initiate to distribute wealth and income to the poor. Without social programs aimed at the poor, economic growth will tend to benefit only the rich, and growth itself will eventually stagnate.

The disparity between rich and poor is communicated in personal terms in the following statistic. "Today, the net worth of the 358 richest people, the dollar billionaires, is equal to the combined income of the poorest 45% of the world's population—2.3 billion people."[63] As Gandhi said, the earth has enough for everyone's need, but not for everyone's greed.[64]

A rich elite ruling over an impoverished majority is a legacy of colonialism in many developing countries. Brazil, for example, has Latin America's most unequal distribution of land, with 45 percent of the land owned by 1 percent of the population, but this is a familiar pattern throughout Latin America and much of the Two-Thirds World.[65] From 1990 through 1994 Latin America experienced annual economic growth of over 3 percent, but the number of families living in poverty, 38 percent, remained constant. There was economic growth, but no reduction in poverty. The rich got richer.[66] Mexico's economic inequity is among the worst in the world. "Today the richest 10 percent of Mexicans control 41 percent of the country's wealth, while the bottom half of the population receives only 1 percent of all national income."[67] Thailand has the most skewed distribution of income outside Latin America, and its economic growth has only widened the gap. "Twenty years ago the richest 20 percent of the population earned just under half of the national income; today they earn 63 percent. The share of the poorest fifth of the population dropped from 6 percent to 3.4 percent."[68]

One useful way of comparing economic disparity internationally is to look at the poorest 20 percent of the population in each country, comparing their average per capita income with the national average (see Table 2.2). "In Guatemala the per capita income of the poorest 20% is only a tenth of the average per capita income, while in Bangladesh it is nearly half."[69] The poor are more marginal in Brazil, Chile, Guatemala, Guinea-Bissau, Tanzania, and the United States—less in Bangladesh, Hungary, Indonesia, Nepal, and Japan. In the Two-Thirds World as a whole, the poorest 20 percent of the people only receive about 7 percent of the total income, but in Latin America they receive only 3 percent.[70]

Table 2.2
Per Capita Income of the Poorest 20%, 1993 (PPP$)

Country	Average per capita income	Per Capita income of the poorest 20%
United States	24,240	5,814
Japan	20,850	9,070
Netherlands	17,330	7,105
United Kingdom	17,210	3,958
South Korea	9,630	3,563
Chile	8,400	1,386
Hungary	6,050	3,297
Brazil	5,370	564
Guatemala	3,350	352
Indonesia	3,150	1,370
Nigeria	1,400	357
India	1,220	537
Bangladesh	1,290	613
Nepal	1,020	464
Guinea-Bissau	840	88
Tanzania	580	70

Source: *Human Development Report 1996*, p. 13.

Recent studies have demonstrated that there is no conflict between growth and equity (fair distribution), indeed there is a correlation between them. Neither can be sustained without the other. And there are clear strategies that governments could pursue to insure that economic growth results in genuine human development:[71]

1. A political commitment to increasing *job* opportunities and employment that pay a living wage. Success in lowering unemployment does not happen automatically, but it occurs more often when this is a central policy objective of the government. A country with a growing population and high unemployment should obviously seek patterns of growth that are labor intensive. Creating job opportunities in the private sector is generally preferable to establishing a large public sector bureaucracy.

2. Social spending that enhances human capabilities, particularly *education* and *health*. Investment in human resources is a key to both human development and economic growth. South Korea, for example, has a literacy rate and an average years-of-schooling per child rating comparable or better than some OECD countries.[72] "The Republic of Korea invests $160 per person a year in health and education, Malaysia $150. India, by contrast, invests only $14, Pakistan $10 and Bangladesh $5."[73] An educated and skilled workforce is essential to meet the needs of a high technology economy.

3. Increasing access to productive assets, especially *land* and financial

credit. Land reform is key to rural development, which is in turn essential to feeding hungry people and slowing the migration to the cities. Peasant families have worked the land for generations. Once it was their land, but at some point it was taken from them. It seems only fair to return it. (Plantation owners, of course, usually take a different view.)

The Grameen Bank in Bangladesh, founded by Muhammad Yunus, has demonstrated that small loans to poor women for micro-enterprises can significantly reduce poverty and make a profit for the bank. Since 1976 Grameen Bank has made micro-loans to two million families in 35,000 villages in Bangladesh. The repayment rate exceeds 90 percent. Many of these loans have provided the stimulus for enterprises that have enabled the poor to satisfy their basic needs and even come to employ others in small businesses.[74]

4. A focused investment in *women*'s capabilities through education, child care, credit, health care, and employment. Until recently most development projects tended to focus on men as the generators of capital. But actually it is women who are key to meeting the basic needs of their families and who often do the productive, but uncompensated, work in the village or household. Empowerment of women is also key to controlling population growth.[75]

5. A responsible *government* that gives high priority to the needs of all the people and controls corruption.[76] Such governments tend to be or to become participative or democratic, but authoritarian governments genuinely committed to national productivity and prosperity have achieved economic growth and human development. Corrupt, self-serving governments have not.[77]

For economic justice to be realized and human development to happen for the poor there have to be changes both in the global economic system and within the countries of the Two-Thirds World.

POVERTY AND THE U.S. ECONOMY

It is scandalous that significant poverty exists in the United States, one of the wealthiest countries in history. The final sections of this chapter examine the income disparity in the United States and two issues that especially affect poor Americans—health care and welfare.

The United States is an extraordinarily wealthy and powerful country. It is the world's largest economy, with a GNP more than a third greater than that of Japan. The U.S. standard of living is one of the highest in the world. Its technological sophistication, scientific research, and higher education are unparalleled. It has the world's strongest armed forces.

At the same time, in the United States the gap between the rich and the poor is the largest among the world's industrial nations. The wealthiest 1 percent of American households own nearly 40 percent of the nation's wealth, the top 10 percent own 70 percent of the wealth, and the top 20 percent, over 80 percent of the wealth. "Income statistics are similarly skewed.

At the bottom end of the scale, the lowest-earning 20 percent of Americans earn only 5.7 percent of all the after-tax income paid to individuals in the United States each year."[78] The top 20 percent receive 55 percent of all after-tax income. This disparity is increasing, and income is becoming more concentrated all the way up the scale. "The top 5 percent have gotten richer compared with the next 15 percent; the top 1 percent have gotten richer compared with the next 4 percent."[79] Although the United States has experienced steady, if modest, economic growth with low inflation and high employment in recent years, the real wages of American workers have stagnated since 1992 and were actually 6 percent lower in 1996 than in 1988.[80] "Over the period from 1983 to 1992, the top 20 percent of wealth holders received 99 percent of the total gain in wealth and the top 1 percent 58 percent of wealth growth."[81] Meanwhile the number of Americans living in poverty has increased from 33 million to almost 37 million.[82] One out of every four children in America is born into poverty, and the U.S. child-poverty rate is four times the average of Western Europe.[83] Such economic inequality in the world's wealthiest country is a moral outrage.

Also disturbing is the fact that the United States has not only lost its status as the world's leading lender, it is now the world's largest debtor nation. The national debt was $1 trillion in 1980, grew to $3 trillion by the end of the decade, and in 1996 is about $5 trillion, but growing more slowly. The reasons for this increasing indebtedness are large budget deficits and large trade deficits. The government is spending more than it takes in through taxes, and the United States is importing more goods than it exports. The huge budget deficits during the Reagan years in the 1980s were due to tax cuts and increased military spending. Since 1992 the Clinton administration has decreased the annual budget deficit from over $250 billion in 1992 to about $110 billion projected for 1996 through tax increases, mainly on the wealthy, and spending decreases.[84] The U.S. government hopes to have a balanced budget in 2002. In the meantime the national debt keeps growing, although more slowly. The debt is approaching the equivalent of one year's GDP, and in fiscal year 1994 about 18 percent of the federal budget ($300 billion) went to paying interest on the debt. The U.S. debt service is beginning to consume much of its annual economic growth, similar to the way population growth absorbs economic growth in developing countries. Even for an economy as large as that of the United States, these deficits and this debt are disturbing economic realities.[85]

The United States faces a number of social problems related to political economy and to poverty: homelessness, crime,[86] urban violence, drugs,[87] racial tension, the feminization of poverty, the breakdown of the family, declining test scores and increasing school drop-out rates.[88] During the first Clinton administration, however, two problems dominated the national debate—health care reform and welfare reform. Both of these are enormously complicated issues and a thorough examination is beyond the scope of this chapter, but they deserve at least a word in that they reveal the direction of discussions about poverty in the United States.[89]

Health Care Reform

During the 1992 Presidential campaign health care reform re-emerged as a pressing national issue for two reasons: the need to control the increasing costs of health care and a significant and growing number of Americans without health insurance.

In 1992 the United States was spending about 12 percent of its GNP, or about $750 billion, on health care. This was about double the amount of GNP spent for health care by other industrial countries. What's more, the cost of health care was rising much faster than the rate of inflation. Nearly everyone agreed that strong measures were needed to control the cost of health care.

At the same time there were 37 million Americans who did not have health insurance and therefore were without access to health care. Because the Medicaid program provides health care to the very poor and Medicare insures the elderly, the uninsured in the United States tended to be the working poor and the unemployed. Typically, Americans receive their health insurance through their employment. Many small businesses, however, cannot afford to offer health insurance to their employees, and the unemployed can seldom afford a personal insurance policy. Thus the United States was paying more for health care than any other Western nation, but was the only Western nation without universal health care, and often ranked rather low in comparison with peer countries in health indices such as infant mortality.[90] While the United States led the world in medical technology, a significant number of Americans did not have access to even basic health care. Something needed to be done.

The difficulty here, of course, is that these two goals—cutting costs and providing universal access—appear to directly oppose one another. Insuring 37 million more people is likely to cost more, not less. Furthermore, the politics of health care reform is complicated and conflictual. Some people consider health care a commodity and focus on cutting costs; others think health care is a right and stress universal access to quality care. Some think government intervention can respond to the problem; others prefer to rely on the marketplace. The health care system is complex with many competing interest groups such as physicians, hospitals, insurance companies, suppliers and drug companies, and consumers.

In the end, by 1994, the Clinton administration's attempt to reform health care had failed. It foundered on a combination of the administration's own political mistakes (the overly complex plan was developed in secret), opposition by powerful interest groups (especially by the insurance industry), and partisan politics.

Thus, in 1996, there were 40 million Americans without access to health care, and the cost of health care had grown to about 14 percent of GNP, or nearly $1 trillion a year. The United States still pays the most for health care, but it may be of some consolation that other Western nations are also struggling to control costs.[91]

Health care spending did grow more slowly in 1994 than in any other year since 1960.[92] This was because of managed care and managed competition and the rise of for-profit medicine in the United States. Thus the health care discussion stimulated by the attempt to reform the system, in effect, prodded the marketplace to cut costs. Managed care, however, has raised troubling questions regarding the doctor-patient relationship and the quality of care, and it has done nothing to directly increase access to care for the uninsured. Congress has passed a health-insurance reform bill that makes health insurance portable from one job to the next, but this is a weak response to a much broader problem.[93] Health care reform no longer seems to be on the national agenda; it was largely absent as a topic of discussion in the 1996 Presidential campaign.

In the face of these discussions, we must insist that health care is not a commodity. Human beings have a right to basic health care that prevents disease and cures sickness. The United States remains the only industrial nation that does not have universal health care for all of its citizens. This is an injustice that still needs to be corrected.

Welfare Reform

In the 1992 Presidential campaign, Bill Clinton promised to "end welfare as we know it," and that pledge elicited a chorus of "Amens." Welfare reform, however, means different things to different people, even though most everyone agrees the system needs to be reformed. Some contend that it costs too much and burdens taxpayers too heavily. Others think that welfare contributes to the breakdown of the family. Many agreed with President Clinton that "the current welfare system undermines the basic values of work, responsibility, and family, trapping generation after generation in dependency. [Welfare should be] a second chance, not a way of life."[94] For their part, welfare recipients find the system bureaucratic, humiliating, and inadequate, and often agree that its stipulations can result in dependency and a culture of poverty.

"Welfare" generally refers to Aid to Families with Dependent Children (AFDC), but U.S. poverty programs also include food stamps, housing subsidies, Supplemental Security Income for the elderly poor and the disabled, and Medicaid. Federal and state governments share the cost of many of these programs, and some states share the cost with local governments. "All welfare programs, including AFDC, food stamps, housing subsidies, and supplemental income for the disabled elderly, cost a total of $53.4 billion to the Federal Government—about 4% of the federal budget. (The states kick in another $15.3 billion.)"[95] AFDC costs about $25 billion a year total (federal and state) and represents only 1 percent of the federal budget. Its costs have remained steady for 25 years, although the number of women and children receiving AFDC rose 31 percent, to a record 14 million, from 1989 through 1994. If Medicaid, the health care program for the poor is factored in, the cost of responding to the poor increases significantly. In 1993 Medicaid, which is also split between federal and state governments, cost $132 billion. Unlike AFDC, the cost of Medicaid has been rising steadily, doubling in the first four years of the 1990s.[96] Thus the debate on welfare reform is tied to the one on health care reform.

Welfare, then, is obviously a complicated hodgepodge of programs that vary from state to state. It is even difficult to calculate what percentage of tax monies supports programs for the poor. Nevertheless it is clear to me at least that the amount of tax dollars spent on the poor is hardly excessive, and that cutting poverty programs will not yield savings that significantly lower the U.S. budget deficit. AFDC, for example, is a mere drop in the federal budget bucket (1 percent). If taxpayers want to save big bucks, both reason and compassion would bid them look elsewhere.

Moreover, "most of the big antipoverty programs have done what they were meant to do."[97] They have reduced hunger and malnutrition, prevented illness and cured sickness, subsidized decent shelter, contributed to education and child development, supported the disabled and the elderly, and reduced the misery of children unlucky enough to be born into poverty. They have not eliminated poverty in America, but that has not been the objective of these programs. AFDC benefits, for example, have always been set well below the poverty line.

Mostly the poor in America are children and their mothers. Two out of three recipients of AFDC are children (9 million); nearly all the rest are their mothers. Thirty-nine percent of welfare mothers are black, 38 percent are white, and 17 percent are Hispanic.[98] In the discussion of the evils of dependency it is worth remembering that children *are* dependent on adults, and very often mothers of young children who are not poor depend on their husbands for income and support.[99] The disabled and those too old to work are also dependent. A good society cares for those who are unable to care for themselves.

Nevertheless, it may well be that welfare programs have fostered a culture of poverty or a cycle of dependency in the United States which needs to be addressed. For the majority of recipients, welfare is a temporary support over a tough period—37 percent will be on welfare less than two years in their lifetime and another 19 percent less than four years. But one in four will receive AFDC for over eight years, and sometimes there are three generations on welfare in the same home.[100]

In searching for the causes of poverty and the increasing numbers of poor people in the United States, two factors stand out. The first is the disappearance of manufacturing jobs from northern cities and from America itself. These low-skilled jobs which provided a living wage for working-class families first moved to the South, and then out of the country. This phenomenon leaves those with less education and skills unemployed and impoverished. It also degrades their dignity and leads them toward despair. Poverty, then, is rooted in the economy. The solution seems obvious. Create jobs that pay a living wage, both in inner cities and rural areas that have been abandoned by industry, and educate people for a high-tech economy. Doing this is difficult and expensive. It requires an investment in human beings and in communities.[101]

The second factor is the dramatic increase in out-of-wedlock births. "Nearly a third of American children are born out of wedlock, and those children are four times as likely as the others to be poor."[102] By the end of the decade, it is projected that nearly 40 percent of all births and 80 percent of minority births will be out-of-wedlock.[103] Both conservatives such as Charles Murray and liberals such as David Ellwood agree that single parents face the strong probability of being poor.[104] Many conservatives tend to view "illegitimacy" as morally wrong and think that welfare subsidizes it. Their response is to stop welfare and stigmatize illegitimacy again.[105] Perhaps the elimination of welfare for single parents will induce women not to have children they cannot care for on their own, but there is a lack of data to demonstrate this.[106] Such a policy risks punishing innocent children for the bad judgment of their parents.

Others are genuinely baffled by the number of out-of-wedlock and teenage births, but are not sure what to do about it.[107] This phenomenon is not limited to the United States, but the U.S. rates are comparatively quite high. Unwed teenage pregnancy is more a product of than a cause of poverty. The multiple causes of unwed teenage pregnancy include limited education and lack of skills, a sense of hopelessness and meaninglessness, lack of contraceptive and sex education, media pressure, poor self-esteem, and male joblessness.[108] "The drop in marriage rates parallels the drop in employment prospects."[109] Young people with no sense of hope and little positive sense of self tend to live for the moment rather than plan for the future. Any adequate response would include the improvement of education and the creation of jobs.

The politics of welfare reform during the Clinton administration were acrimonious. Clinton focused on health care in his first two years, then was faced with a Republican Congress in 1994 whose agenda was the radical reduction of welfare spending. Both Clinton and the Congress shared the goal of transforming welfare recipients into workers, but the Republican plan for doing this focused on time limits on receiving benefits, while Clinton believed in including more funds for job training and job creation. Throughout the Clinton administration the Federal Government gave many states waivers from federal guidelines in order for states to experiment with their own welfare reforms.

Clinton twice vetoed legislation passed by Congress before finally signing a compromise bill in August of 1996, in the midst of the Presidential campaign. The "Personal Responsibility and Work Opportunity Act of 1996" does indeed change the welfare program. Its provisions are complicated and it allows many exceptions, but basically it eliminates AFDC and replaces it with federal block grants to the states which each state can use for its own welfare and work programs. This eliminates a poor person's entitlement to federal aid. Federal spending on welfare and food stamps will be cut by $60 billion over six years. Non-citizens, including legal immigrants, will no longer be eligible for assistance. Every adult recipient of welfare would have to have a job within two years or lose benefits, and there is a five-year lifetime cap on receiving benefits. States can provide assistance to a mother under 18 only if she resides at home and stays in school. Funds for child care are increased slightly. The Medicaid program is not affected by this new law.

Critics of this legislation, such as New York Senator Daniel Patrick Moynihan and former top administration official Peter Edelman, contend that the result will be increased misery for a significant number of poor children. They point out that, while the law requires work, it does not increase funding for education or job training or for job creation. Clinton was successful in getting Congress to increase the minimum wage by 90 cents, to $5.15 an hour, but minimum wage jobs are inadequate for supporting a family and even these jobs are hard to come by in inner cities and rural areas.[110] Moreover, a recent study indicates that working mothers with comparable skills and education fare even worse than those on welfare, because their increased income is eaten up by work-related expenses such as clothing, child care, and transportation.[111] It seems that this legislation will punish poor children as it tries ineffectively to empower their parents.[112]

POVERTY AND CONFLICT

Finally, an observation that is perhaps obvious, but that needs to be stated: poverty is an important cause of revolutions, wars, and violence; and war results in poverty. There is an interrelationship between poverty and conflict.[113]

During the Cold War most conflicts and revolutions in the Two-Thirds World were viewed by the United States and the Soviet Union through the prism of the East-West conflict, as a struggle between communism and democratic capitalism. But very often, once the ideological shell was stripped away, these conflicts represented a struggle by a poor majority of people for justice and a better life. In many of the conflicts and revolutions in Latin America during the 1960s through the 1990s, a crucial element was the struggle of the poor for justice. This was true in Nicaragua, El Salvador, and Guatemala, in Haiti, Jamaica, and the Dominican Republic, in Chile, Brazil, and Colombia. Poverty was an important ingredient in the struggle against apartheid in South Africa, the people power revolution in the Philippines, the troubles in Northern Ireland, the overthrow of the Shah of Iran, and the Palestinian question in Israel.

Poverty is in itself a violence against human dignity, and it sometimes leads the poor to violently respond to their desperate situations. A revolution by the poor generally begets a disproportionately violent response by the army to protect the status quo. Poverty can set off a spiral of violence.[114]

The destructiveness of violence and war results in poverty. War creates refugees, people who leave their homes and often their homeland to escape the violence. Refugees leave behind their belongings and resources; they become instantly impoverished. War destroys cities, homes, schools, hospitals, crops, offices and factories. War perversely reverses the corporal works of mercy, creating conditions in which people's basic needs are not met. Crops are defoliated and people go hungry. Reservoirs are contaminated and people go thirsty. Homes are destroyed and people are without shelter or clothing. People are injured and sickness is sown. Prisoners are taken. Sometimes even the dead are unburied.[115] Economic growth and human development are clearly impossible under conditions of war and violence.

The overwhelming majority of people on Earth live in poverty, unable to meet their basic needs and fulfill their God-given potential. This reality is a tremendous obstacle to the dream of creating a just and peaceful world order. It is even more of a scandal because it need not be. The poverty of the many exists in sharp contrast with the affluence of the few. The Parables of the Rich Fool (Lk 12:13-21), of the Rich Man and Lazarus (Lk 16:19-31), and of the Great Feast (Lk 14:15-24) stand as a warning to contemporary Christians who are comfortable with their riches in a hungry world. God invites humanity to a great banquet, but everyone must be included at the table.

STUDY QUESTIONS

1. Have you experienced or observed poverty? What does poverty do to the human spirit?
2. When Jesus says, "Blessed are the poor in spirit, for theirs is the kingdom of heaven," (Mt 5:3) what does he mean?
3. Why are the countries of the North rich and the countries of the South poor?
4. What are the lessons for human development of the Newly Industrialized Countries (NICs)? Do the "structural adjustment programs" imposed on developing countries by the World Bank and the IMF appropriately capture the lessons in the success of the NICs? What sort of structural adjustment program would you suggest for a country that wants to accomplish human development?
5. Do you think the loans incurred by developing countries should be forgiven?
6. When multi-national corporations move into developing countries are they a blessing or a curse for the poor? What can be done to make their presence a blessing?
7. Are multi-national corporations a blessing or a curse for middle-class Americans? for poor Americans?
8. From the perspective of the poor, is NAFTA a good idea or a bad idea?
9. Is economic growth necessary for human development? Is economic growth the same as economic development? What can developing countries do to make sure that economic growth translates into human development? What can developed countries do to aid this process?
10. Is health care a human right? Why did the attempt at health care reform in the United States fail in 1994? How would you propose to reform the health care delivery system in the United States? How could global health care reform be accomplished?

11. What do you think are the benefits and liabilities of the welfare reform enacted by Congress in 1996? What further reforms do you think are needed? What can the United States do to eradicate poverty at home?

12. Do you think that peace on Earth can co-exist with global poverty? Are the rich in the North really threatened by the poor in the South?

CHAPTER THREE

Population Explosion, Resource Depletion, and Environmental Destruction

"Then God said to Noah and to his sons with him: 'As for me, I am establishing my covenant with you and your descendants after you, and with every living creature that is with you, the birds, the domestic animals, and every animal of the earth with you, as many as came out of the ark.'" (Genesis 9:8-10)

"Modern Society will find no solution to the ecological problem unless it takes a serious look at its lifestyle. In many parts of the world, society is given to instant gratification and consumerism while remaining indifferent to the damage which they cause. . . . Simplicity, moderation and discipline, as well as a spirit of sacrifice, must become part of everyday life, lest all suffer the negative consequences of the careless habits of a few."[1]

On a warm Saturday morning in the spring of 1974, shortly after the celebration of the fourth Earth Day, I was walking along 56th Street in New York City. A black Lincoln Town Car, with four big men in black suits and white shirts, windows rolled down, passed me going in the same direction. As the car slowed to stop at a red light, the man riding "shotgun" threw a big styrofoam coffee cup out of the window. It fell at the feet of a young woman who was walking toward me. She picked up the cup, walked over to the stopped car, and threw it back in the window onto the lap of the astonished litterer, with the firm admonition, "New York is not your garbage can." Then she proceeded calmly down the sidewalk.

In some ways this story can function as a parable about environmental issues. I do not know what effect the woman's action had on the car's occupants, but she certainly raised my consciousness and changed my behavior. I admired her conviction and her courage. Indeed the earth is not our garbage can, and we humans have got to take responsibility for our waste, and encourage others to do so as well.

Yet environmental issues are complicated and ambiguous. If the man throws the cup into a garbage can, the city is cleaner and more pleasant. The cup, however, still has to be disposed of, by being buried in a landfill or burned in an incinerator. It takes energy to produce the cup, and styrofoam is potentially harmful to the earth and the atmosphere. Environmental responsibility may mean not buying or producing the cup in the first place.

But are there realistic alternatives for having our morning coffee on the run? Maybe it is our fast food lifestyle that is the root problem. Yet the modern economy depends on that lifestyle. Even a brief reflection on a simple styrofoam cup raises radical questions, and seemingly intractable problems.

Here is the conundrum that humanity faces regarding environmental and economic justice. The earth's ecosystem is wondrously diverse and resilient, with a capacity to create and maintain life in countless forms. But the planet itself is finite, and the balance of its resources is fragile. The human species has been so successful in reproducing of late that we are beginning to radically alter or destroy the ecosystem on which all life depends. The sheer number of humans is leaving a deep impression on planet Earth. At the same time, as we have already noted, in order for humans to survive and flourish, in order to have economic and human development, economic growth seems necessary.[2] Indeed, as we shall see, economic development seems to be an essential ingredient in stopping the runaway growth of the human population. But economic growth, through increased industrial productivity, presently requires large quantities of nonrenewable energy and materials. This depletes the earth's resources and heats up the atmosphere, like an engine running faster and faster. "Since 1900, the number of people inhabiting the earth has multiplied more than three times. The world economy has expanded more than 20 times. The consumption of fossil fuels has grown by a factor of 30, and industrial production has increased by a factor of 50; four fifths of that increase has occurred since 1950."[3] How does society meet the needs of the 6 billion people now alive, the majority of whom are poor, without compromising the prospects of future generations by harming the ecosphere? Economic growth seems essential, but increased productivity may alter the biosphere in disastrous ways. This chapter will address the issues packed into this dilemma.

VALUES AND CONCEPTS

As mentioned in the Introduction, three interrelated levels of analysis (situation/information, interpretation/evaluation, and response) are involved in this examination of ecological problems. As we shall see, science yields tentative, ambiguous information, which further complicates the politics of environmental justice. Humanity's relationship with the earth, however, raises complex ethical and conceptual questions as well.

Christianity has been accused of being the culprit in the ecological crisis through its conception of human dominion over the earth and its creatures.[4] "God blessed them, saying: 'Be fertile and multiply; fill the earth and subdue it. Have dominion over the fish of the sea, the birds of the air, and all the living things that move on the earth.'"[5] This anthropocentric (human-centered) perspective encourages the exploitation of the earth, and Western cultures have done just that.

In response, many Christian theologians, while acknowledging a history of abuse, have interpreted the creation stories in terms of stewardship[6], or more recently, companionship[7], rather than dominion.[8] Others, such as Thomas Berry, have moved toward an earth-centered perspective, drawing on sources outside the Christian tradition.[9] Philosophers have had their own version of this debate in the clash between "deep ecology,"[10] with its eco-centric approach, and the mainstream environmental movement, which calls for human responsibility toward the earth in the interests of humanity.[11]

It is not the purpose of this chapter to enter into this important discussion, but, of course, values and perspectives are the foundation of any analysis. Environmental issues are theological, philosophical, and ethical, as well as scientific, technological, economic, and political in nature. Neither a *biocentrism* that asserts the equal value of a person and a fly, nor an *anthropocentrism* that assigns only instrumental value to the natural world, make much sense. A *theocentric* vision sees the universe and the earth as created by God who calls humanity into right relationship with God, one another, and all of creation. This seems at once more biblical and more realistic. Humanity is neither above, nor below, nor over against creation. We are embedded in creation, and in relationship with the natural world. All of creation is good and valuable in itself; all of creation stands before God in profound poverty as creatures; and all of creation is a sacrament of God's goodness and creative power. Many Christian theologians feel that, in responding to the needs of the poor and in respecting the value of earth, humanity is seeking a right relationship with God, each other, and the natural world. "Right relationship" is what God has created us for and called us to.[12]

POPULATION EXPLOSION

Global population reached a record high today, and tomorrow it will break the record once again.[13] Most of the history of the human species has been a struggle to survive, to multiply and fill the earth. It took most of human history to reach a population of 1 billion (around 1825), but only 100 years to add a second billion people. Fifty years later, in 1975, global population had doubled again to 4 billion, and in fifty more years, in 2025, the population is expected to double again to at least 8 billion people[14] (see Figure 3.1). Only in the twentieth century has any human being witnessed the doubling of human population during his or her lifetime.[15] In 1998 the population will reach 6 billion. Over 90 million people (the equivalent of the population of Mexico) are being added to the global population every year, more than 200,000 every day.[16] Humanity has been very successful at multiplying and filling the earth in the twentieth century. Human flourishing and the survival of our fellow species now depends on stabilizing the human population.

To understand both population growth and economic growth and their twin threat to the earth's ecosystem, it is important to grasp the concept of *exponential growth*. "Exponential growth occurs when some quantity continuously increases by a constant percentage over a given period of time—when, for example, a population grows by 2 percent every year."[17] This is

Figure 3.1
World Population Growth

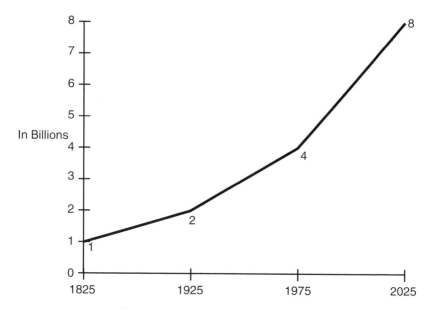

In Billions

the principle behind compound interest on a savings account. At an annual growth rate of 1 percent, a quantity, such as population or savings, will double in 70 years. The doubling time at a 2 percent rate of growth is 35 years; 4 percent—18 years; 5 percent—14 years; 10 percent—7 years. The global population growth rate has been steadily declining. In the 1990s it has averaged about 1.48 percent, or a doubling time of about 50 years. Now, however, the *number* that may double during the next fifty years is 5 billion.[18] Even a low rate of exponential growth of a population within a finite ecosystem cannot continue indefinitely without negative consequences. Either the birth rate will have to decrease or the death rate will increase.[19]

Another way of viewing demographic trends is through the *fertility rate.* "The total fertility rate refers to the average number of children a woman would have in her lifetime on the basis of fertility rates in a given year."[20] A fertility rate of about 2 means that each couple is replacing itself, and population growth has stabilized. (See the Appendix for the fertility rates of the countries of the world.) This does not mean, however, that population growth levels off immediately. There is a "demographic momentum" that increases population for some time before it finally levels off because there are many couples in their reproductive years in the population. In other words, although each woman is having fewer children, there are more women having children.[21] Worldwide, the fertility rate is about 3, and steadily declining. In developed countries, the average is below 2. "For developing countries as a whole, [the fertility rate] has dropped from 6.2 in 1960 to about 3.4 today. In the poorest developing countries, however, it is still about 5.6."[22]

Obviously there are regional differences in the growth of population. Over 90 percent of the growth is occurring in the Two-Thirds World. "The developing countries add a million people every five days to lands already overworked and depleted of water and cheap sources of energy."[23] Every other person on earth is an Asian, and Asia's population is expected to increase by 40 percent, from the current 3.46 billion to 4.9 billion, by 2025.[24] The largest absolute increases in numbers are taking place in Asia, but the fastest population growth rate (3.1 percent a year) is in Africa.[25] In 1950, Africa's population was half that of Europe; by 1985, their populations had drawn even at about 480 million each; and by 2025, Africa is expected to have about three times as many people as Europe (1.58 billion to 512 million).[26] In a historical perspective, however, the present growth spurt in Africa and Asia simply returns the global balance to what it was prior to European and North American growth during the Industrial Revolution. Thus, in 1650 Asia and Africa accounted for 78.4 percent of the world's population; in 2050, according to U.N. projections, these two regions will account for 78.5 percent.[27]

The populations of the countries of the former Soviet Union and of Central Europe are actually declining, and the population of most developed countries is stable or projected to decline. The big exception is the United States, whose population continues to grow at a rate of about 1 percent, the same rate as China. This means that the number of Americans will increase from the current 263 million to about 331 million in 2025.[28] While this increase is not especially significant in terms of the sheer numbers of global growth, an increase in the number of Americans is bad news for the planet's ecosystem. "According to one calculation, the average American baby represents twice the environmental damage of a Swedish child, three times that of an Italian, thirteen times that of a Brazilian, thirty-five times that of an Indian, and 280(!) times that of a Chadian or Haitian because its level of consumption throughout its life will be so much greater."[29] While each American or Canadian consumes the equivalent of over forty barrels of oil per year, a Chinese consumes less than four barrels, and an Indian or Nigerian, about two barrels.[30] What, then, is the significance of population growth for the ecosystem? Is the population explosion itself the problem?

Proliferating populations contribute heavily to the stresses on both social systems and the ecosystem. Population growth can effectively cancel out the benefits of economic growth and other attempts to alleviate poverty. To meet the needs of ever more people, an economy has to create ever more jobs and wealth. But to do this, the economy must use more energy and more resources, which depletes the goods of the earth and produces more pollution.

Overcrowding can be another problem. The population density of Asia and Europe is ten times that of North America.[31] A friend who traveled to Calcutta in India said that when she arrived, she thought that there must be some huge national festival going on to account for all the people who were there. Some days later, it finally dawned on her that shoulder-to-shoulder people was the everyday norm. Bangladesh, one of the most densely populated territories on earth, with 810 people per square kilometer, will need to find room to accommodate twice as many people by the middle of the twenty-first century, despite relatively successful efforts to curb population growth.[32] North America has well over two acres of arable land to support each inhabitant, but Asia has little more than a third of an acre per person.[33] (See the Appendix for the population density of the countries of the world.)

In developing countries, the struggle for survival often results in damage to the environment. Trees, for example, are cut down for firewood. This deforestation often leads directly to soil erosion, which results in flooding and the washing away of valuable topsoil.[34] The result is a desert, incapable of supporting agriculture or grazing. This further impoverishes the people who depend on the land for their livelihood. The "slash and burn" farming methods of growing numbers of indigenous people in Brazil or the Philippines contribute to the destruction of tropical forests, although corporate logging and agribusiness are by far the greater culprits. In many places, land and water are becoming scarce resources.

As natural environments deteriorate from overuse, people *migrate* from rural areas to overcrowded cities, and, globally, from the South to the North.[35] While urbanization tends to lower fertility rates in the long run, the influx of people often overwhelms the capacity of cities to provide basic social services, such as housing, sanitation, water, education, health care, and work.[36] Mexico City, for instance, which could have a population of nearly 40 million by 2034, already faces air pollution that is a grave threat to human health.[37] Yet, while population pressure may play some part in the complex phenomenon of immigration, it is not the principal cause.[38]

Although it is true that the growing populations in the Two-Thirds World stress the ecosystem, we in the North must realize that most of the planet's problems are caused by the production and consumption patterns of the First World. "The industrialized countries of the Northern Hemisphere are home to one-fifth of the world's population, yet they consume two-thirds of the world's food, three-quarters of its energy and minerals and 85 percent of its wood."[39] The United States alone, with less than 5 percent of the world's population, consumes about 60 percent of the world's natural gas, 40 percent of coal and aluminum, and 30 percent of nickel, copper, and petroleum. The United States accounts for a quarter of global energy consumption and produces a quarter of the world's air pollution.[40] "Numbers per se are not the measure of overpopulation; instead it is the *impact* of people on ecosystems and nonrenewable resources. While developing countries severely tax their environments, clearly the populations of rich countries leave a vastly disproportionate mark on the planet."[41] Thus, it is the affluence and over-consumption of people in developed countries that is the major threat to the earth's ecosystem.

Population growth occurs when the birth rates exceed the death rates in a society. The process of economic development results in a fairly universal pattern known as the "demographic transition." First, death rates fall, mostly due to public health measures, such as better sanitation and diet, and immunization against diseases. As an immediate result, the population increases. Later, birth rates fall because people become more educated, more secure, more urbanized, and women's status in society rises. It then becomes reasonable to have fewer children, and population stabilizes. Great Britain went through this demographic transition with the Industrial Revolution. Other developed countries have followed the same pattern.[42]

Agrarian people are acculturated to having large families because children are assets: their labor contributes to the family and they provide security in the parent's old age. An infant mortality rate of 50 percent, as is often the case in developing countries, means that half of all children die before age five. Having many children, then, makes sense for the rural poor. To make it more reasonable to have fewer children, economic development is necessary.[43] Thus, economic development seems to be the ordinary way to move through a demographic transition and stabilize population.

Thus we enter into an ecological and economic conundrum: economic growth is necessary (but not sufficient) for economic development, which is, in turn, necessary for stabilizing population growth. But economic growth, at least initially, tends to boost population growth. And, as we have seen, population growth can make economic growth very difficult to accomplish. Furthermore, industrialization (presently an important ingredient in economic growth) depletes resources and damages the environment. Yet economic development seems necessary to stabilize population growth, lest the human population exceed the carrying capacity of earth.

It should be noted that some developing countries have been successful in lowering the rate of population growth through aggressive government programs aimed at doing so.[44] Thailand's population growth was cut from 3.2 percent to 1.6 percent in only 15 years, in part through the efforts of Mechai Viravaidya, a dynamic and creative former government economist who has promoted various methods of contraception. Over 70 percent of couples in Thailand practice family planning.[45] Bangladesh has lowered the fertility rate from 7 to 4.5 through the efforts of family planning workers. In 1993, 45 percent of couples practiced family planning, while only 6 percent did so in 1974.[46] Zimbabwe has used a similar program to slow the growth of its population "from catastrophic to merely dreadful."[47] China reduced its fertility rate from 6 to 2.5 in a single decade (the 1970s) through what many consider a Draconian policy of "one child per couple." India has had mixed success with a less coercive approach.[48]

Some government family planning programs, like China's, seek to override a family's personal decision, while others try to collaborate with families through education, access to birth control, and even incentives to limit family size. Public policies that expand education, health care, economic security, and access to contraceptives are surely necessary, but a central ethical concern is whether the programs increase or significantly reduce the choices open to parents and especially women.[49] Coercion is morally suspect even in a legitimate cause.

Religion and culture interact with population policy in complex ways. Included in the mix are cultural understandings of gender roles, and the status of women. The Catholic Church's well known opposition to artificial methods of birth control is based in an interpretation of natural law philosophy, rather than in a directly pronatalist position. In practice, it results in Church opposition to most family planning programs. However, both in terms of natural law philosophy and especially of the desperate need to stabilize population growth, some theologians have questioned the wisdom of the Catholic Church's position.[50]

Conservative Muslim clerics often oppose contraception as well, although the teaching of Mohammed on birth control is ambiguous at best. In Iran, for example, the politically influential Muslim religious leaders now officially approve of birth control. An educational session on birth control is required in Iran in order to get a marriage license, and condoms, pills, and sterilization are free.[51]

Most religious teachings were developed at a time and in a context in which procreation was essential for survival. Past cultural norms were logically pronatalist. Today the situation is quite different. Stabilizing population growth may be necessary for future human flourishing.

Economic development remains the primary way to accomplish the demographic transition, but it is also clear that aggressive government programs that make available a variety of contraceptive methods and provide education and incentives for family planning, can lower the population growth rate. In particular, "if there is a single key to population control in developing countries, experts agree, it lies in improving the social status of women."[52] Population control is not a mystery; it is a difficult cultural, economic, and political task. In essence it requires the alleviation of poverty and raising the standard of living.

> **For Reflection**
>
> An Irish missionary was asked how long he had been in the Philippines. "Longer than most Filipinos," he said, "fifteen years." He was correct. More than 50 percent of the population of many developing countries, including the Philippines, is under the age of fifteen. Developed countries, which have moved through the demographic transition, face the opposite problem of an aging society. Both situations are ripe for social conflict.

RESOURCE DEPLETION

Nearly everyone agrees that it is essential to control the growth of population, but Julian Simon, an economist at the University of Maryland, is an exception. Simon, an ecological optimist, or Cornucopian, argues that human ingenuity is the ultimate resource, the key to ecological stability and human well-being. Therefore, population growth is ultimately an asset because human ingenuity will develop the technology to respond to environmental problems, and to create the wealth necessary for economic development. The more humans, the better.[53]

Simon's nemesis has been Paul Erlich, an ecologist at Stanford University, an eco-pessimist or Malthusian. Erlich argues that population growth is like a bomb that threatens the carrying capacity of spaceship earth by overextending its supplies of food, fresh water, and minerals.[54]

In 1980, Erlich and Simon chose a refreshingly unacademic way to resolve their differences. They bet $1,000 on the future price of five metals—chrome, copper, nickel, tin, and tungsten. If in 1990 the price had gone up, Simon would pay Erlich the difference. If the price went down, Erlich would pay Simon. During the 1980s the population grew by more than 800 million, the greatest increase in history, and the earth's stock of metals stayed the same.

In the fall of 1990, however, Erlich sent Simon a check for $576.07. Each of the five metals had declined in price when adjusted for inflation. "Prices fell for the same Cornucopian reasons they had fallen in previous decades—entrepreneurship and continuing technological improvements."[55] New lodes were found, greater efficiency in mining and using the metals was implemented, and other materials, such as plastics, replaced metals in industries such as communications. As might be expected, Erlich was neither chastened nor silenced by losing the bet. "Julian Simon is like the guy who jumps off the Empire State Building and says how great things are going so far as he passes the 10th floor," said Erlich.[56] Simon proposed raising the wager on any other resource for any year in the future. Erlich passed.

The lesson of this story is not that ecological prophets such as Erlich and Lester Brown (of the Worldwatch Institute) can be ignored. The one point on which both Simon and Erlich could agree is the value of pointing out problems, of raising issues. Without an awareness of potential problems, human ingenuity cannot work to prevent or solve them. The subtlety of environmental changes and the complexity and uncertainty of scientific evidence can make it difficult to effect changes in people's behavior or to marshall the political will necessary to change social practices.

Energy: The Master Resource

Energy fuels industrialization and economic growth. Energy runs machines; it propels cars, trains, and airplanes; it heats and cools houses and offices, lights lamps, refrigerates and cooks food, and powers computers. Energy is consumed by industry, domestic use, and transportation. It has been called the master resource.[57]

"The commercial fuels that power the world's industrial economies are *oil* (39 percent of world energy consumption), *coal* (32 percent), *natural gas* (24 percent), and *hydroelectric and nuclear power* (5 percent). The fossil fuels (coal, oil, gas) thus account for 95 percent of world energy consumption."[58] As we shall see below, this reliance on fossil fuels is largely responsible for potentially catastrophic climate change. Overuse is also rapidly depleting these nonrenewable sources of energy. Humankind consumes in one year an amount of fossil fuel that it took nature a million years to produce.[59] In 1993 global energy production was 40 percent higher than in 1973, but global energy consumption was 49 percent greater.[60] It has been projected that world energy consumption will rise over 50 percent within the next 20 years.[61] "If energy consumption were to remain constant at current levels, proved reserves would supply world petroleum needs for 40 years, natural gas needs for 60 years, and coal needs for well over 200 years."[62] Sometime in the future it seems quite probable that the generations of the twentieth and twenty-first centuries will be remembered as "the oil age," the time in human history when oil was discovered, developed, and depleted.

The developed countries, with 15 percent of the global population, consume 50 percent of the energy.[63] On average North Americans consume the energy equivalent of 10 metric tons (22,000 pounds) of coal per person per year. In comparison, Western Europeans consume 5 tons per capita and Japanese 4.5 tons, mostly because of greater efficiency. Latin Americans consume 1.2 tons per person, South Asians .4 of a ton, and Africans .3 of a ton because they are less industrialized. (see Figure 3.2). Much of the growth in energy consumption in the future, however, will take place in developing countries as they industrialize. While the urban American is distinguished from the Asian peasant by vastly different levels of industrialization and domestic consumer goods, it is the amount and mode of movement—transportation—that make the most difference in energy consumption. The 500 million automobiles on the planet burn an average of 2 gallons of fuel a day. One-third of the world's oil consumption goes for this purpose. The United States consumes twice as much oil per person as does Western Europe.[64]

Although developed countries consume more than half of all commercial energy, they produce only slightly more than a third of it. Thus, most industrialized countries, including the United States, and especially Japan, depend on imported oil for the smooth functioning of their economies. The United States is dependent on imports for well over 40 percent of the oil it uses. Over 60 percent of the known reserves of petroleum are found in the politically volatile Middle East.[65]

Despite two oil crises in 1973 and 1979, the Gulf War in 1991, and increasing scientific evidence of global warming, the United States still has no coherent national energy policy.[66] On the contrary, there was a proposal in the summer of 1996 to *reduce* the national tax on gasoline by 4 cents. At that time, Americans were paying about $1.40 a gallon for gas, and national and state taxes accounted for only about 27 percent of the cost. At the same time, drivers were paying about $4.00 a gallon in Europe and Japan, where taxes accounted for 74 percent and 51 percent of the price on average respectively[67] (see Figure 3.3). With gasoline in the United States cheaper than it was in the 1950's (after adjusting for inflation), Americans are embracing gas-guzzling vans, pick-up trucks and utility vehicles with a vengeance.[68]

Figure 3.2
Annual Energy Consumption per Capita

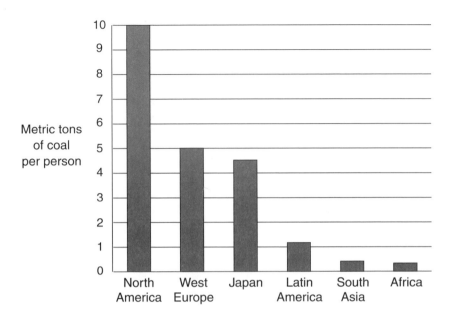

Figure 3.3
Price at the Pump

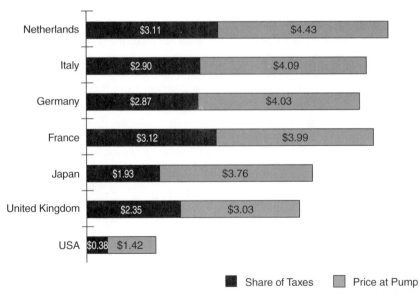

■ Share of Taxes   ☐ Price at Pump

Note: Prices as of April 15, 1996   Source: Energy Information Administration, *Network,* July/August, 1996, p.11.

Any rational U.S. energy policy would raise the tax on gas significantly, mandate higher fuel efficiency, and support the use of alternative sources of energy and alternative modes of transportation, such as mass transit and bicycles.[69] The goal would be to reduce dependence on oil imports, the consumption of a nonrenewable resource, and the pollution of earth's atmosphere.

Fossil fuels are not the only nonrenewable resources. The bet between Simon and Erlich should caution against predicting the depletion of energy resources and other minerals. "Still, there are limits. A 1985 U.S. government study projected that with the 1985 rates of usage and even assuming *five times* the amount of known reserves, there were only 53 years of tin reserves, 72 years for lead, and 149 years for iron ore."[70] Technology and human ingenuity may well respond satisfactorily to the depletion of mineral resources, yet this generation should reflect on its moral responsibility for what may be a sin of gluttony.

Forests

"An important paradox to bear in mind when examining natural resource trends is that so-called nonrenewable resources—such as coal, oil, and minerals—are in fact inexhaustible, while so-called renewable resources can be finite."[71] Scarcity of nonrenewable resources will generally increase prices and stimulate the development of alternative resources so that they will not be totally depleted. Trees, however, can sometimes be cut so quickly and extensively that a desert is formed, and the forest cannot be replenished. Forests, fresh water, and arable land are crucial resources at risk. What is happening all over the planet is the destruction of whole ecosystems.

The Amazon rainforest in Brazil has been called "the lungs of the earth." Since the 1970s, an estimated 20 percent of this tropical forest has been wiped out.[72] "Already the [tropical] forest has been reduced to approximately 55 percent of its original cover . . . , and it is being further reduced at a rate in excess of 100,000 square kilometers a year. This amount is 1 percent of the total cover, or more than the area of Switzerland and the Netherlands combined."[73] The tropical deforestation rates were highest in Asia. Worldwide, forest, woodland, and scrub cover declined by 2 percent during the decade from 1980–1990.[74]

The deforestation of tropical forests, that is, the attempted conversion of the forest to cropland or fields for grazing herds, makes no sense because it creates a desert. Indeed, the emerald beauty of a rainforest is only skin deep. The luxuriant vegetation and canopy of 200-feet-tall trees is supported by the constant decay of its moist ground surface. When the vegetation and trees are cleared, the soil stops being replenished and quickly becomes barren. After only six or seven years it is worthless for agriculture or grazing.[75] Thus, such deforestation is the worst of both worlds—economically shortsighted and ecologically devastating. Clear-cut logging, while yielding a one time profit, has a similar devastating environmental effect. The ancient temperate forest in the American northwest is being stripped and shipped to Japan.[76]

Forests are ecologically valuable as regulators of global climate, as conservators of soil and water resources, and as repositories of species and potentially valuable new products.[77] Trees and plants (and the oceans) absorb carbon (about 3 billion tons a year) and produce oxygen. Forests absorb fresh water and prevent soil erosion and flooding. But perhaps the greatest ecological tragedy of deforestation is the loss of biodiversity or the depletion of species of insects, plants, and animals.

Most people are now familiar with the notion of endangered species. The danger, of course, comes from humankind, sometimes through direct killing, as with buffalo and whales, but more often indirectly through the alteration or destruction of habitats, as with the spotted owl in the northwest or the timber rattlesnake in Connecticut. A few concerted efforts have managed to reverse the pattern of destruction, as in the case of the American eagle and some species of whale. But when we destroy huge swathes of tropical forest, we terminate thousands of species whose existence will never be known to us.

"Tropical forests cover only 7% of the earth's surface, but they house between 50% and 80% of the planet's species."[78] There is a prodigious variety of species, and especially of insects. Harvard biologist E.O. Wilson tells of finding on one tree in Peru as many species of ants as exist on the whole of the British Isles.[79] No one knows how many living species there are on earth. Estimates range from 4 million to 111 million, with 14 million an often cited number, of which only about 1.7 million species have been identified.[80] Species naturally evolve and sometimes disappear. Human activity, however, in polluting lakes and rivers, in consuming land through urban sprawl, and especially in cutting and clearing tropical forests, is extinguishing species at a rate thousands of times faster than the natural pace of evolution.[81] In doing this we are vastly diminishing the genetic heritage of earth, and we are hurting the interests of humanity itself. "Some 25% of the pharmaceuticals in use in the United States today contain ingredients originally derived from wild plants."[82] Who knows what miracle cures are going up in smoke today? Both economically and ecologically it would make much more sense to harvest carefully the genetic and biological fruits of the forest, rather than to cut them down.[83]

Fresh Water and Ocean Fisheries

Water, water, everywhere, and not a drop to drink![84] The lament of Coleridge's Ancient Mariner, stranded on a listless sea, is becoming a description of the human predicament today. Less than 1 percent of the water on earth is fresh water that is usable for consumption, agriculture, and industry.[85] "Worldwide, agriculture uses about 65 percent of all the water removed from rivers, lakes, and aquifers for human activities, compared with 25 percent for industries and 10 percent for households and municipalities. It takes about 1,000 tons of water to produce a ton of harvested grain."[86] To produce a pound of beef requires between 2,500 and 6,000 gallons of water. The manufacture of one automobile takes 100,000 gallons of water. "Water usage grows faster than population. It is estimated that water usage triples as population doubles."[87] The typical American consumes more than 70 times as much water every year as does the average Ghanian.[88]

Water pollution (caused by domestic sewage, industrial waste, chemical run-off from agriculture and mining, and soil erosion), and increased use (due to irrigation, industrialization, and population growth) have resulted in a scarcity of fresh water in some regions. Aquifers in regions such as the Western United States, the Arabian Peninsula, Northern Africa, and Southeast Asia are being irreparably drained by the overuse of groundwater at rates faster than rains can replenish them. The Ganges River in India, the Colorado River in the United States, and the Jordan River in the Middle East often run dry before they reach the sea. The Aral Sea (between Kazakhstan and Uzbekistan, former Republics of the Soviet Union), once the world's fourth largest lake, has lost half its area and three-fourths of its volume because of river diversions to grow cotton in the desert.[89]

Fresh water scarcity threatens three fundamental aspects of human and ecological security: food production, the health of the aquatic environment and those who consume the water, and social and political stability.[90] Since agriculture uses two-thirds of fresh water supplies, it is not clear where more water will come from for irrigation in regions where aquifers have collapsed from overuse, or where rivers and lakes have been drained. And without water, crops will not grow.

Rivers and lakes are ecosystems with a delicate balance of life. Human, industrial, and agricultural waste and pollution can damage these aquatic ecosystems and the life that teems within them. Ultimately, this reduces the recreational and utilitarian value of rivers and lakes for humans. Fortunately, damaged aquatic ecosystems, unlike aquifers, can sometimes be restored to life.

In his ecological classic, *The Closing Circle*, Barry Commoner tells the story of the demise of Lake Erie, a 12,000-year-old natural wonder so polluted since the beginning of the twentieth century that it actually burst into flames at one point.[91] When Commoner wrote in 1971, Lake Erie's beaches had been closed. Each summer huge mounds of decaying fish and algae rotted on its shores, and the once sparkling water was dense with muck. There were few fish to be caught, and those fish were inedible. Happily, in the last 25 years, a concerted effort to clean up Lake Erie has been at least partially successful: beaches have been re-opened, and the fish are returning.

The remarkable transformation of the Hudson River in New York is a similar story. "Only 30 years ago, this magnificent river was little more than a 350-mile sewer stretching from the Adirondacks to Manhattan's Battery, choked with untreated human wastes, industrial chemicals, and agricultural runoff. Today the Hudson pulses with life."[92] The restoration of the Hudson is neither complete nor certain, but it is a resounding success story for energetic citizen action and careful government regulation.

Ecosystems can also be vulnerable to the introduction of foreign life forms that then wreak havoc. For example, the water hyacinth from Brazil's Amazon region somehow found its way to Lake Victoria in Africa. With no natural enemy around, the weed has thrived in the warm, nutrient-rich waters of the lake, blocking ports, clogging hydroelectric pipes, choking engines, jamming propellers, and sucking oxygen out of the water.[93] Similar stories could be told about kudzu in the American South, or zebra mussels in Lake Michigan.[94]

Finally, the scarcity of fresh water can cause conflict within and between countries. States in the American West, for example, argue over who should have access to scarce water in aquifers and rivers and for what purpose. Egypt is utterly dependent on the Nile River, but the sources of the Nile are in Sudan and Ethiopia. Ethiopia now has the political stability to plan to use the water for irrigation and hydropower production. Egypt is clearly prepared to go to war if Ethiopia diverts Nile waters. Syria and Iraq are in a similar situation with regard to Turkey, which contains the source of both the Tigris and the Euphrates Rivers. Turkey is also planning a huge hydropower and irrigation scheme that will reduce the flow of the rivers and pollute them as well.[95]

Water is often underpriced or subsidized by the government, thus reducing the incentive to conserve it. Since agriculture uses so much water, better irrigation efficiency can be a modest step in preserving the supply of fresh water.[96] The concept of a "water stress index," measured as the annual renewable water resources per capita available to meet the needs of agriculture, industry, and domestic use, might be a way of highlighting vulnerable regions. A benchmark of 1,000 cubic meters per capita per year would seem to indicate places where chronic water shortage can be expected. Several countries in the Middle East and North Africa, in particular, fall well below this benchmark.[97]

Salt water oceans and seas cover 70 percent of the earth's surface and provide 8 out of every 10 fish caught. Fish provide 16 percent of the animal protein consumed by humans and are especially important in the diet of people in many developing countries. "Of the total global fish harvest of 101 million metric tons in 1993, 78 percent was caught by the marine fishing fleet, 6.8 percent was caught inland, and 15.5 percent was raised artificially through aquaculture."[98]

Despite a record high global fish harvest in 1993, there are clear signs that ocean fisheries are in trouble, due primarily to overfishing, as well as to coastal degradation. While the marine harvest actually peaked in 1989, the decline has been made up for by aquaculture. Many fish stocks, such as cod, have declined dramatically (25 percent), and the price of seafood has been rising.[99] "In fish farming, it takes about 2 kilograms of grain to produce 1 kilogram of fish."[100] Such costly inefficiency means that it is unlikely that aquaculture will be able to replace significant declines in ocean fisheries. Given the reality of overfishing, then, it makes little sense for governments to continue to subsidize high-tech marine fishing fleets, which often displace local subsistence fishing boats.[101]

Oceans are clearly part of the global commons, and thus there is the temptation for some to take more than is fair from the sea's bounty. One response is to enclose the commons by deciding who has jurisdiction over them. Negotiations sponsored by the United Nations Conference on the Law of the Sea (UNCLOS), from 1973–1982, resulted in a treaty that expanded the territorial waters of nations to 12 miles for shipping and 200 miles for economic activities such as fishing and mining. The treaty also affirmed the principle that the oceans are the common heritage of humankind by establishing international rules for using territorial waters and for sharing the wealth extracted from the ocean floor beyond 200 miles. The United States blocked the ratification of the treaty for over a decade, finally signing it in 1994.[102] It remains to be seen whether nations will practice the restraint necessary to allow fish and seafood stocks to renew themselves.

Food Security

The essence of the trap that Malthus predicted (see chapter 1) was that population would outstrip food production, resulting in massive famine. At present, one out of every five people on earth is hungry and chronically malnourished, and another 20 percent is undernourished. Thus far, however, hunger seems to be caused by poverty and the maldistribution of resources, not by scarcity. Now, as in the time of Malthus, food production has increased even faster than population. There are some signs that this trend may be reversing, and we can only speculate as to the number of people that a finite planet can feed.[103]

Food production is another area where optimists and pessimists come to different conclusions. The Food and Agriculture Organization of the United Nations (FAO) and the World Bank predict that food production will be able to keep pace with population growth in the near future. Lester Brown of the Worldwatch Institute, an organization that researches and reports on the ecological conditions of the earth, is critical of their projections and calls food scarcity the defining issue of the next decade.[104]

Everyone agrees that the rate of growth in annual food production is slowing. We have seen that growth in the world fish catch has apparently ended.[105] "From 1961 to 1992, the growth of world agricultural production slowed, dropping from 3 percent annually in the 1960s to 2.3 percent per year in the 1970s and to 2 percent during the 1980–92 period."[106] Whether this is the beginning of an ominous long-term trend in which population grows faster than food production is the question.[107]

The reason for the growth in agricultural production is the "green revolution," that is, the development of high-yielding, high-input seeds. These modern varieties of rice, wheat, and corn yield many times the produce of traditional varieties, but they also require the intensive use of fertilizers, water, and pesticides.[108] High-input agriculture has both ecological and economic costs. Since fertilizers are often petroleum based, developing countries using modern varieties of grains were hard hit by the oil shocks of the 1970s.

This sort of farming tends to wear out the soil, and we have already seen that water scarcity is an increasing problem in many regions of the world. Pesticide application and runoff have negative consequences for human health and aquatic ecosystems.

Lester Brown bases his dire predictions of food scarcity on three trends: "a gradual decline in grainland area since 1981, little or no growth in irrigation water supplies since 1990, and a decline in world fertilizer use since 1989."[109] While it is true that topsoil is being eroded and degraded in many places, and that desertification is a real problem,[110] it is also true that there is arable land that can be put to productive use, and that steps can be taken to minimize soil degradation.[111] In some regions, water scarcity will limit food production, but greater efficiency in irrigation can partially address the problem. Fertilizer use may be declining, but there is no reason why it has to decrease, and why organic, rather than chemical fertilizer cannot be used. Moreover, biotechnology is primed to increase yields through genetic alteration, and perhaps even eliminate the field and the farmer altogether. Advances in biotechnology, however, while increasing food production, may also increase rural unemployment, and raise other environmental and health issues.[112]

In sum, although it seems possible that food production—through greater efficiency, less waste, and new technology—may keep up with population growth, food security is more an issue of access than of scarcity. Already about 40 percent of humanity lacks access to adequate nourishment, and, especially in Africa, it appears that trend will get worse in the near future. While agricultural and aquatic productivity are essential, access to food is more of an economic and political issue.[113]

ATMOSPHERIC POLLUTION

Ozone Depletion

When chlorofluorocarbons (CFCs) were first synthesized in the 1920s, they seemed too good to be true. They were nontoxic and inert, cheap and simple to manufacture, and useful as coolants, propellant gases in spray cans, and in the production of plastic foam materials such as Styrofoam.[114] They were thoroughly tested and found to be benign, but their effect on the atmosphere and the remote stratosphere was never even considered. In the atmosphere each CFC molecule is 20,000 times as efficient at trapping heat as is a molecule of carbon dioxide, thus contributing to the greenhouse effect and global warming. In the stratosphere the long-lived CFCs destroy ozone molecules. The ozone layer, between 10 and 30 miles up, prevents harmful ultraviolet radiation from the sun from reaching the earth. Ultraviolet radiation is very dangerous to life on earth. It can cause skin cancer in humans and blindness in animals, kill vegetation, lower agricultural yields, and disrupt ecosystems.[115]

Scientists in the 1970s discovered the potential for CFCs to destroy ozone and warned of the danger to the ozone layer. Then in 1985 researchers documented the existence of a huge hole in the ozone layer over Antarctica.[116] This set in motion a series of diplomatic conferences that resulted in the signing of the Montreal Protocol in 1987 to reduce the production of CFCs. In 1990, in London, 93 countries agreed to end production of ozone damaging chemicals by the year 2000. A follow-up meeting in 1992 in Copenhagen moved the date up to 1996. Thus, developed countries have now ceased production of CFCs, and have set up a fund to enable developing countries to stop production within a decade.[117] This very constructive and cooperative response by the nations of the world is a model of environmental responsibility. The clarity of the danger and the development of effective and inexpensive substitutes for CFCs were important factors in accomplishing this remarkable ecological victory.[118]

Global Warming

Destruction of the stratospheric ozone layer lets harmful ultraviolet rays in; the buildup of specific gases in the atmosphere does not allow heat to get out. The net effect is that the atmosphere begins to function like a greenhouse, therefore warming the temperature of the earth. The greenhouse gases are: CFCs, carbon dioxide, methane or natural gas, and nitrogen oxides. Since CFCs account for an estimated 15 percent of the greenhouse effect, it is good news that the world has stopped producing them. Methane is produced by a number of sources, including bacteria living in the stomachs of cattle and termites, the muck of rice paddies, and the rotting garbage of landfills. Although burning methane produces carbon dioxide, methane traps 20 times as much heat as carbon dioxide. Thus, burning methane produced by landfills would reduce the greenhouse effect.[119]

Carbon dioxide is released from the burning of wood and of fossil fuels—coal, oil, and natural gas.[120] "Fossil fuel burning is now releasing about 6 billion tons of carbon into the air each year, adding 3 billion tons annually to the 170 billion tons that have accumulated since the Industrial Revolution."[121] By the late 1800s atmospheric carbon dioxide had risen to about 285 parts per million. Now it is 350 p.p.m., and it could reach 500 to 700 p.p.m. by 2050.[122] Better exhaust technology has significantly reduced the amounts of lead, nitrous oxide, and carbon monoxide emitted by automobiles, but there is no filter that can reduce carbon dioxide emissions. A well-tuned car releases five-and-a-half pounds of carbon in the form of carbon dioxide for every gallon of gas it burns.[123]

Because economic growth requires more energy, most of which comes from burning fossil fuels, the emission of carbon dioxide has increased by about 40 percent over the past 20 years, and is projected to increase by the same amount in the next two decades. The United States accounts for nearly 25 percent of carbon dioxide emissions and the OECD countries for about 45 percent. In gross amounts the United States emits nearly twice as much carbon dioxide as China or Russia, and nearly four times as much as Japan. The United States also has the highest per capita emissions of carbon dioxide—19.1 metric tons per person per year—compared with the average of all OECD countries of 11.5 tons in 1992. As developing countries industrialize, their share of air pollution is projected to increase from one-third today to one-half in 2010.[124] China already has the second highest total emissions of carbon dioxide in the world, mostly from burning coal to power its industry. Imagine China with the same number of cars per capita as the United States!

The projected result of the accumulation of greenhouse gases in the atmosphere will be to raise the average world temperature by between 1.5 and 4.5 degrees Celsius (2.7 and 8.1 degrees Fahrenheit) over the next 50 years.[125] While there is some scientific ambiguity about global warming, the evidence that global warming is taking place is mounting. The temperature of the earth has increased by 0.6 degree Celsius in the twentieth century, and 10 of the warmest years of the century have occurred since 1980. Events such as the melting of a large chunk of Antarctica, the warming of Siberia, warmer winters in Northern Europe, and heat waves in India are disconcerting signs. There is no doubt that greenhouse gases are accumulating in the atmosphere; the debate is about the potential seriousness and consequences of this phenomenon.[126]

The effects of global warming include: coastal inundation from rising sea levels, disruption of rainfall and therefore water use patterns, agricultural effects due to heat stress, the spread of disease, and ecosystem damage, such as the loss of biodiversity and habitat disruption.[127] There would be winners and losers from the disruption of weather patterns. Some deserts might bloom from greater rainfall, while in other places farmland might turn to desert. Nearly 50 percent of the world's population live in coastal regions. Rising sea levels could have a catastrophic effect on their lives, and even eliminate some island nations, such as the Maldives (off the southern coast of India). Bangladesh and Egypt, for example, would be severely affected, as would the United States with its long, heavily populated coastlines. Developed countries could afford to adapt to changes more readily than poor countries.[128]

Besides the very serious threat of global warming, air pollution has the more apparent effect of smog, which burns the eyes, causes difficulty in breathing, harms health, sullies and erodes buildings and monuments, and damages trees and plants. There are convincing short term and long term reasons for controlling air pollution.

Carbon emissions are tied to energy use, and energy is necessary for economic growth. Thus, curbing air pollution will be neither simple nor cheap because of the conflict between the need for economic development and for environmental responsibility. Pollution controls make production more expensive. Developed countries often seem to apply a double standard when they urge developing countries not to harm the environment as they industrialize.

An important element in any strategy to reduce carbon emissions would be the efficient use of energy. One way to measure the energy efficiency of a nation is the amount of carbon emitted per million dollars of economic output. According to this standard some of the republics of the former Soviet Union have the worst records, including Kazakhstan, Ukraine, and Russia, although all of these countries report decreasing emissions because of slowing economies. Japan is nearly twice as efficient as the United States. Canada, the United States, and Australia—with their patterns of low energy prices, large houses, and heavy use of cars to travel greater distances—all show more rapid increase in emissions and lower energy efficiency than the countries of Western Europe or Japan.[129]

The Intergovernmental Panel on Climate Change (IPCC), a group of more than 1500 scientists assembled from 60 nations by the United Nations, has recommended an immediate 60 percent reduction in fossil fuel use to prevent global warming. Achieving this goal would require more than energy efficiency; it would require a change in the lifestyle of those who live in the rich countries. It would mean fewer cars and more bicycles, smaller and better insulated houses and buildings, a commitment comparable to the one that put a human on the moon to develop alternative energy sources such as solar and wind power, higher prices for energy and a tax on carbon emissions, and expanded research on and monitoring of the climate. "Addicted to growth, busily spreading our vision of the good life around the globe, we are sprinting in the opposite direction."[130]

"The challenge of reducing carbon emissions is not so much technical or even economic as it is political, led by strong opposition of industries deeply vested in the fossil fuel economy."[131] Energy and automobile companies are among the largest multi-national corporations in the world. Their tremendous wealth and profit are tied to fossil fuels. They tend to resist the development of the sun and wind as sources of energy, as well as the construction of bicycle paths, and the imposition of taxes on carbon emissions. At international climate conferences, the United States, with its profligate use of energy, has resisted setting international limits on carbon emissions.[132] The good news, in a fairly bleak international political picture, is that at the 1995 Berlin Conference on Climate Change, a coalition of the insurance industries (which have begun to face escalating claims from bad weather associated with global warming), the Alliance of Small Island States, and the Group of 77 (developing countries) began to call forcefully for serious change.[133] While the ending of the production of CFCs is a positive step, significantly reducing carbon emissions and other greenhouse gases is more complex and much more costly. Preventing global warming touches us where we live, work, and drive.[134]

Another controversial ethical issue related to global warming and energy development is *nuclear power*. Nuclear energy does not emit any greenhouse gases, and does not contribute to global warming. Thus, it could be an alternative energy source to fossil fuels. Nuclear energy, however, is saddled with another set of environmental and health problems. The two major concerns are safety and waste disposal.

The uncontained meltdown at Chernobyl in Ukraine, in 1986, and the accident at Three Mile Island in Pennsylvania, in 1979, demonstrate the safety issues surrounding the operation of nuclear power plants. The release of radiation is very damaging to human health and to the environment. High doses of radiation can cause death, and lower doses can result in cancer and genetic defects.

One of the by-products of the nuclear fission of enriched uranium is plutonium, one of the most carcinogenic substances known. Even a millionth of a gram of plutonium, ingested into the lungs, can cause lung cancer in 15 to 30 years. Nuclear power plants produce 400–500 pounds of plutonium and other highly radioactive wastes a year. Plutonium has a half-life of 24,400 years, which means it lasts virtually forever.[135] Although Congress, in 1982, mandated the construction of a permanent storage site for high level radioactive wastes by 1998, no state wants such a site in its backyard, and no facility has been approved to store the 30,000 tons of spent fuel already in existence in the United States alone.[136] The safe storage of such toxic and corrosive substances for tens of thousands of years may be an impossible assignment for fallible human beings in an ecosystem in flux. To make matters worse, plutonium can also be used to make nuclear weapons. Storing plutonium clearly raises some serious issues of security.

Since there is no place to store these highly radioactive wastes, they are being "temporarily" housed in cooling tanks adjacent to nuclear power plants. These spent fuel tanks, like the reactor core, pose a threat of a meltdown. A courageous engineer blew the whistle on both Northeast Utilities of Connecticut and on the Nuclear Regulatory Commission (NRC), which is mandated to protect public safety, because of unsafe practices in the storage of spent fuel rods. Northeast Utilities has been forced to shut down its nuclear plants until essential repairs are made, costing the company hundreds of millions of dollars. This problem seems systemic to the industry, rather than specific to Connecticut.[137]

Although nuclear power accounts for 20 percent of the electricity consumed in the United States (and more in countries such as France and Japan), it costs twice as much as fossil fuel generated electricity. It is for economic reasons, then, that no new plants have been ordered in the United States since 1978.[138]

WASTE DISPOSAL

Highly radioactive wastes are so toxic and dangerous that they pose extremely difficult, and thus far unresolved, disposal problems. The disposal of toxic chemicals is similarly costly and difficult, and the disposal of more ordinary refuse is complex and controversial.

In September of 1986 the freighter *Pelicano* was loaded with 14,000 tons of toxic ash from Philadelphia's trash incinerator. The intended recipient refused to take the toxic ash, and the ship spent over two years traveling the world seeking a country that would accept its cargo. Finally, with the ash mislabeled as fertilizer, 4,000 tons of it was dumped on a beach in Haiti. The rest was illegally spilled into the Indian Ocean. The long voyage of the

Pelicano is a symbol of the difficulty of disposing of toxic wastes and of the potential environmental exploitation of poor countries by the rich.[139]

The 1980 Superfund Act authorized and funded the Environmental Protection Agency (EPA) to locate toxic waste sites and to force the responsible parties to clean them up. While over 27,000 sites have been identified, with 2,500 requiring immediate action, only a few hundred have received attention.[140]

There are several problems with cleaning up toxic waste. It can be expensive and dangerous. There are precious few effective methods of disposal, and each has its own environmental and economic drawbacks.[141] Burning it, for example, can pollute the air and still leave a toxic ash that needs a dump site. Which chemicals are toxic, and how dangerous they are (for example, how carcinogenic) is often not known. Clearly, it is a good idea to reduce the production of toxic chemicals, even if that might add to the cost of products. Industries should be required to properly dispose of toxic wastes, and they should contribute to cleaning up past messes. International agreements now prohibit dumping toxic and nuclear wastes at sea, and global norms now constrain the export of toxic wastes, a practice perceived as exploitative of developing countries.[142]

Garbage is another problem. The consumer society in the United States is also a throw-away society. It is estimated that the average American produces over three-and-a-half pounds of garbage a day or 1300 pounds a year. Each year Americans discard 16 billion disposable diapers and 220 million tires. All together, we produce 160 million tons of refuse a year.[143]

In the late 1980s, many regions of the United States seemed to be faced with a landfill crisis. In only a decade, 70 percent of the approximately 14,000 solid waste landfills had closed, many others were nearing their capacity, and few were being opened. It was projected that a handful of states—Connecticut, Florida, Massachusetts, New Hampshire, and New Jersey—would close virtually all active landfills within a decade.[144]

Because landfill space became scarce, the price rose. This encouraged companies to construct more landfills. Today landfills are scarce in just a few places, notably in the Northeast and near some cities, where land is expensive. There still is ample opportunity for Northern cities to ship their garbage to landfills in the South and Midwest. This arrangement, which might grate at first (take care of your own garbage!), can be beneficial to all concerned. Cities get rid of their refuse, and rural areas and distant regions benefit by the creation of jobs and the expansion of their tax base. Moreover, Federal regulations require that new landfills be lined with clay and plastic, equipped with drainage and gas-collection pipes, covered daily, and regularly monitored. Modern landfills are much safer than their older, leaky, smelly counterparts.[145] Incinerators and hazardous-waste facilities, however, can be much more perilous for human health and the environment, and they are too often found in poor neighborhoods or areas.[146]

In the midst of the landfill crisis many places latched onto the idea of recycling as a response to the possibility of drowning in their own garbage. In

1988, the United States was recycling about 10 percent of its waste. The Environmental Protection Agency (EPA) suggested that a five-year goal of 25 percent was reasonable, and some state and municipal legislatures enacted laws mandating recycling and setting even higher goals. Today the national rate is 25 percent, but it has been a costly achievement, since recycling programs routinely lose money.[147]

In the summer of 1996, New York City debated the benefits and costs of recycling. A 1989 municipal law mandated that the city recycle 25 percent of its garbage by 1994. Since the city was only recycling 14 percent of its 13,000 tons of daily residential refuse, environmentalists went to court to force the city to do better. Mayor Rudolph Giuliani argued that recycling may be more expensive than it is worth, and that the city budget could not afford the extra costs associated with increased recycling.[148]

It is a fact that collecting recyclables in New York costs three times more per ton than collecting ordinary refuse. Because recyclable refuse cannot be compacted, collecting it takes more time and space. Because the processing costs of most recyclable material exceed the resale value, the city also has to pay between $10 and $40 a ton to vendors for recycling the refuse. This is, however, less than the $42 it costs to dump a ton of garbage in a landfill, and that cost is likely to go up considerably when the city has to transport its waste to more distant landfills. Thus, while recycling costs more at the moment, in the long term its costs are likely to compare favorably with dumping garbage in landfills. Recycling also employs people in productive work.[149]

Waste disposal may be one of those problems ripe for a capitalist solution. Putting a price on garbage and making the consumer pay for it could go a long way toward resolving local problems of solid waste disposal. Some cities have tried this approach to good effect. When the cost of garbage disposal is clear rather than hidden in city taxes, people are less apt to take for granted their garbage. They throw away less, remove their names from junk mail lists, shop differently, start a compost pile, and recycle.[150]

ENVIRONMENT, CONFLICT, AND SECURITY

Resource scarcity and environmental issues can be a source of international and civil conflict and violence. Seldom is the environment the principal cause of a war or an insurgency, but it is often an important variable. This has been true throughout history: nations have gone to war over important resources. The Gulf War (1991), for example, was fought, in large part, to insure the access of developed nations to Middle East oil. The increasing rate and scope of environmental change is likely to increase its importance as a source of conflict.[151]

Humanity effects environmental change in three ways: the degradation and depletion of renewable resources, population growth, and changes in resource distribution among groups. Alone or in combination these three human activities produce "environmental scarcity." This, in turn, results in three sorts of social disruptions which can be sources of conflict. (1) Expanding populations can cause deforestation, soil degradation, and water depletion, all of which can decrease agricultural production. Food scarcity can be a source of conflict, as can land and water scarcity. (2) Poverty and environmental degradation can form a negative spiral, each creating more of the other. Economic decline is a major factor in the weakening of governments and in the strengthening of insurgencies. (3) Environmental scarcity can be an important factor in population displacements and migration. Migrants and refugees often cause social tension and ethnic conflict.

There are three kinds of conflicts that are influenced by environmental scarcity. The first is *scarcity conflict*. The scarcity of water, for example, can be a major factor in conflicts among nations and within countries. The Middle East and North Africa present several examples of conflict over water: between Turkey and Syria over the Euphrates River, between Egypt and Ethiopia over the Nile River, among Israel, Syria, and Jordan over the Jordan River, and between Israel and the Palestinians over the aquifer under the West Bank.

The second is *ethnic conflict*. For example, a combination of population density and scarce arable land in Bangladesh has resulted in the migration of perhaps 15 million Muslim Bengalis into the Assam province of India. The native Lalung tribe has long resented the new arrivals whom they felt were usurping some of the best land. In 1983 Lalung tribespeople hacked to death 1700 Bengalis in one five-hour rampage. The strife between the Tutsi and Hutu tribes in Rwanda and Burundi has been exacerbated by similar pressures from population growth and resource scarcity. High population growth rates among a minority or a migrant people can disturb a majority or native people.[152]

The third type of conflict is *deprivation conflict*, that is, insurgencies on the part of the poor. The decades-long insurgency in the Philippines, for example, has surely been strengthened by the deforestation resulting from intense logging and the unfair distribution of land dating from the colonial period. The long guerilla conflict in El Salvador was also intensified by the severe scarcity of land in proportion to the population, and its unfair distribution.

One result of the growing awareness that environmental scarcity and social and economic deprivations are sources of conflict has been a "greening of U.S. diplomacy."[153] American intelligence agencies are paying much closer attention to phenomena such as the water hyacinths choking Lake Victoria, droughts in Somalia or Senegal, overcrowding in Chinese cities, and the AIDS epidemic in East Africa in trying to anticipate the global crises of tomorrow.

Not only is environmental scarcity a source of international conflict, but war and preparation for war are also sources of environmental degradation. The environmental effect of war was highlighted during the Gulf War when Iraqi forces spilled large amounts of Kuwaiti oil into the Persian Gulf and blew up hundreds of Kuwaiti oil wells, leaving them burning as they retreated. Burning crops, defoliating fields, and poisoning water are common practices in warfare. Even in preparing for war, military industries pollute the earth, use excessive amounts of energy, and deplete natural resources. The nuclear and chemical weapons programs have created a plethora of radioactive and toxic wastes, which are often stored in deteriorating facilities. A nuclear war would be the greatest potential environmental disaster imaginable.[154]

Another type of insecurity resulting from population growth and global warming is the spread of deadly viruses. Overcrowding, poverty, disrupted ecosystems, and accelerated climate change are having profound and destabilizing impacts on the control of infectious disease. Illnesses thought to be under control, such as tuberculosis, dengue fever, and cholera, are making strong comebacks, and new viruses, such as HIV and ebola, are posing unforeseen threats to human health. Because of modern transportation, viruses can spread rapidly and widely. Infectious diseases are still the number one killer worldwide.[155]

SUSTAINABLE DEVELOPMENT

The web of life in any ecosystem is interconnected and interdependent, and this is clearly true of the earth's ecosystem as a whole. The most serious ecological problems, such as atmospheric pollution, deforestation, and the depletion of ocean fisheries, are related to the global commons and require cooperative global responses. The interdependence of humanity and of the whole earth community is an ecological truth.

Two of the laws of an interconnected, closed ecosystem are: "everything must go somewhere," and "there is no such thing as a free lunch."[156] Unfortunately, the industrial and technological society, achieved by the First World and sought by the Two-Thirds World, has not paid attention to these laws of ecology. Exponential economic growth, through increased industrialization, threatens to damage, or at least radically alter, the earth's ecosystem.

Optimists may be correct in their belief that human ingenuity and technology will allow humanity to adapt to ecological transformations, even transcend the limits that seem to be set by a finite ecosystem. The pessimists, however, while sometimes excessively bleak in their predictions of doom, certainly raise ominous questions about limits to economic growth.

If everyone's basic needs were being fulfilled and every human being had an opportunity to flourish, it might be reasonable and fair to stop economic growth. But that is not the case. A third of humanity lacks even basic needs and another third is not able to flourish. Economic growth, along with a more just distribution of goods, is thought to be essential for overcoming poverty.[157] Such economic development also seems to be a requirement for stabilizing the growth of world population. But economic growth might also irreparably damage earth's ecosystem. This is a dilemma.

"Sustainable" development has been suggested as a way through the conundrum posed by the contradictory goals and consequences of economics and ecology. A Native American proverb expresses the vision and values necessary for sustainable development: "We do not inherit the earth from our parents; we *borrow* it from our grandchildren." Sustainable development means economic development that meets the needs of the present generation in a way that does not compromise the needs of future generations.[158]

A sustainable fishing policy, for example, would limit the catch to that amount that enables the remaining fish to replenish the stock for next year. Overfishing can diminish the ecological capital of fish to the point of extinction. While ever-increasing catches of fish might reap short term profits, the practice becomes unsustainable. Similarly, if groundwater is used at a rate much faster than it can be replenished, the aquifer itself can compact, eliminating the pores and spaces that held the water. While large quantities of water can be important for economic growth, such activity can be ecologically unsustainable. The tension remains: an ecologically sustainable practice or policy might not allow sufficient economic growth for economic development.

Any serious resolution of the dilemma must address poverty. Not only is this a moral imperative, but economic development is fundamental to stabilizing population growth, which is a key ingredient in alleviating the plight both of the poor and of the earth.

Instead of concentrating on economic growth as a strategy for alleviating poverty, perhaps the focus should be on increasing economic equity. "Development strategies based on more equality within nations and across the entire globe could greatly improve living conditions of the world's poor. This improvement could be bought at a relatively modest cost."[159]

Life expectancy (expected life span at birth) is a key indicator of the quality of life and of human development in low income countries. There is a correlation between life expectancy and income levels (Gross National Product per capita). Life expectancy goes up about a year for every $50 increase in income per capita, up to a GNP per capita of about $3,000. At that point, life expectancy usually rises to about 65, after which it takes a $1,000 increment in income to add another year of life expectancy. Beyond a $6,000 GNP per capita there is almost no relationship between income and life expectancy.

"This pattern implies that major improvements in health and living conditions for the poor could be bought at a price not requiring major sacrifices by people in the rich countries. A transfer of income from rich countries to the poor need not hurt very much and could have an enormous impact."[160] Indeed, cuts in military budgets, in both the developed and developing countries, given the post-Cold War world, could underwrite this significant reduction in poverty. The cost would not much exceed the doubling of current nonmilitary international development assistance. The aid would have to be carefully targeted to meet public health, education, and nutrition needs. It would be complicated and would require some sacrifice, but it could be done.[161] There is enough wealth in the world to alleviate poverty without huge strides in economic growth, but it needs to be creatively transferred to those who need it. A focus on economic equity and the fair distribution of goods, with less pressure for economic growth, may be the ticket to the future.

It would be ecologically disastrous for the Two-Thirds World to reach the standard of living of North Americans. Given a concern for reasonable human equality, this reality raises serious questions about the lifestyle of the North and about economic growth to "improve" that lifestyle. Sustainable development, if taken seriously, means a new way of thinking and a different way of living for the North.[162]

Human flourishing includes the satisfaction of basic needs, intellectual challenge, creative expression, meaningful activity, healthy relationships, supportive community, and spiritual growth. Perhaps there are already more than enough goods for a meaningful and satisfying human life. Less might be better for the global North, and it will surely be beneficial for the Earth.

Sustainable development is a radical idea that is more rhetoric than reality in today's public policy discussions.[163] There is a need for political, religious, and moral leaders who embody and proclaim these values and this vision. The words of Pope John Paul II, quoted at the beginning of this chapter, are challenging indeed. What if affluent Christians took seriously the call to simplicity, moderation, discipline, and a spirit of sacrifice? That would indeed be good news both for the poor and for the Earth.

STUDY QUESTIONS

1. What are the practical implications of the different cosmologies (views of the universe): human-centered, biocentric, earth-centered, God-centered? What is your cosmology?
2. From an ecological perspective, has the Judeo-Christian tradition been a part of the problem? the basis of the problem? Can the Judeo-Christian tradition be part of the solution?
3. Do you think that the growth of the human population is approaching the carrying capacity of the Earth? What proposals would you suggest to respond to population growth?
4. Discuss the bet on planet Earth between Erlich and Simon. What are its implications regarding resource depletion and environmental issues?
5. What are the pros and cons of a significantly higher tax on gasoline in the United States?
6. Do you think global warming is a real problem? What steps should be taken to address the issue?
7. Discuss waste disposal.
8. Can you name some places where you think environmental issues will lead to violent conflict? How should U.S. foreign policy take "environmental security" into account?
9. Do you think there is a direct conflict between the need for economic development for the poor and the need to protect the environment? How can sustainable development be accomplished?

CHAPTER FOUR

Human Rights

*"So God created humankind in his image, in the image of God he cre-
ated them; male and female he created them." (Genesis 1:27)*

*"Any human society, if it is to be well-ordered and productive, must
lay down as a foundation this principle, namely, that every human
being is a person; that is, his nature is endowed with intelligence and
free will. Indeed, precisely because he is a person he has rights and
obligations flowing directly and simultaneously from his nature. And
these rights and obligations are universal and inviolable, so they cannot in any way be surrendered."[1]*

Throughout history humans have oppressed one another. On the basis of
some accident—such as race, color, ethnicity, birth, nationality, gender,
sexual orientation, age, class, caste, or religion—people's humanity itself has
been violated. Oppression and discrimination can take many forms—slavery,
imprisonment, torture, violence, impoverishment, exclusion, humiliation—
but at its heart is dehumanization. The full humanity of the victim is denied,
and, paradoxically, the oppressor becomes less human in the denial. Too
often citizens have been persecuted by the state with the blessing of religion.
Prejudice and discrimination are not new, but in the last 50 years the human
community has begun to name this oppression as a violation of human rights
and, at least in theory, to condemn these practices. Unfortunately, violations
of human rights continue to plague our world, but there has been some
progress, and there is the possibility of more.

The Nobel Prize for Peace has been awarded to several individuals who
have been activists and advocates for human rights: Martin Luther King, Jr.
(1964), the American civil rights leader; Mairead Corrigan and Betty Williams
(1976), two women from Belfast, Northern Ireland, who sought a dialogue
between Protestants and Catholics; Mother Teresa of Calcutta (1979) for her
work among the poor; Adolfo Perez Esquivel (1980) for resisting the repression of Argentina's military dictatorship; Lech Walesa (1983), the leader of
the Polish trade union Solidarity; Bishop Desmond Tutu (1984), the South
African anti-apartheid leader; Holocaust survivor and witness, Elie Wiesel
(1986); the exiled Tibetan leader, the Dalai Lama (1989); Daw Aung San
Suu Kyi (1991) who is opposing the military rule of Burma (Myanmar);
Nelson Mandela and F. W. de Klerk (1993) for their leadership in ending
apartheid in South Africa; and Bishop Carlos Ximenes Belo and Mr. José
Ramos-Horta (1996), for their struggle for independence for East Timor.

Amnesty International, an organization that monitors human rights abuses throughout the world and advocates on behalf of political prisoners, received the Nobel Peace Prize in 1977. In 1992, the recipient was Rigoberta Menchú, a native of the Quiché people of Guatemala, who has campaigned courageously for the rights of indigenous people in her country and against the repression of the rural poor by the Guatemalan military. Her story is a fitting introduction to the reality of the violation of human rights in the contemporary world.

Rigoberta Menchú and her family were poor peasants working on cotton and coffee plantations in rural Guatemala. Two of her brothers died on the plantation, one from disease and the other from pesticide poisoning. Her father became a catechist and a leader of the community. When he resisted the landowners' attempt to take the little land owned by the community, his home was burned and he was imprisoned, tortured, and beaten many times. In 1979, the military kidnapped Rigoberta's 16-year-old younger brother, whom they accused of being a guerrilla fighter. The military tortured him by beating him, pulling out his fingernails, and cutting off parts of his ears and lips. Then they publicly burned him alive, along with 20 others, as a warning to the community. Rigoberta and her mother witnessed his execution. Both of her parents were killed in the repression that followed, and Rigoberta fled the country to exile in Mexico.[2]

Rigoberta Menchú's experience is an all too common one in our world. Similar events have taken place in countries such as El Salvador, Nicaragua, Cuba, Haiti, Argentina, Chile, South Africa, Sudan, Nigeria, Zaire, Rwanda, Algeria, Iran, Iraq, Syria, Israel, Great Britain, the former Soviet Union, Afghanistan, Indonesia, the Philippines, China, India, Singapore, North Korea, South Korea, and elsewhere. The United States, with its tradition of racism, its record of support for military dictatorships, and as one of the few Western nations that practices capital punishment, is hardly immune to the charge of human rights violations. In some places the repression has stopped or lessened, but in others it continues. This chapter will explore the struggle for human rights in all its complexity.

HISTORY AND CONTEXT

Before World War II, human rights were viewed as a purely domestic matter and not a topic for international relations. The horror of the Holocaust and the attempt to hold German army officers accountable at the Nuremberg trials gave international validity to human rights concerns.

The United Nations has played an important role in setting the standards for human rights. On December 10, 1948 the newly formed United Nations issued its "Universal Declaration of Human Rights." No country voted against the Declaration, although some abstained—the U.S.S.R. and its allies because there was not enough emphasis on social and economic rights, South Africa because of race, and Saudi Arabia because of gender issues.[3] Because the Declaration did not have the binding force of a treaty, the United Nations developed the International Covenant on Economic, Social, and Cultural Rights and the International Covenant on Civil and Political Rights.[4] Together these three documents are often referred to as the "International Bill of Human Rights." They summarize the minimum social and political guarantees internationally recognized as necessary for a life of dignity in the contemporary world. Table 4.1 lists the human rights that have been recognized by the community of nations.[5]

The U.N. has also released several other Conventions on particular aspects of human rights: on the Elimination of All Forms of Racial Discrimination (1965), on the Suppression and Punishment of the Crime of Apartheid (1973), on the Elimination of Discrimination Against Women (1979), against Torture and Other Cruel, Inhuman, or Degrading Treatment or Punishment (1984), and on the Rights of the Child (1989). None of these Conventions has enjoyed universal ratification, but together they have established clear norms regarding human rights. The United Nations has also issued a (nonbinding) Declaration on the Right to Development (1986).

The United Nations has been less effective in redressing violations of human rights because of the doctrine of national sovereignty. The U.N. Commission on Human Rights, a permanent subsidiary body of the Economic and Social Council, is the world's most prominent forum for protesting infractions of human rights by states, but its hearings on individual countries are strictly confidential, and it has no enforcement authority. Many of the Conventions regarding aspects of human rights also have implementation or monitoring committees, but they all depend on the cooperation of states. While these monitoring and enforcement mechanisms are admittedly weak and ineffective, the consciousness and behavior of some governments have been changed, and victims have been aided.[6]

The Cold War twisted the principled concern for human rights into a tool in the ideological battle between the East (the Soviet Union and the Warsaw Pact nations) and the West (the United States and NATO). The West focused its rhetoric on civil and political rights, such as freedom of the press and the right to peacefully assemble and protest, decrying the failure of Communist countries to honor these rights. The East emphasized social and economic rights, such as employment, housing, and health care, disparaging the condition of the underclass in the United States. Since both superpowers had logs in their own eyes, it was difficult to remove the log in the eye of the adversary. Peoples in the Two-Thirds World, meanwhile, were struggling toward self-determination in a global context that forced them to choose sides.

The Cold War period (1945–89) yields a paradox regarding human rights. It was an era when violations of human rights were routine and ubiquitous, and it was the time when the concept of human rights became established and accepted, and even extensively monitored.[7] The United Nations, as we have seen, was largely responsible for establishing human rights as an international norm. Non-Governmental Organizations (NGOs), such as Amnesty International and Human Rights Watch, built sterling reputations for impar-

Table 4.1
Internationally Recognized Human Rights

The International Bill of Human Rights recognizes the rights to:

Equality of rights without discrimination (D1, D2, E2, E3, C2, C3; P30, 44, 48, 65, 86, 89)
Life (D3, C6; P11)
Liberty and security of person (D3, C9; P11)
Protection against slavery (D4, C8)
Protection against torture and cruel and inhuman punishment (D5, C7)
Recognition as a person before the law (D6, C16; P27 "juridicial protection of [human] rights.")
Equal protection of the law (D7, C14, C26; P69)
Access to legal remedies for rights violations (D8, C2)
Protection against arbitrary arrest or detention (D9, C9)
Hearing before an independent and impartial judiciary (D10, C14)
Presumption of innocence (D11, C14)
Protection against ex post facto laws (D11, C15)
Protection of privacy, family, and home (D12, C17)
Freedom of movement and residence (D13, C12; P25)
Seek asylum from persecution (D14; P103–08)
Nationality (D15)
Marry and found a family (D16, E10, C23; P15)
Own property (D17; P21)
Freedom of thought, conscience, and religion (D18, C18; P12,14)
Freedom of opinion, expression, and the press (D19, C19; P12)
Freedom of assembly and association (D20, C21, C22; P23)
Political participation (D21, C25; P26, 73, 146)
Social security (D22, E9; P11, 63–64)
Work, under favorable conditions (D23, E6, E7; P18, 19)
Free trade unions (D23, E8, C22)
Rest and leisure (D24, E7)
Food, clothing, and housing (D25, E11; P11)
Health care and social services (D25, E12; P11)
Special protections for children (D25, E10, C24)
Education (D26, E13, E14; P13)
Participation in cultural life (D27, E15; P12, 13, 64)
A social and international order needed to realize rights (D28; P60–63, 75–77, 139, 141)
Self-determination (E1, C1; [P42, 43, 94])
Humane treatment when detained or imprisoned (C10)
Protection against debtor's prison (C11)
Protection against arbitrary expulsion of aliens (C13; P103–08)
Protection of minority culture (C27; P56, 94–97)
[Assistance in development (P121–25)]

Note: This list includes all rights that are enumerated in two of the three documents of the International Bill of Human Rights or have a full article in one document. The source of each right is indicated in parentheses, by document and article number. D = Universal Declaration of Human Rights. E = International Covenant on Economic, Social, and Cultural Rights. C = International Covenant on Civil and Political Rights.
Source: Jack Donnelly, *International Human Rights* (Boulder, CO: Westview Press, 1993), p. 9. The author has cross referenced Donnelly's list with Pope John XXIII, *Pacem in Terris* (*Peace on Earth*, abbreviated P in the list) in David J. O'Brien and Thomas A. Shannon, eds, *Catholic Social Thought: The Documentary Heritage* (Maryknoll, NY Orbis Books, 1992), pp. 131–62. Numbers refer to paragraphs in the document.

tially investigating human rights transgressions and accurately reporting their findings.

There was plenty of work for these NGOs to do. Communist countries were totalitarian societies. Two-thirds of the world was desperately poor, and those countries, with few exceptions, were ruled by brutal dictators or repressive militaries. Many of those countries were in a state of civil war characterized by guerrilla insurgencies and military counterinsurgency warfare. Innocent civilians were often caught in the middle, violated by both sides. While the world was coming to conceptual clarity that it is wrong to violate a person's human rights, such abuse was pervasive.

Happily, since about 1986, the world has experienced a remarkable transformation regarding civil and political rights. In Asia the "People Power" revolution deposed the conjugal dictatorship of the Marcoses in the Philippines, while South Korea, and then Taiwan moved toward representative government. Pakistan and Bangladesh have had free elections and peaceful transfers of power. Except for Cuba, elected governments hold office in every country in the Western hemisphere, although the democratic credentials of some, such as Paraguay, remain suspect. The political imprisonment, torture, and disappearances that were commonplace in Latin America in the early 1980s have abated.[8] Africa too has been touched by this wave of liberalization, although more lightly. The enfranchisement of the black majority in South Africa is the most startling success story, but other countries, such as Benin and Zambia, have moved from one man or one party rule to genuine elections. Africa and the Middle East, however, remain civil rights backwaters, as do such Asian countries as China, North Korea, Vietnam, Indonesia, and Singapore.

The "Velvet Revolution" (1989–91) converted Eastern Europe and the former Soviet Empire from police states into fledgling democracies. The human rights transition, however, has not been smooth. In the former Czechoslovakia, for example, a commission charged with investigating over 150,000 informants of the old secret police paid scant attention to due process. Merely turning the tables does not represent genuine progress toward respect for human rights. Indeed, *the treatment of the guilty and the despised is the litmus test of human rights in a society.*[9] The 1994 split of Czechoslovakia into the Czech Republic and Slovakia was due, in part, to concerns about the fair treatment of minorities. Old habits and ingrained prejudices are hard to change.

THE UNITED STATES

While there is no comparison between the human rights records of the United States and the former Soviet Union, Washington's actions during the Cold War were problematic regarding human rights. U.S. foreign policy during this period submerged human rights concerns in order to combat the threat of communism. Thus, the United States showered anticommunist dictators with economic assistance and military aid throughout the Cold War, even to those who were oppressive and corrupt. The United States supported, for example, the Shah in Iran, Marcos in the Philippines, Somoza in Nicaragua, Duvalier in Haiti, Stroessner in Paraguay, and Mobutu in Zaire. None of these men shied away from imprisoning, torturing, or even murdering their opponents. There are even disturbing examples of U.S. efforts to overthrow freely elected governments, in Guatemala in 1954, Chile in 1973, and Nicaragua after 1984, for example. The Soviet record was equally appalling, backing, for example, the Mengistu regime in Ethiopia, among the most barbaric on record.[10] The difference is that the United States is supposed to be committed to the principles of freedom and justice.

There were nuances of difference among the American administrations during the Cold War, but anticommunism was the cornerstone of U.S. foreign policy. President Jimmy Carter (1976–1980) did give human rights an important role, but global realities often made it difficult for his administration to practice this principle. Ronald Reagan campaigned against the Carter human rights policy and on behalf of a single-minded focus on overcoming communism, and he acted on these values once elected. Congress, however, gradually reasserted human rights as a foreign policy consideration during the 1980s.

The end of the Cold War could mean a more prominent place for human rights as an international interest, and, as we have seen, there has been a decrease in political repression. National sovereignty, however, remains in tension with intervention on behalf of human rights, and the benefits of trade also impinge on legitimate concerns about violations of human rights. China's repression of political protestors in Tiananmen Square in 1989 stands as a symbol of human rights abuse in the post-Cold War world, yet neither the Bush nor the Clinton administrations have taken substantive action against China's human rights violations. While ideology no longer justifies allowing repression, sovereignty and economics continue to be obstacles to international advocacy for human rights.

The Soviet Union's criticism of the U.S. *domestic* record on social and economic rights was generally dismissed, but it contains more than a grain of truth. In the late 1980s, for example, the case could be made that Cuba's health care system performed better than America's in terms of meeting the basic needs of their entire populations. Homelessness in one of the richest nations on earth is a moral outrage. The United States seems to be afflicted with a certain blindness, perhaps born of self-righteousness, to its domestic failures in the area of human rights. "The United States, however, is said to suffer from, for example, police brutality, civil rights problems, or a health care crisis, which are spoken of as if they are qualitatively different from torture, racial discrimination, or denial of the right to health care."[11] The history of slavery and segregation and the near genocide of the indigenous peoples should certainly caution America about self-satisfaction regarding human rights, and urge on us a genuine watchfulness and a sense of reform.

THE MEANING OF HUMAN RIGHTS

Human rights make strong claims. Right is not a word to be thrown around loosely. If a person has a right, then the community and other persons have a duty to respect and fulfill that right. Because a right confers an obligation on the community, it is not surprising that various societies have contested the foundation, meaning, and scope of human rights.

During the Cold War, each of the three "worlds" was said to emphasize a different aspect of human rights. The First World stressed civil and political rights and the right to private property. The Second World gave priority to social, economic, and cultural rights as prerequisites to civil and political rights. The Third World also emphasized social, economic, and cultural rights, as well as the right to self-determination and the right to development.[12] These, however, are self-serving, ideological distinctions that have little basis in any sound theory of rights. *All* of these rights are affirmed in the International Bill of Human Rights (Table 4.1), based on U.N. documents, and all of them require respect and satisfaction if human beings are to flourish.

There is a remarkable parallel between the formulation of human rights by the United Nations and that found in contemporary Catholic social teaching. The clearest expression of the meaning and scope of human rights in Catholic thought appears in the encyclical *Peace on Earth* by Pope John XXIII, written in 1963 while the Second Vatican Council was in progress. Pope John's list of human rights closely parallels that of the U.N. Universal Declaration of Human Rights (see Table 4.1). The convenings of the United Nations (1948) and of the Second Vatican Council (1962–1965) both produced transnational bodies with a focus on issues of justice and peace in a pluralistic world. "The need to find consensus on a normative basis for international justice and peace without suppressing the legitimate differences within regions and social systems led both bodies to a human rights focus."[13] Both Catholic social teaching and the standards set by the United Nations adopted human rights as a normative framework for a pluralistic world. Human rights have become the moral parameter within which a society must be ordered. There can be many legitimate ways of organizing a government and a society, but all of them have to recognize and respect human rights.[14]

Human rights are rights that a person has simply because one is human. Such rights are held equally by all humans, and they are inalienable. Human rights are rooted, then, in a theory of human nature. Various philosophical systems provide stronger or weaker foundations for a concept of human rights.[15] The dignity of the human person, realized in community is the foundation of Catholic social thought and its theory of human rights.[16] Thus, the Catholic conception of human rights is personalistic and communitarian, not individualistic as some Enlightenment philosophers would have it. The theological foundations of human dignity and human rights include creation in the image of God, the trinitarian concept of God,[17] redemption by Jesus Christ, and the call to a transcendent destiny. The Christian tradition provides a solid foundation for a theory of human rights. The concept of human rights, however, can find healthy roots in all of the major religious traditions.[18]

There are several ways of describing human rights. One is the Cold War division of rights into three "worlds." Perhaps a better way is to differentiate rights according to three sectors or spheres of the human person essential to the preservation of human dignity: basic needs, freedom, and relationship. Human beings, for example, need food and shelter for bodily existence. Similarly, the freedom to associate with others, to participate in political decisions, and to express religious beliefs are fundamental to human dignity. Every person depends on community—the relationships into which we are born and the ones we form and choose—for his or her development and flourishing. To each of these essential areas of human existence—needs, freedom, and relationship—corresponds a set of human rights which defend human dignity within that sector.[19]

Rights can also be differentiated according to the way they are mediated by society and social institutions. Here too there are three dimensions:

First there are *personal rights* which protect fundamental characteristics of the person as such. Life, bodiliness, self-determination, sociability, work, sexuality, family, and core values are characteristics of every person that are shielded by personal rights. These personal attributes, however, can be actualized in different ways in different societies and cultures, and can be realized and safeguarded by a variety of institutional structures.

Second there are *social rights* which specify the positive obligations of society toward all its members for providing conditions that enable human beings to grow and thrive. These would include the rights to health care, political participation, adequate working conditions, education, and assembly.

Finally, there are *instrumental rights* which promote participation in forming the institutions that shape and structure human life, such as the government, the economy, the health care and educational systems, and the law. Instrumental rights require the structuring or institutionalizing of human rights, through, for example, court systems that protect one's personal and social rights or some system of social security (see Figure 4.1).

These two ways of elaborating human rights—according to sectors or spheres of the human person and according to the kinds of personal, social, and institutional relationships involved—are helpful keys for unlocking the inner logic of the Catholic human rights tradition.[20] The result is a list of human rights like that found in *Peace on Earth* and in the International Bill of Human Rights.

These schema can also be helpful in identifying the sorts of policies that can best promote human rights. The framing of the discussion that arose during the Cold War set up a conflict between civil and political rights versus economic and social rights. The conflict, however, is not between political participation (voting) versus economic participation (jobs). The conflict in most societies is between the elite who are both politically and economically powerful versus the marginalized who are neither.

Constructive human rights policies, then, should focus on establishing the full set of social rights for the protection of human dignity. The full set of social rights would include the following: the rights to food, clothing, shelter, health care, and rest; the right to political participation; the rights to nationality and to migration; the rights of assembly and association; the rights to work, to adequate working conditions, and to a just wage; the right to found a family or live singly; the rights to freedom of expression, to education, and to religious expression[21] (see Figure 4.1).

Three principles have been proposed to guide the development of human rights policies toward overcoming the marginalization of the poor, minorities, and the oppressed:

1. The needs of the poor take priority over the wants of the rich.
2. The freedom of the dominated takes priority over the liberty of the powerful.
3. The participation of marginalized groups takes priority over the preservation of an order which excludes them.[22]

Figure 4.1
Personal, Social and Instrumental Rights:
An Interpretation of *Pacem in Terris*

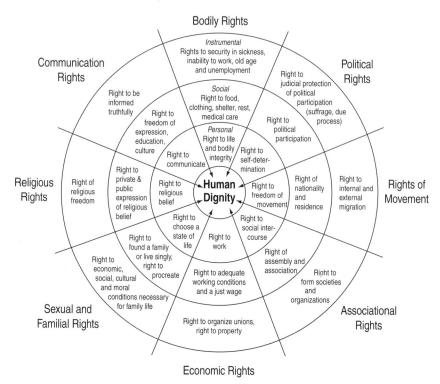

Source: Adapted from the Yale Task Force on Population Ethics (D. Christiansen, R. Garet, D. Hollenbach and C. Powers), "Moral Claims, Human Rights and Population Policies," *Theological Studies 35* (1974), p. 102 (with permission).

These principles are helpful yardsticks for measuring the human rights impact of legislative or policy proposals, and for assessing foreign policy. They highlight the value of human rights as moral norms in a pluralistic world, and they expose the fundamental questions that human rights standards can raise in every sort of political and economic system.

CULTURAL RELATIVISM

The United Nations called its Declaration of Human Rights "Universal," that is, applicable to and binding on all nations and people. The claim of universal human rights, however, is controversial in a pluralistic world. Some nations have claimed that the International Bill of Human Rights, with its affirmation of equal rights for women, for example, is too Western in its conception and articulation, and American conservatives have been reluctant to affirm some of the social, economic, and cultural rights, such as the right to work or the right to health care. Thoroughgoing relativists would deny the theoretical possibility of universal norms, noting the sometimes radical differences among cultures.

In arguing in favor of universal norms regarding human rights, it is not necessary to take an extreme absolutist position. Not every value is absolute; indeed, there may be conflicts among and exceptions to universal norms. The fact of cultural relativism, however, does not mean that whatever a culture sanctions is right. There may well be universal norms that adhere to humans as human, and that transcend and critique culture.

In sorting out the tension between universal standards and the different practices of various cultures, it can be helpful to distinguish three levels of specification regarding human rights.[23] The first level is the *concept* of a human right, such as the right to work. This general statement of principle admits to little cultural variability. Secondly, there is the *interpretation* of the principle. A guaranteed job or unemployment insurance might be two legitimate interpretations of the right to work. Finally, there may be many different ways to *implement* an interpretation of a right. A government might employ a large percentage of the population in a wide network of civil service jobs, or it might stimulate the economy to provide ample employment opportunities for its people.

The right to political participation might be interpreted as the right to vote, but voting can take place in a two-party system or a multi-party system, for individual candidates or for slates of candidates, or through direct referenda. But a one-party system that really admits of no choice may violate the right to political participation.

In Western societies, standards of modesty require women to cover their chest, while Muslim customs require women to wear a veil, often covering their entire bodies. It would seem, however, that the rights to equality of treatment without discrimination and to education would require every society to offer equal opportunities for education to women and men.

If the norms regarding human rights are not universal, then they are arbitrary, and they offer little moral guidance for a pluralistic world.[24] While sensitivity is certainly called for in addressing clashing cultural values, caution should not be equated with indifference or inaction. Even if we are not entitled to impose our values on others, we are responsible for owning our values, witnessing to them, and acting on them. Practices such as female infanticide, apartheid, anti-Semitism, slavery, sexual exploitation of children,[25] female genital mutilation, and torture deserve neither respect nor tolerance.[26]

DISCRIMINATION AGAINST WOMEN

The oppression and subjugation of women is worldwide. Sexism is characteristic of every society and culture on earth. Indeed, only recently has feminism (the belief in the equality of the sexes) meaningfully challenged patriarchy (the institutionalized belief that men are superior to women and should dominate them). Although some nations have made significant progress toward the goal of gender equality, no society has reached that goal.

The *Human Development Report* recently devised the *gender-related development index* (GDI) which adjusted the three factors in its human development index (HDI)—life expectancy, educational attainment, and income—for gender inequality. On a scale of 0 to 1, with 1 representing perfect equality, the highest score is .929 by Sweden. (The United States ranks fourth with a GDI score of .923.) That no country scores 1 is remarkable because nearly everywhere in the world women's life expectancy is higher than that of men. Even given this edge, and, in most industrial countries an equal achievement in basic education, the disparity in income is enough to lower the GDI to below 1.[27] (See the Appendix for a listing of the GDI rank and value of the countries of the world.)

The *Human Development Report 1996* draws several conclusions from the GDI rankings: 1) No society treats its women as well as its men. 2) The pursuit of gender equality is not necessarily associated with high growth in income, and it can be pursued at all levels of income. 3) Progress in gender equality can be attained by nations characterized by different political ideologies, economic conditions, cultures, and stages of development.[28] The key to progress toward gender equality seems simply to be the will to succeed, that is, an awareness that discrimination exists, is wrong, and needs to change, followed by the removal of restrictions on women and targeted social programs on women's behalf.

The *Human Development Report* also introduced the *gender empowerment measure* (GEM) which focuses on women's participation in economic and political decision-making by noting the percentage of women who hold seats in congress or parliament, administrative or managerial positions, professional or technical jobs, and women's share of earned income. The highest score, with 1 representing perfect equality between men and women, is Norway's .786. The United States ranks ninth in the world with a score of .645. In 1995, only 10 percent of the seats in the U.S. Congress were held by women, and women's share of earned income in the United States was only

40 percent.[29] Only 10 countries have a GEM rating higher than .600, and 29 countries have a GEM lower than .300. Surprisingly, some industrial countries, such as Japan and France, are actually behind some developing countries such as Barbados, Cuba, China, Costa Rica, and Mexico.[30] Female government leaders are still rare in the modern world. While women have led Israel, the Philippines, Pakistan, Bangladesh, Sri Lanka, and Great Britain, for example, they have not occupied the highest office in the United States, Japan, France, Russia, or China.

Women's rights are denied in nearly every aspect of life. Wherever people are oppressed, women suffer more, first as members of the oppressed group, then as women. When people are hungry, it is often the custom for the men and boys to eat first, and for the women and girls to eat what is left over. Thus in India, where this practice is common, the rate of female mortality is higher.[31] The "feminization of poverty," that is, the much higher incidence of poverty among households headed by women, is a reality in both industrial and developing countries.[32] This is due in part to economic exploitation and wage discrimination. Women suffer discrimination in employment, salaries, and promotion—the "glass ceiling" phenomenon. It is no accident that sweatshops in Latin America and Asia employ mostly women because they can be paid less and are more vulnerable to exploitation. In the United States, women doing work comparable to men are paid on average about two-thirds of what men are paid. Women are often excluded from educational opportunities.[33] In Saudi Arabia women are prohibited from driving a car.

It was only in 1910 that women in the United States received the right to vote. Political participation is still restricted for women, either through law or common practice, in countries such as Kuwait, Iran, South Korea, Turkey, Egypt, Morocco, Congo, Pakistan, Nigeria, Togo, and Mali.[34] In 1997, women held only 11.7 percent of all the seats in the world's 179 parliaments, even though females make up 49.6 percent of the world's population.[35]

In many countries women do not enjoy the full protection of the law. Wives and daughters are not allowed to inherit the property or wealth of their husbands or fathers, for example, or women do not have the standing to be granted credit in their own name.

In many countries of the world, women do not fare any better at home than they do in public life. The life of a poor peasant woman is one of unending menial labor: gathering wood for cooking, hauling water, washing clothes by hand, preparing food from scratch, working the fields, while caring for perhaps a half-dozen children. In industrial countries, some of the drudgery has been eliminated from household duties by washing machines and vacuum cleaners, but most women have jobs, and then come home to their "second shift" of cooking, cleaning, and child care. In many cultures, women remain subject to the rule of their father or husband, and can be forced to marry the husband chosen by their father. Throughout much of the world, the dependency of women on men and the inferiority of women to men is socially constructed and institutionalized, so much so that it seems natural to women and men. Such attitudes and practices, deeply embedded in culture, are very difficult to change.

Perhaps the most shocking common problem of women is their everyday experience of violence and brutality and the threat of violence. In nearly every country, across all classes, women are beaten by their husbands and fathers, assaulted and raped by relatives, acquaintances, and strangers, and harassed and intimidated on the street, in school, and at work. Muslim women were systematically raped by Serbian soldiers in Bosnia, as were Tutsi women during the slaughter by the Hutu in Rwanda. This sexual violence is not random; it is aimed at women as women, and meant to frighten and control them. It amounts to "sexual terrorism," a system perpetuated by men for the domination of women.[36]

The most abhorrent custom related to gender violence and men's inordinate desire to control female sexuality is the practice of female genital mutilation. Female genital cutting is practiced by a wide variety of ethnic groups, whether their religion is Christian, Muslim, or Traditional, in a band of 28 countries in north-central Africa, from Egypt and Somalia to Senegal and the Ivory Coast.[37] An estimated 100 million women today have undergone this centuries-old practice, and each year about 2 million more girls endure the procedure.[38] One form of the procedure involves a clitoridectomy, the removal of the clitoris and sometimes some of the labial tissue. In some countries, such as Mali, Ethiopia, and Sudan, infibulation, a more severe form of genital mutilation is practiced. The clitoris and all of the woman's external genitalia are removed and the wound is sewn shut until she is married, leaving a small opening for urination and menstruation.[39] In some places genital cutting is done on girls aged 4 to 10; among other peoples it is a ritual of adolescence. It is done, usually without anesthesia, by local excisers, midwives, barbers, or relatives using a razor blade or crude knife. Female genital mutilation diminishes or eliminates a woman's ability to experience sexual pleasure. Besides the physical and psychological trauma of the procedure itself and its primary consequence, the cutting can result in difficult childbirth, serious infections, and even death.[40]

The purpose of the cutting, according to a local exciser in the Ivory Coast, is to insure a woman's fidelity to her husband and her family. A woman's role in life is to care for her children, keep house, and cook. If she has not been cut she might be distracted by her own sexual pleasure.[41] Many people who practice genital cutting believe that a woman will be sexually aggressive, even promiscuous, without the procedure. As an Egyptian farmer explained, "If a woman is more passive it is in her interest, it is in her father's interest and in her husband's interest."[42]

The story of Fauziya Kassindja[43] (see sidebar) illustrates many of the aspects of the oppression of women in the Two-Thirds World: their narrow domestic role definition, their subjection to patriarchal rule, their vulnerability to violence, and their lack of protection under the law.[44] While a government official in Togo admitted that excision is a problem, he insisted that poverty is the primary problem. Human rights and economic development, however, are not mutually exclusive goals, nor is development a prerequisite for respecting the human rights of women. Female genital cutting is mutilation. Education campaigns can be developed aimed at changing attitudes, policies and laws can be enacted to prohibit female genital mutilation, and they can be enforced.

This is true not only in Togo or Egypt, but also in the United States. Immigrants who practice the custom of female genital mutilation have imported it to the United States from Africa and the Middle East.[45] This practice has been illegal in most of Europe for over a decade. In the fall of 1996, the U.S. Congress also outlawed female genital mutilation. The new law

---

One Woman's Story

In the spring of 1996, the story of Fauziya Kassindja, a 19-year-old woman who had fled from Togo in West Africa to the United States in order to avoid genital mutilation, became public. Ms. Kassindja arrived in the United States in December of 1994 and requested asylum. She was immediately imprisoned where she remained for sixteen months. Finally, public pressure led to her release, and her request for asylum was eventually granted.

Fauziya is the youngest of a family of seven children—two sons and five daughters—born to Muhammad and Hajia Kassindja. Among the Muslim Tchamba people in her city in rural Togo, polygamy is common, and female genital cutting is nearly universal. Her mother's older sister died as a result of the practice, so Hajia was spared the procedure. Muhammad Kassindja started a trucking business that made his family rich by local standards, and allowed him to thwart some of his people's traditions. He took only one wife; he made sure all of his children were educated; and, one by one, his daughters married men of their own choosing without being cut, until Fauziya was the only one remaining at home.

The situation changed drastically when Muhammad Kassindja died in 1993. Fauziya was then 16. According to Tchamba custom, Mrs. Kassindja was required to hand over her home and to cede the responsibility for Fauziya to her husband's widowed sister, Hadja Mamoude. The Kassindja family gave the widow an inheritance of about $3,500. Mouhamadou Kassindja, the family patriarch and a cousin of Muhammad, and Mrs. Mamoude promptly took Fauziya out of school and began negotiating with Issakah Ibrahim for her to become his fourth wife. Mr. Ibrahim insisted that Fauziya be cut, and the family readily agreed. Fauziya resisted both the marriage and the cutting. Her mother and an older sister helped Fauziya to run away on the eve of her wedding, and literally minutes before her genital mutilation. Haija's inheritance had been given to Fauziya so she could flee the country.

After Haija Kassindja was sure that her daughter was safe, she went before the family patriarch begging his forgiveness and asking to be allowed to live in his plain cement compound. Some male members of her family accompanied her to the formal apology. Because she is a woman, she did not speak; a male cousin apologized on her behalf. She sat mute and motionless, head hung low, while Mouhamadou Kassindja upbraided her before finally accepting her apology. That afternoon she moved into his compound with two of the patriarch's four wives (the other two wives live in two different cities). The compound with its dingy courtyard will define her existence from now on, because the patriarch does not allow his wives to leave it.

requires federal authorities to inform immigrants that parents who arrange for their children to be cut here, and those who perform the cutting, face up to five years in prison. The law also requires U.S. representatives to international financial institutions to oppose loans to countries where the practice is common and whose governments have not carried out educational programs to prevent it.[46]

Violence and discrimination against women are among the most pervasive problems facing the global community, yet in many parts of the world women's rights are not commonly classified as human rights.[47] Sexism is often fostered by religion, yet is seldom intrinsic to religious beliefs or tenets.[48] The dignity and equality of women need to be tenaciously fostered through education, public policy, and law.

RACE AND CASTE

Discrimination also can be based on race, caste, and ethnicity. Ethnic conflict has become such a problem in the post-Cold War world that it will be the subject of the next chapter. The present section will focus on the denial of human rights based on race or caste.

Race is rather difficult to define. Biologically and psychologically, the human species is more alike than different, and the differences among individuals of a given race are far greater than the differences among races.[49] Theologically, there is one human family, with God as our common parent; we are all brothers and sisters to one another. But this theological affirmation of solidarity and community could just as well be based in biology. There are different blood types, but they are found throughout the human species. Any female human being can theoretically procreate with any other male human being. Tissue type and size, not race, are the obstacles to organ transplantation. Genetically humans are one people. Nevertheless, race refers to the physical characteristics, primarily skin color, that can distinguish one group of humans from another. While race may be a social fabrication rooted in skin color, it is a differentiation that has led to much conflict, injustice, and suffering.

Race, then, is not the problem; racism is. Racism consists in a *belief* that one racial group is inherently superior to another racial group. In the twentieth century there has been much attention paid to white racism—the attitude of superiority and supremacy of whites toward peoples of other colors—and justly so, since the European colonizers brought an insufferable belief in their innate superiority to their conquest of the world.[50] Racism is not the sole preserve of whites, but white racism has a particularly sordid modern history.

The Europeans who settled the United States developed a belief in "manifest destiny"—that they were a people chosen by God to rule this land given to them by God—to justify taking the land inhabited by the indigenous people and slaughtering the native Americans. Dee Brown tells this story from the Indian perspective in his bestselling book, *Bury My Heart at Wounded*

Knee.[51] It is a story of broken promises and savage massacres.

One example is the massacre at Sand Creek in Colorado in November of 1864. Cheyenne and Arapaho Indians had camped at Sand Creek, about forty miles from Fort Lyon, with the assurance that they were safe from attack. Major Anthony, the commander of Fort Lyon, had encouraged the warriors to hunt buffalo to feed their tribes. Most of the men, therefore, were away from the camp when 700 U.S. cavalry, under the command of Colonel Chivington and Major Anthony, descended on the camp at sunrise, firing randomly at the Indians. Chief Black Kettle came out of his lodge and raised an American flag and a white flag of surrender on a long lodgepole. He called to his people not to be afraid, that the soldiers wouldn't hurt them. As hundreds of women and children gathered under Black Kettle's American flag, the soldiers opened fire from two sides of the camp. The cavalry indiscriminately slaughtered men, women, and children. Most of the dead Indians were scalped by the soldiers, and many were mutilated. Although lack of discipline, drunkenness, cowardice, and poor marksmanship allowed many of the Indians to escape, when the shooting ended 105 Indian women and children and 28 men were dead. Most had been unarmed and had offered no resistance. Of the 47 casualties among the soldiers, most were the result of their careless firing on each other.[52] This is sadly characteristic of the way the West was won.

Those native Americans who still live on reservations experience the highest rate of poverty and the shortest life span of any group of Americans. A few tribes, such as the Mashantucket Pequot and the Mohegan in Connecticut, have exploited loopholes in the law to open casinos that have been financially successful. Native peoples have been victims of white racism in the United States, and, as we saw in the section on colonialism in the first chapter, throughout the world.

One of the most repulsive examples of racism was the trade in African slaves. As many as nine million Africans were captured and shipped to the New World prior to 1863, nearly half of them to the southern United States.[53] Many died from the horrid conditions on slave ships. When they arrived, human beings were bought and sold like cattle. Their labor was key to the plantation system in the southern United States, the Caribbean, and South America. African slaves were beaten, tortured, and raped by their white masters. Families were broken asunder, and living conditions were abominable. In the movie *Roots*, a captured runaway slave is given the choice between castration and having his foot cut off. Human beings were stripped of all dignity.

In the United States, when the system of slavery was abolished after the Civil War (1861–65), it was replaced with a system of segregation which lasted more than a hundred years. Blacks in the South were kept separate from whites. Blacks received an inadequate education, were excluded from better paying jobs, denied the vote, and confined to substandard housing with few public services. "Whites Only" signs forced blacks to use different restrooms, public parks, drinking fountains, and restaurants.[54] The Civil

Rights Act of 1964, enacted after years of non-violent protests led by Rev. Martin Luther King, Jr. and others, prohibited segregated public facilities in the United States, and the Voting Rights Act of the following year enfranchised blacks in America.[55]

Slavery and the system of segregation have been abolished in the United States, but racism and its effects persist. Progress has been made, but intermarriage and genuinely integrated neighborhoods, schools, and churches remain rare, while discrimination, direct or systematic, is still too common.[56] At present, the United States remains a multi-racial society rather than a truly integrated community. America's history of white racism will not be easy to transform.

Racism is a belief in racial superiority. Once it has been taught and ingrained in a person's consciousness and a culture's structure, it is very difficult to change. Since racial superiority is believed, it tends to be immune to evidence to the contrary and selective in reflecting on experience. Thus, for instance, if a white person believes that blacks are stupid, the white will tend not to notice a brilliant black physicist or a competent black businessperson. Because racism is a belief, not a logical conclusion, it is difficult to correct. This is even more true when racism is embedded in and reinforced by culture.

South Africa's recently ended system of apartheid (separateness in Afrikaner) provides another particularly appalling example of white racism. This system of state-enforced segregation, which was the last bastion of white supremacy in Africa, allowed a white minority—only 18 percent of a population of over 40 million—to keep strict control of the black majority. Apartheid guaranteed 87 percent of the land and 75 percent of the income to the white minority. Blacks were legally allowed to live only in one of twelve "bantustans" (so-called homelands), and were required to have a special permit to live and work in the other 87 percent of the country. Blacks were required to carry a valid passbook with them at all times or be imprisoned. Public facilities, schools, and residences were strictly segregated. Blacks had no civil or political standing in the Republic of South Africa. Resisting the system of apartheid could result in arrest, detention, torture, and death. Nelson Mandela, the first black president of a reformed South Africa, spent nearly forty years of his life in prison for resisting apartheid.[57]

The formal system of apartheid in South Africa collapsed in 1994 because of courageous resistance from blacks, and because of economic, social, and political sanctions imposed by the world community. As in the United States, the system has been abolished, but racism and its effects persist.

While Europe has long been split by ethnic conflict, racial tensions were less noticeable until recently. Now racism is rearing its ugly head in response to the immigration of people of color. Asians, Africans, and Caribbean blacks from the Commonwealth countries of the former British Empire are flowing into Great Britain, changing the complexion of British society, and causing a conflict of cultures. Prejudice is sometimes being expressed violently toward immigrants—who often respond with more violence. France is experiencing an influx of immigrants and refugees from former colonies in Africa, and especially Algeria, and is having similar problems in integrating them into French society. Neo-Nazis and skinheads in Germany have attacked "guestworkers" from Turkey and immigrants and refugees from developing countries.[58]

Anti-Semitism is widespread in Europe and in much of the world. It found its most horrific expression in the Holocaust during World War II,[59] and unfortunately it continues to the present. The Ku Klux Klan in the United States persecuted blacks, Jews, and Catholics.

Because of the slave trade, Brazil has the largest African population outside of Africa itself. Blacks comprise one-third to one-half of Brazil's 160 million people. Because there has been considerable intermarriage among Brazilians, there are over twenty terms to describe the various hues found among Brazil's people. Such color consciousness has been developed by a social preference for light-skinned persons and a subtle pattern of discrimination which has relegated blacks to the bottom of the economic order. The percentage of blacks in college or public employment, for example, is minuscule.[60]

Only 1 percent of Peru's population is black, but they are employed almost exclusively in menial jobs, such as pallbearers and doormen, where their skin color is thought to add prestige to the work. The country's Indian majority suffers much of the same racism from the Hispanic elite, but hostilities born of colonial history keep Indians and blacks from uniting against discrimination. In fact they often discriminate against each other.[61]

Racism, unfortunately, is hardly a white prerogative. Reverse racism in response to racial oppression, while perhaps understandable, is still racism, and it is unjust. At least some elements of the Black Muslim movement in the United States have engaged in reverse racism. Asian shopkeepers in black communities in the United States have sometimes experienced discrimination, and there is a documented tension between black and Hispanic communities.

In Central and East Africa, black Africans treated Asian immigrants with harsh discrimination in the years after independence. The Asians were descendants of Indian immigrants who had come to Kenya, Malawi, Tanzania, Zambia, and Uganda as part of the free immigration policy of the British Empire in the late nineteenth century. Many of them became shopkeepers and traders. When these countries gained their independence, the Asians found themselves excluded in the effort to Africanize the management of the government and local companies. The discrimination was most blatant in Uganda, where the dictator Idi Amin expelled all Asians from the country and confiscated their property.[62]

There is resentment in the Philippines and Malaysia of the families of Chinese origin who have often enjoyed business success in these countries. In recent history the Japanese have exhibited xenophobic tendencies, especially in their conquests of Korea and China during the period around World War II. Racism, prejudice, and discrimination are universal temptations.

Caste refers to prejudice and discrimination based on the idea that one's position in life is determined by one's birth family. It is similar to class, which is an economic distinction between groups of people, but it is even more insidious in that caste implies little possibility of improving one's lot in life. It imposes a kind of predestination.

In India's Hindu culture, people were born into one of four castes. But about 15 percent of India's population were born below any of these into a fifth caste called the "Untouchables." These people were considered unclean, and they were relegated into the lowest occupations—waste removal, disposing of dead animals, or working with leather. They were made to live on the margins of the village or city, and excluded from temples and public facilities. Mahatma Gandhi called the Untouchables, Harijans, that is, the children of God, and he vigorously campaigned for their inclusion into society. India's constitution completely outlaws the exclusion of Untouchables, making the observance of this practice a crime. Specific laws forbid discrimination and set up affirmative action programs for the Harijan. But the laws are hard to enforce and implementation has been slow.[63]

While the plight of the Untouchables in India is perhaps the clearest example of discrimination based on caste, it is practiced in more subtle forms in many other societies. Caste and class can often largely determine one's fate in life.

HAITI: A CASE STUDY

Haiti is a tragic example of the deprivation of civil and economic rights in the post-Cold War world and of the complexities of intervening in a country on behalf of human rights.

After the United States, Haiti was the second country in the Western hemisphere to establish its independence from colonial rule. A revolt by African slaves established the Republic of Haiti by 1804. But the new country was immediately isolated, ignored, and discriminated against by its slave-owning neighbors and the slave trading countries of Europe. In addition, chaos and corruption have characterized Haiti's politics since its inception. "Paralleling the isolation and discrimination of the international community," says Anthony Maingot, "was the pervasive absence of any sense of national or political cohesion."[64] In the first 75 years of its existence, Haiti experienced 69 "revolutions."

The United States sent the marines into Haiti in 1915 and controlled the country for 19 years, until 1934. The cover story for this invasion was political anarchy in Haiti, but the real reason was to control "America's Lake" (the Caribbean), and to protect access to the Panama Canal.[65]

During most of the Cold War, Haiti was ruled by the Duvalier family, one of the most corrupt regimes in history. François "Papa Doc" Duvalier seized power in 1957, and his son, Jean-Claude "Baby Doc" Duvalier succeeded him in 1971. "One United States administration after another held its nose against the stench but tolerated [and supported] the Duvaliers as the alternative to possible communist penetration."[66] The Soviet Union, however, showed no interest in the morass of problems that comprised Haiti.

Papa Doc Duvalier instituted the Tontons Macoute, a private army of goons to enforce his will, and a paramilitary national security force larger than the Haitian army. The Duvaliers ruled through a policy of repression that included political imprisonment, torture, and murder. They also amassed a huge fortune for themselves and a few of the light-skinned mulatto elite through pervasive corruption and greed, in the process making Haiti the poorest country in the Western hemisphere.[67] When Jean-Claude Duvalier was finally forced to leave Haiti (he escaped to the French Riviera) in 1986, the country was thrown into another period of chaos and coups.

In December, 1990, after several violently aborted attempts, Haiti chose its first democratically elected president, Jean-Bertrand Aristide, a former priest and a charismatic advocate for the poor. Although the United States had some reservations about the popular priest's ability to govern, the Bush administration was quietly supportive. No doubt Aristide made some mistakes in his attempt to revive Haiti's economy with a genuine focus on the poor, and there were some instances of mob violence on the part of his supporters, but his administration seemed to be genuinely trying to reconcile the rich and poor in Haiti and to improve the lot of the poor. In October 1991, after less than a year in office, President Aristide was overthrown in a military coup led by General Raoul Cédras. Aristide received asylum in the United

States, which condemned the coup and called for his restoration to power.

The next three years under Cédras and his military cronies were some of the worst in Haiti's bleak and violent history. The regular military, along with a paramilitary group called FRAPH, systematically attacked and intimidated supporters of Aristide and his "Lavalas" (which means "a cleansing flood" in Creole) political movement. The poor were subject to arbitrary arrests, beatings, and torture. Prominent Aristide supporters, such as Antoine Izmery and Haitian Justice Minister Guy Malary, were assassinated in broad daylight. As many as 4,000 civilians were murdered by the military during this period.[68]

Haiti's already poor economy declined precipitously during the military regime. In part, this decline was caused by a hemispheric trade embargo imposed by the Organization of American States and other economic sanctions imposed by the United Nations and the United States in an effort to pressure the military government to restore the democratically elected president to Haiti. Unfortunately, these economic sanctions hurt the poor rather than those in power. Per capita income fell from $390 to $240 and real GDP declined by 34 percent during the three years of military rule. Both exports and imports dropped by roughly half. The inflation rate rose from 8.4 percent in 1991 to 48 percent by the end of 1993. By mid-1994, 75 percent of the nation's workforce was unemployed or underemployed and more than 100,000 jobs had been lost.[69]

Persecuted and destitute, some of the poor crowded into astonishingly unseaworthy vessels for the perilous trip to the United States. A few actually made it; others perished at sea. Both the Bush and the Clinton administrations decided it was best to interdict these refugees at sea, and either return them to Haiti or detain them at the Guantanamo Bay Base in Cuba.

On July 3, 1993, after intense pressure by U.S. and U.N. officials, Aristide and Cédras signed an accord that promised to return Aristide to power on October 30. The Haitian military, however, had no intention of honoring the accord. When the American troop ship, *Harlan County*, approached Port-au-Prince on October 11, carrying lightly armed American and Canadian military engineers, it was greeted by an armed mob on the dock. Since this happened little more than a week after 18 U.S. soldiers had been killed in Somalia, President Clinton decided to order the ship to retreat. Cédras and his cronies were cynically manipulating the world community.[70]

Less than a year later, in September 1994, President Clinton, having procured a U.N. resolution authorizing the use of force to remove the military regime, ordered 20,000 American troops into Haiti. Two days before the troops were to invade, former President Jimmy Carter, accompanied by Senator Sam Nunn and retired General Colin Powell, went to Haiti to try to convince Cédras to resign and leave the country. These negotiations reached a resolution literally hours before the troops landed. Instead of having to fight their way into Haiti, the troops received a tumultuous welcome by joyful crowds of Haitians.[71] The next day American TV-viewers witnessed the brutality of the Haitian military when another crowd celebrating the arrival of the troops was attacked and beaten.

Cédras and his family flew into exile in Panama. On October 15, Aristide returned to Haiti and was reinstalled as president. The new constitution in Haiti does not allow the president to be re-elected to a second successive five-year term. Thus, although he spent three years of his term in exile, Aristide was not eligible to run for re-election. In February 1996, the newly married Aristide turned over the presidency to his close associate René Préval, who won the December election as the Lavalas candidate. This orderly, democratic transfer of power was another first for Haiti.

By March, most U.S. troops had left Haiti, although about 1,500 U.N. troops were scheduled to remain until November. Haiti's 7,000 troop military has been disbanded, as have the paramilitary organizations that terrorized the populace. In their place is a new but inadequately trained and ill-equipped police force of 5,000 officers. The good news in Haiti is that at this writing the violence and terrorism have subsided.[72] Arbitrary arrests, random beatings, and political murders in the middle of the night are nearly a thing of the past. Lifting the veil of political repression is important progress in terms of respect for human rights in Haiti. It makes a big difference in people's lives when this fear is removed.

But this is not to say that law and order has been established in Haiti. "A brutal dictatorship, a repressive army and organized political violence have been banished, but crime and mob rule are filling the vacuum of authority."[73] It is reported that the police, whom many Haitians have dismissively dubbed *ti police* or little police, are afraid to patrol Cité Soleil, the largest and most notorious slum in Port-au-Prince, at night.[74] The soldiers and paramilitary thugs of the military regime, many of whom date back to the Duvalier reign of terror, have not been totally disarmed, and have recently shown a new boldness that threatens Haiti's democratic government. An effective and fair justice system, a necessary complement to a better prepared police force, simply does not exist in Haiti.[75]

Aristide's seemingly realistic promise to move Haiti "from misery to poverty" remains unfulfilled.[76] Although the economy is growing at a rate of 4.5 percent a year and the inflation rate has been halved to about 25 percent, there are few signs of real economic growth or of human development in Haiti. Three-quarters of working-age Haitians are unemployed or underemployed. Nearly 80 percent are illiterate. Per capita income, at $260 a year, remains the lowest in the Western hemisphere.[77] There are virtually no public services and little infrastructure. Human refuse floats in open channels through the streets of Cité Soleil. Disease is widespread. There is no garbage collection. There are few roads and virtually no electricity, phones, or running water. The countryside is almost completely deforested, and thus it is often ravaged by floods, and the land is seriously eroded. Little investment is coming into Haiti. The United States gave Haiti $235 million in 1995. Clinton asked Congress for only $115 million for 1996, and Congress did not approve even that much. International lenders have refused aid to Haiti unless the government implements a structural adjustment program (see chapter 2). The masses of Haitians remain mired in misery.[78]

The new (1997) president, René Préval, is practical, plainspoken, and deci-sive, unlike Aristide, who aroused the people with powerful metaphors and an inspirational vision. Préval does not have the charisma or the popular sup-port enjoyed by his predecessor and likely successor. Unless he can deliver on his promises, Haiti could revert to its traditional pattern of violence and political chaos.[79] There are many obstacles to a healthy democracy and eco-nomic recovery in Haiti: its violent history and lack of a cohesive culture attentive to the common good, the gang violence and criminal activity already present, armed and disgruntled former soldiers and paramilitary thugs who have not been brought to justice for past crimes, a denuded and eroded land that cannot support the food needs of its growing population of 7 million, a greedy, corrupt, and powerful elite, non-existent public services and infrastructure, and leery foreign investors and fickle friends.[80]

The United States has to be numbered among those friends of Haiti which are unreliable and inconsistent. The Haitian people have every reason to be suspicious of American "help," given the U.S. occupation from 1915–1934 and U.S. complicity in the Duvalier reign of terror. Indeed, there were long-standing ties between American military and intelligence agencies and many of the top Haitian military officers, including some involved in the coup that overthrew Aristide.[81] The United States immediately sent troops into the Persian Gulf to protect its oil-rich friend, Saudi Arabia, and eventually to lib-erate its oil-rich friend, Kuwait, under the cover of the principle of sover-eignty in the post-Cold War world. However, the U.S. response to the trampling of the principle of democracy by a military coup in its own back-yard was more timid. While Aristide was given sanctuary, and the coup was condemned, it took three years to send the troops into Haiti. In the mean-time, the United States and the world community imposed ineffective eco-nomic sanctions which hurt the poor but spared those in power.

While the Clinton administration has counted the Haitian intervention as a success story in foreign policy, it is worth remembering that the President's decision to lead a U.N. approved invasion force was opposed by Congress and questioned by the American people at the time. "The critics said that although morally reprehensible, Cédras's continuation in power, the heinous violations of human rights by his forces, and his defiance of U.N. resolutions, did not justify American military intervention."[82] This amounts to an isola-tionist foreign policy.

To call the Haiti intervention a success is to define success very narrowly. The Clinton administration achieved the three limited goals that it set for itself:

- to restore Aristide, the legitimate Haitian President, to power, and in so doing to stop the flow of boat people toward the United States;
- to insure a fair democratic election and a peaceful transfer of power;
- and to leave.

If this operation was a success, however, why is the patient dying?[83] While it was certainly a good thing to stop the brutal repression of the Cédras military regime, the Haitian people are still in misery.

For this intervention to be truly humanitarian, it might need to engage in "nation building." In Haiti this might require the following:[84]

- not only disbanding, but disarming the Haitian military and paramilitary thugs and bringing them to justice for their brutality;
- training and equipping a respectable and effective National Police Force;[85]
- establishing a judicial system;
- massive economic investment (public and private) that is creatively focused on providing productive jobs that pay a living wage;
- foreign aid and technical assistance directed at grassroots empowerment, and at improving Haiti's infrastructure (roads, electricity, etc.)

Obviously, nation building is expensive. It usually requires a long-term investment of human and financial resources. At the same time, such nation building efforts run the risk of infringing on Haiti's sovereignty. Given that the United States has played no small role in making Haiti among the poorest countries in the world, such U.S. intervention would open the United States to the charge of self-interested exploitation with the net result that even for positive, nation-building efforts, the United States might well be resented by Haitians.

The situation in Haiti has raised the question of the place of human rights in foreign policy and the controversy about humanitarian intervention. The next chapter will focus on another aspect of human rights, revolving around ethnicity, nationalism, and self-determination, and it will continue to explore the question of humanitarian intervention in the post-Cold War world.

While human rights are widely recognized in the contemporary world, they are just as widely abused. Violations of human rights, whether caused by poverty, prejudice, or politics, injure the victim and dehumanize the violator. The value of human dignity calls us to work for universal respect for human rights. When this involves the policies and practices of states, however, intervention on behalf of human rights can become complicated and risky. Whether, when, and how to intervene on behalf of human rights are among the most difficult questions facing countries and communities today.

STUDY QUESTIONS

1. How do you explain the paradox that human rights are increasingly recognized in theory, yet continue to be abused in practice?
2. Should human rights be a cornerstone of U.S. foreign policy? What would be the implications of a principled human rights foreign policy for trade policy with countries such as China, Indonesia, Myanmar (Burma), Nigeria, and Syria, for example?
3. Is the idea of "rights" now being taken too far in U.S. society? What are the rights of human beings?

4. Discuss the cultural practice of female genital mutilation. Is this a legitimate cultural practice or a violation of human rights? What makes a practice relative to a particular culture? Are there universal human rights whose violation can never be justified?

5. Discuss the inequality between men and women, in the world and in U.S. society. Is religion a cause of the inequality?

6. Many contend that the United States continues to be a society deeply divided along racial lines. What do you think? How can racism be addressed in the United States?

7. Do you think armed intervention on behalf of human rights, as in Haiti, is ethically justified? wise? sound foreign policy? Should nation building be an objective of such interventions?

CHAPTER FIVE

Ethno-Nationalist Conflict

"You shall not wrong or oppress a resident alien, for you were aliens in the land of Egypt." (Exodus 22: 21)

"One of the most disturbing threats to peace in the post-Cold War world has been the spread of conflicts rooted in national, ethnic, racial, and religious differences. . . . Precisely because of their intractable and explosive nature, ethnic conflicts can be resolved only through political dialogue and negotiation. War and violence are unacceptable means for resolving ethnic conflicts; they serve only to exacerbate them. Nor are political solutions alone sufficient. Also needed is the commitment to reconciliation that is at the heart of the Christian and other religious traditions. For religious believers can imagine what some would dismiss as unrealistic: that even the most intense hatreds can be overcome by love, that free human beings can break historic cycles of violence and injustice, and that deeply divided people can learn to live together in peace."[1]

Ethnic hatred is resulting in especially barbaric behavior throughout the contemporary world:

- On April 6, 1994, Rwanda's Hutu government unleashed the bloodiest 100 days in the second half of the twentieth century. At least 500,000 Tutsi (and their sympathizers) were slaughtered, mostly with machetes.[2] The world was aghast when a river of their bloated bodies emptied into Lake Kivu. Nearly 100,000 Hutu and Tutsi have also been killed in neighboring Burundi. There were well over 1 million refugees from this ethnic conflict in central Africa, which spilled over into Zaire late in 1996.
- The pre-war (1991) population of Bosnia was 4.3 million people. During the war (1991–95), 3.4 million people (or three out of every four people) became internal or external refugees.[3] Ethnic cleansing there meant that Serbs, Croats, and Muslims killed or drove out their neighbors (literally the family living next door), and blew up their houses. Serbian soldiers systematically raped an estimated 20,000 Muslim women,[4] snipers intentionally shot children in Sarajevo, and Serbs put Muslims into concentration camps.
- News reports from the war in Chechnya (December 1994-August 1996), a section of southwestern Russia, showed that the capital city of

Grozny had been reduced to rubble. Homeless Chechnyans were living on the streets of Grozny amidst the bricks and stones of their former residences.[5]

- In Sri Lanka, an island country off the southern coast of India, battles between the Sinhala majority and rebels of the Tamil minority have resulted in over 50,000 casualties and displaced a half-million Tamil civilians since 1983.[6]
- On February 9, 1996, the Irish Republican Army broke a cease-fire that had been in effect in Northern Ireland for 17 months by detonating a huge bomb in the eastern dock area of London. One person was killed and over 100 injured.[7]
- Throughout the world there are over 25 million refugees fleeing from 17 different ethnic wars that have killed roughly 4 million people.[8]

The decade of the 1990s may well be remembered as ushering in an era of ethno-nationalist conflict. When the Cold War ended many expected a period of peace and prosperity to follow. One analyst even proclaimed "the end of history."[9] History, however, has not moved into a peaceful reign of democratic capitalism, but has degenerated into a morass of ethnic conflict. The international community is torn between the principles of national sovereignty, territorial integrity, and nonintervention on the one hand, and the principle of self-determination on the other hand, and so has not known how to respond. Ethnic conflict, in its many apparitions, is the current source of the grossest violations of human rights, and may be the most serious barrier to peace in the contemporary world.

Although, in a sense, ethnic conflict is as old as human history, nationalism gives it a new tinge. Clans and tribes have always fought one another over territory or resources, or sometimes simply out of fear of people outside of their own group. Peoples have united to form empires by conquering other peoples. But the idea of a sovereign state is relatively new in history, and the principle of self-determination that decrees that nations should be states is even newer.

Americans tend to have a difficult time grasping ethno-nationalist conflict. Because the European colonizers nearly annihilated the indigenous people in North America, and because the United States has been settled by wave after wave of immigrants, the United States has always been a multiethnic society. Most large American cities have their "little Italy," "Germantown," or "Chinatown" sections, but today that usually designates a cluster of good ethnic restaurants rather than a genuine ethnic enclave. There is much debate about whether America is truly a melting pot, and there are surely ethnic, and especially racial tensions and conflicts, but the American reality is quite different from that of most countries in the world. Since every ethnic group has come here to establish a new home, no ethnic group in the United States (except the remaining indigenous people) can claim that this is their ancestral home. In most other countries several competing ethnic groups do make precisely that claim. Thus, to understand the power of ethno-nationalism in other countries, Americans often have to disregard their own experience.

WHEN NATIONS WANT TO BECOME STATES

Ethnicity is difficult to define, with no strictly objective criteria essential for its existence. Rather, ethnicity is subjective, a conviction of commonality. Groups of people can distinguish themselves from other groups by characteristics such as language, religion, social customs, physical appearance, and region of residence, or by a combination of these features.[10] In a way, ethnic groups are "psychological communities" whose members share a persisting sense of common interest and identity that is based on some combination of shared historical experience and valued cultural traits.[11] When an ethnic group becomes politicized and begins to claim a certain territory as its homeland, it becomes a "nation."[12]

Technically, there is a difference between a "nation" and a "state," as well as between nationalism and patriotism, although the terms are often used interchangeably. Properly speaking, "nation" refers to a group of people who believe they share a common ancestry, or to the largest human grouping predicated on a myth of common ancestry. It is close to the notion of a fully extended family.[13] There is no need for the belief in a common ancestry to be factual or historical. Indeed, as Walker Connor, an expert on ethnicity and nationalism, says, "the myth of common and exclusive descent can overcome a battery of contrary fact."[14] In another place, Connor puts it this way, "It is not chronological or factual history that is the key to the nation, but sentient or felt history. All that is required for the existence of a nation is that the members share an intuitive conviction of the group's separate origin and evolution."[15] Thus, the existence of a nation, a people, is subjective, subconscious, sometimes even sentimental in nature. It is based on blood and belonging. It is a phenomenon of the masses, not a proclamation of an elite.[16] Nationalism, then, is the love and loyalty one feels for one's nation or people.

An important aspect of nationalism is the sense of a homeland. There are a few immigrant societies, such as the United States, Argentina, and Australia, but most of the land masses of the world are divided into ethnic homelands: a Scotland, land of the Scots; Poland, Finland, Zululand, Kazakhstan ("stan" means "land of"), Afghanistan, and the like. Nations have a strong attachment to a place—where they feel they originated, where their ancestors are buried, where their blood has been spilled. Again, this perception need not, and often will not, accord with historical fact, but that in no way diminishes a people's attachment to the "land of their fathers." Since a nation feels a sense of primal ownership for a place, its people view others, who may have lived there for centuries as well, to be aliens or outsiders in their homeland.[17] Nationalism, then, when stirred by some change or current event, comes to mean the reclamation of a people's homeland by ejecting aliens who have taken up residence there. In the period 1991–95, in the villages of the Krajina section of Croatia and in much of Bosnia, this meant literally the elimination and expulsion of one's neighbors.[18]

A "state," on the other hand, is a legal and political entity, a government that exercises control over a defined territory.[19] Contemporary states are recognized as sovereign, both internally and externally. States exercise control over the people within their territory, and they interact autonomously with one another, signing treaties, joining organizations, setting trade policies, and the like. The love and loyalty one feels for one's country or state is properly called patriotism.

Thus, one may correctly refer to British patriotism, but to Scottish, Welsh, or English nationalism; to Canadian patriotism, but to Quebecois nationalism; to Belgian patriotism, but Flemish nationalism, and so on. The difficulty is that in a world with perhaps 5000 nations, there are only about 190 states. Of those states only about fifteen, such as Japan, Iceland, and Portugal, are ethnically homogeneous, or genuine nation-states. Thus, more than 90 percent of all states are ethnically heterogeneous, that is, they are comprised of more than one significant ethnic group. In 40 percent of these states, there are five or more significant ethnic groups, and in nearly one-third the largest ethnic group is not even a majority (e.g., Kazakhstan). The state of Nigeria contains more than 100 different ethnic groups, as did the former Soviet Union.[20]

Many ethnic groups coexist amicably within a single state, as do Swedes who live in Finland, for example. Others become assimilated into multi-ethnic societies, such as the Irish in the United States. But when an ethnic group begins to coalesce to take political action, whether because of its swelling sense of identity, or because of its victimization through discrimination, the resulting conflict can threaten to rip apart a state. The principle of national self-determination, which says that nations or peoples should be autonomous and free to control their own destiny, can wreak havoc in multi-national states.[21]

Ethno-national conflict does not always lead to violence or civil war. Since the end of the Cold War, for example, Czechoslovakia has amicably split into the Czech Republic and Slovakia. The breakup of the Soviet Union into its fifteen constituent republics created fifteen new states by political fiat rather than by war. Most of these new states, however, face internal ethnic conflicts, and these have not always been peacefully resolved, as the war in Chechnya illustrates.

When ethno-national conflict does become violent, the struggle is often protracted and brutal. States do not readily cede territory or authority, and ethnic groups who have power do not easily accede to the demands of a minority or an oppressed group. Thus, fighting can continue for decades as it has in Northern Ireland, Israel, and Sri Lanka. Furthermore, ethnic conflict is often motivated by hatred of the other group. The conflict is polarized, and the out-group is often dehumanized and stripped of all human rights. Atrocities by one group provoke atrocities by the other group in a destructive spiral of violence. Any restraints called for by the rules and conventions of war fall by the wayside. Genocide—killing members of an ethnic group with the intent to destroy in whole or in part the group itself[22]—becomes the logic of much inter-ethnic warfare. Because such conflicts are not only about politics or economics but are filled with personal and cultural animosity, they tend to be extremely difficult to resolve.[23] The trust necessary for negotiation and conflict resolution is often absent.

Although there may be as many as 5000 "nations" in the contemporary world (since there are at least that many linguistic groups)[24], Ted Robert Gurr, director of the Minorities at Risk project, counted 292 communal groups in 1994 which were taking political action to assert their collective interests against the states that claim to govern them. This number includes both national peoples asserting their need for autonomy or independence and minority groups trying to protect or improve their status within a state. These 292 politically active ethnic groups comprise nearly a billion people, or about one-sixth of the world's population. While no region of the world is immune from serious ethnic conflict, sub-Saharan Africa has the greatest concentration of minorities at risk—81 groups incorporating half of the regional population. In this respect, Latin America is the least troubled region.[25]

Contemporary ethnic conflict is often part of the heritage of history. Israel, for example, was at the crossroad of empires and civilizations dating back to the Egyptians, Assyrians, and Babylonians, then the Greeks and Romans. Jerusalem has changed hands dozens of times. The Balkans marked the dividing line between the Ottoman Empire in the East and the Roman Empire in the West. Thus, division and conflict in Bosnia go back at least a century.

Not surprisingly, colonialism is key to many of the ethnic conflicts in the Two-Thirds World. In the first chapter it was noted that the European powers arbitrarily divided up Africa among themselves at the Congress of Berlin in 1884, drawing boundaries on a map with little regard for ethno-national territories.

The legacy of colonialism has also left its mark on South Asia. India, a patchwork of principalities and a tapestry of tribes tied to villages, was united only by British rule (1757–1947). Religious conflict between Hindus and Muslims led to the creation of Pakistan in 1947, and then to the war that resulted in Bangladesh in 1971, and ongoing conflicts with Sikh and Kashmir rebels seeking independence from India. The potential for other ethnic rebellions in the region is ripe.

The 36 million indigenous peoples of the Americas comprise only 5 percent of the total population, but they account for half the population in Bolivia, Peru, and Guatemala. In addition, as a consequence of colonialism, Africans were transported as slaves to the new world and immigrant workers were moved from colony to colony (from India to Africa, for example) for their managerial or commercial skills or for their labor. Thus did colonialism plant the seeds of ethnic conflict: "Conquered peoples seek to regain their lost autonomy; indigenous peoples ask for restoration of their traditional lands; immigrant workers and the descendants of slaves demand full equality."[26]

Contemporary ethnic conflict, however, is not inevitable. Imperial conquest and colonial rule provide a historical backdrop, but past division or discrimination do not necessarily determine present conflict. As recently as World War II, the United States and Germany and Japan were enemies, but now these countries are allies and peaceful competitors. During the Cold War Russians and Americans were ready to annihilate one another, but today they are global colleagues. Similarly, ethnic conflict cannot simply be ascribed to human nature. Humans are capable of transcending the social psychology of in-group/out-group violence. While belonging to a community of like-minded persons is important for healthy human development (identity and relationships), it does not follow that other communities must be hated and fought. Ethnic conflict, although all too common, is neither historically inevitable nor biologically determined.

CHRISTIAN ETHICS AND THE IDOLATRY OF NATIONALISM

Christian theology and ethics can provide a critical perspective for evaluating ethnic conflict and nationalism. In the Christian framework the particular and the universal are not in opposition to one another; both are affirmed.[27] An ethic faithful to the Gospel must be universal in scope, extending love to each and every person. Since all of humanity shares a common Creator, Redeemer, and Sanctifier, we are one human family, brothers and sisters all. Christian love cannot discriminate; it must embrace every person, near and far.

The teachings of Christian tradition are also incarnational and sacramental, particular and practical.[28] Christian love is concrete and real, and Christian living is essentially relational and communal. The church is catholic (universal) and apostolic (a tradition inherited from our ancestors in the faith), but it is also local—incarnated in the lives of those who gather together to hear the story, share a meal, and become the body of Christ in the world. As we will see in chapter 8, contemporary Catholic social thought has used the virtue and principle of "solidarity" to try to capture the concrete, communal, and universal nature of the Christian faith. "[Solidarity] is not a feeling of vague compassion or shallow distress at the misfortunes of so many people, both near and far. On the contrary, it is a firm and persevering determination to commit oneself to the common good; that is to say to the good of all and of each individual, because we are all really responsible for all."[29]

In light of this framework, patriotism and nationalism can be good, but neither is an absolute good. When loyalty and love for country or nation become absolute and fanatical, they become idolatrous and can be harmful. Love of country or nation is good and valuable. It is a source of identity and of relationships and community that create special duties and obligations, just as the special relationships of marriage, parenthood, and friendship create special responsibilities. But neither patriotism nor nationalism should be an ultimate or primary loyalty, exercising unquestioned authority in our lives. State or nation can become an idol, and that sort of allegiance needs to be guarded against, resisted, and rejected.

Our devotion to state or nation should be characterized by a certain emotional detachment that tempers its passion. Loyalty to one's country or people must be balanced by other commitments, both more intimate and more universal.[30]

A distinction between civic nationalism and ethnic nationalism, made by Michael Ignatieff, can be helpful. Civic nationalism is capable of uniting diverse people around a political creed and a civic ethos. It is based on a constitutional rule of law that facilitates the participation of every citizen and of every community in the public life of the state. One chooses to be loyal to the state because of one's experience of justice and order in this society. Ethnic nationalism, in contrast, claims that an individual's deepest attachments are inherited, not chosen. Such allegiance tends to be uncritical, even idolatrous.[31]

A commitment to human rights can reconcile loyalty to a particular state or nation with a global ethic that encourages a universal love. Patriotism or nationalism can be embraced only as part of a larger morality of solidarity and human rights. Love of country or nation can no more justify hatred of foreigners than friendship can legitimize despising those with whom one is not acquainted. National sovereignty is, then, a real, but relative value: patriotism and nationalism are real values, but they are relative to respecting the human rights of every person in the human family.[32] In given circumstances, human rights claims can override the principles of territorial sovereignty and nonintervention. Belief in the theory of human rights points to minimal requirements for right relationships with one another in a just society. Protecting human rights is a helpful way to articulate what it means to reverence the dignity of the human person and to embrace all of humanity as family.

In more practical terms, this ethical analysis would suggest that communal or group rights need to be recognized in international law. Thus far the declarations and covenants promulgated by the United Nations focus on individual rights and the rights of states. Formal international recognition of the rights and responsibilities of ethnic groups or communities within states, the rights of "nations,"[33] would help to balance the needs of individuals with the common good.

Religion seems to be an important factor in many ethnic conflicts: between Catholics and Protestants in Northern Ireland, Jewish Israelis and Muslim Palestinians, Buddhist Sinhala and Hindu Tamils in Sri Lanka, and among Catholic Croats, Orthodox Serbs, and Bosnian Muslims. Religion is one of the features that can distinguish one ethnic group from another. Since religion pertains to core values, it can inflate the intensity and intractablity of ethnic conflict.[34] Religious belief can even be used to legitimate or authorize intolerance toward another ethnic group.[35] Most analysts, however, have concluded that while religious divisions can be a contributing factor, religion itself is seldom the root cause, main motivation, or principal reason for ethnic conflict.[36]

While it may be true that religion is more peripheral than central to ethnic conflict, the use of religion to inflame nationalism remains troubling. Religious traditions profess universal love, forgiveness, and reconciliation. Ethno-nationalism preaches hatred, revenge, and division. How is it that religion can be co-opted to espouse hatred and violence? Why isn't religion a powerful force for forgiveness, reconciliation, and peace in Bosnia, the Middle East, or Sri Lanka? The American Catholic Bishops deserve to be heard and heeded when they proclaim:

> Every child murdered, every woman raped, every town "cleansed," every hatred uttered in the name of religion is a crime against God and a scandal for religious believers. Religious violence and nationalism deny what we profess in faith: We are all created in the image of the same God and destined for the same eternal salvation. "[N]o Christian can knowingly foster or support structures and attitudes that unjustly divide individuals or groups."[37]

Having developed a general understanding of ethno-nationalist conflict and a basic critique of it from the perspective of Christian ethics, it will be helpful to analyze some particular instances of such conflict, such as the situations in Bosnia, Sri Lanka, Rwanda, Northern Ireland, and Kurdistan. Each of these ethnic conflicts has been characterized by significant violence, and has been well documented. Obviously the following descriptions give only summaries of these very complex conflicts.

BOSNIA-HERZEGOVINA

U.S. Senator Daniel Patrick Moynihan has said, "Ethnic conflict does not require great differences, small will do."[38] That certainly applies to the brutal ethnic conflict among the nations in what was the state of Yugoslavia. There is no apparent difference among the peoples who once lived together in harmony. They are all southern Slav (Yugoslav) people. They speak basically the same language, Serbo-Croatian, but the Serbs use a Cyrillic alphabet, and the Croats use a Roman alphabet. Most Serbs are Orthodox Christians, most Croats are Roman Catholics, and the majority of Bosnians are Muslim (45 percent). But there are significant Serbian (33 percent) and Croatian (18 percent) minorities in Bosnia, and a significant Serbian minority (15 percent) in Croatia. These peoples who have so much in common once again began massacring each other shortly after the end of the Cold War, primarily because of their ethnic differences and their fear and hatred of each other.

The Balkan Peninsula is the section of southeastern Europe bordered by the Adriatic, Mediterranean, Aegean, and the Black Seas. In the fourth century, the Balkans became the dividing line between the Roman and the Byzantine Empires. Since then, the area has been a battleground between the forces of empires rising in the West and in the East. The Croats identified with the West and the Serbs with the East.[39]

In 1389 the Turks conquered Serbia at the Battle of Kosovo and estab-

lished five centuries of rule under the Ottoman Empire. It was during this period that some of the Slavs in Bosnia converted to Islam.

In the nineteenth century, the Austro-Hungarian Empire gained ascendancy in the area, and kept a wary eye on an expanding Serbia, then newly-free from the crumbling Ottoman Empire. This conflict became the match that sparked World War I when, in Sarajevo in 1914, a Serbian nationalist assassinated Archduke Ferdinand, heir to the Hapsburg (Austrian) throne. Both the Austro-Hungarian and the Ottoman Empires were dismantled after World War I, and a repressive Serbian dictatorship gained control over Croatia and Slovenia and renamed the country Yugoslavia.

World War II provided a backdrop for a Balkan civil war that raged from 1941 to 1945. Croatian "Ustashe" forces, allied with Nazi Germany, slaughtered Serbs, while Serbian "Chetnik" forces, allied with Russia, slaughtered Croats. Muslims in Bosnia fought both Croats and Serbs during this period. In some sense, the current conflict is a continuation of that unresolved civil war.[40]

Yugoslavia was re-established under Tito (Josip Broz), a communist partisan who emerged victorious from the fractious fighting following World War II. Although a communist and totalitarian, Tito declared his independence from the Soviet Union and found himself courted and aided by both the West and the East during the Cold War.[41] Under Tito's rule, Yugoslavia consisted of eight republics: Slovenia, Croatia, Bosnia-Herzegovina, Serbia, Macedonia, Montenegro, Vojvodina, and Kosovo (see map). Tito died in 1980 and, with the collapse of communism in 1990, the republics began to break away from the Serb-dominated Yugoslav federation.

According to today's Balkan nationalists, their history is their fate. There is no doubt that the peoples of the Balkans have often been at war with one another, and that their record of atrocities against one another was as recent as the World War II period. But it is also true that the Serbs, Croats, and Muslims lived in a multicultural peace as neighbors and friends during the Cold War period, working together and often intermarrying. Sarajevo, the site of the 1984 winter Olympic Games, was often touted as a model of multi-ethnic cooperation. As Michael Ignatieff says, "It is not how the past dictates to the present but how the present manipulates the past that is decisive in the Balkans."[42] The ethnic hatred holding sway in the Balkans toward the end of the twentieth century is the result of the fear stirred up by the disintegration of the legitimate authority of the multinational state that was Yugoslavia. As Yugoslavia broke apart, the Serbian minorities living in Croatia and Bosnia perceived themselves to be endangered by the rule of past enemies. Both Serb and Croat leaders played on this fear and on the dream of nationalist glory and power through the creation of a Greater Serbia or a Greater Croatia. They were successful with a vengeance. The result was "ethnic cleansing" and a seemingly intractable ethno-nationalist conflict.

The trouble came to a head in June 1991 when Slovenia and Croatia declared their independence from Yugoslavia.[43] The Yugoslav People's Army (JNA), dominated by Serbs, made a half-hearted attempt in a ten-day war to keep Slovenia, an ethnically homogeneous republic, in the federation. In the end, the Serbian leader, Slobodan Milosevic, was willing to let Slovenia go and to allow the breakup of Yugoslavia.

The real fight was between Serbia and Croatia. Serbs comprise 15 percent of the population of Croatia, mostly clustered in two pockets along the borders between Croatia and Bosnia (Krajina) and between Croatia and Serbia (Slavonia). The fighting in Croatia was fierce with both Croats and Serbs practicing ethnic cleansing in the areas they controlled. The Serbs, however, benefitting from the better-equipped JNA, gained the upper hand and seized about 30 percent of Croatia. Meanwhile, the international community, prodded by Germany, a traditional ally of Croatia, recognized the independence of Slovenia and Croatia and the dissolution of Yugoslavia.

This left multi-ethnic Bosnia with little choice but to declare its independence under Muslim leadership, which it did in February of 1992. The Bosnian Serbs, led by Radovan Karadzic and supported by Milosevic, immediately declared a separate state, promptly took over military control of about 70 percent of Bosnia, and began their siege of Sarajevo. Atrocities, mostly committed by the militarily more powerful Serbs against the relatively defenseless Muslims, followed in rapid succession: shelling the cities of Vukovar and Dubrovnik, ethnic cleansing, concentration camps, systematic rape, and bombing and sniping of civilians in Sarajevo led to the displacement of millions of refugees.

The response of the international community was weak and ineffectual. The United States, with no direct interests at stake, waited for the European Union or the United Nations to respond. Neither was united or clear about what to do to respond forcefully. Milosevic and Karadzic shamelessly manipulated peacemaking efforts to their advantage, promising again and again to stop attacking the Muslims and then continuing their attacks. Bosnian Croats first sided with the Muslims, then attacked them, then re-allied themselves with the Muslims. Peace plans proliferated, but none was acceptable to the Muslims or to the Serbs.

U.N. troops entered the scene to offer humanitarian relief and to secure so-called safe areas, but in some ways they seemed only to complicate the conflict. These troops were on a peacekeeping mission where there was no peace to keep. Their presence often prevented NATO air strikes, especially after Serbs took troops hostage. Nor were the U.N. troops able to effectively protect safe areas from some of the worse massacres of the war.

Early in the conflict an arms embargo was placed on all of the republics of the former Yugoslavia, and international trade sanctions were imposed on Serbia. The embargo resulted in temporarily freezing the military imbalance between Serbs and Muslims. Ultimately, the trade sanctions were important in moving Milosevic to the negotiating table.

In August of 1995, Croatian forces rapidly pushed Serb troops and civilians out of the Krajina section of Croatia and from parts of Slavonia; the Croatian forces also undertook ethnic cleansing, creating thousands of Serbian refugees. The Croat-Muslim alliance simultaneously put military pressure on Bosnian Serbs in northwest Bosnia. Suddenly the Serbs were losing big chunks of territory and no longer had the upper hand. At the same time, NATO finally decided to strike Serb positions around Sarajevo and to force the still defiant Serbs to retreat. Milosevic, anxious to end the Western sanctions that were crippling Belgrade's economy, decided to negotiate.[44]

At the invitation of U.S. diplomat Richard Holbrooke, the three leaders—Croatia's Franjo Tudjman, Serbia's Slobodan Milosevic, and Bosnian Muslim's Alija Izetbegovic—met for three weeks in Dayton, Ohio, where they reached a complex agreement. Sixty thousand NATO troops, including a U.S. contingent of 20,000, were sent into Bosnia to monitor the cease-fire and to ensure the compliance of the parties with the Dayton Agreement. The U.S. commitment of troops was due to expire after one year, or around Christmas, 1996, but it became clear that the prospects for peace required a longer stay. President Clinton extended the U.S. commitment shortly after his re-election in November, 1996.

"The Dayton agreement codified a series of compromises among the adversaries that left each of the parties partially dissatisfied."[45] Milosevic made several of those compromises on behalf of the Bosnian Serbs, whose interests he did not fully represent. Such an agreement is a shaky basis for lasting peace.

The elections held in accordance with the Dayton Agreement produced three ultra-nationalist leaders representing the three ethnic communities in the central government. But these very leaders and their ultra-nationalist ideologies are precisely what caused the problem in the first place. Throughout this civil war, while the Serbs appear to have committed the biggest crimes and the Muslims seem to have been most victimized, all sides have engaged in ethnic cleansing when given the opportunity, and all are guilty of unspeakable acts. "All factions in the former Yugoslavia have pursued the same objective—avoiding minority status in Yugoslavia or any successor state—and all have used the tools most readily available to achieve that end."[46] Such atrocities are not easily forgotten, especially when all the factions continue to have the objective of avoiding minority status, and all seem willing to commit more crimes against humanity to achieve their goal. There is little reason for optimism in the Balkans.

The war in Bosnia and Croatia was not the result of centuries of hatred. It was the product of greed, ambition, fear, and incompetence—both local and international. In retrospect, the blame for this horrific ethnic war can be shared by many parties. First of all, the leaders who fanned the flames of fanatical nationalism are responsible for this debacle—Milosevic, Karadzic, and Tudjman in particular. Secondly, Slovenia's precipitous move toward independence kindled this ethnic explosion.[47] Thirdly, the international community, in recognizing the independence of Slovenia and Croatia, contributed to the crisis, and then sat on its hands while women were raped, cities were shelled and sieged, and people were exiled and massacred simply because of their ethnicity.[48] Last but not least, religion (Orthodox, Catholic, and Muslim), while not the direct cause of the war, is tragically intertwined with nationalism in the Balkans.

SRI LANKA

One of the longest and most brutal ethnic conflicts in the modern world has taken place in Sri Lanka, a teardrop-shaped island off the southern coast of India. This tropical island is about 250 miles long, 125 miles wide, and has a population of about 18 million people. The conflict between the Sinhala majority (75 percent) who are predominantly Buddhist, and the Tamil minority (18 percent) who are mainly Hindu, emerged only in the twentieth century. For centuries the Sinhala (or Sinhalese) and Tamils had lived together in respectful peace. But an enmity between the two peoples, kindled during the last decades of British colonial rule, was stoked by political leaders after independence in 1948. In 1983 it exploded into a civil war which has resulted in approximately 50,000 deaths and nearly a half million refugees.[49] Both sides have been guilty of human rights violations.

Sri Lanka was first colonized by the Portuguese (1505–1568), then by the Dutch (1568–1796), then by the British (1796–1948). The aggressive Catholicism of the Portuguese and the militant Calvinism of the Dutch introduced religious intolerance to the island. The British launched a full-scale

attack on Buddhism and Hinduism that was institutionalized in the creation of a colonial Christian education system. The British also introduced divisive racial theories that contended that the Sinhala were Aryan people, not as superior as the British, of course, but better than the Tamil. Thus did colonialism sow the seeds of ethnic resentment and division in Sri Lanka.[50]

The search for an identity other than that imposed by the British resulted in a revival of Sinhala Buddhism during the first decades of the twentieth century. This Buddhist revival imitated the tactics of the Christian missionaries by creating a politicized and aggressive Buddhism that championed the Sinhala as a chosen people destined to govern Sri Lanka. It also laid the groundwork for the Sinhala crusade to assert their dominance in the first decade of independence during the 1950s.[51]

The Tamil response was to create for Hindus a mirror image of Sinhala Buddhist nationalism.[52] Based on British racial theory, which asserted that the Tamil culture of South India was superior to that of the Brahmins in the North of India, Sri Lankan Tamils promoted a myth of Tamil sovereignty from prehistoric times through the colonial period. Thus, at the time of Ceylon's independence (in the early 1970s the name was changed to Sri Lanka, the Buddhist name for the island), the contending communal groups, each believing in their own superiority and sovereignty, were primed for conflict.

Since the Sinhala comprise an overwhelming majority of the population (75 percent), they can easily control a national vote. The pattern that has developed since independence is that Sinhala political leaders inflame Buddhist nationalism in order to get elected, and then are politically unable to accommodate reasonable compromises with the Tamil.[53] For example, in 1959 the island's second prime minister was assassinated by a Buddhist monk after the prime minister tried to enter into a reasonable pact with a Tamil leader. By 1972, tension between the two ethnic groups had escalated into increasingly violent conflict. Tamil leaders called for a separate state in the northeastern province where Tamil are a majority, and the Sinhala government responded with more chauvinism and repression.

During the 1980s, militant Tamil opposition groups coalesced into the Liberation Tigers of Tamil Eelam (LTTE, Eelam means state) and began trading atrocities with the Sri Lankan army in a descending spiral of violence. The violence came to a head in 1983 when a funeral for Sinhala soldiers killed in the fighting in the north erupted into a horrific riot with rampaging Sinhala slaughtering Tamil in Colombo, the capital city. In response the LTTE began a partially-successful campaign to control the north, and especially Jaffna, the Tamil capital.

In 1987 the Indian government, which had been supporting and arming the Tamil rebels, intervened, pressuring the Sinhala government to accept an Indian Peacekeeping Force (IPKF) stationed in the north. Both militant Sinhala youth and the Tamil LTTE resented India's intrusion and began attacking the IPKF. By 1990, India pulled out its beleaguered forces, and the LTTE took over effective control of the northeast. A year later an LTTE suicide bomber assassinated Rajiv Gandhi, the Indian leader.

Terrorist acts, such as suicide bombings aimed at Sinhala political leaders and other government targets, often killing dozens of bystanders, have been a specialty of the LTTE. On the other side, "disappearances" and torture have been common practices of the Sri Lankan army and of the death squads they sponsor. Civilians on both sides, but especially the Tamil, who have been victimized by both the Sri Lankan army and the extremist LTTE, have suffered the most.[54]

By 1995 the country was tired of the violence, and a newly elected President arranged a cease-fire agreement and peace talks. Within three months, however, the LTTE broke the cease-fire, and the government responded with an aggressive, bloody campaign to re-take Jaffna. That campaign created hundreds of thousands of Tamil refugees. In early 1996, the LTTE bombed the Central Bank building in Colombo killing 80 and wounding 1400. To date, this ethnic conflict has resulted in over 50,000 casualties, and there is no end in sight.[55]

The enmity between the Sinhala and the Tamil is not a manifestation of an ancient hatred. The two communities lived together for centuries. Rather, it is an enmity invented in response to colonialism, and fueled by the rhetoric and repression of nationalist leaders. It is not a religious war per se, but it is rooted in an intolerance that is perversely justified by the religious convictions of the two communities.[56] That Buddhism and Hinduism have been twisted to condone political violence and ethnic hatred is perverse indeed. A more orthodox interpretation of these two great religious traditions could become a foundation for tolerance, justice, and peace in Sri Lanka. At the moment that prospect seems dim.

RWANDA

The bloodiest ethnic conflict in the post-Cold War world has occurred in central Africa between the Hutu and Tutsi peoples, mostly in Rwanda, but also in Burundi and Zaire. The massacre of over 500,000 Tutsi and their sympathizers by extremist Hutu in Rwanda during the spring of 1994 is rightly regarded as an act of genocide.[57] This complex conflict is rooted in the colonial history of the region and is motivated by politics, resource scarcity, and ethnic enmity.

With a population of eight million people in an area smaller than Haiti, Rwanda is the most densely populated country in Africa. Prior to 1994, about 84 percent of the population was Hutu and 14 percent were Tutsi.[58] Thus, the massacre probably killed about half of the Rwandan Tutsi population.

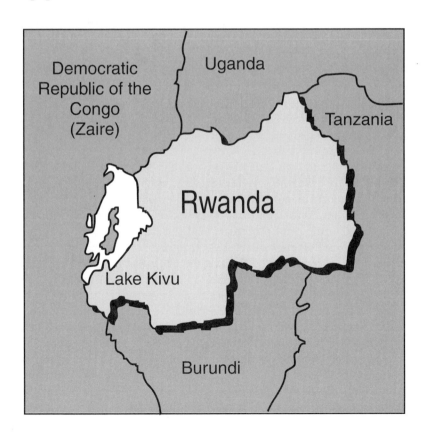

In about the sixteenth century, the Tutsi, a nomadic, cattle-raising people, moved from the north and settled in what is now Rwanda. The Hutu, an agricultural people, had arrived centuries earlier. When German Catholic missionaries arrived in the nineteenth century, they found an advanced culture that was well integrated and organized around a Tutsi king and ruling class. After the German defeat in World War I, Rwanda became a Belgian colony. Both the Germans and the Belgians administered the colony through the Tutsi.

Scholars differ on the nature and character of the distinction between Tutsi and Hutu. Some contend that they are two different ethnic groups, but others suggest the difference is more like that of caste or class. They speak the same language and share the same cultural practices. About 90 percent of Rwandans are Christian, and 62 percent are baptized Catholics.[59] The Tutsi were thought to be tall and thin and the Hutu short and stocky, but intermarriage has diminished these physical differences today. European racial theories identified the Tutsi as related to Aryans, and therefore destined to rule over the Hutu in Rwanda. In the 1930s, the Belgians decided to clarify who belonged to which group. They conducted a census and issued identity cards. Apparently the main way of differentiating the groups was by counting the number of cows (the primary sign of wealth) that each person owned. Those owning ten or more cows were designated Tutsi. After that original classification, one's identity depended on whether one's father was Tutsi or Hutu.[60] Thus European colonial rule stratified Rwandan society, further privileging the Tutsi.

In the period from 1959–1962, as Rwanda struggled toward decolonization and independence, there was a "social revolution," abetted by the church and the departing Belgian government, in which elite Hutu supplanted the ruling Tutsi. During this violent transition about 10,000 Tutsi were massacred, and another 150,000, perhaps 40 percent of the Tutsi population, fled to neighboring countries.[61]

The ruling Hutu party kept the system of ethnic identity cards in place, but reversed the benefits and privileges accorded to the two groups. The majority Hutu instituted a quota system for education, state jobs, and government positions, favoring themselves. The Hutu government blocked the return of Tutsi refugees and confiscated their pastures for Hutu farmers.[62] Hutu rule was characterized by widespread corruption, and by the vilification and periodic massacre of Tutsi. Meanwhile, Belgium and France gave the Hutu government massive economic and military assistance.[63]

By 1990, three developments were threatening the Hutu grip on power. First, an economic crisis, perhaps precipitated by a structural adjustment program required by the International Monetary Fund, resulted in food shortages, unemployment, and increasing poverty, especially among youth coming of age in a rapidly-growing population. Second, there was both internal pressure from excluded Hutu groups and external pressure from the international community to further democratize and share power. Third, there was an invasion from Uganda by the Rwandan Patriotic Front (RPF), a well-trained organization founded and led by Tutsi exiles from the early 1960s.[64]

The Hutu government responded to these threats by deliberately reviling and further repressing the Tutsi. A Hutu militia, the *interahamwe*, was recruited from the ranks of disgruntled and despairing youth and equipped by the French-trained Presidential Guard. Through the print media and over the radio (a chief form of communication in Rwanda), Hutu propaganda incited ethnic hatred of all Tutsi.[65] In 1992–1993, the Presidential Guard and the *interahamwe* massacred thousands of Tutsi and planted bombs and mines to instill a climate of fear. The Hutu government attempted to scapegoat the Tutsi, polarize society, and normalize violence.[66]

Internal and international pressure on the Hutu government finally led to a comprehensive peace agreement signed at Arusha, Tanzania in August, 1993. The Arusha Agreement provided for power sharing with the RPF and civilian opposition parties in all government institutions and the army, guarantees on human rights, and the dispatch of a U.N. force of 2,500 troops—the U.N. Assistance Mission to Rwanda (UNAMIR)—to oversee the peace process. Although Hutu extremists encumbered the peace process, the government finally pledged to hand over power at a meeting of African heads of state in Tanzania on April 5, 1994. When the plane carrying the Presidents of Rwanda and Burundi was shot down the next day as it returned to Rwanda, the Hutu extremists set in motion their "final solution."[67]

Aided by the police and the army, the *interahamwe* systematically rounded up and slaughtered Tutsis and any Hutus whom they suspected of sympathizing with the Tutsi. Most of the killing was done with machetes imported for the purpose. The killing began in the capital, Kigali, and rapidly spread to the countryside. Roving bands of Hutu thugs hacked to death Tutsis and coerced others into joining the butchery or be killed themselves.[68] Tutsi who gathered in churches seeking asylum from the pogrom were sacrificed around the altar. Hundreds of thousands of women were raped,[69] and hundreds of thousands of people were murdered.

The U.N. troops stationed in Rwanda abandoned the civilian population to their fate. On the first full day of the genocide, ten U.N. Belgian troops and a moderate Hutu government official whom they were trying to protect were brutally killed by a throng of military and militia. Belgium immediately withdrew its contingent of UNAMIR troops and pressured other governments to follow suit. By April 21, 1994, the U.N. Security Council had voted to reduce the 2500 UNAMIR troops to 270.[70] The international community thereby abandoned a civilian population to genocide.

With the breakdown of the peace process and the beginning of a massacre, the Rwandan Patriotic Front immediately renewed its invasion of Rwanda and rapidly advanced across the country. By July, 1994, despite the constant calls for a cease-fire on the part of the international community, the RPF had soundly defeated the Hutu military and militia and gained control of Rwanda. As the RPF advanced, millions of Hutu, either fearing reprisals or coerced by armed Hutu extremists, fled from Rwanda into Burundi and

Zaire. Although there were some reprisals, the RPF showed restraint and discipline and set up an inclusive government.

The world community was then faced with over a million Hutu refugees huddled in the rugged hills of eastern Zaire. Hunger, cholera and other diseases spread through the camps. The Hutu supremacists responsible for the genocide soon began using the refugee camps as a base for insurgent operations against Tutsi in western Rwanda, provoking an anti-guerrilla campaign on the part of the Rwandan government.[71] In retrospect, it seems clear that international relief agencies, by focusing almost exclusively on humanitarian assistance rather than condemning the massive violation of human rights represented by the genocide of Tutsi, had allowed themselves to be used by the Hutu supremacists.[72]

In 1995, as many as 700,000 Tutsi refugees, descendants of Tutsis displaced in the early 1960s, returned to Rwanda with their cattle.[73] The government settled many of them in the houses abandoned by Hutu.

The Hutu militia based in refugee camps in Zaire were also stirring up resentment and attacking a Tutsi community, called the Banyamulenge, which had settled and prospered in eastern Zaire two centuries earlier. In September 1996, a Zairian provincial official announced that the Banyamulenge would be expelled from the country. Instead these Tutsi, who had long been armed and well-organized, attacked and routed the unpaid and undisciplined Zairian Army.

The fighting in eastern Zaire in the fall of 1996 threatened the refugee camps and the international relief organizations that served them, precipitating yet another humanitarian crisis. Then, in November 1996, the Banyamulenge attacked the Hutu militia based in the refugee camps, and routed them into the mountains of Zaire. With the retreat of the Hutu militia, hundreds of thousands of Hutu returned en masse to their villages in Rwanda. Many of them found their houses, abandoned over two years before, now occupied by Tutsi. Furthermore, among the returning refugees were some of those who killed the families and friends of Rwandan Tutsi during the genocide.[74]

In 1997, the Tutsi-dominated Rwandan government faced overwhelming problems:[75]

- *Housing.* This densely populated country has a severe shortage of housing, with nowhere for the returning refugee, Hutu or Tutsi, to live.
- *Economy.* Civil war, genocide, and general chaos have decimated an already failing economy.
- A *System of Justice.* Nearly 75,000 people—accused, often summarily, of participation in genocide—filled Rwandan jails, in appalling conditions, even before the mass return of Hutu refugees.[76] More will be added to their number. Yet Rwanda has no judicial system. How can so many people, accused of horrendous crimes, be accorded fair trials and just punishments? Without justice how can there be reconciliation?
- *Ethnic Hatred.* Ethnic hatred has a decades-long history in Rwandan

society.[77] Now there are new scores to settle, more reasons to stereotype and hate. Overcoming these prejudices and healing these psychological and social wounds remains a daunting task.

The role of the church in the crisis in Rwanda was very complex and ambiguous. While the church was at least indirectly complicit in the genocide, it was also a church of martyrs. Unfortunately, the church's local history of evangelism resulted in intensifying rather than challenging the ethnic distinctions between Hutu and Tutsi. The church itself was divided along ethnic lines in Rwanda. While some church leaders called for negotiation and reconciliation, and criticized human rights violations, others clearly identified with the Hutu regime or were pro-Tutsi. Whether the church in Rwanda can yet become a force for healing and reconciliation remains to be seen.[78]

The international community, and especially the West with its colonial stakes in central Africa, failed miserably in responding to the crisis in Rwanda. While prior to April 1994 the United Nations worked for a peace agreement, it abandoned hundreds of thousands of Rwandans to genocidal slaughter when that process broke down. The international community, often willing to haltingly and clumsily provide humanitarian aid to refugees, still seems stubbornly unwilling to constructively aid the fledgling Rwandan government in nation building. This is admittedly a more complex, costly, and controversial assignment than providing emergency relief to refugees, but it seems essential.

It is worth noting that in 1997 the situation in Burundi, Rwanda's neighbor to the south, is tragically similar to that in Rwanda. The Hutu are a majority (84 percent) and the Tutsi are a minority (14 percent) who have historically ruled. Burundi's history since independence has been characterized by more frequent changes in government than in Rwanda, and while the power between the Hutu and the Tutsi communities seems more balanced, Burundi has also had a history of massacres and violent reprisals that have produced 150,000 deaths since 1993. It is not surprising, then, that at the beginning of 1997 the political situation in Burundi was extremely precarious.[79]

In May of 1997 the central government of Zaire, under longtime dictator Mobutu Sese Seko, was overthrown by a revolutionary army under Laurent Kabila. Kabila has re-named the country the Democratic Republic of the Congo. Although rich in resources, this third largest country in Africa is among the world's poorest countries. While its diverse population does have some sense of national identity, Congo's government faces economic and political problems at least as daunting as those in Rwanda or Burundi.[80]

NORTHERN IRELAND

What are referred to as "the troubles" began in 1969, but in a real sense the roots of the conflict stretch back to 1169 when the Irish King of Leinster sought help from the English king in fighting his enemies, thus initiating "eight hundred years of British oppression" in Ireland; and to 1609 when

James I sent English and Scottish settlers to establish plantations on confiscated Irish lands in the north of Ireland; and to 1690 when the Protestant William of Orange defeated the Catholic James II and his Irish and French allies at the Battle of the Boyne.[81] The basic division in Northern Ireland is the native people versus the colonial settlers. "Politically, the natives were nationalists and the settlers unionists; socially, the nationalists were deprived and the unionists privileged; and religiously, the deprived were Catholic and the privileged Protestant."[82] This is a conflict about power and privilege, participation and justice. In this case, the antagonists happen to be Protestant and Catholic.

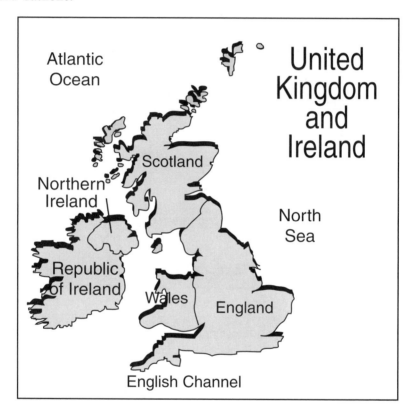

The Protestants in Northern Ireland are descendants of the seventeenth-century colonial settlers. They are loyal (Loyalist) to the union (Unionist) between Northern Ireland and Great Britain. They identify themselves as citizens of Ulster (Ulstermen), the northern region of Ireland. On July 12 the Orange Order (Orangemen) celebrate the victory of William of Orange at the Battle of the Boyne with marches and bonfires in their own neighborhoods, and in those of Catholics as well.[83] They fly the Union Jack flag of Great Britain and the Red Hand flag of Ulster. Most Protestant Christians attend the Church of Ireland (Anglican), although some are Presbyterian. About 60 percent (950,000) of Northern Ireland's 1.6 million people are Protestant.

The Catholic minority (650,000) in Northern Ireland identify with the Republic of Ireland, and with the Roman Catholic Church. They consider themselves Irish, and think that Northern Ireland should be re-united with the Republic of Ireland. The majority of them are Nationalist, that is, they favor a legal and constitutional approach to unification. Republicans share the same goal, but think that force is necessary to accomplish unification.[84]

British colonial rule in Ireland was characterized by harsh repression and periodic rebellions by the Irish. The English imposed their language, extirpated the native culture, and expropriated the land, leaving the Irish powerless, poor, and prone to pestilence and famine. During the Great Famine of the 1840s some one million Irish were sent to the grave while another million fled the country in order to survive. Every generation produced a major "rising" against British rule.[85]

As Ireland gradually moved toward Home Rule or independence in the last decades of the nineteenth century and the first decades of the twentieth, the Unionists of Ulster vehemently resisted. When the Irish Free State (which evolved into the Republic of Ireland) was established in 1921, six of the nine counties of Ulster—those counties where there was a Protestant majority—were partitioned off into Northern Ireland, and remained part of the United Kingdom.[86]

In Northern Ireland the Protestant Unionists developed a system that kept them in an economically and politically superior position. They rejected proportional representation, and created a fundamentally undemocratic state specifically designed to keep Protestants in power. Even though their greater numbers guaranteed them control over Stormont, the parliament in Northern Ireland (abolished in 1972), they still restricted the power of Catholics by limiting them to two votes per household. At the same time, they enhanced the power of Protestants by giving extra votes to businesses and universities which were dominated by Protestants. In the town of Derry (called Londonderry by Unionists), where Catholics had a two-thirds majority of the population, Protestants gerrymandered the election districts to effectively control the local government. The town and county councils distributed public housing and public jobs. Catholics faced long waiting lists for both. Protestants dominated the Royal Ulster Constabulary (RUC)—the police force—and the B-Specials—an official Protestant militia—both of which repressed the Catholic population.[87]

> **For Reflection**
>
> Tim Pat Coogan in *The Troubles* (p. 25) says, "In many ways the hard-working, God-fearing fundamentalists of the Six Counties resembled the Boers of South Africa. They developed the same *laager* mentality and a system of administration very similar to apartheid, albeit based on religion rather than colour." Is apartheid a fitting designation for Protestant rule in Ulster?

The violence of the current "troubles" was precipitated by a nonviolent civil rights movement in 1969. In the mid-1960s, Catholics, inspired by the wave of civil rights agitation in the United States and elsewhere, decided to temporarily table the goal of unification with Ireland in favor of a civil rights movement. Catholics contended that if Northern Ireland was to belong to the United Kingdom, they were entitled to their rights as British citizens. These rights included a right to vote for all adults, fair representation in government, legislation barring discrimination in jobs and housing, and freedom from harassment by the police and militia. Catholic demonstrations for their civil rights were met by violent resistance on the part of the RUC and the Unionists, forcing Britain to send in troops to maintain order.[88] The situation quickly degenerated into a cycle of violence that persisted until the cease-fire declared in September of 1994.

The Official Irish Republican Army (IRA), built up by Michael Collins (regarded as the father of modern urban guerilla warfare)[89] at the time of the Irish struggle for independence from British colonial rule (1916–1922), had laid dormant for nearly 50 years. But the violence that the Ulster police and militia unleashed on unarmed Catholic demonstrators made clear the need for protection and for retaliation. Thus, young Catholic men formed the Provisional IRA, dedicated to uniting the North to the Republic of Ireland through the use of force, fear, and terror. At the same time, the Loyalists formed the Ulster Defense Association (UDA) and resurrected the Ulster Volunteer Force (UVF) to use the same violent tactics to preserve the union with Great Britain.[90] Britain's armed forces, sent to restore order, at first tried to keep the two sides separate, in effect protecting the Catholic demonstrators from Protestant violence. Soon, however, mistakes and mishandling of the population by the British troops resulted in their becoming targets of the IRA.[91] By 1972, the chaos was such that Britain abolished the Ulster Parliament and established direct rule, sending in 17,000 troops to augment the Ulster police. These military and paramilitary forces have been killing each other and civilians, in Northern Ireland and Britain, for over twenty-five years now.

The toll has been staggering. By the time of the cease-fire in 1994, 3,173 people had been killed in the sectarian warfare, about half of them Protestant and half Catholic, roughly two-thirds of them civilians and one-third members of the security forces.[92] Over 35,500 people had been wounded in over 33,350 shootings and 9,760 bombings.[93] For example, the death toll was 24 in one week near the end of October 1993. A young member of the IRA placed a bomb in a crowded fish store in the Protestant Shankill area of West Belfast. When it apparently exploded prematurely, it killed the bomber and nine others. Unionist death squads retaliated by killing seven Catholics, including two brothers watching TV after their sister's birthday party. Then two Loyalist gunmen walked into the Rising Sun pub in the town of Greysteel on Halloween night, yelled "Trick or Treat!" and opened fire with automatic weapons, killing seven people and wounding six.

Such indiscriminate violence terrorizes both the Protestant and the Catholic communities and inculcates hatred. When the funeral processions for the IRA bomber and for a thirteen-year-old girl, one of his Protestant victims in the fish shop, passed one another, a Protestant shouted, "You're yellow pigs, all of you!" A Catholic held up nine fingers, one for each Protestant killed and yelled back, "We got nine of you! We can't kill enough of you!"[94]

This terrible cycle of violence was interrupted in the fall of 1994 when the IRA unilaterally declared a cease-fire and the Protestant paramilitary groups followed suit a month later. The intent of the IRA cease-fire was to get its political arm, Sinn Fein ("We Ourselves"), led by Gerry Adams, invited to the negotiating table about the future of Northern Ireland. In 1993, Great Britain had promised that if the violence ceased, Sinn Fein could join the dialogue between the governments and the political parties.

The United States had been a key player in boosting the status and acceptability of Sinn Fein. President Clinton reversed the policy of his predecessors and issued a travel visa for Gerry Adams to visit the United States. Clinton also sent former Senator George Mitchell to head a commission to facilitate all-party talks in Northern Ireland. For his efforts President Clinton received an enthusiastic reception when he visited Belfast and Derry in Northern Ireland in November 1995.[95]

Prime Minister John Major of Great Britain, however, responded to the cease-fire by insisting that the IRA disarm as well before Sinn Fein could sit at the negotiation table. Mr. Major's Conservative government had the thinnest of majorities in the Parliament and was therefore beholden to the nine Unionist representatives from Ulster to govern. When the Mitchell Commission seemed to finesse the disarmament stumbling block by suggesting a commission to plan and monitor mutual disarmament while the peace talks progressed, Mr. Major ignored the idea and called for elections prior to negotiations—another condition on admitting Sinn Fein to the table. The IRA ended the cease-fire with a February 9, 1996 bomb blast in the eastern dock area of London, and followed it up with other bombs in London and Manchester. Although the return to terrorist violence was reprehensible, Britain had dawdled over negotiations for seventeen months, breaking promises made in 1993. And the government still refused at that point to sit at the negotiation table with Sinn Fein.[96]

In May 1997 a Liberal government headed by Tony Blair replaced John Major and the Tories in Great Britain. Mr. Blair once again offered a place at the negotiating table to Sinn Fein if the IRA ceased its campaign of violence. At this writing, after a bloody and conflictive "marching season" (July), the IRA has renewed its cease-fire, opening the possibility of all-party talks in September, 1997.[97]

The central obstacle to peace is, of course, that the non-negotiable demands of the Protestant Loyalists and the Catholic Nationalists are in direct opposition to one another. Protestant Unionists insist that Northern Ireland remain part of the United Kingdom, while Catholic Nationalists demand unification with the Republic of Ireland. At the heart of the Protestant position is their desire to maintain control and to preserve their superiority over Catholics, on which their identity depends. By contrast their history and experience of Protestant repression convince Catholics that Unionists will never recognize them as equal or respond to them with justice. Nor do Nationalists find any convincing reason for the partition of Ireland.[98]

Another obstacle to a just peace in Northern Ireland is the complexity of the politics of the parties involved. There are at least four major participants in the negotiations: Protestant Unionists, Catholic Nationalists, Great Britain, and the Republic of Ireland. Within each of these there are opposing factions and vested interests. Within both the Protestant and the Catholic communities there are moderates and extremists. Both Unionists and Nationalists will find themselves sitting at the table with representatives of groups who have terrorized them—killing their family and friends, bombing their houses and businesses, harassing them day and night. Moreover, the extremists of the Provisional IRA and the Ulster Defense Association do not really believe a settlement can be negotiated. Since they do not plan on compromising, and they do not expect the enemy to compromise either, they think this is simply a war that must be won.

It should be noted that both Catholic and Protestant paramilitary groups have gone beyond the violence of sectarian strife and entered into criminal, mafia-style violence within their own communities. The "hard men" of the IRA and the UDA/UVF are deeply involved in protection rackets in Belfast, where they are making a great deal of money through extortion. Genuine peace would remove the sectarian cover under which they conduct this dirty business.[99] The paramilitary groups thus have a vested interest in continuing the troubles.

Unionist identity is tied to their superiority and control and to anti-Catholicism. From their perspective, to compromise is to lose their very self. Unionists consider themselves loyal to an imperial concept of Great Britain that the British government itself has relinquished. They suspect and fear that Britain will ultimately betray them.[100]

Thus far, British policy has always supported Protestant domination in Ulster, even though military and economic support for Ulster is costing Britain about $3 billion a year. Hundreds of British soldiers have died in Ulster in the last 25 years, and the IRA has brought its terror tactics to the heart of London.[101] Yet Britain has declared that as long as a majority of the people of Ulster wish to remain in the union, Northern Ireland will be part of the United Kingdom. In that regard demographic trends that indicate higher birth rates among Catholics also concern Protestants.[102]

The Republic of Ireland, although supportive of the nationalist cause, is no friend of the IRA and could not afford the economic support for Ulster that Britain is currently providing. While opposed to the partition of Ireland, it has no great desire to inherit the ethnic strife in the North.

While the majority of Catholics in Northern Ireland do not support the terrorist tactics of the Provisional IRA and Sinn Fein, they do agree on the goal of re-unification with the Republic of Ireland. The Catholic community is convinced that if they remain a minority in Northern Ireland, they will continue to be oppressed by the Protestant majority with the backing of Britain.

Although Ireland is partitioned, the churches in Ireland are not. Each of the main churches (Catholic, Anglican, and Presbyterian) is a united, all-Ireland organization. Precisely because the church is not partitioned, it has been a unifying factor in the conflict. The recent development of ecumenical organizations and of efforts at reconciliation rooted in the churches are positive signs that the churches are responding to the challenge to overcome segregation and sectarianism in Northern Ireland.[103]

Both Protestants and Catholics are guilty of murder and mayhem. Whether Northern Ireland remains in the United Kingdom, unites with the Republic of Ireland, or settles on a different arrangement, the protection of human rights for all people, and particularly the minority population, is a key to a just peace. The churches, whose vocation is conversion, forgiveness, and reconciliation, need to play a constructive role by courageously condemning oppression and violence wherever it is found, by steadfastly working for justice and promoting human rights, and by boldly calling for reconciliation and community.

THE KURDS

The Middle East is home to much violence and conflict, much of it ethnic in nature. The best-known example is the on-going struggle between Israel and the Palestinians (who have been supported by the surrounding Arab countries). Even this complex and bitter conflict, which began with the establishment of Israel in 1948, turned in the direction of peace with the 1993 agreement between Israel and the Palestinian Liberation Organization (PLO). However, continuing strife suggests that their journey toward peace and security is perilous and precarious.

Another conflict in the Middle East that deserves more than the peripheral attention of the world community is the situation of the Kurds.

Kurdish clans have lived in the Caucasus Mountains for some four thousand years. The Kurds are clearly a nation without a state: "The Kurds' identity is based on a number of shared traits: a common homeland and culture, a myth of common origin, a shared faith in Islam, similar languages, and a history of bitter conflict with outsiders."[104] Kurdistan, their homeland, is divided among five states: Turkey, Syria, Iraq, Iran, and Armenia. The Kurds have had the misfortune of living at a major intersection or crossroads: of two empires—the Ottoman and the Persian; of three significant peoples—Turks to the northwest, Persians (Iranians) to the east, and Arabs to the south; and of four aggressive nationalisms—Turkish, Syrian, Iraqi, and Iranian.[105] The riptides of these rivalries have resulted in the violent repression of the Kurds, and have thwarted their desire for recognition as a nation-state.

Historically, the Ottomans and the Persians manipulated the Kurds, taking advantage of internal frictions to divide and control them. The Kurds were left out when the Ottoman Empire disintegrated after World War I. The promise in the Treaty of Sevres in 1920 that the Kurds would receive a homeland was betrayed in the Treaty of Lausanne in 1923. Thus, the 25 million

Kurds became a significant and backward minority that threatened the aspirations toward modernity and regional power of Turkey, Iraq, and Iran.

The Kurds in Iran have fared better than their compatriots in Turkey or Iraq, but their lot has still been deplorable. Kurds represent only 10 percent of Iran's rather diverse and multi-ethnic population. In the early 1970s, the former Shah, in concert with Israel and the United States, armed the Kurds and used them in a war against Iraq. He then betrayed them to the wrath of Saddam Hussein after Iran and Iraq signed an accord. As Sunni Muslims the Kurds received no better treatment from the Shiite Islamic fundamentalists who overthrew the Shah in 1979. The Iranians slaughtered over 50,000 Kurds and focused on assassinating their exiled leaders.[106]

In Turkey the repression of the Kurds began in the late 1920s and continues through the 1990s. Turkey tried to force the Kurds to assimilate by prohibiting the public expression of Kurdish culture and identity. Kurds were not allowed to speak their language in public, nor was it to be used in education. The Turks passed legislation that prohibited Kurds, who represent 23 percent of Turkey's population, to comprise no more than 5 percent of the population in any place they inhabited; their dispersal and re-settlement was enforced by the Turkish army. By 1937, frustrated that these measures were not having the desired results, the Turkish government began direct military repression of the Kurds, massacring tens of thousands at a time.

Such measures led to the formation of the Kurdistan Worker's Party (PKK), a radical Marxist liberation group, which began a campaign of terror aimed at Turks and at Kurds thought to accommodate the government. Turkey responded with yet more brutal repression, and Kurdish civilians in the countryside were caught in the crossfire between the aggressive terrorism of the PKK guerrillas and the ruthless counter-insurgency of the government. At least 18,000 people have been killed in Turkey in the decade since 1984, and hundreds of thousands have been displaced. A 1991 anti-terrorism law allowed the imprisonment of anyone speaking on behalf of Kurdish rights.[107]

In northern Iraq, although Kurds were at least recognized as a significant minority (23 percent of Iraq's population) and granted some autonomy, Saddam Hussein committed acts of genocide against the Kurds in two periods in the 1980s. In 1983 Iraqi troops entered the town of Barzan and rounded up every male over the age of 13, some 8000 men, paraded them through the streets of Baghdad, and then executed every one of them. The Barzani clan are the traditional leaders of the struggle for a Kurdish homeland. In 1988 alone, 200,000 Kurds were killed. During that horrible year, the Iraqi army killed the 5,000 people in the town of Halabja—every man, woman, and child—by dropping poison gas on them.[108]

After the U.S.-led victory over Iraq in 1991, the Kurds again rebelled in the expectation that Saddam Hussein would be overthrown. But the U.S. army stopped its advance short of Baghdad, leaving much of the Iraqi army intact. Hussein then unleashed his army with a vengeance on the over-matched Kurds. International shock at the treatment of the Kurds forced the United Nations to establish a "no fly" zone and safe haven for the Kurds in the north of Iraq in 1991. This humanitarian intervention, in spite of state sovereignty and territorial integrity, was a first for the United Nations.[109]

Unfortunately, Iraqi Kurds have been hampered by the traditional weakness of the Kurdish peoples—infighting and division. Historically, Kurdish clans have more often fought among themselves than they have against an outside force. There are two rival parties among the Iraqi Kurds—the Kurdish Democratic Party (KDP), and the Patriotic Union of Kurdistan (PUK).[110] In the fall of 1996 the PUK invited the Iraqi army to help it get the upper hand over the KDP, resulting in a serious breach in the safe haven, and in mutual Kurdish killing and displacement. This incident reinforced the notion that Saddam Hussein is poised to pounce on the Kurds should international protection be relaxed.

In part, the Kurd's legitimate desire for a homeland is the victim of regional and international power politics. Kurdistan is surrounded by aggressive regimes bent on dominating the region, and that are not about to yield sovereignty or territory to the Kurds. In the aftermath of the Cold War and the wake of the Persian Gulf victory, the United States has an important influence in the region. The United States, as it has done before, may be using the Kurds to achieve a certain balance of power in the region. If the Iraqi Kurds were to establish an independent state in northern Iraq, Iraq's power in the region would be diminished, and Iran, which has been hostile to the United States since the 1979 Islamic revolution, might be able to dominate the Persian Gulf. Thus, U.S. interests in this strategic area may be better served by a Kurdish irritant than by an independent Kurdistan.[111]

But the Kurds themselves are also partly responsible for their failure to create meaningful ethnic unity or coherent national organizations.[112] If Kurdistan were to be recognized as an independent state tomorrow, it would likely disintegrate into civil war among the various clans and factions soon thereafter. Thus, the Kurds are the victims of self-serving, manipulative leaders—among themselves, their neighbors, and the international community.

The Kurdish people have suffered egregious violations of their human rights, manipulation by regional and outside powers, and the denial of a homeland. Their internal divisions can partly be explained by external oppression, and they are unlikely to be healed as long as they continue to be divided among five states.

CONCLUSION

Ethnic conflict is primarily about power and oppression. Although antagonisms between ethnic groups or nations may have a long history, such enmity is neither natural nor inevitable. Ethnic enmity is invented. In each of the conflicts examined above national leaders have fanned the flames of ethnic hatred with little regard for the common good or for constructive solutions to complex conflicts. Self-serving leadership is often responsible for ethnic conflagrations and the brutal violence that too often characterizes them. In order to prevent and to constructively resolve ethnic conflict it would seem there is no substitute for leaders who have not only the genuine interests of their people at heart, but who also are able to recognize that other people have genuine interests at stake as well. The world needs more statesmen and stateswomen and fewer demagogues; more like Nelson Mandela (South Africa), Vaclav Havel (Czech Republic), Anwar Sadat (Egypt), and Yitzhak Rabin (Israel), and fewer like Slobodan Milosevic (Serbia), Franjo Tudjman (Croatia), Rev. Ian Paisley (Ulster), and Saddam Hussein (Iraq).

In three of the cases surveyed above (Bosnia, Sri Lanka, and Northern Ireland) religion has been used to add fuel to the fire of nationalism. Since both religion and nationalism relate to core values, it is understandable that they become intertwined, but when religion legitimizes ethnic nationalism, religion becomes bastardized. Authentic religion should critique the absolutization of any value save God and any ideology that inculcates hatred and division. Religious communities should be advocates for conversion, forgiveness, and reconciliation; they should be forces for justice, solidarity, nonviolence, and peace. Religious communities should produce leaders who serve their communities and work for the common good—like Gandhi in India, Martin Luther King, Jr. (United States), Bishop Desmond Tutu (South Africa), Dag Hammarskjold (United Nations), Cory Aquino (Philippines), and Jimmy

Carter (United States). And when those in power spew hatred and do violence, religious communities should produce prophets and martyrs, like Bishop Oscar Romero in El Salvador and Franz Jaegerstaetter and Dietrich Bonhoeffer in Nazi Germany. Religion can and should become a constructive force for justice and equality, reconciliation and peace in situations of ethnic conflict.

Finally, it may be that the international community will have to evolve different conceptions of state, nation, and sovereignty and different institutional arrangements for civil societies.[113] The reality of sovereign states is, after all, only a few centuries old. Thus, different conceptions and arrangements are surely possible and may even be better. But it seems that key to any arrangement of civil society are the twin values of the *participation of citizens* in decisions that affect their well being and *respect for human rights*. When people have a real share in the exercise of power by the government, ordinarily change can be accomplished without demagoguery, polarization, or resorting to violence. When human rights are honored, especially the rights of minorities and the marginalized, violent conflict is rare. Any scheme that attempts to reorganize states and nations will need to pay particular attention to participation and human rights.

STUDY QUESTIONS

1. Distinguish between a nation and a state. Do you think every nation should be a state?
2. Is nationalism a danger in the contemporary world? How can nationalism be harnessed as a positive force and be reined in as a negative force?
3. Explain the situation in Bosnia. What do you think that NATO and/or the United Nations should do in response to the situation? How can religion be a constructive force in Bosnia?
4. Why care about the ethnic conflict in Sri Lanka?
5. Was the slaughter of Tutsi by the Hutu in 1994 in Rwanda an act of genocide? Should other nations have intervened to stop the slaughter? How?
6. Can there be peace in Northern Ireland? Is this a religious conflict?
7. Why isn't there a Kurdistan?

CHAPTER SIX

Weapons and Disarmament

"Finally, be strong in the Lord and in the strength of his power. Put on the whole armor of God, so that you may be able to stand against the wiles of the devil. . . . Stand therefore and fasten the belt of truth around your waist, and put on the breastplate of righteousness. As shoes for your feet put on whatever will make you ready to proclaim the gospel of peace. With all of these, take the shield of faith, with which you will be able to quench all the flaming arrows of the evil one. Take the helmet of salvation, and the sword of the spirit, which is the word of God." (Ephesians 6: 10-11, 14-17)

"We must re-emphasize with all our being, nonetheless, that it is not only nuclear war that must be prevented, but war itself. Therefore with Pope John Paul II we declare:

Today, the scale and the horror of modern warfare—whether nuclear or not—makes it totally unacceptable as a means of settling differences between nations. War should belong to the tragic past, to history; it should find no place on humanity's agenda for the future.

Reason and experience tell us that a continuing upward spiral, even in conventional arms, coupled with an unbridled increase in armed forces, instead of securing true peace will almost certainly be provocative of war."[1]

World security analyst Michael Klare says there is a "deadly convergence" of three trends in the post-Cold War world.[2] One trend is the emergence of ethno-nationalist conflict, the subject of the previous chapter. The other two are the proliferation of weapons of mass destruction (nuclear, chemical, and biological weapons) and the spread of ever more sophisticated conventional weapons and delivery systems through the arms trade. These three trends are likely to increase the number and severity of regional conflicts unless the global community takes decisive steps to defuse them. Previous chapters have looked at some of the motives for war in the post-Cold War world: empire building and exploitation, poverty and the gap between the rich and the poor, environmental scarcity, violations of human rights, and ethno-nationalism. This chapter will address the means to conduct war, exploring first the issues of nuclear weapons and other weapons of mass destruction, and then the traffic in conventional arms and military spending.

LEST WE FORGET: UNIMAGINABLE DESTRUCTION

The forty-five years of the Cold War (1945–1990) were characterized by a nuclear stalemate between the Union of Soviet Socialist Republics (U.S.S.R.) and the United States, the East and the West. The watchword for U.S. foreign policy was "containment." Communism was to be contained and resisted wherever possible. This led the United States into wars in Korea in the 1950s and Vietnam in the 1960s to keep the nations of Southeast Asia from falling "like dominoes" into communist hands. The policy of containment also led to interventions in Latin America (Cuba, Chile, El Salvador, Nicaragua, etc.) during the 1970s and 1980s.

The two superpowers divided the world up into "spheres of influence," and competed with one another for the allegiance of unaligned states. Foreign aid, especially in the form of weapons and military assistance, was a major tactic in this strategy. For example:

- When Anwar Sadat decided to expel the Soviets in 1972 and switch allegiance to the United States, Egypt quickly became the second largest beneficiary (after Israel) of U.S. foreign aid.
- Cuba was heavily subsidized by the Soviet Union in recognition of Castro's allegiance to communism. Cuba then became a conduit for Soviet aid to rebel armies in Central America and Africa.
- In the 1970s Ethiopia and Somalia, neighbors and combatants over disputed territory, each switched allegiances between the two superpowers. When Marxist guerrillas took control of Ethiopia, that country dropped its close relationship with the United States and turned to Moscow. Somalia, which had forged close links with the Soviet Union, then allied itself with the United States in 1978, which showered its dictatorship with the weapons later used in the civil unrest and against U.N. and American troops in the early 1990s.[3]
- In the 1980s the United States backed rebel armies in the Soviet-allied states of Angola and Nicaragua.

Thus, during the Cold War, the world map was like a chessboard for the superpowers.

The arms race, however, was the major field of competition between the superpowers. Each tried to build bigger, better, and more nuclear weapons than the other. The paradoxical strategic doctrine that made this insane arms race marginally rational was deterrence through "mutually assured destruction" (MAD). MAD meant that both blocks would be deterred from using nuclear weapons by the assurance that the victim of a nuclear attack could literally destroy the aggressor in retaliation. The populations of the United States and the Soviet Union were, in effect, hostages in a situation of nuclear terrorism.

The word terrorism is not used lightly here. It is important to remember and appreciate the fear that characterized the Cold War in order to understand the relief when it ended, as well as the task that still remains. The fall of communism in Eastern Europe and the former Soviet Union dispelled the political tensions that produced this terror, but most of the weapons themselves still exist. While we no longer live in daily fear that we will suddenly be engulfed in a nuclear firestorm, as long as nuclear weapons exist, the unimaginable could happen.[4]

The power of nuclear weapons is truly awesome. The blast effect from a one megaton (a million tons of TNT) warhead exploded over a major city would crush and vaporize everything within a one-and-a-half mile radius. The temperature at the center of the fireball would be eight times hotter than the sun. All human beings within this zone would immediately die. A shock front with winds exceeding 600 miles per hour would create a vacuum that would be filled with inrushing winds of greater than hurricane force. Nearly everything would be destroyed in a three-mile radius from ground zero. Asphalt paving would melt; wood and clothes would ignite. Trucks would be thrown about like giant Molotov cocktails. Over eight miles from ground zero, winds would reach hurricane force, and most people would suffer second or third degree burns from this firestorm. People and animals dozens of miles away who saw the flash from the explosion would be blinded or suffer eye damage. Much of the rubble near the blast would be highly radioactive.

Survivors would envy the dead. Many would die slowly from radiation sickness, severe burns, broken bones, and lacerations. Hospitals and health care personnel would be destroyed, disabled, or overwhelmed, as would fire departments, water treatment plants, and food stores. Many of the uninjured would die from epidemics or hunger. Some, no doubt, would commit suicide out of grief or shock. Radioactive particles, pulled into the upper atmosphere by the mushroom cloud, would fall hundreds or even thousands of miles away, contaminating milk or food and causing cancer decades later. Survivors of the atomic bomb dropped on Hiroshima in 1945 lived in fear of falling victim to cancer because of their exposure to radiation from the bomb. This radiation effect of a nuclear bomb makes it utterly indiscriminate. In a nuclear war, of course, a city could be hit with several warheads. The cumulative effect of a full-scale nuclear war would most likely produce a nuclear winter, lowering the temperature of earth so that little food could be produced.[5]

At the height of the arms race the two superpowers possessed over 50,000 nuclear bombs. Humanity still has the power to undo creation as the twen-

For Reflection

During the 1950s, Senator Joseph McCarthy stirred anti-communist sentiment in the United States to the point of blacklisting writers and celebrities. At the same time, Americans were building bomb shelters and conducting air raid drills in schools. Those who have no experience of this fear of communism and of nuclear weapons might want to interview someone about the climate in the United States during the Cold War, or see films such as "The Front" (1976) or "Testament" (1983).

tieth century draws to a close. Jonathan Schell hauntingly reflected on the meaning of this in *The Fate of the Earth*.

> Four and a half billion years ago, the earth was formed. Perhaps a half billion years after that life arose on the planet. For the next four billion years life became more complex, more varied, and more ingenious, until, around a million years ago, it produced mankind—the most complex and ingenious species of all. Only six or seven thousand years ago—a period that is to the history of the earth as less than a minute is to a year—civilization emerged, enabling us to build up a human world, and to add to the marvels of evolution marvels of our own: marvels of art, of science, of social organization, of spiritual attainment. . . . And now, . . . we hold this entire terrestrial creation hostage to nuclear destruction, threatening to hurl it back into the inanimate darkness from which it came. And this threat of self-destruction and planetary destruction is . . . here now, hanging over the heads of all of us at every moment. The machinery of destruction is complete, poised on a hair trigger, waiting for the "button" to be "pushed" by some misguided or deranged human being or for some faulty computer chip to send out the instruction to fire. That so much should be balanced on so fine a point—that the fruit of four and a half billion years can be undone in a careless moment—is a fact against which belief rebels. And there is another even vaster measure of the loss, for stretching ahead from our present are billions of years of life on earth, all of which can be filled not only with human life but with human civilization. . . . And yet we threaten, in the name of our transient aims and fallible convictions, to foreclose it all. If our species does destroy itself, it will be a death in the cradle—a case of infant mortality. The disparity between the cause and the effect of our peril is so great that our minds seem all but powerless to encompass it. . . . It is almost an illusion. Now we are sitting at the breakfast table drinking our coffee and reading our newspaper, but in a moment we may be inside a fireball whose temperature is tens of thousands of degrees. Now we are on our way to work, walking through the city streets, but in a moment we may be standing on an empty plain under a darkened sky looking for the charred remnants of our children. Now we are alive, but in a moment we may be dead. Now there is human life on earth, but in a moment it may be gone.[6]

The horrific weapons and the policy of deterrence are still with us. It is still possible for "some misguided or deranged human being or faulty computer chip" to launch nuclear warheads. It is still possible for the commander of a Trident submarine, with its capacity to deliver over 190 warheads on as many targets, to blackmail the world or to effectively destroy a continent. And as quickly as the political rationale for nuclear terrorism dissolved, it could return, if, for example, the precarious Russian experiment with democracy were to fail.[7] The weapons themselves, apart from the threat or the will to use them, are terrifying.

The end of the Cold War, which has given the world a window of opportunity for nuclear disarmament, ironically saps the motivation to do so. The citizen anti-nuclear movement which ebbed and flowed in intensity from the 1960s through the 1980s seems to have lost much of its momentum in the 1990s. Since it is highly unlikely that nuclear weapons will be used today, it is difficult to generate much concern about the existence of such destructive power, or much debate about the meaning or wisdom of deterrence in such a changed political context. We need to remember the power of these weapons, and that atomic weapons were used at Hiroshima and Nagasaki. Surely the world should take advantage of this opportunity to move toward a policy of minimal deterrence and the much fewer warheads this would require as a first step toward living in a nuclear-free world.

DETERRENCE OR DISARMAMENT

As the arms race developed so did efforts at arms control, and these efforts bore fruit in various treaties and agreements. The 1963 Limited Test Ban Treaty prohibited above-ground testing of nuclear weapons. It was signed in the aftermath of the Cuban Missile Crisis, one of the tensest moments in the Cold War. In 1968 most nations joined in signing the Non-Proliferation Treaty (NPT), which has been effective in keeping the nuclear club (the nations with nuclear weapons) rather exclusive. The Anti-Ballistic Missile treaty (ABM) of 1972 severely curtailed the development of defensive systems to counter a nuclear attack and effectively closed off a whole new direction for the arms race. The Strategic Arms Limitation Talks (SALT), which resulted in the 1972 SALT I and 1979 SALT II agreements, slowed the arms race, but they did not result in the destruction of any nuclear warheads, missiles, or bombers.[8]

The Reagan years (the early and middle 1980s) brought a lull in arms control agreements, a leap in the arms race, and a corresponding surge in nuclear anxiety. This impasse ended when Mikhail Gorbachev, the Soviet Premier, accepted the U.S. position regarding intermediate-range ballistic missiles in Europe. These were missiles on both sides of the Iron Curtain that could reach targets in Western Europe, or in the Soviet Union. Although the U.S.S.R. had a substantial lead in the number of missiles and warheads, Gorbachev agreed that both sides would destroy *all* of their intermediate nuclear forces (INF). The INF treaty (1987) was the first treaty that actually reduced the number of missiles and warheads.[9]

After that historic agreement, the superpowers began Strategic Arms Reduction Talks (START) which resulted in two agreements that substantially reduced the strategic weapons on both sides—START I (1991) and START II (1993). If these agreements are implemented the United States and Russia will each reduce their stockpiles to about 3,500 strategic nuclear warheads early in the twenty-first century. Each side will also reduce their stockpiles of tactical nuclear warheads. This would mean that about 42,000 warheads (and the missiles meant to deliver them) would be dismantled in the decade 1993–2003.[10]

The U.S. Senate finally ratified START II in January 1996, but by 1997 the Russian Duma (Parliament) had not ratified the treaty and may no longer be willing to do so. When the treaty was negotiated in 1993, the United States drove a hard bargain with Russian President Boris Yeltsin who was desperate for Western aid. The treaty could be interpreted as favoring the United States in allowing it to maintain a numerical advantage, and in requiring Russia to dismantle all of its big land-based missiles while allowing the United States to keep many of its advantageous submarine-based missiles. By 1997 President Yeltsin had neither the popularity nor the control that he did in 1993, and the United States proved to be rather parsimonious with aid. While the United States has been reluctant to implement the treaty until it is ratified by Russia, Washington has suggested a START III process as a way to deflect Russia's concerns.[11] A golden opportunity to dismantle many nuclear warheads and their delivery systems may have slipped away.

Even if the treaty is ratified and implemented, there are significant problems related to this positive process:

- Elaborate procedures for *verification* were built into the START agreements, but the process is hampered by a hangover of suspicion from the secrecy of the Cold War.
- Breaking down the warheads and the missiles, storing or recycling the fissionable material, and verifying that this is being done is very *expensive*. This is a particularly difficult problem for the former Soviet Union. Its struggling economy cannot bear the cost of this process.
- Atomic know-how and nuclear material are scarce assets that can earn Russia hard currency. Official export (for example, to Iran[12]) or black-market profit are constant temptations. There have already been cases of *fissionable material being sold or stolen.*[13] The dispersion of fissionable material can, of course, result in the proliferation of nuclear weapons, either to "rogue" states or terrorist groups.[14]
- It is difficult to dismantle nuclear weapons in a *safe and environmentally responsible way*. In the United States this is being done at the Pantex plant in Amarillo, Texas. Workers who once built bombs are now carefully taking them apart. Yet this is hazardous, and questions have been raised about adherence to safety procedures at the plant.[15] If the United States is struggling with safety issues, there is little doubt that Russia, with a weaker economy and lax government controls, is having an even harder time.
- Storing or *disposing* of fissionable uranium and plutonium in bomb-grade form is even more difficult than disposing of highly radioactive waste from nuclear power plants (see chapter 3). As long as it remains in bomb-grade form, a warhead can be quickly re-assembled. The United States has agreed to purchase much of the former Soviet Union's

fissionable material for use in nuclear power plants, but that arrangement seems to be in jeopardy.[16] The United States already has a surplus of uranium and plutonium for its stalled nuclear energy program, and has yet to solve the problem of how to safely store or dispose of this highly radioactive and virtually everlasting material.[17] Dismantling nuclear weapons is an expensive and hazardous process. In a period of chaos in the Russian economy and of budget cuts and an aversion to tax increases in the United States, implementing progressive disarmament continues to be problematic.

The nuclear arms race between the two Cold War superpowers has been costly. Although the atomic arms program was touted by the Pentagon as being cheaper than spending on conventional weapons, a 1995 study contends that the United States spent about $4 trillion (in 1995 dollars) over a fifty year period for its nuclear arsenal. This amounts to more than a fourth of all United States military spending since World War II.[18] As the Second Vatican Council pointed out as early as 1965, "the arms race is an utterly treacherous trap for humanity, and one which injures the poor to an intolerable degree."[19] Even without being used, the development of nuclear weapons represents a theft from the poor and creates a threat to the earth.[20]

The more fundamental question facing policymakers and citizens, however, is not technical, financial, or environmental; it is political. Should the goal be a non-nuclear world or should the doctrine of deterrence, based on a limited stockpile of nuclear weapons, continue to guide U.S. foreign policy?

If it is decided that deterrence is the more secure policy (and it appears to have worked thus far), a few hundred or a thousand nuclear warheads probably would be sufficient. Thus, deterrence could be achieved at a level less than a third of that allowed by the START II treaty. Since the credibility of deterrence depends on a country's ability to strike back after an attack, mobile submarines and bombers would be superior delivery vehicles to missiles in fixed silos, which are more vulnerable to a first strike attack.

But if nuclear weapons are unusable in *any* moral or rational approach to warfare, and if they are dangerous and terrifying in themselves, then why have them at all? Would not our country and our world be more secure if nuclear weapons were abolished? The difficulty, of course, is that the nuclear genie cannot be put back in the bottle. Humankind will always have the capability of making a nuclear bomb.

While the design of a bomb is not especially daunting, producing bomb-grade fissionable material is a complex process that requires sophisticated and scarce equipment.[21] Thus a non-nuclear world could be maintained through strict controls on producing weapons-grade material. Indeed, although it has not been foolproof, the International Atomic Energy Agency (IAEA) does keep track of fissionable material throughout the world. Protocols for managing this doubly dangerous material are already in place, although they undoubtedly should be strengthened.

Catholic social teaching certainly leans in the direction of nuclear disarmament. In their 1983 Pastoral Letter on *The Challenge of Peace*, the American Catholic bishops, following statements by Pope John Paul II, arrived at a "strictly conditioned moral acceptance of nuclear deterrence . . . as a step on the way toward progressive disarmament (#186–187)." Ten years later in their anniversary statement titled *The Harvest of Justice Is Sown in Peace*, the bishops continued to accept deterrence, but only as a step toward a post-nuclear form of security that lies in the abolition of nuclear weapons and the strengthening of international law. Pope John XXIII seemed to be well ahead of his successors when he wrote in his 1963 encyclical *Peace on Earth*: "Justice, then, right reason and consideration for human dignity and life urgently demand that the arms race should cease, that the stockpiles which exist in various countries should be reduced equally and simultaneously by the parties concerned, that nuclear weapons should be banned, and finally that all come to an agreement on a fitting program of disarmament, employing mutual and effective controls (#112)." The Catholic Church, then, calls for nuclear disarmament, but allows deterrence to stand in the meantime.[22]

Remarkably, a growing number of diplomats, military leaders, and defense experts in the United States (such as General Andrew Goodpaster, former Commander of the North Atlantic Treaty Organization [NATO], Paul Nitze, former arms negotiator, and Robert McNamara, former Secretary of Defense) have urged "a fundamental re-evaluation of long-standing assumptions regarding the benefits of nuclear weapons," and total nuclear disarmament as realistic goals.[23] One of the most outspoken proponents of this view is General Charles A. Horner, head of the United States Space Command, leader of the North American Aerospace Defense Command (which is responsible for defending the United States and Canada from nuclear attack), and commander of the coalition air forces during the Persian Gulf War. General Horner says nuclear weapons are "obsolete and unusable," and the United States should take "the high moral ground" and "get rid of them all." "It's kind of hard for us to say to North Korea, 'You are a terrible people, you're developing a nuclear weapon when we have, oh, 8000.'"[24] Didn't Jesus suggest that we get the log out of our own eye before we try to remove the speck from our neighbor's eye (Mt 7:1-5)?

If our nation decides on a policy of minimal deterrence we will need the proposed START III process to move us in that direction. Perhaps, however, it is time for Nuclear Weapons Elimination Talks (NWET), which would need to move beyond the bilateral approach of START and include all the members, official and de facto, of the nuclear club.

NUCLEAR PROLIFERATION

The nuclear age dawned because of a race, in the midst of World War II, to create an atomic bomb. The United States tested the bomb on July 16, 1945, and used it a few weeks later, on August 6 at Hiroshima and August 9 at Nagasaki, Japan. Shortly thereafter, Japan surrendered.[25]

When the Soviet Union developed its own bomb in 1949, the numerical and technological arms race was off and running. In the arms race, the United States always maintained a creative and technological lead, and the U.S.S.R. effectively played catch-up, mimicking each American advance and even building more and bigger warheads and intercontinental ballistic missiles (ICBM). After the early 1960s, when both superpowers could totally obliterate the other, it became ludicrous to speak of winning the arms race. From that point on, each superpower was simply adding to its overkill capacity and making sure that its nuclear weapons (not its people) could survive a first strike by the other side. Soon, however, the two superpowers, locked into their strategy of mutual nuclear terrorism (deterrence), became concerned about the spread of nuclear weapons to other nations.

Great Britain and France developed their own nuclear weapons and delivery systems to further deter the Soviet Union from attacking Western Europe, to enhance their prestige as major players in the world, and to maintain their independence. China, feeling threatened by its Soviet neighbor and desiring global prestige, developed nuclear weapons. These three nations together have about 1,200 nuclear warheads. With the United States and Russia they constitute the nuclear club, that is, acknowledged nuclear powers. These countries also happen to be the five permanent members of the United Nations Security Council.

> **For reflection**
>
> The controversy over whether the use of the atomic bomb was morally right and historically necessary still rages. Opponents contend that Japan was on the verge of surrendering anyway, and that the bomb was used to prevent the Soviet Union from sharing in the victory in the Pacific. They also question the morality of using an indiscriminate weapon with the intention of killing civilians. Proponents contend that a bloody invasion would have been necessary before Japan would have surrendered, and that the use of the atomic bombs saved tens of thousands of American lives. This controversy was publicly rekindled when the Smithsonian Institute developed a display to commemorate the 50th anniversary of the Hiroshima and Nagasaki attacks in 1995.

Three other countries are thought to be nuclear weapons states. Israel, although it does not officially admit it, has built and stockpiled nuclear weapons. India was the first country to exploit Atoms for Peace—a program which assisted countries in the development of nuclear energy—to develop a nuclear bomb. India's neighbor and nemesis, Pakistan, now has the capability of producing an atomic weapon. None of these three signed the Non-Proliferation Treaty (NPT). At this time, although their nuclear capability is troublesome, all of them are relatively stable democracies.

When the Soviet Union splintered into fifteen independent republics, Ukraine, Kazakhstan, and Belarus became nuclear powers by virtue of having Soviet missiles based in their territories. All three agreed to have these weapons dismantled and removed to Russia, with the aid of Russia and the United States, and this has now been accomplished.[26] Thus, all three countries have disarmed and joined the NPT protocol. This is good news given the historical and current tensions between these "near-abroad" countries and Russia, as well as the continuing ethnic and political turmoil within these states.

Today's nuclear "wannabes," however, present a definite cause for alarm. The aftermath of the Persian Gulf War made it clear that Iraq, despite signing the NPT, was closer to developing a nuclear bomb than most experts had thought. Iraq also has stockpiles of chemical and biological weapons, and it has used chemical weapons in its conflict with Iran and on its own Kurdish minority. Iran has made little secret of its desire to develop a nuclear weapon. Syria, Libya, and Algeria are also known to be envious of nuclear capability. All of these five Middle Eastern or North African states could be considered "loose cannons" ruled by ruthless, power-hungry tyrants. The thought of Iraq's Saddam Hussein, or Syria's Hafez al-Assad, or Libya's Muammar al-Qaddafi with his finger on the nuclear button is terrifying indeed. The Middle East is a volatile area that contains multiple fault lines for war: Israel vs. the Palestinians and the Arab countries, Iraq vs. Iran or Kuwait or Saudi Arabia, the Kurdish struggle for independence, tensions between the Sunni and Shiite branches of Islam and with Muslim fundamentalists, various other ethnic and religious tensions, and a gap between the oil-rich minority and the poor majority. Introducing weapons of mass destruction and sophisticated delivery systems such as ballistic missiles and high-tech fighter-bombers into this region is an invitation for trouble and tribulation.

An equally troubling situation is North Korea's attempt to acquire nuclear weapons. North Korea is a deeply impoverished, heavily armed, and totally repressive communist dictatorship that in 1997 faced the possibility of a massive famine. Since 1953, a precarious standoff has existed between North Korea and South Korea, its increasingly democratic and economically prosperous better half. Enmity also exists between North Korea and Japan. These relationships are further complicated by the proximity of China. North Korea's development of nuclear weapons could trigger an Asian nuclear arms race, and radically change the politics of the Far East for the worse. Certainly Japan, South Korea, and Taiwan have the technological capability of rapidly becoming nuclear powers if they so desire. In 1994, the United States declared that it will not allow North Korea to make a nuclear bomb. After strained negotiations, North Korea has agreed to dismantle its nuclear program in exchange for assistance in developing alternative energy sources less amenable to bomb making.[27] This is a shaky agreement, however, that in 1997 awaits full implementation.

It is important to note that there have been some successes in regard to nuclear non-proliferation. South Africa developed, tested, and stockpiled a small number of bombs, then decided to destroy them, and is now nuclear-free. At one time, Argentina and Brazil seemed poised to embark on a nuclear arms race like that between India and Pakistan, but the replacement of their military governments with democracies has eased the tension between the two countries and resulted in the termination of their nuclear weapons programs. Most nations seem comfortable without nuclear weapons, but all are wary of those that do exist and of the countries that possess them.

The spread of nuclear weapons has been curbed primarily by the Nuclear Non-Proliferation Treaty (NPT). This 1968 accord took effect in 1970, and in April 1995 the nations of the world gathered to discuss its future. The NPT binds together the acknowledged nuclear powers with non-nuclear nations. Those without nuclear weapons pledge not to acquire them and to submit to the purview of the International Atomic Energy Agency (IAEA), which monitors their compliance. Nuclear powers agree to share nuclear energy technology with other nations, under the watchful eye of the IAEA, and to take steps toward reversing the arms race, nuclear disarmament, and a treaty on "general and complete disarmament" (Article VI). Israel, India, and Pakistan have not signed the NPT, but nearly all other nations have. Iraq has violated the accord, and Iran seems ready to do so. North Korea momentarily left the accord, as its provisions allow, but is now back in the fold.

At the meeting to renew the NPT on its 25th anniversary, the nuclear powers pushed for its indefinite extension. Some of the non-nuclear nations—notably Mexico, Venezuela, Nigeria, and Indonesia—argued for extending the treaty for fixed periods of time, as in the past. These countries argued that the nuclear powers had not lived up to the nuclear disarmament provisions of the treaty and were unlikely to do so unless they were subjected to continued pressure. The treaty was indefinitely and unconditionally renewed in 1995, but the arguments of the non-nuclear nations retain considerable merit. The NPT regime will only work if there is a genuine consensus of opinion and an effective implementation of its provisions. The nuclear weapons states, in particular, must make good-faith efforts toward the abolition of nuclear weapons. The path toward disarmament is clear; movement down that path has been halting at best.[28]

The first step toward nuclear disarmament is a comprehensive test ban (CBT) on nuclear weapons. In order to win the vote for an indefinite extension of the NPT the nuclear powers agreed early in 1996 to reach an accord banning nuclear testing. The road leading to a CBT accord was full of twists and turns. The United States began quibbling about the definition of a nuclear test, and then France decided to hold its first tests in three years in the fall of 1995.[29] China set off a nuclear test in July 1996, but then agreed to join a CBT accord. This meant that the five official members of the nuclear club had all declared moratoriums on testing, and were ready to support a CBT treaty. India, however, adamantly refused to approve the treaty unless the nuclear powers set a deadline for the total elimination of nuclear weapons. In September 1996, the United Nations overwhelmingly endorsed the CBT treaty as a vehicle to halt all nuclear testing. In order for the treaty to become universal law, however, all forty-four nations possessing nuclear reactors must sign and ratify the treaty. At the time of this writing, India refuses to do so, and Pakistan will not sign unless India does.[30] The end result of this arduous process is a de facto ban on nuclear testing, with the possibility that this moratorium might become international law in a few years.

Other steps toward nuclear disarmament would include a global ban on the production of fissionable materials for use in nuclear weapons and strengthening the IAEA, whose role is expanding beyond the constraints of its limited budget. The United States and Russia should implement START II and also begin discussion of further reductions of their nuclear stockpiles or, even better, enter into multilateral discussions aimed at the elimination of nuclear weapons.

The world is at a turning point regarding nuclear weapons. Humanity can go in three different directions: first, the international community can continue to rely on a reduced nuclear deterrent controlled by today's Great Powers; second, we can witness the spread of nuclear weapons to many more nations, some of which are rogue states; or, third, the international community can create a nuclear-free world. As usual there has been far too little serious public discussion about which direction U.S. leadership should take.

The U.S. foreign policy establishment seems to vacillate on the issue of nuclear weapons, decrying the efforts of others to acquire them, but clinging to our own like a security blanket. But nuclear weapons are more like a grenade than a security blanket. The nuclear Non-Proliferation Treaty clearly commits the nuclear powers to disarm. India has a point when it demands that this commitment be taken seriously and a deadline be set for its implementation. If the United States is a country of integrity that honors the treaties it signs, then the United States has chosen the path of nuclear disarmament. The American Catholic bishops point this out in their 1983 Pastoral Letter, *The Challenge of Peace* (#208). If this were acknowledged with conviction by the President and the State Department, the United States would be moving steadfastly down the path toward a safer world order, one without the fear of a nuclear holocaust shadowing the future. The contours of that path are clear: adherence to the Comprehensive Test Ban treaty, a global freeze on the production of weapons-grade fissionable material, strengthening the IAEA, and dismantling all nuclear weapons and their delivery systems.

In the NPT, the nations of the world have committed themselves to nuclear disarmament. This is a remarkable achievement. It is time to honor that commitment and become a nuclear-free world.

In light of this commitment to nuclear disarmament, a renewed debate about building a missile defense system, similar to President Reagan's Strategic Defense Initiative, called "Star Wars" by the press, makes little sense. The Republican Congress of the mid-1990s and conservative pundits argue that without a system to protect the country from missile attack, the United States is defenseless.[31] These legislators and strategic thinkers are most concerned about being blackmailed by a rogue state that has acquired nuclear weapons. But since countries such as Iraq, Iran, and Libya do not have intercontinental ballistic missiles, a missile defense system would protect our missiles from an imaginary threat. A more plausible threat, although farfetched, would be a nuclear bomb in a suitcase or a pick-up truck.[32] Moreover, a missile defense system is technologically very complex and therefore intrinsically unreliable, yet extremely expensive, estimates are around $60 billion. In building a missile defense system, the United States would be violating the Anti-Ballistic Missile Treaty (ABM) of 1972, which prohibited such systems and prevented both the Soviet Union and the United States from pursuing that very expensive direction in the arms race during the Cold War. It would seem folly to reopen this door in the post-Cold War period. Nuclear disarmament would be a much surer path to security than throwing money at a Star Wars fantasy.[33]

CHEMICAL AND BIOLOGICAL WEAPONS AND LAND MINES

Although nuclear weapons are the most destructive, chemical and biological weapons share many of the same characteristics: they are indiscriminate and can cause the horror of mass death, they are difficult to control, they are prone to proliferation, and they are problematic to destroy.

Chemical weapons release chemicals, such as nerve gas or tear gas, that kill or disable people. They have been called the "poor country's atom bomb" because they represent an inexpensive way for a country to acquire weapons of mass destruction for potential leverage in international conflicts. Protective clothing and gas masks can often defend against a chemical threat. Chemical weapons are intrinsically indiscriminate, and they have sometimes been intentionally used to massacre civilians—as in the gas chambers of the concentration camps during the Holocaust, and against Iraqi Kurds in 1988.

Chemical weapons have only rarely been used in warfare. The results of their use during World War I were so horrible that the use of chemical weapons was banned by the 1925 Geneva Convention. It seems that only Iraq has clearly violated this prohibition during its war with Iran in the 1980s. In 1992, a new Chemical Weapons Convention was introduced through the United Nations to ban the production and possession of chemical weapons.[34] This Convention, signed by 160 nations and ratified by over 65 of them, went into effect in the Spring of 1997.[35]

The United States, Russia, and China have all signed the accord, but none of them had ratified it at the beginning of 1997. The United States Senate tabled the vote on the treaty in the midst of the 1996 election campaign, even though the Convention had bi-partisan political support and the endorsement of the American chemical industry as well as the Pentagon. Since the Convention mandates severe restrictions on chemical purchases from countries that have not ratified it, procrastination would have cost the United States chemical industry billions of dollars in lost exports.[36] Opponents of the Convention argued that the treaty would be impossible to verify, given the dual use of many chemicals, and that it may even contribute to the proliferation of chemical weapons by allowing freer exports to countries that have ratified it.[37] During the Bush administration congress had already committed the United States to destroying its chemical weapons stockpile by 2004. Thus, even if verification is difficult, it seemed to make sense to put the weight of international law behind the total ban on chemical weapons. In late April of 1997, the deadline for ratification, the U.S. Senate ratified the Chemical Weapons Convention; the Russian parliament, however, pleading poverty, failed to ratify the treaty.[38]

Because many chemicals have both a peaceful use and can also be used in weapons (for example, the bomb set off in Oklahoma City in 1995 was made from chemicals used in the manufacture of fertilizer), it is very difficult to control the proliferation of chemical weapons. For example, U.S. intelligence sources say that Libya is building the world's largest underground chemical weapons plant in a hollowed-out mountain 40 miles from Tripoli. Col. Qaddafi, Libya's tyrannical leader, says this is an irrigation project. In another instance, he claimed a suspected chemical weapons plant was a pharmaceutical installation company.[39] Without on-site inspection, such claims are difficult to refute.

As with nuclear weapons, the dismantling and disposal of chemical weapons has proved to be costly and hazardous. Congress has mandated the destruction of America's 30,000 tons of chemical weapons by 2004. These weapons are stored at eight sites in the United States, and since transporting them is particularly dangerous, it has been decided that they will be incinerated on site. Thus far only one incinerator has been made operational, at Tooele, Utah, where about 40 percent of the United States chemical arsenal is stored in underground igloos. Serious questions have been raised by the facility's dismissed manager and other critics about its safety, and the plant has experienced three emergency shutdowns in its first hundred days of operation. Meanwhile, 30-year-old M-55 rockets containing the deadly poison sarin are corroding and beginning to leak. At this point, it is probably less risky to continue with the incineration than to continue to store the leaky chemical warheads.[40] The program to destroy America's chemical weapons is expected to cost over $12 billion. Again, paralleling the problems associated with nuclear weapons are concerns that Russia's weak economy cannot afford to safely dispose of Moscow's chemical weapons, nor to maintain adequate security around the storage sites.[41] Other countries, especially in the Two-Thirds World, face similar problems.

Biological weapons use micro-organisms or biologically derived toxins instead of chemicals. Some organisms, such as the ebola virus, can cause fatal diseases; others, such as influenza, could be incapacitating. Deadly viruses could cause an epidemic that would be impossible to control, and that might rebound to destroy the nation that used the weapon. To date, biological weapons have not yet been used in warfare. The development, production, and possession of biological weapons are prohibited by the 1972 Biological Weapons Convention, but the treaty makes no provision for inspection or verification. The United States and perhaps a dozen other countries all engage in biological weapons research, which is not banned by the treaty, ostensibly to deter each other from developing such weapons.[42]

Land mines, although they do not threaten mass destruction, have actually claimed more victims than nuclear, chemical, and biological weapons together, and they kill and maim civilians long after the conflict in which they were sown has ended.[43]

In 1997, there are perhaps 110 million mines buried in 64 countries around the world, and they kill or maim about 30,000 people, mostly civilians, each year. A new mine costs as little as $3, but uprooting a mine can cost between $200 and $1000, and an arm, a leg, or a life. Only about 100,000 mines are removed each year, but as many as 50 are sown for each one removed.[44] The heaviest concentrations of mines are in poor countries such as Egypt, Angola, Cambodia, the former Yugoslavia, Mozambique, Somalia, and Sudan.[45] In Cambodia, a country of 8 million people, there are an estimated 10 million mines, rendering about 20 percent of fertile land uncultivated. Approximately one out of every 20 Cambodians is an amputee, the highest rate in the world.[46]

The civilian casualties caused by mines are a strong argument for their condemnation, but mines can serve a defensive military purpose. Bernard E. Trainor, a retired Marine lieutenant general and director of the national security program at Harvard's Kennedy School of Government, conveys the ambiguity of land mines in recounting his experience in the Korean War. As his platoon was taking Hill 59 from Chinese communist forces, Trainor tripped on a wire. "I heard a 'thip' as it activated a mine, and I steeled myself for the explosion that would rip off my legs. Nothing happened. The mine had failed to function." Two nights later, when the enemy forces tried to recapture the hill, the mines his platoon had planted to protect their position saved them from being overrun. Trainor thinks that trying to outlaw mines would be futile and unverifiable, and, since mines can protect American troops in certain circumstances, perhaps immoral.[47] He and others favor the use of sophisticated, so-called "smart," mines that automatically deactivate after a few months, along with restrictions on the sale of mines. Other American military officers, however, including General Norman Schwarzkopf, the commander of the war against Iraq, and General David Jones, a former chair of the Joint Chiefs of Staff, argue that antipersonnel land mines are not essential in modern warfare and ought to be banned.[48]

An international conference in the spring of 1996 produced an agreement that called for curtailing the use of mines and for moving toward making them more detectable and self-deactivating. Those who had been campaigning for a ban on land mines found this pact weak and inadequate.[49] In November, the United States introduced a nonbinding resolution at the United Nations to ban the use, stockpiling, production and transfer of antipersonnel land mines. This resolution was also weak, and it went well beyond current U.S. practice.[50]

The Clinton administration seems to want to exercise some leadership on this issue but, at the same time, does not want to tie its own hands on the use of land mines. For example, every official U.S. statement allows an exception on any ban for the demilitarized zone in Korea. But other nations will have their own exceptions, which will undermine the meaning of a ban on land mines. The United States cannot have it both ways. Concern for discriminate warfare and civilian casualties should motivate the United States to stop using or producing antipersonnel mines, and to destroy its stockpile of these weapons. Only then will other nations take seriously U.S. statements on banning land mines.

FUEL TO THE FIRE: THE TRADE IN CONVENTIONAL ARMS

The end of the Cold War has barely slowed the traffic in conventional arms. Few would argue that weapons in themselves start wars. While the arms trade is not the match that ignites conflict, the proliferation of weapons adds fuel to the fire.[51]

The availability of armaments can encourage potential belligerents to rely on a military rather than a political solution to their dispute. And once combat has begun, the influx of weapons tends to prolong the dispute and magnify it. One thinks of the almost total destruction of Grozny, the capital of Chechnya, in the early months of 1995, or the annihilation in Bosnia since 1992. (Rwanda teaches us, however, that, while artillery may be necessary to destroy buildings, simple machetes and small arms are sufficient for slaughtering hundreds of thousands of human beings.)

Arms transfers have also contributed to escalating a war. The acquisition of missiles, for example, enabled both Iran and Iraq to engage in a variety of escalatory moves during their conflict (1980–88), such as bombing each other's ports and cities. Both sides used chemical weapons. What if one or both had possessed nuclear weapons?

The proliferation of conventional arms, therefore, leads to more, longer, and worse wars.[52] Adding fuel to the fire of international conflict is hardly conducive to a more peaceful world order. The arms trade, however, is very profitable, and thus the weapons industries and their governments have a vested interest in its continuation. A rudimentary understanding of the mechanics and motivation for the arms trade is essential for deciding whether and how to curtail it.

Global arms sales average $40 to $50 billion a year. For decades the Soviet Union exported the most weapons (usually accounting for about 40 percent of the world market), while the United States was second, with about a 20 percent share of the sales.[53] In 1991, however, with the decline of the Russian economy and with the display of the technological superiority of U.S. weapons in the Gulf War, the United States raced past Russia to become the world's premier arms exporter, controlling over 60 percent of the global market in arms exports by 1994.[54] The five permanent members of the U.N. Security Council supply 75 percent of all arms sold.[55]

These first-tier merchants are full service suppliers. A second-tier of sellers tend to specialize in certain types of weapons and carve out a market niche for themselves. They include other countries in Europe, such as the Netherlands, and some of the newly industrialized nations, including Singapore, South Korea, Israel, Brazil, and China, which has a reputation for a willingness to sell anything to anyone.[56]

Given both the free market and the black market, it is not unusual to find American weapons on both sides of a particular war. In the decade 1985–1995, the United States supplied more than $42 billion worth of weapons to parties involved in 45 of the 50 global conflicts. Among the recipients were Turkey, Somalia, Liberia, Zaire, Pakistan, Indonesia, Haiti, Guatemala, Colombia, Mexico, and the Philippines. Often American-made weapons have been used to slaughter poor peasants who have rebelled against repressive regimes. Ironically, U.S. fighter planes, stationed in Turkey, protect Kurds in northern Iraq, while American-financed fighter planes sold to Turkey are used to bomb Kurdish villages in Turkey.[57]

The threat of American-made weapons being turned against U.S. troops is known as the "boomerang effect" or "blow-back" in military jargon. "In virtually every conflict into which the United States has sent troops since the 1989 collapse of the Soviet Union—Panama, Haiti, Somalia, Iraq and, to a limited extent, Bosnia—American forces have faced American-made weapons."[58]

Traffic in conventional weapons steals from the poor even more directly than the nuclear arms race. Those countries that can least afford it are buying bombs when their people need bread. In the 1980s the developing countries consumed about three-quarters of the arms traded in a given year, but the market for arms in the developing world has shrunk from $61 billion in 1988 to $15.4 billion in 1995.[59] The largest market for weapons is the Middle East. With about 3.5 percent of the world's population, this area purchases about 33 percent of the arms traded in a given year. For consumers of weapons a combination of means and motive is key, and the oil-rich countries of the Middle East have both.[60] In 1995 Russia regained the position as the largest arms seller to the developing world, and Russia's best customer was China, which had received no arms from America since the Tiananmen Square massacre in 1989.[61]

Selling Weapons

The motives for arms transfer involve a push (supply) and a pull (purchase). Suppliers push weapons for political and economic reasons. Suppliers want to arm their allies, or to create friends through the transfer of weapons. But it is largely the profit motive that inhibits the restraint that the politics of the post-Cold War period would seem to warrant. The United States suffers from a serious trade deficit that would be much worse without its arms sales. Thus the U.S. government, under Presidents Bush and Clinton, has vigorously supported the United States arms industry through easing restrictions and fees on foreign weapons purchases, financially assisting friendly nations in buying American armaments, and aiding the U.S. defense industry in research and development.[62] For Russia, the sale of weapons is one of its few sources of hard currency, and indeed one of the few products it can export.

The military-industrial complex in both superpowers, facing declining government purchases of their wares in the post-Cold War environment, turned their attention to increasing their share of the global market. The arms industry in the United States has elicited government support for selling its weapons to the world market by arguing that American jobs depend on their success. Ironically, the global success of the American arms industry has been accompanied by deep cuts in its workforce due to government-subsidized mergers within the industry, and arms agreements abroad (known as "offsets") which transfer production and jobs, along with weapons, to buying countries. "The defense industry has lost more than a million jobs since 1989, according to Department of Defense statistics. And 700,000 more jobs are expected to be gone by 1997."[63] At the same time the highest paid CEO in the defense industry, James Mellor of General Dynamics, which cut over 35,000 jobs from 1990–1995, made $11.3 million in 1994.[64] Still, arms manufacturers contend that even more jobs would have been lost if they were not exporting arms to the world.

The Bush administration tried to lobby the five permanent members of the U.N. Security Council to join a system of multilateral controls on the arms market after the Persian Gulf War (1991). The system broke down after the United States announced billions of dollars of sales to Israel, Kuwait, Saudi Arabia, Turkey, and Taiwan—contrary to the agreed-upon regime.[65] This in spite of the reality that the arming of Iraq, mostly by Russia and Western Europe, was an important ingredient in Iraq's invasion of Kuwait, which resulted in the Persian Gulf War. Arms sales are a clear case of profit eclipsing prudence.

Buying Weapons

Buyers purchase armaments for security and symbolic reasons. Some nations have neighbors or other enemies against which they need to defend themselves. The repressive governments of many countries need to defend themselves against their own people. High-tech weapons can function as symbols of power, pride, and modernity for developing countries.

There can be irony in the convergence of these two purposes for procuring weapons. The Shah of Iran, for example, developed a very sophisticated air force by purchasing top-grade American planes in the early 1970s. But these were of little use when his own people rebelled against him. He could not bomb his own capital. The fighter-bombers were put to use, however, by the Islamic fundamentalists, who ousted the Shah, in defending Iran against an opportunistic attack from Saddam Hussein's Iraq.[66]

Both profits and politics make the arms trade very difficult to control. Since the United States is now the world's top arms exporter, it is logical to expect American leadership in developing a policy to control the arms trade.

The four components of an arms control regime are relatively clear. The first is *transparency*. The nations of the world need to declare and account for their arms imports and exports, probably through the United Nations. Records need to be kept in order to understand the dynamics of the arms trade and to curtail the black market in weapons. Second, there need to be *supply-side restraints*. Although high-minded and principled, it is bad business for a country to refuse to sell arms when other nations are eagerly in line to do so. Rather than try to cut off sales "cold turkey," it is probably more realistic to set incremental goals toward the objective of disarmament. For example, a ceiling on volume could be set based on current percentage of the market. Certain types of high-tech weapons could be banned from trade. Third, *economic conversion* is essential. Unless the military-industrial complex is converted to serve civilian markets, suppliers will not be restrained, and politicians will continually be faced with the unhappy prospect of the loss of domestic jobs when efforts are made to reduce the arms trade. Finally, *regional arms control agreements* can begin to restrain recipients from filling their perceived need for more arms.[67]

Obviously such an arms control regime will need to be connected to a broader effort toward building common security, preventing and resolving conflict, recognizing human rights, diminishing poverty, and promoting democracy. Putting out fires and preventing them are at least as important as cutting off the fuel.

U.S. DEFENSE SPENDING: WHAT HAPPENED TO THE PEACE DIVIDEND?

The Reagan administration (1980–88) dramatically increased U.S. military spending in order to counter the perceived threat of the Soviet "evil empire." Some analysts argue that the Soviet Union was not able to match the American spending spree, and that Reagan's strategy was in part responsible for ending the Cold War. Whether or not that is true, the deficit spending required by huge military budgets and simultaneous tax cuts was responsible for turning the United States debt (over $4 trillion in 1997) into the world's largest. Thus, many people expected that the demise of the Soviet empire would yield a large "peace dividend" by dramatically reducing military spending.

U.S. defense spending did, in fact, decrease through both the Bush and the first Clinton administrations, and it is projected to continue a gradual decline, dropping about 10 percent in inflation-adjusted dollars from 1996 to 2002. The Defense Department budget called for $263 billion in fiscal year 1995, $265 billion in 1996, and $256.6 billion in 1997. This represents about 3.6 percent of the gross domestic product (GDP), a significant decrease from the 6.3 percent of GDP in 1986, the peak of the Reagan build-up. Since 1990, the number of personnel in uniform has declined by about 25 percent.[68] In 1996, military spending—which includes the Defense Department budget plus other related military costs such as military retirement, veterans' benefits, and military-related interest on the national debt—represented 26.5 percent of the total federal budget, and 39.6 percent of income tax dollars (the federal budget minus mandatory social security deductions).[69]

In inflation-adjusted dollars, defense spending has gradually decreased from its peak peacetime years under Reagan, and is now holding steady at about the same amount as the average peacetime budgets during the Cold War.[70] In other words, there has been no peace dividend. The United States continues to spend about as much for defense now as it did during the Cold War.

When U.S. spending is compared to that of competing nations, it becomes clear that the United States is spending a disproportionate amount on defense. In 1995, the United States Defense Department budget was $263 billion. That was roughly equal to the amount spent by the next six nations combined: Russia spent about $80 billion, Japan $54 billion, France $40 billion, United Kingdom $35 billion, Germany $34 billion, and China $29 billion on defense (see Figure 6.1). Rogue states that might oppose the United States, such as Iran, Iraq, Libya, Syria, North Korea, and Cuba, spent $15 billion combined.[71]

Figure 6.1
United States Military Budget Compared to Next Eight Countries
1995 military budgets in billions of dollars

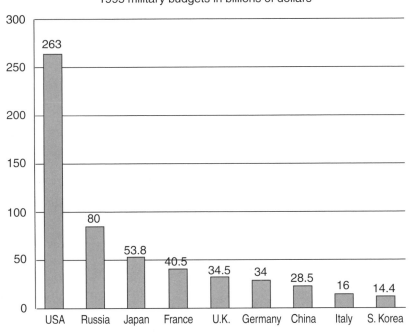

U.S. spending is roughly equal to that of the next six nations combined.

Source: military budget figures from *The Military Balance 1995/96*, published by The International Institute for Strategic Studies (IISS). IISS 1995 military budget totals used in most cases. Military expenditures listed when military budget appears to understate spending. Charles M. Sennott "Armed for Profit," *Boston Globe*, February 11, 1996, section B. Prepared by Council for a Livable World Education Fund, February 1996 and revised by author.

As with the arms trade, the military-industrial complex justifies defense spending in part by arguing that cuts will jeopardize jobs. We have already seen that the arms industry is radically downsizing despite high defense

Table 6.1
America's Political/Economic Choices

$114 billion =	650 new F-22 fighters the Air Force is asking for	or	modernization and expansion of all U.S. mass-transit systems
$100 billion =	Trident II submarine and F-18 jet fighter programs	or	cleaning up the 3,000 worst hazardous U.S. Waste Dumps
$25 billion =	a fleet of C-17 jet cargo planes	or	rehabilitation for more than 1 million public housing units
$4.9 billion =	the ATACM and Hellfire Missile programs	or	funding to allow all eligible children to enter the Head Start program
$3.7 billion =	the Tow-2 missile program	or	funding to extend Medicare to an additional 4 million adults and 2 million children
$2.9 billion =	extra funding recommended by the Senate Appropriations Subcommittee on Defense for two Seawolf submarines	or	subway lines for three U.S. cities
$2 billion =	a single B-2 bomber	or	400 new elementary schools
$2 billion =	annual operating cost of one of the army's heavy-tank divisions	or	textbooks for 16 million students
$1.66 billion =	39 F-15E fighter bomber aircraft	or	funding to extend the WIC program to cover all eligible women, infants, and children
$1.4 billion =	1 Trident submarine	or	global 5-year child immunization programs against six diseases, preventing 1 million deaths a year
$942 million =	973 Patriot missiles	or	cost of providing medical/social services to AIDS patients to reduce hospital stays and increase life expectancy
$940 million =	80 Apache Attack helicopters	or	Pell grants to all eligible college students
$479 million =	28 F-16 fighter aircraft	or	40,000 new teachers for U.S. schools
$263 million =	14 AV-8B Harriers Ground Attack aircraft	or	amount needed by states to meet the EPA's Safe Drinking Water Act standards
$224 million =	136 Tomahawk cruise missiles	or	a domestic program to encourage solar energy development and home energy conservation
$12 million =	1 nuclear weapon test	or	80,000 hand pumps to give Third World villages safe water

Sources: Department of Defense, *Selected Acquisitions Report*, 1990; and *Program Acquisition Cost by Weapon System, FY 1990–91*; Congressional Budget Office, *Selected Weapons Cost*, 1989; Employment Research Association, *Converting the American Economy*, 1991; S. Kufson and J. Yang, "Congress Set to Tackle Issue of War's Cost," *Washington Post*, January 24, 1991; D. Evans, "How the 'Pentagon Tax' Is Bleeding America's Cities," *Chicago Tribune*, May 8, 1992; R. Sivard, *World Military and Social Expenditures* (World Priorities, 1988); Fund for Renewable Energy and the Environment, *State of the States*, 1987. (From Seymour Melman, "Book Review of *World Military and Social Expenditures, Annual, 1974–1991* by Ruth L. Sivard," in *Peace & Change* 18 [January, 1993], pp. 86–87)

spending and healthy arms sales. Furthermore, while it is true that decreases in defense spending will cost jobs in the short run, it will have a long term economic benefit. This is so because military spending produces goods that have little economic benefit. (Tanks and submarines drain the economy rather than contribute to it, like trucks and fishing boats do.) And it is so because military spending creates fewer jobs per dollar than does civilian spending, either public or private. (Teachers, social workers, nurses, and construction workers make less on average than do defense workers who weld submarines or program guided missile systems, and defense work tends to be less labor intensive than most civilian employment.)[72]

If the United States is the world's lone remaining military superpower, and if there is no country that seriously threatens the United States in the foreseeable future, and if military spending actually hurts the economy in the long run, why then is there no peace dividend? As the Republican Congress and the Clinton administration endeavor to cut government spending, reduce the annual deficit, and balance the federal budget in 1997, why is defense spending regarded as sacrosanct and untouchable? It seems that a serious national effort focused on economic conversion and drastic reductions in defense spending to reasonable and strategically justifiable levels would immensely strengthen the American economy. And it may be that a healthy economy will be the real measure of a superpower in the twenty-first century (see Table 6.1).

STUDY QUESTIONS

1. Should you fear that nuclear weapons will be used in the contemporary world?
2. Should the international community be working toward the goal of minimal deterrence or total nuclear disarmament?
3. If it became clear that, for example, North Korea or Iraq were building a nuclear bomb, would the world community be justified in undertaking a military intervention to prevent this? Would unilateral U.S. intervention be justified?
4. Some pundits (George Will, for example) think the Chemical and Biological Convention ratified by the U.S. Senate in 1997 is a bad idea. What are the arguments pro and con? What do you think?
5. Should land mines be banned?
6. Who benefits from the trade in conventional weapons? Whom does such trade harm? What should be done about it?
7. Does the United States spend too much on defense? How would you prioritize the needs and budget allocations if you were the U.S. president?

CHAPTER SEVEN

Peace and Security in the Post-Cold War World

"In days to come the mountain of the Lord's house shall be established as the highest of the mountains, and shall be raised above the hills; all the nations shall stream to it.

Many peoples shall come and say, 'Come let us go up to the mountain of the Lord, to the house of the God of Jacob; that he may teach us his ways and that we may walk in his paths.'

For out of Zion shall go forth instruction, and the word of the Lord from Jerusalem.

He shall judge between the nations, and shall arbitrate for many peoples; they shall beat their swords into plowshares, and their spears into pruning hooks; nation shall not lift up sword against nation, neither shall they learn war anymore." (Isaiah 2:2-4)

"Building peace, combating poverty and despair, and protecting freedom and human rights are not only moral imperatives, but also wise national priorities. They can shape a world that will be a safer, more secure, and more just home for all of us. Responsible international engagement is based on the conviction that our national interests and the interests of the international community, our common good, and the global common good are intertwined."[1]

During the Cold War (1945–1989) the foreign policy of the United States had a clear focus and philosophical foundation. The doctrine of containment directed foreign policy, that is, to contain the spread of communism. U.S. anti-communism was rooted in the political philosophy called *realpolitik* or realism.

With the collapse of communism in Eastern Europe in 1989 and the disintegration of the Soviet Union in 1991, the policy of containment became irrelevant and useless. The United States had defined itself in opposition to communism, as the antithesis of the Soviet Union, and now there was nothing to oppose, no enemy to stand against. The foreign policy establishment, the State Department, and military planners—men and a few women who had built their careers around anti-communism—suddenly faced a new world that required fresh ideas.[2]

This chapter joins in the search for a new vision or a new template that can give direction to foreign policy in the post-Cold War world.[3] It suggests

that a principled foreign policy that focuses on peacemaking is more adequate than realism in responding to and managing the complexity and chaos
of the interdependent, yet divided, contemporary world.

FROM REALISM TO COMPREHENSIVE SECURITY

The theory of international relations called realism has deep roots in thinkers
such as the ancient Chinese strategist Sun Tzu, the ancient Greek historian
Thucydides, the Renaissance adviser of Italian princes Niccolo Machiavelli,
the seventeenth-century English philosopher Thomas Hobbes, and the nineteenth-century German military strategist Karl von Clausewitz. Realism rose
to dominate political and strategic thinking during the Cold War period in
reaction to the idealism or liberalism of the period between the World Wars.
The policies of appeasement that led to the sobering experience of the Second
World War signaled the failure of liberalism. Twentieth-century exponents
of realism have included the scholar Hans Morgenthau, the scholar-states-
men George Kennan and Henry Kissinger, and the Protestant theologian
Reinhold Niebuhr. The foreign policy establishment—those who developed
international political theory, those who translated theory into policy, and
those who implemented policy through strategic decisions and tactical
deployments—were predominantly practitioners of *realpolitik* during the
Cold War period.[4]

Political realists tend to be pessimistic about human nature and even more
suspect about the behavior of groups. Four propositions can summarize the
realist framework:

1. The sovereign state is the most important actor in world affairs.
2. States rationally pursue their own national self-interest, defined as
   power, in competition with other states.
3. In an international system with no central government (anarchy), a balance of power is a realistic way to ensure a precarious order and stability, and a situation of relative peace.
4. Conflict and war are always possibilities, and a credible military defense
   is essential for the security of the state.

Realists, thus, hold to a Darwinian view of the law of the jungle (rather than
the rule of law) where only the strongest survive and win. National security,
in the realist perspective, is the province of each individual state, pursuing
its own self-interest and power, in competition with other states.[5]

There were many thoughtful critiques of realism during the Cold War, but
realpolitik dominated American foreign policy and global statecraft. Now,
however, critiques of realism, old and new, are gaining currency and influ-
encing policy, as well they should.

A consistent criticism of realism is that it tried to exclude or marginalize
the role of ethics in decisions about foreign policy and national security. In
a realist framework power eclipses all other considerations, including morality,

ideology, culture, and economics. Thus realism is more or less openly Machiavellian. This amounts to an ethics of consequentialist self-interest, that is, national self-interest is the overriding value by which the consequences or results of a policy or choice are evaluated. This is not so much amoral as it is a sort of national egoism. Obviously, a Christian ethic rooted in human dignity and human rights, solidarity and community, justice and equality might not have much in common with a realist foreign policy.[6]

While the ethical shortcomings of realism have long troubled its critics, in the late 1990s realism seems politically inadequate to address the spectrum of issues posed by the post-Cold War world. Realism is narrowly focused on issues of security and power, the military and war. Of the issues covered thus far in this book, weapons and security (chapter 6) would dominate the interest of a realist. "A conceptual framework for the study of international relations that has nothing to say about the challenges of development, of the environment, of refugees, of population growth, or about the new religious and cultural antagonisms, or that reduces these phenomena to traditional interstate confrontations is necessarily incomplete, and therefore inadequate."[7] Realism is too reductionistic, too constricted to handle the complexity and chaos, the interdependence and divisions of the post-Cold War world. Human security depends on factors that go well beyond military strength and political power.[8]

Clearly a new paradigm is needed. Michael Klare and Daniel Thomas reject the "national security" model of realism with its focus on competition among the individual nation-states for power. They propose instead a "world security" framework that recognizes the global interdependence of nation-states and seeks to develop structures and institutions that support cooperation in the interest of human security.[9] Several scholars of international relations have fleshed out this world security paradigm by articulating it in terms of "three Cs": collective security, common security, and comprehensive security.[10]

The concept of *collective security* is most clearly incarnated in the contemporary world by the United Nations. The idea is to bind together all or most of the major actors in an international system for the purpose of jointly opposing aggression by any of them. Collective security goes beyond the solitary security of each state that is the logic of realism. Collective security depends on the members of the alliance keeping their commitments to the group and on agreement among the members as to what constitutes aggression. The U.N.-sponsored rebuff of Iraq's invasion of Kuwait in 1990–1991 is a successful example of collective security in action. The case of Bosnia, however, turned out to be too complex and too costly for collective security to be effective.[11]

Common security moves a conceptual step beyond collective security. Common security is the notion that no country can be secure unless every country, especially one's enemies, is secure. The security of nations is interdependent: actions by one state that threaten the security of another state diminish the security of all, including that of the aggressor. If this concept were to gain more currency, its effect would be to move the world community beyond war and toward structures and institutions designed to facilitate international conflict resolution.

Comprehensive security means that *all* of the perils and problems of our world need to be addressed if humanity is truly to be secure. Comprehensive security enlarges the scope of security concerns to include issues such as the gap between rich and poor, ecological concerns, human rights, ethno-nationalism and minority rights, as well as arms races and power politics. America, for example, clearly has the military strength to defend itself against any foreseeable threat to its borders or its interests, but is vulnerable nonetheless to global warming and ozone depletion, to resource scarcity, to economic collapse, to terrorism, and to internal class divisions. Indeed, all humankind, inhabiting what is really a global village, is vulnerable to a variety of threats to its security and well-being. "Rather than fortifying or defending borders, a successful quest for peace must entail strategies for easing and erasing the rifts in society, by eliminating the causes of dissension or finding ways to peacefully bridge the gap between mutually antagonistic groups."[12] A muscular military will hardly be enough to insure human security in the twenty-first century.

A PRINCIPLED FOREIGN POLICY FOR A JUST WORLD ORDER

A number of analysts of international relations have suggested that "global chaos" may be an apt description of the contemporary world. The editors of *Managing Global Chaos* put it this way: "[This book] argues that there are new forces operating alongside more familiar conflict sources at both the domestic and the international levels, forces that are increasing the potential for conflict at both the intrastate and interstate levels in ways that almost certainly will have long-term, systemic implications."[13] They highlight seven factors that they consider important in producing this new and complex global situation:

1. the proliferation of weak, internally-divided states, so-called "failed states";
2. the growing importance of the politics of identity, that is, ethno-nationalist movements;
3. religious and cultural militancy;
4. the impact of environmental degradation as a result of population pressure on scarce resources and large-scale population movements across borders;
5. the growing contribution of scarce resources, renewable and nonrenewable, to international conflict;
6. the globalization of the world economy; and
7. the destabilizing impact of new military technology on regional security.[14]

Viewed together and alongside traditional causes of conflict, these factors point to a world that is increasingly fragmented and disordered, to global chaos.

Yet these authors are confident that this chaos can be managed. With imaginative leadership and concentrated effort, the global community can move closer to a just world order, which is a foundation for peace. Being a peacemaker and working for justice, however, are particularly challenging when global chaos characterizes the world.

Specialists in international affairs, who are in tune with this vision, suggest a *principled* world policy to guide the Christian vocation for global responsibility, to manage global chaos, and to create a more just world order.

There are at least three reasons to base foreign policy on stated principles. First, a conscious declaration of the principles underlying foreign policy can solidify commitment to acting on those principles and can give national policy consistency and constancy. This would normally be preferable to the apparently spontaneous crisis management style that seems to have characterized U.S. foreign policy since the Cold War. Second, principles can focus foreign policy on its proper constituency—humanity in its entirety, rather than narrow national interests. Third, a principled world policy can yield clear common standards of conduct to which every nation is held accountable. This can enhance a sense of fair play for all in world affairs.[15]

The principles that might direct world policy can be articulated in four "Ds": diplomacy, sustainable development, democratization, and demilitarization.[16]

Diplomacy

The principle of diplomacy means a commitment to *conflict resolution and peacemaking* and to the structures, institutions, and regimes that will promote a peaceful resolution of conflict. The spirit of diplomacy places war in the position of an absolute last resort, and commits the world's nations to negotiate in good faith toward a constructive resolution of disputes and conflicts.

The skills and techniques of conflict resolution are well known, and the subject of much academic reflection.[17] The difficult part is approaching conflict constructively—by letting go of the need to win, and by honestly acknowledging our own faults and selfishness. Then it is possible to seek a creative solution that incorporates the legitimate interests of all of the parties involved. This requires a sensitivity to the other, rather than anger, hatred, and self-righteousness. It demands a sense of the common good and a willingness to dialogue, holding to the justice of one's own cause, but attending to the justice in one's adversary's position as well.

The principle of *reciprocity* is a good foundation for diplomacy. Basically reciprocity refers to the Golden Rule—do unto others as you would have them do unto you (Lk 6:31).[18] Each state should evaluate its own actions by the same standards it holds for the behavior of other nations.[19] Reciprocity can foster the sort of self-critical reflection necessary for constructive conflict resolution. For example, if the United States does not want North Korea to possess nuclear weapons, then it must be willing to dismantle its own nuclear weapons. Otherwise the United States is holding North Korea to a standard it is not willing to heed itself. The nuclear Non-Proliferation Treaty (NPT) realistically requires the members of the nuclear club to disarm, while it prohibits other states from procuring nuclear weapons. The NPT incorporates the principle of reciprocity.

An interdependent world requires *international institutions* and agencies to enhance the world's capacity for multilateral peacemaking. "This means, first of all, improving the United Nations' ability to conduct the many critical tasks it has been saddled with over the past fifty years, including its peacekeeping functions, international mediation services, nonproliferation and disarmament activities, refugee assistance, health protection services, and its work for the advancement of human rights."[20] To be more effective in peacemaking the United Nations will need more financial assistance (the United States is nearly a billion dollars in arrears at the United Nations) as well as administrative and organizational reform. Under the leadership of Secretary General Boutros Boutros-Ghali (1991–1996), the United Nations became less bureaucratic and more efficient, and his successor, Kofi Annan, has made a commitment to move further along this route.

Changes in organization that might make the United Nations more representative and democratic, such as restructuring the make-up of the Security Council and the veto power of the permanent members, might also improve the effectiveness and consistency of the United Nations. At the heart of any organizational reform is the willingness of all nations to accept the legitimate authority of the United Nations and to strengthen its capacity to enforce international law. Secretary General Boutros-Ghali, in his 1992 *Agenda for Peace*, suggested a standby peacekeeping force for rapid deployment to areas of incipient violence. This idea deserves serious consideration.[21]

The virtual deadlock on the Security Council during the Cold War, with the two superpowers routinely vetoing each other's proposals, prevented the United Nations from fulfilling its founding promise of making and keeping peace. In the post-Cold War period, the United Nations has been utilized much more often, but with mixed success. The key to the U.N.'s future success seems to be clarity about its goals and functions and support of its authority by member states.[22]

The principle of *subsidiarity* (rooted in Catholic social thought) suggests the resolution of problems and conflicts at the lowest or most local level possible. Global issues require the attention of a global institution such as the United Nations, but regional disputes and difficulties might best be addressed by *regional organizations*. Therefore, world policy should support regional organizations, such as the Conference on Security and Cooperation in Europe (CSCE), the Organization of American States (OAS), and the Organization of African Unity (OAU), and their peacemaking and development efforts. The United States and others should assist in establishing such bodies where they do not now exist, such as in Asia. *Nongovernmental organizations* (NGOs), such as human rights groups, humanitarian organizations, and religious bodies should also be encouraged in appropriate efforts to resolve conflict, aid victims, and alleviate poverty.[23]

Sustainable Development

Injustice and inequity are fundamental causes of conflict and violence. Chapter 2 documented the disparity between the rich and the poor, between the North and the South. "Today, less than one-fifth of the world's people have more than four-fifths of global wealth, but the poorest billion have less than one-fiftieth." More than half of the earth's food is consumed by rich nations, while every day a half billion people go hungry, and a billion and a half are chronically ill.[24] Poverty stimulates population growth, and pressures people into environmentally destructive behavior, resulting in deforestation, desertification, and resource depletion. These ecological calamities, in turn, force people to migrate in search of food, water, and land (see chapter 3). These social, economic, and environmental burdens contribute to conflict and violence in a descending spiral of suffering.

The principle of sustainable development aims to expand economic opportunity, to achieve a fairer distribution of wealth and power, and to satisfy basic needs without jeopardizing the prospects of future generations.[25] One-third of the global population cannot hope to live in peace and security when two-thirds of the world's people suffer in poverty. No one can be secure unless humanity takes the necessary steps to protect the earth, our home.

Sustainable development also needs to be implemented through structures and institutions developed to abolish poverty and to protect the environment. International institutions such as the World Bank, the International Monetary Fund (IMF), and the General Agreement on Trade and Tariffs (GATT) need to be reformed to focus more on reducing debt and promoting equitable development. Robert Johansen suggests a development fund, supported by a progressive tax on the nations of the world, with the goal of abolishing extreme poverty in twenty-five years. Johansen also proposes an Environmental Council within the United Nations to better coordinate global efforts and regimes aimed at managing climate change, ozone depletion, and other global environmental issues.[26] Nongovernmental institutions will continue to play a key role in sustainable development and will need the support of states and their citizens.

Democratization

Participation in the state (civic) and in society (economic and cultural) is key to human dignity and human rights. The principle of democratization, which aims at increasing every government's and every society's accountability to its people, enhances civic and social participation.

This principle embraces a strong commitment to securing and defending a wholistic conception of *human rights*. If minority peoples and oppressed people can truly participate in government and society, their grievances are much more likely to be addressed without violence and strife. World policy aimed at implementing human rights treaties and strengthening human rights institutions will contribute to global peace and security.[27]

It has been observed that established democracies have fought no wars against each other in the twentieth century.[28] Democratization, then, would seem to enhance security and peace. About half of the world's nations (91 of 183) can be described as democracies, and some thirty-five others are in some stage of transition toward democracy. World policy should support and promote progress toward democracy wherever it can, without the contradiction of imposing or forcing democracy on a nation. This is especially crucial in the formerly communist countries of Eastern Europe and the former Soviet Union. In general, it seems that economic development is a key factor in the stabilization of blossoming democracies.[29] The United Nations and regional organizations can also offer support such as election monitoring and technical assistance.[30]

Demilitarization

The principle of demilitarization includes, but also transcends, the idea of disarmament. It means reducing the role of military power in international relations. "Demilitarization aims at dismantling national and international military culture and replacing it with a culture of legal obligation and nonlethal forms of dispute settlement."[31] In a sense, weapons are the tip of the iceberg in the militarization of global culture.

Demilitarization includes many of the topics addressed in the previous chapter. Nuclear disarmament is essential if the world is to be weaned from its reliance on "gods of metal." Controls on other weapons of mass destruction, such as chemical and biological weapons, and on weapons that destroy the masses one at a time, such as land mines, are also urgent.

Demilitarization requires the global community to drastically curb the international traffic in conventional armaments. While weapons seldom cause war, they contribute to the initiation and escalation of wars. Despite the dangers of a proliferating traffic in weapons, the United States and the other permanent members of the United Nations Security Council continue to sell arms, and to reap scandalous profits. "However expedient in the short term, American arms sales are contributing to a global glut in military hardware and facilitating the efforts of future belligerents to gear up for war. It is essential, therefore, that the United States work with other arms suppliers to establish new multilateral restraints on the weapons trade."[32] The world community is in need of gun control if it is to have security and peace.

The size and configuration of the U.S. military and the amount the United States spends on defense should depend on the goals and strategies of U.S. foreign policy. During the Cold War, the doctrine of containment and an anticommunist foreign policy were used to justify spending large amounts on defense. Michael Klare suggests that the Pentagon has substituted a "rogue doctrine" for the doctrine of containment in order to keep United States military spending and military preparation at Cold War levels.[33] The new doctrine contends that so-called rogue states yearning to become regional powers, such as Iran, Iraq, Syria, and Libya, are threats comparable to that

Figure 7.1
United States Military Budget vs. Potential Enemies
1995 military budgets in billions of dollars

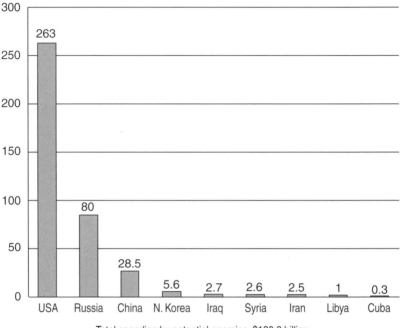

Total spending by potential enemies: $120.2 billion

Source: military budget figures from *The Military Balance 1995/96,* published by The International Institute for
Strategic Studies (IISS). IISS 1995 military budget totals used in most cases. Military expenditures listed when military
budget appears to understate spending. Charles M. Sennott "Armed for Profit," *Boston Globe,* February 11, 1996, section B.
Prepared by Council for a Livable World Education Fund, February 1996 and revised by author.

of the Soviet Union during the Cold War. Each of these rogue states has developed a military capable of fulfilling the dream of being a regional hegemon. In response, U.S. defense strategy calls for a military force capable of fighting two major regional wars simultaneously. The result is defense spending at levels similar to peacetime years during the Cold War, a strong military establishment, and a powerful military presence in American life.

Klare's careful analysis concludes that the strategy that demands a military ability to fight two major regional conflicts at the same time is wrongheaded, unrealistic, and profligate (see Figure 7.1). He calls for a reconfiguration of defense doctrine to conform to the realities of the post-Cold War world.

Because the greatest threat the United States faces today arises from the worldwide proliferation of local conflicts and their potential escalation into regional conflagrations, it is essential that military strategy—like all other components of national policy—be focused on efforts to prevent, contain, abate, and terminate violent conflicts. In essence, this means developing a military trained and equipped for a wide variety of peacemaking and crisis control activities—including multilateral peace-keeping operations, enforcement of U.N. arms embargoes, and humanitarian aid and rescue—in addition to traditional military activities.[34]

The implications of this re-focused defense strategy would be a leaner and more mobile military that is trained and equipped for peacekeeping and crisis intervention, zealous efforts at nuclear disarmament and curbing the global arms trade, and significantly reduced military spending. The latter can free funds for the reconstruction of the domestic educational and industrial infrastructures, and for sustainable development and peacemaking efforts. A sensible and realistic military strategy can produce a peace dividend.

The function of the military in the post-Cold War world should also change. Humanitarian intervention and peacekeeping require military skills that are more like those of police or even social workers. This requires different education, training, and equipment. Perhaps this function could even be separated from the traditional defense role with more clearly-defined types of forces.[35]

The United States Army School of the Americas (SOA) at Fort Benning, Georgia, stands as a symbol of the ill effects of militarization. It was established in 1946 at the U.S. base in Panama and moved to Fort Benning in 1984. The SOA's ostensible purpose was developing ties with Latin American militaries to educate them in the virtues of democracy and civilian control over the military. Instead, it trained them in counter-insurgency warfare, recommending torture, extortion, censorship, false arrest, execution, and "neutralizing" of enemies. Among its nearly 60,000 graduates were some of Latin America's most notorious strongmen, including Panama's drug-dealing dictator, Manuel Noriega, and Roberto D'Aubuisson, a leader of El Salvador's death squads. Other alumni included the military officers who did the bidding of such leaders—the Salvadoran officers linked to the rape and murder of four U.S. missionaries and to the slaughter of six Jesuit priests, six Peruvian officers involved in killing nine students and a college professor, and the Guatemalan colonel who covered up the murder of an American innkeeper and condoned the killing of a captive revolutionary married to an

> **For Reflection**
>
> During the Cold War, U.S. foreign policy was clear. The Soviet Union was the enemy, and the policy was to contain the spread of communism. Since the end of the Cold War, the United States has been searching for a new foreign policy and an appropriate defense strategy. If you were the Secretary of State, what would you propose as the key themes for a renewed U.S. foreign policy? Which states, if any, do you think are potential foes: rogue states? Russia? China? a re-united Germany? Japan? What is the relative importance of military and economic strength in the twenty-first century? How much should the United States spend on defense? What sort of military does the U.S. need?

American lawyer.[36] The values being taught to Latin American military personnel at the School of the Americas are hardly "liberty and justice for all." Many people, including Representative Joseph P. Kennedy II and actress Susan Sarandon, feel the school, which they see as anachronistic and injurious, should be closed, and that the values and techniques it teaches should be expunged from the American military.

Disarmament and economic conversion are essential aspects of demilitarization, but they are not sufficient. Because war and the military pervade so much of our contemporary thinking and culture, this influence needs to be critically examined and changed. During the Cold War, for example, colleges and universities became sites for military research, and for training military officers through the Reserve Officers' Training Corp (ROTC) program. Whether military training and research should continue to be an integral part of higher education in this country is an important question. Violent metaphors or sayings, such as "killing two birds with one stone," or being "blown away," permeate our language and influence our thinking. Violence is pervasive in the media, numbing its viewers to human suffering and death. Military training is steeped in extreme machismo which, in turn, has reinforced sexism in society, thereby making the integration of women into the armed forces more difficult.

The demilitarization of American and world culture will require a deep transformation. However, such a conversion will be an important step toward a more secure and peaceful world.

These four principles—diplomacy, sustainable development, democratization, and demilitarization—could be the cornerstones of a United States foreign policy, and of a world policy that could move the global community toward a just world order. Realism's balance of power is subject to shifts and disequilibrium. A just world order, based on a principled international policy, seems a surer foundation for security and peace.

IS HUMANITARIAN INTERVENTION JUSTIFIED?

One of the most vexing questions for foreign policy in the post-Cold War world is whether and when military intervention on behalf of human rights might be justified. Humanitarian intervention can be defined as "the forceful, direct intervention by one or more states or international organizations in the internal affairs of other states for essentially humanitarian purposes."[37]

There is nothing new about intervention, but the post-Cold War context poses the question in a fresh way. Both superpowers indulged in interventions during the Cold War—in Korea, Vietnam, Afghanistan, Central America, and the Caribbean, for example—but for reasons of power politics and national self-interest. In terms of justice, democracy, and peace, most of the Cold War interventions, in hindsight, turned out badly.

Today, tensions such as ethnic conflict, chaos and anarchy in states where the government appears to have failed, the proliferation of weapons of mass destruction, and gross violations of human rights, raise the question of intervention on behalf of human life and human rights, rather than for purposes of national self-interest. This question has caused some interesting switches in ethical and political positions among pundits and scholars. Some who were "doves" during the Cold War, that is, who were vocal critics of U.S. intervention, now advocate humanitarian intervention; some Cold War "hawks" have now taken a much more isolationist position; and sometimes Cold War adversaries now find themselves taking the same position regarding a particular intervention.

The principles of the *sovereignty* of states and, therefore, of *nonintervention* in the internal affairs of a sovereign state stand against the right or the duty to intervene on behalf of human rights. Sovereignty and nonintervention have imposed some semblance of order upon an international system with no central government.[38] Sovereign states resent interference in their internal affairs. (How would Americans have reacted if China or France had sent troops to protect civil rights protesters on their march from Selma to Montgomery in 1965?) Such intervention could easily result in escalating regional wars.

A second reason against intervention is the tendency of states to rationalize national self-interest under a cloak of humanitarian rhetoric.[39] Colonial powers always thought of themselves as benevolent, bringing a "higher civilization" to primitive peoples, while in fact taking their land, wealth, and resources. Although the United Nations authorized the U.S.-led intervention in Haiti in 1994, the Organization of American States did not approve because of well-founded suspicions of previous U.S. interventions in Latin America.[40]

A third set of concerns about intervention has to do with the difficulty of developing a policy that is clear and consistent, rather than arbitrary and selective. What violations of human rights would justify intervention? Who would authorize it? What would be the feasible goals of humanitarian intervention? Would short-term actions create worse long-term problems?[41]

Arrayed against these reasons for nonintervention are the horrors of genocide in Rwanda, ethnic cleansing in Bosnia, famine caused by the collapse of the state in Somalia, repression by military rulers in Haiti, and pogroms against the Kurds in Iraq and Turkey. Such human suffering cries out to the conscience of the international community.

Christian ethics can be helpful in working through this foreign policy dilemma. First of all, Christian ethics would contend that the sovereignty of the state is a real, but relative value (see chapter 5). State sovereignty is conditioned from below by human rights and from above by the international common good. Thus, when states grievously abuse the human rights of their citizens, they cannot use sovereignty to silence the concern of others.[42] Neither sovereignty nor nonintervention are absolute principles, although both carry real moral weight. The challenge, then, is to develop clear criteria for justified military intervention into the internal affairs of states.

The Christian tradition offers two perspectives on war and military intervention—nonviolence (or pacifism), and just war—although it has long been dominated by the just-war position.[43]

Christians and others who adhere to nonviolence have been perplexed by the question of military intervention for humanitarian purposes. Pacifists oppose warfare in principle. During the Cold War, with every conflict a possible spark for a nuclear holocaust and with power politics the primary purpose of military interventions, Christian pacifists passionately resisted America's military excursions abroad. But humanitarian interventions in the post-Cold War world often are motivated by efforts to remedy injustice and alleviate human suffering. When these cherished values are genuinely the purpose of intervention, and when the violence of the armed intervention is expected to be minimal, can a pacifist condone it?

Many pacifists have been able to justify humanitarian interventions, such as those in Somalia, Haiti, and Bosnia, under the rubric of police actions rather than warfare. Most pacifists are not opposed to all uses of force (although some are), and see the threat of force, or the limited use of force in these cases as justified by the greater human good that can be accomplished. It is analogous to the force used by the police to protect the community from violent criminals.[44] Although it is true that there is a real difference between humanitarian armed intervention and aggressive warfare, the willingness to use violence will continue to trouble pacifists. Once violence is justified, one has inevitably crossed the line into just-war thinking.

The criteria developed by the just-war tradition can offer a framework for justifying humanitarian intervention. The transition from nonviolence to justified force yields the first point in a revised ethic of intervention: military intervention should be a *last resort*. The just-war tradition has always maintained that war is evil, a rule-governed exception to the presumption in favor of peace. Preventative efforts and nonviolent remedies should be applied before force is justified.[45] Economic sanctions can be effective and should be considered, although these too are fraught with ethical problems. The economic sanctions applied against Haiti, for example, seemed to cause the most suffering among poor children, while the wealthy ruling elite escaped their sting. The last resort criterion also gives the necessary weight to the principles of sovereignty and nonintervention. "Because of the diversity of states and the dangers of rationalization, the wisdom of Westphalia [regarding respect for the sovereignty of states] should be heeded. Intervention may be necessary, but it should not be made easy."[46] The burden of proof should always rest on those who are in favor of military intervention.

It is the *just-cause* criterion that makes humanitarian intervention tempting. Everyone agrees that genocide merits an exception to the nonintervention principle, but how serious and egregious must a violation against human rights be in order to justify intervention? This judgment no doubt looks different from the perspective of the victims than from that of the offenders, or of the potential intervenors. The famine in Somalia, ethnic cleansing in Bosnia, the slaughter of Kurds in Iraq, and the military repression in Haiti all appear to be just causes for intervention. Just cause, while necessary, is not, however, a sufficient criterion for intervention.[47]

The just-war tradition insisted that war must also be declared by a *legitimate authority*, based on the idea that only the state could be allowed to authorize the taking of life. Because of the danger of rationalization on the part of individual states, the decision to intervene should ordinarily be authorized by an international organization such as the United Nations and/or a regional security organization. The decision should be multilateral, not unilateral. Given the power differential among states, this does not guarantee probity in judgment, but it does enhance it through procedural restrictions.[48]

The just-war criteria of *right intention* and *the probability of success* are also important as parts of a framework of ethical analysis regarding humanitarian intervention. These criteria focus attention on clearly defining the political goals of the intervention, and on the feasibility of effective intervention.

There is no such thing as an apolitical military intervention, and it is a dangerous delusion to pretend that political goals can be avoided while only humanitarian aid is offered. It is also cruel to bring a people back from the brink of death, through famine aid, for example, only to have them continue to suffer from government oppression or social chaos. Thus, it may be that for intervention to be truly humanitarian and just, in many cases it will need to go beyond mere aid or even peacekeeping. It may have to engage in constructive nation-building, that is, in reforming or creating the social and political structures necessary for honoring human rights.[49] This means some sort of ongoing assistance in reorganizing government, disarming military or paramilitary forces, establishing safe enclaves, re-establishing civic peace, supporting negotiated settlements of grievances, punishing the perpetrators of genocide or ethnic cleansing, instituting a judicial system, training and equipping an impartial police force, and so on.[50]

Such goals may require a lengthy commitment of personnel and resources. Such an expanded agenda opens the intervenors to the charge of a sort of colonial control over other nations or even of naked imperialism. Yet, to exclude such political goals from intervention is to risk doing more harm than good, or not enough good to really matter. It is perhaps necessary to go a step beyond humanitarian intervention to nation-building.

This, of course, raises the question of feasibility. If armed intervenors must have clearly defined political goals and must be prepared to see the process through to completion, then humanitarian intervention is likely to be rare indeed. By its very nature, humanitarian intervention does not directly serve the national interests of the intervenors. Thus, the intervenors are sending their soldiers into harm's way, and expending talent and treasure for no real direct national benefit. Nor will criminals quickly come to heel, nor chaos easily be corrected where havoc is being wreaked. Nation-building will not always be possible, and it will nearly always be difficult to gain popular support for it. Indeed, popular support for the U.S. interventions in Somalia, Haiti, and Bosnia has been lukewarm or non-existent. Perhaps, however, this is partly due to the lack of a clearly-argued foreign policy on behalf of intervention.[51]

Finally, the just-war tradition requires that the *means be proportionate*, and that the conduct of the intervention should also be just. The principles of noncombatant immunity and of proportionality have traditionally governed the conduct of warfare. Since the Vietnam debacle, U.S. military strategy has maintained that, in an intervention, massive military power should be brought to bear on an enemy for a short, defined period of time in the pursuit of a clearly-defined and limited objective. This strategy seemed to work in the Persian Gulf War, but even there questions of proportionality persist. This hit-and-run strategy poses both moral and political concerns. Massive firepower suggests problems of indiscriminate and/or disproportionate attacks, and quickly withdrawing from the scene precludes the commitment necessary for nation-building activities.[52]

Humanitarian intervention can be ethically justified, although it will need to be decided on a case-by-case basis. The just-war tradition provides a framework for the ethical analysis of situations where military intervention is being considered. A public articulation of this framework, and of the reasons that might justify intervention, could build public support for a foreign policy willing to take risks and pay the costs for a just world order.

This chapter has raised the issue of the vision and direction of American foreign policy in the post-Cold War world. It has suggested that a theory of collective, common, and comprehensive security is more suitable for contemporary international relations than the realism or *realpolitik* that held sway during the Cold War period. It has argued for a principled foreign policy organized around four themes: diplomacy, sustainable development, democracy, and demilitarization. And it has proposed "humanitarian intervention," justified and conditioned by the principles of the just-war tradition, as an ethically appropriate strategy for moving toward a more just and peaceful world order.

STUDY QUESTIONS

1. Discuss realism or *realpolitik*. What are its strengths and weaknesses? Is it an adequate theory of international relations in the post-Cold War world?
2. How would comprehensive security (the three Cs) differ from realism? Which do you think would be better?
3. Explain the meaning of a principled foreign policy. Is such a foreign policy realistic in a world of competing states? Aren't principles a luxury that the United States cannot afford in foreign policy?
4. Discuss whether and when humanitarian armed intervention might be ethically and practically justified.

CHAPTER EIGHT

Jesus, Catholic Social Teaching, and Christian Citizenship

"You are the light of the world. A city built on a hill cannot be hid. No one after lighting a lamp puts it under the bushel basket, but on the lampstand, and it gives light to all in the house. In the same way, let your light shine before others, so that they may see your good works and give glory to your Father in heaven." (Matthew 5:14-16)

"To set out on the road to discipleship is to dispose oneself for a share in the cross (cf. Jn 16:20). To be a Christian, according to the New Testament, is not simply to believe with one's mind, but also to become a doer of the word, a wayfarer with and a witness to Jesus. This means, of course, that we never expect complete success within history and that we must regard as normal even the path of persecution and the possibility of martyrdom."[1]

This book has highlighted issues of justice and peace that face humanity in the post-Cold War world. Christians need to understand these issues in order to respond to them, in order to create a global community that is more just and at peace. This chapter will try to make explicit *why* Christians should work for justice and make peace and *how* Christians can begin to become constructively involved in justice and peace issues.

CHRISTIAN FAITH

Faith is a *relationship* with God; Christian faith is a relationship with God who is revealed by Jesus, the Christ. It is important to understand faith as a relationship and not primarily as a set of beliefs nor a checklist of moral requirements. Creeds and commandments are important for persons of faith because they begin to name the God who loves us and they guide us in our response to God. But the relationship of each person with God is primary and central.

As with any relationship, faith is rooted in experience. Since God is spirit, it is sometimes difficult for modern people, convinced of the scientific method and closed to mystery and transcendence, to open themselves to experience the Spirit. There are human experiences that tend to pull us beyond ourselves, such as falling in love or the birth of a child or the death of someone we love or a breathtaking sunrise, but faith always requires the leap that acknowledges the presence of God's Spirit.

Like lovers bursting to recount the experience of being in love,[2] an encounter with transcendent mystery begs to be shared, reflected upon, and responded to. Religious believers gather with other people of faith (community) to tell stories of God, to seek to understand their relationship with God (do theology), to celebrate their faith (worship), and to respond to it (right living). Thus is "church" formed and tradition passed on. Eventually the narratives about God and faith are written down in scripture. Creeds are formulated, worship is established, and principles are put into practice. All of this happens in response to the human relationship with God which rightfully becomes the core and compass of human life.

JESUS AND THE SPIRIT

Jesus was a person of faith. "The most crucial fact about Jesus was that he was a 'spirit person,' a 'mediator of the sacred,' one of those persons in human history to whom the Spirit was an experiential reality."[3] At the center of Jesus' life was an intimate and continuous relationship with the divine Spirit. Jesus was the culmination of a stream of spirit persons in the Jewish tradition—Abraham and Moses and the prophets; others followed in Jesus' wake—Peter and Paul, Benedict and Ignatius, Francis of Assisi, Theresa of Avila, and Teresa of Calcutta.

Jesus knew God. He had visions at his baptism by John (Mt 3:13-17), in the desert (Mt 4:1-11), and on the mountaintop (Mt 17:1-13).[4] Jesus sought out isolated places where he prayed through the night (Mt 14:23; Mk 1:35). In a culture afraid to utter the Almighty's name, Jesus called God *Abba* (Mk 14:35) Aramaic for "Papa." The Spirit's healing and liberating power flowed through Jesus, and he taught about God and faith "with authority," that is, on the basis of his own profound experience of the divine mystery at the heart of reality. At the beginning of his public ministry Jesus applied the words of Isaiah the prophet to himself:

> The Spirit of the Lord is upon me,
> because he has anointed me
> to bring good news to the poor.
> He has sent me to proclaim release to the captives
> and recovery of sight to the blind,
> to let the oppressed go free,
> to proclaim the year of the Lord's favor. *(Lk 4:18-19)*

Jesus invited everyone he met to faith, to encounter the same Spirit he knew and to live in relationship with God.

THE POLITICS OF COMPASSION

Who is the God whom Jesus knew and obeyed and revealed? "For Jesus, compassion was the central quality of God and the central moral quality of a life centered on God."[5] "Be compassionate as your Father is compassion-ate" (Lk 6:36).[6] Moreover, Jesus, "God-with-a-face,"[7] is the embodiment of the divine compassion in the world.[8]

The Hebrew word translated as "compassion" is the plural of the word for womb. It connotes giving life, nourishing, caring, and tenderness, a warm and gentle embrace. It is often used in referring to God in the Hebrew Scriptures. For Jesus, then, God is like a mother who feels for and loves the children of her womb; as followers of Jesus, Christians are to imitate God, being compassionate toward each other. Compassion is both a feeling, being moved by the suffering of others, and a way of being, a willingness to share that suffering and do something about it.[9] In and through Jesus, God shares the suffering of humanity and transforms it into new life. Christians are to be compassionate as the Father is compassionate.

For Jesus, compassion was neither sentimental nor an individual virtue; rather compassion was political. When compassion led Jesus to touch a leper, heal a woman with constant menstruation, feed the hungry, forgive sinners, and share a meal with tax collectors and prostitutes, it was moving him to challenge the dominant sociopolitical paradigm of his social world. Thus, Jesus was engaged in what might be called the "politics of compassion" in contrast to the "politics of purity" that dominated his social world.[10]

Jewish society in the first century was structured around avoiding any-thing that would make one religiously unclean. The biblical roots of this purity system were found in the Book of Leviticus, especially in the verse, "You shall be holy, for I the Lord your God am holy" (Lev 19:2). Set in the context of laws about ritual and religious purity, the holiness of the Jewish community was defined in terms of purity.

This purity system tended to be hierarchical and exclusionary. It divided those who were born into the tribe of priests and Levites from those who were not, the righteous who observed the purity laws from sinners who were unclean and impure, the whole and the well from the handicapped and the ill, the rich (blessed by God) from the poor, males from females, and Jews from Gentiles. In effect, the purity system created a world with sharp social boundaries, a world where many were treated as outcasts.[11]

In opposition to the teaching of the Pharisees and of the Jewish leaders to "Be holy (pure) as God is holy," Jesus proclaimed, "Be compassionate as God is compassionate." Jesus' call to compassion can be seen as a radical challenge to the theology and the politics of the dominant social system of his time, a social structure that was an oppressive burden on the poor and the marginalized.

Jesus' parables and sayings often indicted the purity system and those who used it for power and privilege. In the parable of the Good Samaritan (Lk 10:29-37), for example, it is probable that the priest and Levite pass by the man beaten by robbers because they were afraid of becoming ritually unclean by drawing too close to him. The Samaritan who is by definition impure acts compassionately toward the wounded man and becomes the model of love of neighbor. Jesus prophetically denounced the Pharisees and other religious leaders for their rigorous following of the religious codes, to the neglect of practicing "justice and mercy and faith."[12] Indeed, the string of Jesus' denunciations of the Pharisees and leaders collected in Luke 11 and Matthew 23 are dense with allusions to the purity system and the Pharisees' preoccupation with the outside and external, the law and duty, to the neglect of the spirit and the heart, justice and compassion.

Here Jesus stands in the tradition of the Hebrew prophets who reminded the people of Israel that God was more concerned with justice and mercy and righteousness than with correct ritual or periodic fasting.

> I hate, I despise your festivals,
>   and I take no delight in your solemn assemblies. . . .
> But let justice roll down like waters
>   and righteousness like an ever-flowing stream.
>   *(Am 5:21,24)*

> Is not this the fast that I choose:
>   to loose the bonds of injustice,
>   to undo the thongs of the yoke,
>   to let the oppressed go free,
>   and to break every yoke?
> Is it not to share your bread with the hungry,
>   and to bring the homeless poor into your house.
>   *(Is 58:6-7)*[13]

Sincere worship and humble fasting are, of course, good and important, but the Hebrew prophets and Jesus pointed out that they became outrageous hypocrisy if not accompanied by justice and mercy for the oppressed and the poor.

Jesus' healings and exorcisms and table fellowship shatter the purity boundaries of his social world. Jesus touches lepers who were so unclean that they were literally cast out of the city, he is touched by a hemorrhaging woman (Mk 5:25-34), and he has his feet washed by an unclean woman when he is at dinner at Simon's house (Lk 7:36-50). Jesus enters a graveyard to free a man of a "legion" of unclean spirits who enter a herd of unclean pigs (Mk 5:1-20). Jesus frequently "reclined at table" with impure social outcasts such as tax collectors and sinners.[14]

AN INCLUSIVE EARLY CHURCH

The Christian movement in the early church was characterized by the inclusiveness of compassion rather than the exclusiveness of the purity system. Even an Ethiopian eunuch, a man at the bottom of the purity system, was baptized into the church without hesitation (Acts 8:26-40). And Paul, in his letter to the Galatians, resoundingly declared the unity of all in the Spirit of Christ: "There is no longer Jew or Greek, there is no longer slave or free, there is no longer male and female; for all of you are one in Christ Jesus" (Gal 3:28).

The apostles, filled with the spirit of Christ, founded communities that were inclusive and egalitarian, generous and loving. The Acts of the Apostles describes the Christian community at Jerusalem in this way:

> All who believed were together and had all things in common; they would sell their possessions and goods and distribute the proceeds to all, as any had need. Day by day, as they spent much time together in the temple, they broke bread at home and ate their food with glad and generous hearts, praising God and having the good-will of all the people. And day by day the Lord added to their number those who were being saved. (Acts 2:44-47)[15]

Evangelical theologian Ronald Sider characterizes the practice of the Jerusalem community as "unlimited liability" for each other and "total availability" to each other.[16]

When, through a unique set of historical circumstances, the Jerusalem community became impoverished, Paul took up a great collection from the Gentile churches to bring to the church in Jerusalem. Thus Paul logically enlarged the scope of Christian unity and generosity to the universal church, giving us a model of inter-church sharing. And when Paul heard about class divisions in the eucharistic celebration at Corinth, he angrily declared that if wealthy Christians were feasting while poor believers went hungry, then they were not eating the Lord's Supper at all, but profaning the Body of Christ (1 Cor 11:17-34). On the basis of the practice of the early church and the meaning of the eucharist, Sider concludes, "As long as any Christian anywhere in the world is hungry, the eucharistic celebration of all Christians everywhere in the world is imperfect."[17] Along the same lines, we might legitimately wonder if Christ is really present at a racially segregated eucharist, noting that ten o'clock Sunday morning probably remains the most segregated hour in the week in the United States.

JESUS' THIRD WAY

Jesus' politics of compassion addressed not only the Jewish purity system, but also the oppression of the Roman Empire.[18] In the first century, Israel was occupied by the Romans, who ruled somewhat indirectly through the Jewish leaders. Roman rule was still domineering and exploitative, and the Jews understandably resented it. Thus, revolutionary sentiment and messianic expectations were high in Jesus' social world.

The Jewish people were expecting God to send them a messiah, someone like David who would throw out the Romans and re-establish the kingdom of Israel. And there were Jewish groups, some of them called Zealots, who were ready to engage in violent resistance to Roman rule. The politics of Jesus' world were highly charged. Indeed, the Pharisees and the Essenes hoped that their faithful following of the purity laws and the holiness code would persuade God to send the messiah.[19]

Thus, the ordinary people—the peasants, shepherds, housekeepers, fisherfolk, shopkeepers, and merchants—experienced a double oppression by both Jewish and Roman leaders. The taxes paid to the Romans, which amounted to as much as 40 percent of their income, drove many people into debt. These taxes were collected by fellow Jews who not only collaborated with the hated Romans but enriched themselves in the process. And the religious leaders encumbered the people with the onus of the purity system, adding religious guilt to their economic woes.[20]

In this oppressive context Jesus proclaimed the good news that the reign of God was at hand, offering liberation, justice, and compassion. It was a welcome message. This doubly oppressive and tense revolutionary context helps to make sense of some of Jesus' sayings and of events that at first seem strange to contemporary Christians.

Jesus' Sermon on the Mount as collected in Matthew 5-8 and Luke 6:20-49 is a challenging statement of his alternative way and of the politics of compassion. This teaching of Jesus has been a stumbling block for his followers throughout Christian history. Eileen Egan, a longtime advocate of peace and justice in the Catholic Worker tradition, once said that she thought all of theology might be understood as a way to get around the Sermon on the Mount. She, of course, thought Christians should walk through it.[21] Is it possible to practice this ethic outlined by Jesus?

The first step in a realistic interpretation of the Sermon on the Mount is to see it in light of the context of Jesus' social world. Biblical scholar Walter Wink provides surprising insight by applying this method to one of the most perplexing passages in Jesus' discourse.[22]

> You have heard that it was said, "An eye for an eye and a tooth for a tooth." But I say to you, Do not resist an evildoer. But if anyone strikes you on the right cheek, turn the other also; and if anyone wants to sue you and take your coat, give your cloak as well; and if anyone forces you to go one mile, go also the second mile. (Mt 5:38-41) (see also Lk 6:29-31)

Is Jesus asking his followers to be human doormats, cowardly and complicit in the face of injustice?

First, Wink argues persuasively that the Greek word *antistenai*, translated as "Resist not evil" in the King James version of the Bible, should be more accurately rendered "Do not take revenge on someone who does you wrong," as is found in the Good News version. The sense is: do not retaliate against violence with violence. But if Jesus counsels his followers not to *fight* back, neither does he allow *flight* in response to injustice. Rather he calls for courageous and *creative resistance*, and he gives his audience—people who know about injustice first-hand—three examples of his alternative or "third way" to respond.

The detail in the text referring to the right cheek is a key. The ancient world was a right-handed world where even to gesture with the left hand was offensive and insulting. The only way to hit the right cheek with the right hand is with the back of the hand. (Try acting out the scene.) So Jesus is saying: when someone gives you the back of their hand, turn your other cheek to them. A backhand slap was the normal way of reprimanding inferiors, and it still carries the connotation of putting someone down. "Masters backhanded slaves; husbands, wives; parents, children; men, women; Romans, Jews."[23] The expected response is cowering submission. Jesus counsels neither hitting back nor turning tail, but rather turning the other cheek, which is an act of remarkably creative resistance. It allows the inferior in the relationship to assert her or his equal humanity with the oppressor, and it forces the oppressor to take stock of the relationship and perhaps of the social system that supports such inequality. It is risky, to be sure, and demands courage, but it is a creative way to challenge an unhealthy relationship and an unjust system. Gandhi and Martin Luther King, Jr. grasped this, and molded this idea into a tool for resisting social injustice and creating a more just community.[24]

In Jesus' second example someone is being sued for his coat or outer garment by a creditor. Indebtedness was the severest social problem in first century Palestine, and only the poorest person would have nothing but his coat to serve as collateral.[25] Now he is being hauled into court to have even that stripped away.

Jesus recommends clowning and nudity as a creative response. The people of the time wore only an outer garment and an inner garment. In effect, Jesus would have the debtor say, "Here, take not only my coat, but my underwear as well. Then, you'll have everything!" and walk out of the court naked, leaving the red-faced creditor with your coat in one hand and underwear in the other. Thus, the creditor would be embarrassed and shamed. And he is unmasked as not a respectable moneylender, but a loan shark who perpetuates a system that has reduced an entire social class of his own people to landlessness and destitution. This burlesque offers the creditor a chance to see the human consequences of these practices and to repent, and it empowers the oppressed to take the initiative and burst the delusion that this is a just system. It is a brave and ingenious form of resistance.

Jesus' third example refers to a practice of the Roman occupation troops. When the Roman troops were moving about, a soldier could force a civilian to carry his sixty-five pound pack for him, but only for one mile. To force a civilian to go further risked severe penalties under military law. This sort of practice was a bitter reminder to the Jews that they were a subject people even in the Promised Land.

Imagine, then, the soldier's surprise when, upon arrival at the next mile marker, he absent-mindedly reaches for his pack, looking for his next human packmule, and the Jew says with a smile, "That's ok, I'll carry it for another mile," and starts striding off down the road. Going the second mile knocks the oppressor off balance and reveals the injustice of the situation. It also affirms the dignity of the oppressed by allowing the victim to seize the initiative. Without shedding blood or even raising one's voice in anger, the oppressed person has started down the road to liberation.

Given this interpretation, this passage becomes a different sort of stumbling block to Christian discipleship. Rather than being dismayed at complacency and submissiveness in the face of evil and injustice that at first glance seems implied by Jesus' sayings, one can be put off by the courage and creativity called for by Jesus. But if the Christian disciple is to stumble over this teaching, it should be in the direction of the challenge to creative resistance, Jesus' third way between the ordinary options of fight or flight in response to injustice.

In Matthew's gospel Jesus goes on to say,

> You have heard that it was said, "You shall love your neighbor and hate your enemy." But I say to you, Love your enemies and pray for those who persecute you, so that you may be children of your Father in heaven; for he makes his sun rise on the evil and on the good, and sends rain on the righteous and the unrighteous. For if you love those who love you, what reward do you have? Do not even the tax collectors do the same? And if you greet only your brothers and sisters, what more are you doing than others? Do not even the Gentiles do the same? Be perfect [compassionate], therefore, as your heavenly Father is perfect [compassionate]. (Mt 5: 43-48)[26]

Love of enemies is challenging indeed, but love expressed in creative resistance has the power to free the oppressed from docility and the oppressor from sin, affirming the image of God in both. This is the way, says Jesus, that is consistent with the nature of God, who is compassion, and with our relationship with God, who calls us to create a just community through love.

Jesus lived what he taught, as the events of his life attest. He rode into Jerusalem on a donkey rather than a white horse and was crucified at the hands of the Romans at the insistence of the Jewish leaders. The inscription that Pilate put on his cross read, "The King of the Jews." Jesus' suffering in love redeemed humanity from sin, personal and social, and established the Kingdom of God. Jesus rejected dominating power and insisted instead on the power of love.[27]

It is interesting to note that the Christian community eschewed violence and warfare and embraced nonviolence and peace, even in the face of persecution, during the first three centuries of its existence. There are multiple and complex reasons why Christians refused military participation during this period, but the basic reason was its incompatibility with Christian love. This practice of pacifism changed rather dramatically when the Roman Empire became the Holy Roman Empire in 313 after the conversion of the Emperor Constantine.[28]

CHRISTIAN CONVERSION AND SOCIAL TRANSFORMATION

At the beginning of his public ministry, Jesus is presented as traveling through Galilee, proclaiming a message of *metanoia* or conversion in response to the coming of the reign of God.[29] This notion of conversion is central to understanding the message of Jesus and the meaning of Christian discipleship. Basically it means turning from selfishness toward love, placing God and the teachings of Jesus at the center of life. Conversion, then, is a call to "Be compassionate as your Father is compassionate." St. Paul puts it this way: "Let each of you look not to your own interests, but to the interests of others. Let the same mind be in you that was in Christ Jesus, who, . . . emptied himself, . . . and became obedient to the point of death—even death on a cross" (Phil 2:4-5, 7, 8).

Conversion of the heart, then, means that Christians are to be socially subversive, that disciples of Christ work to transform the world.[30] Conversion means to turn around; subversion means to turn over. The implication is that the Christian, like a plow moving through a field, will turn society over, from oppression to justice, from violence to peace. "The Christian is called not only to change his [or her] own heart but also to change the social, political, economic, and cultural structures of human existence. Conversion is not addressed to the heart alone."[31]

CATHOLIC SOCIAL TEACHING

The social teaching of the churches, Protestant and Catholic, attempts to interpret the social dimension of Christian discipleship in the context of the contemporary world. The World Council of Churches (WCC), which includes nearly all of the Orthodox and Protestant churches, has held seven world assemblies since 1948, most recently in Canberra, Australia, in 1991. The documents produced by these world assemblies have emphasized the theme of a "responsible society" and have clearly expressed the notion that justice demands the transformation of social structures.[32] In the last decade there has also been a particular focus on justice, peace, and the integrity of creation. The National Council of Churches (NCC), the comparable body in the United States, has likewise given consistent and concerted attention to issues of justice and peace, as have the national assemblies of the various Protestant denominations.

"Catholic social teaching" refers to the body of work produced by the popes, the Second Vatican Council, the Vatican synods, and the national conferences of bishops, beginning with the encyclical *Rerum Novarum (The Condition of Labor)* by Pope Leo XIII in 1891, and continued through the writings of Pope John Paul II and the various bishops' conferences.[33] The documents produced by the Vatican address global concerns of the universal church, while those of the bishops' conferences tend to take more national or regional perspectives on justice and peace issues.

Catholic social thought has not developed systematically. Sometimes popes and bishops' conferences have decided to address specific issues that seemed pressing at a particular moment in history. Thus Pope Leo XIII addressed the condition of labor in 1891; Pope John XXIII, human rights and the arms race in 1963; Pope Paul VI, poverty and development in 1967; the Latin American bishops, poverty and liberation in 1968 (at Medellín) and in 1979 (at Puebla); and the American Catholic bishops, the arms race and deterrence in 1983, and the U.S. economy in 1986. Other social encyclicals have been produced to mark the anniversary of a previous encyclical, such as *Quadragesimo Anno* by Pope Pius XI, *Octogesima Adveniens* by Pope Paul VI, and *Centesimus Annus* by Pope John Paul II, to mark the fortieth, eightieth, and hundredth anniversaries of *Rerum Novarum* (1891). These documents tend to have a broader, more general scope, while also engaging issues of the day. Although there is much cross-referencing among these documents and a certain consistency both in theory and in positions taken, there is no conscious philosophical or theological foundation adopted and developed, nor is there a clear economic, social, or political theory expounded. Since the Second Vatican Council (1962–1965), Catholic social thought has paid much more attention to its biblical basis, yet its use of scripture has remained uneven. Nevertheless, the Magisterium (pope and bishops) of the Catholic Church has managed to produce a substantial and credible body of social teaching, one that unfortunately has been accurately referred to as "our best kept secret."[34]

The documents comprising Catholic social teaching over the past hundred years fill several volumes, and the theological reflection on this body of thought fill yet more volumes.[35] While it is not possible here to give a thorough overview of Catholic social thought, it is important to note several key themes related to the issues addressed in this book.

First, Catholic social teaching unambiguously affirms that the church and individual Christians are to be *engaged in the work of transforming the world*. This is clearly expressed in a famous sentence from the document produced by an international Synod of Bishops in 1971, *Justice in the World*: "Action on behalf of justice and participation in the transformation of the world fully appear to us as a constitutive dimension of the preaching of the Gospel, or, in other words, of the church's mission for the redemption of the human race and its liberation from every oppressive situation."[36] Working for justice is not peripheral or optional, but rather central and essential for a life lived in relationship with God. Faith affects every aspect of the believer's life, including the social, cultural, economic and political dimensions. "Our faith is not just a weekend obligation, a mystery to be celebrated around the altar on Sunday. It is a pervasive reality to be practiced in homes, offices, factories, schools, and businesses across our land."[37]

Second, the two values that form the foundation of Catholic social thought are *human dignity, realized in community*. The human person is sacred and social. The church's profound commitment to the values of human dignity and community is based on the biblical stories of *creation* and of God's *covenant* with the people of Israel.

Human beings are created in the image and likeness of God (Gen 1:27) and gifted with an unearned and inestimable value and dignity. Each person is obligated to respect this human dignity and to treat one another as sacraments of God and as sisters and brothers.

Through the call of Abraham and his descendants and through God's revelation to Moses at Sinai, God established a covenant with the Hebrew people.

Then Moses went up to God; the Lord called to him from the mountain, saying, "Thus you shall say to the house of Jacob, and tell the Israelites: You have seen what I did to the Egyptians, how I bore you on eagle's wings and brought you to myself. Now therefore, if you obey my voice and keep my covenant, you shall be my treasured possession out of all the peoples. Indeed the whole earth is mine, but you shall be for me a priestly kingdom and a holy nation. These are the words that you shall speak to the Israelites." (Ex 19:3-6)

God acted in the history of the people of Israel, liberating them from their bondage in Egypt and thus demonstrating compassion, faithfulness, and concern for justice and freedom. At Sinai God promises to take care of the people if they will keep the covenant with God. The following chapters (20–23) in the book of Exodus detail the code that is to characterize their lives: faithful worship of God alone, care for one another, creation of a just community, and a special concern for vulnerable members of the community —widows and orphans, the poor and strangers. Thus the people of Israel are called into community, a just community that becomes the norm of their faithful response to God's love for them.[38]

The principles of the community of Israel include the *Sabbatical Year* (the seventh year) and the Year of *Jubilee* (the fiftieth year or the Grand Sabbatical) when Israelites recognize that the land is God's gift to be cared for and that a people liberated from bondage should take care of the poor and oppressed in their midst. During the Sabbatical Year (Ex 23:11; Lev 25:1-7) land was to remain uncultivated, slaves were to be freed, and debts forgiven. During the Year of Jubilee (Lev 25:8-41) all members of the community were to be returned to their rightful place in the community, and property was to be restored to its original owners. Thus, in principle, the tribes of Israel were to be kept in a sort of egalitarian equilibrium.[39]

In the eighth century B.C.E., at a time when idolatry and social injustice had come to characterize the people of Israel, *prophets* called Israel back to the demands of the covenant. The prophets spoke in God's name and functioned as the conscience of the nation. They identified Israel's sin: infidelity to the covenant with God. Israel had turned to other gods and had put its trust in alliances rather than in Yahweh. In Israel, the rich oppressed the poor, and the rulers were corrupt, violent, and exploitative.

> Alas for those who devise wickedness
> and evil deeds on their beds!

When morning dawns, they perform it,
    because it is in their power.
They covet fields and seize them;
    houses, and take them away;
they oppress the householder and house,
    people and their inheritance. *(Mic 2:1-2)*

Hear this you rulers of the house of Jacob
    and chiefs of the house of Israel,
who abhor justice
    and pervert all equity,
who build Zion with blood
    and Jerusalem with wrong!
Its rulers give judgment for a bribe,
    its priests teach for a price,
    its prophets give oracles for money;
Yet they lean upon the LORD and say,
    "Surely the LORD is with us!
No harm shall come upon us."
Therefore because of you
    Zion shall be plowed as a field;
Jerusalem shall become a heap of ruins,
    and the mountain of the house a wooded height.
    (Mic 3:9-12)

Thus, the prophets announced the judgment of God because of the sin of Israel, a punishment meant to correct the people's evil ways and to bring them back to the covenant with God.

    God's requirements for right living in accord with the covenant were clear.

He has told you, O mortal, what is good;
    and what does the LORD require of you
but to do justice, and to love kindness,
    and to walk humbly with your God. *(Mic 6:8)*

The prophets reveal a God who requires fidelity, justice, and righteousness, but who, in the end, is compassionate and merciful, forgiving and faithful.[40] God's steadfast love gives the prophets and Israel reason to hope.

Who is a God like you, pardoning iniquity
    and passing over the transgression
    of the remnant of your possession?
He does not retain his anger forever,
    because he delights in showing clemency.
He will again have compassion upon us;
    he will tread our iniquities under foot.

You will cast all our sins
   into the depths of the sea.
You will show faithfulness to Jacob
   and unswerving loyalty to Abraham,
as you have sworn to our ancestors
   from the days of old. *(Mic 7:18-20)*[41]

Jesus stands in the tradition of the Hebrew prophets. Like the prophets of Israel, Jesus calls his followers to fidelity, justice, righteousness, and community, and he proclaims the presence of God who is faithful, compassionate, and gracious. (See, for example, the parable of the prodigal son and his brother in Lk 15:11-32, or the story of the sinful woman who is forgiven at the house of a Pharisee in Lk 7:36-50.) Through his death and resurrection Jesus renews the covenant, and expands its scope to include all of humanity. Through Jesus, God establishes a *new covenant* with all people and calls on humankind to become a just community throughout the earth. In the new covenant, as in the original one, the way the community responds to the needs of the poor is the "litmus test" of its justice or injustice, of its fidelity to the covenant with God.[42]

These two values, then, human dignity and just community, rooted in the stories of creation and covenant, form the foundation for the major principles developed in Catholic social teaching. Although any listing of those principles will be somewhat idiosyncratic, those most relevant to the themes developed in this book are: human rights, social sin, solidarity, participation, the preferential option for the poor, and peacemaking. Although some of these have been touched on in previous chapters, each will receive at least a brief reflection here.

The meaning of *human rights* and the development of this principle in Catholic social thought was explored earlier (see chapter 4). Clearly the concept of human rights is rooted in the creation of humanity in the image of God and in the obligations of life in community. Pope John XXIII provides the fullest exposition of human rights from the church's perspective in his encyclical *Peace on Earth* (1963).[43]

Whenever the church talks about human rights, it is always careful to give equal attention to human responsibility. Catholic social thought has used human rights as a normative framework for addressing the minimal obligations of any society or polity in a pluralistic world.[44] In other words, the least that can be expected of any government is to create a society where basic human needs (food, water, health care, shelter, safety) are met and where there is the opportunity to develop one's potential and to participate in society through work and through politics. Each person, then, has the responsibility to use his or her gifts for the betterment of society and to participate in creating a more just community.

There is an abiding awareness in Catholic social thought that evil and sin have a tendency to become embedded in the structures and institutions of society, that is, there is a consciousness of *social sin*, or the "structures of sin." This concept is deeply rooted in the theology of the Hebrew prophets who accused Israel of infidelity and who function as the conscience of the nation.

The social sciences, which have convincingly argued that all knowledge is socially constructed—that is, that each person is so immersed in culture and society that it is virtually impossible to understand or know anything outside of our social framework—add an empirical dimension to the concept of social sin. Thus, for example, racism transcends the sum total of individual acts of discrimination and becomes institutionalized and self-perpetuating in a society. The same claim can be made for other social sins, such as sexism, violence, ethnic hatred, and materialism or consumerism.

In his encyclical *On Social Concern*, Pope John Paul II speaks of, "'structures of sin,' which . . . are rooted in personal sin, and thus always linked to the concrete acts of individuals who introduce these structures, consolidate them and make them difficult to remove. And thus they grow stronger, spread, and become the source of other sins, and so influence people's behavior."[45] Pope John Paul II then points to two interrelated actions and attitudes that seem to him to be at the root of structures of sin in the contemporary world— "the all-consuming desire for profit" and "the thirst for power." They give rise to "certain forms of modern imperialism" and to "real forms of idolatry: of money, ideology, class and technology."[46] Certainly race, ethnicity, and gender could be added to the idolatries mentioned by the pope.

> **For Reflection**
>
> It is generally easier to see the social sin of other nations than it is to see the sinful structures of one's own nation. The anti-semitism of Nazi Germany clearly transcended the acts of individuals and became the sin of the nation. The same was true of apartheid in South Africa. What are the social sins of contemporary America? How can social redemption be accomplished?

If evil is structured into society, then its remedy must include social transformation, that is, changing the structures and institutions of society. Christian responsibility, then, must include both *charity*, personal acts of compassion in response to individual suffering, and *justice*, social and political action aimed at transforming the root causes of evil and suffering. Christians should be found in soup kitchens, tutoring programs, and inner-city clinics, and on picket lines, political campaigns, and congressional lobbies.[47]

Pope John Paul II recommends the virtue of *solidarity* as the antidote to structures of sin. He sees solidarity as the moral virtue and social attitude that corresponds to the reality of global interdependence. "[Solidarity] then is not a feeling of vague compassion or shallow distress at the misfortunes of so many people, both near and far. On the contrary, it is a firm and persevering determination to commit oneself to the common good; that is to say to the good of all and of each individual, because we are all really responsible for all."[48] Solidarity is diametrically opposed to the desire for profit or a thirst for power. It calls for a readiness to sacrifice oneself for the sake of the other and to serve the neighbor, as opposed to a willingness to exploit or oppress the other for one's own advantage. Because of the unity and inter-dependence of humanity, the virtue of solidarity is a commitment to recog-nize the equality of persons and peoples, to share the goods of creation with all, and to work with others as partners on behalf of development, justice, and peace.[49]

Increasingly Catholic social thought has understood social justice in terms of *participation*.[50] "Social justice implies that persons have an obligation to be active and productive participants in the life of society and that society has a duty to enable them to participate in this way."[51] The principle of par-ticipation is rooted in the created dignity of the human person, who is endowed with freedom and charged with self-determination, and in the oblig-ations of just community.

As with human rights, the church's understanding of participation is broad and inclusive, and it involves reciprocal obligations on the part of individu-als and society. Pope John Paul II and the American and Canadian bishops have stressed both the right to civil or *political* participation and the right to meaningful work, i.e., *economic* participation.[52] As citizens and workers, per-sons should have the opportunity and the obligation to participate in a whole range of voluntary organizations and associations, including political par-ties and unions, and in the full spectrum of political and economic decisions. Nations, as well, large and small, rich and poor, should have the opportu-nity and the obligation to participate in international organizations such as regional associations and the United Nations.[53] The principle of participa-tion empowers persons and nations to have a voice in decisions that affect them.

There is a balanced appreciation of the role of the government in Catholic social thought. On the one hand, the principle of *subsidiarity*, which insists that larger communities should not usurp the proper role and authority of smaller communities, tends to de-centralize power and to limit the author-ity of central governments.[54] On the other hand, the principle often called *"socialization"* insists on the proper role of central government, especially in the increasingly complex contemporary world, to help promote the com-mon good and to advocate for the poor.[55] Government should not render cit-izens and local communities powerless by throwing its weight around where inappropriate, but government should not fail to exercise power where it is needed. Both individual initiative and government intervention can be proper forms of participation.

In their pastoral letter on the American economy, the U.S. Catholic bish-ops highlight *"the preferential option for the poor."*[56] The bishops say that Christians must judge the morality and the justice of public policies from the perspective of the poor:

> Decisions must be judged in light of what they do *for* the poor, what they do *to* the poor, and what they enable the poor to do *for themselves*.

The fundamental moral criterion for all economic decisions, policies, and institutions is this: They must be at the service of *all people, especially the poor.*[57]

This option for the poor and the powerless is a remarkably challenging way to invite contemporary Christians to "Be compassionate as your Father is compassionate."

The U.S. bishops adapt this principle from their brother bishops in Latin America. In 1968, the Latin American Bishops Conference met at Medellín, Colombia to reflect on the implications of the Second Vatican Council and especially its "Pastoral Constitution on the Church in the Modern World." That document said that, ". . . the church has always had the duty of scrutinizing the signs of the times and of interpreting them in the light of the gospel."[58] The most significant "sign of the time" in Latin America was the crushing poverty of the overwhelming majority of people and the glaring gap between the rich and the poor. At Medellín the church began to move decisively from the side of the rich to stand with the poor. When the Latin American bishops met again in 1979 in Puebla, Mexico, they articulated this move as the preferential option for the poor.[59] This Latin American theology was consistent with Pope Paul VI's encyclical *On the Development of Peoples* (1971), and, after being picked up by the U.S. bishops, was also employed by Pope John Paul II in his *On Social Concern* (1987, #42–45).[60] It is a key principle of Catholic social teaching.

There are deep biblical roots for the option for the poor. God's compassionate and caring concern for the poor is a dominant theme in the Hebrew Scriptures and in the message and ministry of Jesus and the early Christian community. The commitment of God's people to the covenant was manifested in their treatment of the widow, the orphan, and the stranger. Jesus identified himself with the hungry, the thirsty, the stranger, the naked, the sick, and the imprisoned, with "the least of these" (Mt 25:31-46).

Who are the poor? "The poor are the economically disadvantaged, the materially deprived, who as a consequence suffer powerlessness, exploitation and oppression."[61] Poverty, then, is primarily an economic and material reality in this usage. The U.S. bishops acknowledge the many spiritual and physical diminishments affecting people, but add that material poverty compounds these problems.[62] The option for the poor calls Christians and the church to stand with the hungry, the homeless, the unemployed, those without access to an adequate education or basic health care, those on the margins of society.

The "option" for the poor is not optional. "Rather it is a decisive action and a deliberate choice, reflecting values as well as desires, flowing from the core of . . . faith."[63] Standing with the poor,[64] being present to the poor, seeing the world from the perspective of the poor, working with the poor, advocating for the poor, this is *essential* to being a follower of Christ. Christians stand with the poor because God stands with the poor. Given the scandalous extent and depth of poverty in the United States and in the world (see chapter 2), the preferential option for the poor is a radical challenge. How is it possible that there can be rich Christians in a hungry world?[65]

Peacemaking (a central issue in chapter 7) has been another prominent and consistent theme in Catholic social thought. The Catholic tradition, at least from the fourth century on, has not taken a pacifist position. Rather, it has justified war as a rule-governed exception to the moral presumption in favor of peace. Indeed, when the U.S. bishops, in their pastoral letter *The Challenge of Peace*, affirmed nonviolence as a legitimate position for Christians to hold, many hailed this as significant progress.[66] Yet, despite its refusal to say a definite no to war or military intervention as a last resort, the church has been a vocal advocate for peace in four specific ways:

1. By promoting and working for justice—through development, human rights, and participation—the church has sought to overcome the causes of war. Pope John XXIII's advocacy of human rights in his encyclical *Peace on Earth* was an important step in this direction. Pope Paul VI said that "the new name for peace is development," a sentiment reiterated by Pope John Paul II again and again.[67] The church has clearly identified the connection between working for justice and making peace and has not been fooled into thinking that calm in the midst of injustice and oppression, hostility and hatred, is genuine peace.[68] Justice and trust are the only sure foundations for peace.

2. By developing the just-war tradition and applying it to policies and situations, the church has insisted that military intervention and warfare are *moral* questions, not merely tools of the state or techniques of *realpolitik*. And the church's moral analysis has yielded important conclusions, such as the condemnation of "any act of war aimed indiscriminately at the destruction of entire cities or of extensive areas along with their population . . . ,"[69] its prohibition on the use of nuclear weapons,[70] and the "strictly conditioned moral acceptance of nuclear deterrence . . . as a step on the way toward progressive disarmament."[71]

By persuasively articulating the criteria of the just-war tradition, the Roman Catholic Magisterium has provided a moral framework that has significantly influenced public policy discussions and the policies themselves. The decision about military intervention in the Persian Gulf, for example, was debated largely in terms of the just-war tradition, and the Pentagon took pains to persuade the public that it was fighting the war within the bounds of the principle of discrimination.[72] Recently the church has increasingly fostered nonviolence, with its insistence on conflict resolution, diplomacy, and alternatives to violence. Indeed, Pope John Paul II sometimes comes across as at least a practical pacifist in his continual calls for peace and his criticisms of war and violence.[73]

3. By decrying the arms race and the misplaced priorities evident in military spending, the church has functioned as a moral check on an irrational situation. In the words of the Second Vatican Council, "the arms race is an

utterly treacherous trap for humanity, and one which injures the poor to an intolerable degree."[74] Again the church is making the connection between justice and peace, pointing out not only the danger of accumulating weapons of mass destruction, but also the theft from the poor represented by military spending.

4. By supporting institutions designed to promote peace, the church has played a constructive role in creating the conditions for peace. By reminding the world of the fact of interdependence and calling for the virtue of solidarity that is necessary for creating a global just community, the church has advocated a world order that is essential for justice and peace.[75] The church continually supports and suggests strengthening the United Nations and other regimes that foster cooperation and conflict resolution. And the church has been willing, sometimes behind the scenes as in Poland and sometimes more publicly as in El Salvador, to participate in conflict resolution itself.

Finally, it is important to note an omission in official Catholic social teaching—an authoritative statement on the environment and ecology. John Paul II includes passing mention of ecological concern in two of his social encyclicals, and he addressed the issue in his World Day of Peace Message in 1990, but the Magisterium has yet to give this subject sufficient attention.[76] The theological literature on this topic is blossoming. Although principles such as "stewardship," "just and sustainable development," and "humanity as co-creators with God" can be found in Catholic social thought, the Vatican and the U.S. bishops have not yet developed a substantive statement on this issue.

Given that contemporary Catholic social teaching was developed in a Cold War world characterized by a deep polarization of competing ideologies, there is a remarkable *balance* in Catholic social thought. To the polarizations of either/or, Catholic social thought responds both/and. Catholic social teaching affirms both the value and dignity of each human person and the value of the community, both individual freedom and the common good, both human rights and human responsibility, both personal sin and structures of sin and the redemption of persons and nations, both the obligation of society to enable persons to participate in political and economic life and the responsibility of the person to participate in society, both the principle of subsidiarity or de-centralization of decision making and the principle of socialization or the proper role of the central government, both nonviolence and the justified use of force.

There is much to be said for this balance in Catholic social teaching. It focuses on seeking the truth rather than getting trapped in a one-sided ideology that is popular at the moment. It allows the church to criticize both capitalism and socialism and to call for the integral or wholistic development of the human person. It also allows the church to be critical and constructive without being politically partisan.

The danger of such balance, however, is the tendency to be dispassionate or lukewarm when a situation calls for the passionate defense of justice or a burning condemnation of oppression. There are times when the church and

Christians should be prophetic, should take sides. Indeed, the preferential option for the poor and the church's clear stand on behalf of human dignity, human rights, just community, and peacemaking call for precisely such committed advocacy and action. Reason and truth are not obstacles to a passion for justice and peace; selfishness and apathy are the problems.

No doubt there are many who would urge the church to take even stronger stands for justice and peace, but the record of the Christian community as a justice seeker and peacemaker is, on the whole, positive and constructive. Included in that record is the witness and service of individual Christians whose lives have introduced neighbors and friends to Catholic social thought and the social teaching of the churches. Some of these Christian witnesses have become well-known—Dorothy Day, Helder Camara, Oscar Romero, Jean Donovan, Martin Luther King, Jr., Desmond Tutu, Mother Teresa, Cesar Chavez, Helen Prejean, Philip and Daniel Berrigan.[77] Those who practice justice and peace are eloquent witnesses to the healing presence and reconciling power of God in our world.

CHRISTIAN CITIZENSHIP

Christian discipleship requires that one work for justice and make peace. This is the social and global dimension of striving to be compassionate. Christians must be hearers of the Word, that is, attentive to the presence and call of God in their lives, and *doers* of the Word, actively responding to God's call in the world.

Discipleship requires both an inner journey and an outer journey, both contemplation and resistance.[78] There are at least four dimensions to this journey: growing in knowledge and wisdom, personal conversion and changes in lifestyle, working within a faith community, and public policy advocacy or exercising one's citizenship. Growth in each of these areas contributes to living a life of compassion and justice.

In Luke's gospel the transition between the infancy narrative and Jesus' public ministry is accomplished with the statement: "And Jesus increased in wisdom and in years, and in divine and human favor" (Lk 2:52). *To grow in knowledge and wisdom* requires information and education, and it requires the development of a heart and conscience able to discern right from wrong.[79] If knowledge is the queen of virtues, wisdom is the grandmother of virtues—earthy, practical, sensitive, caring, and authentic. Knowledge can be gained from books, but wisdom is born of experience. Wisdom comes from making love, tending to sick children, weathering conflict patiently, and growing older gracefully.

This book has provided a considerable amount of information on global issues. Justice-seekers and peacemakers should crave information, constantly search for truth. In the movie "Gandhi," there is a scene in which hungry peasants oppressed by the landowners ask Gandhi to come and help them. The first thing Gandhi does upon arrival (after persuading the local magistrate that there is no reason to arrest him) is to carefully document the abuses. Gathering information is a critical first step in working for justice.

Karl Barth, one of the twentieth century's great theologians, said that the Christian should face the world with the Bible in one hand and a newspaper in the other. An educated person should read a daily paper or make it a habit to watch the news or subscribe to a weekly news magazine to keep up with what is going on in the world. (See the Resources section for a list of helpful periodicals.)

Those who are working for justice because of their faith often include "contemplation" in their process of reflection, that is, a conscious listening for God's voice by paying attention to the presence and movement of God's Spirit in our lives and our world. Conversion calls for continual growth.[80]

This growth in the Spirit will inevitably affect the way one lives life, one's lifestyle. An awareness of the simplicity of Jesus' life, of the gap between the rich and the poor, and of the way patterns of human consumption injure the earth and its ecosystems will push the Christian to "live simply so that others can simply live."

Materialism or consumerism is one of the most insidious ideologies of the last part of the twentieth century.[81] Its victims are not only the poor and the planet, but its practitioners. It has often been said that consumerism is a form of idolatry that promises personal fulfillment but yields only frustration and alienation—from God, each other, and nature. Thus a simpler lifestyle is good, first of all, for the one who lives it.

Asceticism and voluntary poverty have deep roots in the Christian tradition. A simple lifestyle is not the pursuit of suffering or hardship for its own sake, but rather a conscious effort to live in harmony with God, the community, and nature. The "Shakertown Pledge," first taken by a group of justice- and peace-minded Christians on a retreat at Shakertown, Kentucky in 1973, raises the right questions for intentionally moving toward a life of creative simplicity:

Recognizing that the earth and the fullness thereof is a gift from our gracious God,

---

Researching an Issue

Once one chooses an issue where one wants to make a difference, then specialized knowledge can be sought. A file for articles and news clippings can be begun, and a library of books started. One could take a college course on the subject, or integrate the topic into a college major or minor or as the focus of a graduate degree. One could attend lectures, seminars, or workshops related to a particular justice and peace interest. Eventually the learner will want to make the transition to teacher (since teaching is a great way to keep learning), sharing information informally with friends and family, leading a study group or joining a speaker's bureau, and writing letters-to-the-editor, op-ed pieces, or articles on the topic. And of course one will want to work for constructive change through direct service and public policy advocacy. Reflection, in the context of a community of people with similar interests and commitments, on the information one is gathering and on one's experiences of trying to change society for the better, generates wisdom.

and that we are called to cherish, nurture, and provide loving stewardship for the earth's resources,
and recognizing that life itself is a gift, and a call to responsibility, joy, and celebration,
I make the following declarations:
1. I declare myself to be a world citizen.
2. I commit myself to lead an ecologically sound life.
3. I commit myself to lead a life of creative simplicity and to share my personal wealth with the world's poor.
4. I commit myself to join with others in the reshaping of institutions in order to bring about a more just global society in which all people have full access to the needed resources for their physical, emotional, intellectual, and spiritual growth.
5. I commit myself to occupational accountability, and so doing I will seek to avoid the creation of products which cause harm to others.
6. I affirm the gift of my body and commit myself to its proper nourishment and physical well-being.
7. I commit myself to examine continually my relations with others, and to attempt to relate honestly, morally, and lovingly to those around me.
8. I commit myself to personal renewal through prayer, meditation, and study.
9. I commit myself to responsible participation in a community of faith.[82]

There are many ways for different persons to apply these commitments to their own lives, but a few examples might stimulate further reflection.

Most people are familiar with steps that they can take to lead a more ecologically sound life—buying a fuel-efficient car, using the car less and walking or bicycling more, turning off lights and turning the thermostat down in the winter and up in the summer, and recycling or not buying products that are packaged in ways harmful to the atmosphere. Many states require deposits on cans and bottles to reduce litter and encourage recycling and that residents separate waste from recyclable materials for garbage pickup. It is surprising that these practices are not universal.

Tithing—giving away one-tenth of one's income, to either religious institutions or to other charities—has biblical roots, and represents a practical way to share wealth.[83] Average Americans give only between 1 or 2 percent of their income to charity. Some parishes and churches tithe their collections for the poor and the cause of justice and peace.

Another example is that of a man who discovered that the gospel calls disciples toward nonviolence. His first step, he concluded, would be to disarm himself and his household. He had been in the army and owned three rifles, worth several hundred dollars. But he decided that to sell the rifles would have no impact on disarming the world. So he and his wife took the rifles into the backyard and ceremoniously broke them into a pile of scrap metal and wood and threw it away. For him, this was a powerful symbol of personal transformation and of a commitment to work to disarm the world.

A third example is a white couple, deeply committed to racial equality, who deliberately moved into an integrated neighborhood. They felt that they could not raise their children in the segregated environment of most suburbs.

Occupation or employment can also be signs of Christian vocation. According to Catholic social thought, ideally work should be a meaningful way for us to use talents and gifts to contribute to the community, and it should pay a wage that allows people to meet their needs.[84] "The investment of wealth, talent, and human energy should be specially directed to benefit those who are poor or economically insecure."[85]

Nearly any profession or job can be directed toward justice for the poor. A physician can work in an urban clinic or a remote rural area in need of health care. A lawyer can work for legal aid or promote civil rights or defend the environment. A business person can make responsibility for customers and employees the number-one priority. A salesclerk can treat customers with respect.

Financial investments can also be evaluated with a social conscience. Saving for the future can be reasonable and responsible, but, for example, banks that engage in "redlining" should not receive support. Christians can seek out money market funds or investment portfolios with a social conscience.

Christians usually seek justice and peace through *working within a faith community*. The faith community can support the individual Christian in the sometimes risky and often painful struggle to overcome injustice, and it can challenge its members to continue to strive to transform society into a just community. The institutional church can often add clout to efforts to reform society or change social structures or institutions.

The themes of justice and peace should be integrated into the worship and prayer of faith communities. The connections between, for example, the Eucharist—the Lord's supper—and world hunger and the oppression of the poor should always be apparent.[86] The inclusive table fellowship of the Lord demands that Christians oppose segregation and discrimination and the violation of human rights, that they work to feed the hungry and give drink to the thirsty. The memory of Jesus' crucifixion demands Christians stand in solidarity with those who are imprisoned and tortured and killed because they oppose tyranny and want a better life for their communities. Weaving concerns about justice and peace into the worship and the life of a faith community is the responsibility of every member.

The church should be a model or a sign of a just community in the world,[87] but inevitably this community of sinners falls short in this regard. Thus, working for justice includes efforts to transform the institutional church and local congregations as well as efforts to transform the larger society. Are fair wages paid to church employees? Are there equal opportunities for women? Does the church have an "edifice complex" that distracts it from a commitment to the poor? Is wealth wasted or hoarded or spent on the needs of the community and especially "the least of these"? Are the church's investments made with a social conscience? Is authority exercised in terms of service? Is the faith community engaged in direct service to the poor and courageous advocacy for justice? Are luxury cars in the church parking lot consistent with a preferential option for the poor? Does self-righteousness creep into attitudes and service?

Finally, it must be emphasized that *public policy advocacy* or *the exercise of one's citizenship* is an essential dimension of Christian discipleship. Christian and church involvement in politics is not only appropriate, it is necessary. Social structures are set up through public policy decisions, and they are changed and reformed through public policy decisions. Working for a society that is more just necessarily involves critical participation in these decisions.

It is important for churches to set up shelters for the homeless and soup kitchens for the hungry and for Christians to work at shelters and soup kitchens. But it is just as important for churches to lobby for affordable housing and for welfare policies that ensure that no one is hungry. Indeed fundamental social changes regarding housing and feeding the hungry would make shelters and soup kitchens unnecessary. The more just a society is, the less need there is for charity.

In the United States there is an important constitutional principle that separates the church from the state, but it is often misunderstood. The Constitution takes pains to keep the *institutions* of church and state separate. History has taught us that when the church becomes a secular power, it corrupts the church and harms society. Likewise the state has no business either establishing a particular religion or forbidding the free exercise of any religion, which is a fundamental human right.

The separation of religion from life, however, or of faith from politics is "pure heresy."[88] A Christian's relationship with God should affect every dimension of life, from what we eat to how we vote. Christian faith *should* influence the exercise of citizenship. The Christian community, the church, has as much right to lobby for its perspective and policy choices as does the National Rifle Association, the American Medical Association, or a coalition of insurance companies. Nor does the Constitution prohibit Christians from exercising their citizenship rights or the church from *proper* involvement in public policy discussions and decisions.

It is important, however, that the church influence public policy in a theologically and politically appropriate manner. The following five guidelines can assist the church in properly participating in politics:[89]

1. The role of the church is to lift up for discussion the *moral* dimension of public policy issues. Morality should be the consistent focus of the church's social pronouncements.
2. The church should endeavor to be *persuasive* when it enters public policy debate. The church's social analysis must be competent and informed, clear and reasonable. The church cannot rely exclusively on authority, or revelation, in public debate in a pluralistic society.

3. One of the most persuasive and effective ways for the church to influence public policy is through *example*, by modeling its moral teachings. The church must practice what it preaches. It must incarnate its moral vision through programs and structures that stand as beacons to society.

4. Because of the nature of the church's social mission and the nature of politics, it is almost always prudent for the church to *avoid single-issue politics and to remain clearly non-partisan*. The church's mission is broad and encompassing, and political issues are complex and interconnected. The pursuit of single-issue politics, on the other hand, is narrow and reductionistic; and partisan positions often exclude people of good will and tend to be short-sighted. Thus, ordinarily, the church should avoid endorsing candidates or political parties and avoid evaluating candidates or political platforms on the basis of any single issue.

5. In a pluralistic society public policy and legislation should be able to satisfy the criteria of *feasibility and enforceability*. Politics involves building a consensus around a reasonable and viable position. An unenforceable law is a bad law because it lessens respect for the law. A public policy that is forced on an unwilling public is divisive and alienating.

These five guidelines pertain to the church's official involvement in public policy discussions and decisions. The individual Christian's participation in politics is, of course, less constrained and might be more partisan, since individuals speak and act for themselves and not the community.

The primary act of political involvement is to register and to cast an informed and conscientious ballot for candidates who represent values and positions consistent with Christian faith. Financial support and active campaigning for candidates are important ways to participate in the political process. Committed Christians can also choose to run for local, state, or federal offices. Every country certainly needs politicians of integrity who are willing to serve the public and to work for the common good.

Voting and campaigning are only the first steps in shaping public policy. Just as organizations, corporations, and interest groups *lobby* elected officials in an effort to get their perspective enacted into legislation and policy, so every citizen should lobby their representatives on behalf of their point of view, and Christian citizens should advocate for the poor and oppressed, the powerless and voiceless. Communication with elected representatives through letters, telegrams, e-mail, phone calls, and visits can influence government policy.[90]

Some people are intimidated by the prospect of writing their government officials, but there is no reason for this. Representatives to the House and Senate are, after all, *representatives*. Their job is to represent citizens' views in the government, and if they do not, they are held accountable at election time. Thus they are interested in knowing what people think. Sometimes a dozen or so well-timed letters can have a dramatic impact in getting a representative's attention focused on a piece of legislation and in shaping his or her views.

An effective letter is courteous, brief, and clear. It is usually best to focus on one issue at a time and to be specific about the legislation under discussion. Most legislators will respond to your letter. It is a good idea to write a follow-up letter thanking the representative for making such a wise choice or continuing the dialogue on the issue. An example of a lobby letter follows.[91]

Return Address
Date

Dear Senator ——,

The Women, Infants and Children (WIC) program is in danger of being cut back. I urge you to vote to restore the President's funding request, rather than cut the program by 25 percent.

Every dollar spent on prenatal care under the WIC program saves $3.50 in later Medicaid costs, according the General Accounting Office. Not only does WIC save money, it is also a wise investment in human resources. A 25 percent cut in funding would reduce the number of recipients by nearly 100,000. This simply does not make sense.

I hope you will vote for women, infants, and children, and that you will encourage your colleagues to do so as well. Please inform me of your position.

Sincerely,

Important addresses:

The White House	The U.S. Senate	U.S. House of Representatives
Washington, D.C.	Washington, D.C.	Washington, D.C.
20500	20510	20515

White House phone: (202) 456-1414
Capitol phone: (202) 224-3121

Most senators and congresspersons now have e-mail addresses which are available through internet servers. The president's e-mail address is: president @whitehouse.gov

Writing a letter to the editor of a local newspaper or an informative op-ed piece can also be an effective way to engage in public policy discussion. Such efforts allow citizens to take a public stand and to educate and encourage others as well.

Direct communication with elected officials can be accomplished by arranging a visit with them, either on a trip to Washington, D.C. or in their home district. Government representatives are busy people, but most realize that they must be accessible to the citizens they represent. Their office is more likely to schedule a personal visit with a small group that represents an organization such as Bread for the World or Network (see Resources section).

Even if the representative is not available, it is worthwhile to meet with a member of their staff.

There are times, of course, when public policy advocacy and social change will require steps beyond dialogue. Nonviolent direct confrontation through protest marches, demonstrations, strikes, boycotts, street theater, or civil disobedience can be important steps in transforming society into a just community.[92] Such actions were instrumental in the civil rights and the labor movements, for example. In the United States rights to free speech and to assemble and protest are recognized and generally protected. Still it often requires personal courage to take a public stand or to court arrest on behalf of the poor and for the cause of justice and peace in the midst of controversy. Resistance against tyranny and oppression and standing for liberty and justice for all are the founding principles of the American nation. Christian citizens should not find it extraordinary to engage in public protest in the name of justice and peace.

Christian discipleship requires the maturation of compassion, wisdom, and courage in one who becomes a justice-seeker and a peacemaker. "Go therefore and make disciples of all nations, baptizing them in the name of the Father and of the Son and of the Holy Spirit, and teaching them to obey everything that I have commanded you. And remember, I am with you always, to the end of the age" (Mt 28:19-20).

STUDY QUESTIONS

1. Is the idea that faith is a relationship with God meaningful for you?
2. What is the message of Jesus? What makes you think Jesus was or was not interested in justice and peace issues? Is the gospel message relevant to social and political issues?
3. Is it possible to validly celebrate the eucharist in a church that is divided along lines of race, gender, or class?
4. Can you think of a personal experience where Jesus' Third Way could have offered you an alternative between fighting or fleeing?
5. Should converted Christians be socially subversive?
6. Catholic social teaching has been called the church's "best kept secret." What strategies would you propose for getting this message out to the people in the church and into society?
7. How do you think the church should speak to society on issues of public policy? Does the separation of church and state mean that the church is excluded from public policy discussions?
8. How can Christians follow Christ in a consumer society? How should rich Christians respond to a hungry world? What would it mean to take seriously the "preferential option for the poor?" How might the option for the poor affect your choice of career?
9. In what ways do you think the church has been successful in being a peacemaker and an advocate for justice? In what ways has the church fallen short in these roles?

10. What is the difference between charity and justice? How can Christians be both charitable and just?
11. Is responsible citizenship an obligation for disciples of Christ? What strategies can be used in advocating for the poor in public policy discussions. Can civil disobedience be sometimes justified? sometimes required?
12. What are the responsibilities of a justice seeker and a peacemaker in the contemporary world?
13. Which organizations have you decided to join?

Resources for Involvement and Information

The first part of this Resources section focuses on organizations that feed the hungry, enhance self-reliance, work for structural change, preserve the environment, advocate for human rights, and promote peace and disarmament. The second part lists resources for further information and study. Finally, there are some suggestions for research projects on justice and peace issues.

ORGANIZATIONS

There are many organizations working for justice and peace. Some of them are like comets streaking across the sky, burning brightly, but soon fading from view. Some have a very specific focus. Nearly all have a particular perspective or ideology that motivates their activities and colors their approach. Unfortunately internecine conflict characterizes even the struggle for justice and peace.

The following list is highly subjective and selective, even idiosyncratic. It makes no claim to being thorough or complete. Rather than list hundreds of organizations, I have chosen to list only a few. An exhaustive list of organizations working for justice and peace can be found in the *Encyclopedia of Associations*, edited by Sandra Jaszczak, et al., published annually by Gale Research Co., Detroit. It provides an annotated guide to more than 23,000 national and international organizations, and can be found in many libraries.

Many of the following are Catholic or Christian in their perspective, and most of them have been in existence long enough to have both a solid track record and a probable future. They can provide motivation, information, and guidance in attempting to change things for the better. Many of these organizations have local branches on campuses, in places of worship, or in communities or congressional districts.

Economic Justice

The first two organizations, Bread for the World and NETWORK, engage in public policy advocacy on behalf of the poor. The next two organizations, Oxfam America and Catholic Relief Services, engage in relief work and development efforts.

Bread for the World, 1100 Wayne Avenue, Suite 1000, Silver Spring, MD 20910; (301) 608-2400; Fax: (301) 608-2401
E-mail: bread@igc.apc.org   WWW:http://www.bread.org

Bread for the World is a Christian citizen's lobby on behalf of the poor at home and abroad. Its goal is to influence public policy in a way that benefits the poor. It does no direct relief work. It is organized by congressional district and through Christian congregations, with many local groups throughout the United States. It publishes a very informative monthly newsletter. Bread for the World sponsors an annual "offering of letters" in churches focused on a particular hunger issue. Its board of directors includes activists, academics, farmers, religious leaders, and politicians.

NETWORK: A National Catholic Social Justice Lobby, 801 Pennsylvania Ave., SE, Suite 460, Washington, D.C. 20003-2167; (202) 547-5556; Fax: (202) 547-5510; E-mail: network@igc.apc.org

Founded by Catholic sisters in 1971, NETWORK is the only Catholic registered lobby in Washington, D.C. Although still staffed mostly by sisters of various religious orders, its membership is open to anyone. Rooted in a value-based vision of justice and peace, NETWORK organizes, educates, and lobbies for socially just legislation. Its bimonthly magazine and information packets on timely issues before Congress keep its members up-to-date on public policy issues.

Oxfam America, 26 West Street, Boston MA 02111-1206; (617) 482-1211; (800) 225-5800; Fax: (617) 728-2596; E-mail: oxfamfast@igc.apc.org (There are also offices in Washington, D.C. and Oakland, CA.)

Oxfam America is a member of Oxfam International, begun at Oxford, England and now comprising nine autonomous Oxfams around the world. Oxfam America fights global poverty and hunger by working with grass-roots organizations promoting sustainable development in Africa, Asia, the Americas, and the Caribbean. More than simple relief, Oxfam supports development projects to enable the poor to become self-sufficient. Oxfam also engages in advocacy and education, but its focus is on development projects. Oxfam America works with colleges, schools, communities, and places of worship in promoting an annual "Fast for a World Harvest" every November close to Thanksgiving.

Catholic Relief Services (CRS), 209 West Fayette Street, Baltimore, MD 21201-3443; (410) 625-2220; Fax: (410) 685-1635.

Catholic Relief Services is the global assistance arm of the United States Catholic Conference (USCC). CRS responds to victims of natural and human-caused disasters, provides assistance to meet the basic needs of the poor, and supports self-help programs to lift people out of poverty and restore their dignity. Its reach is global. Recently, for example, CRS has been assisting refugees and helping to rebuild in Bosnia, offering relief to the victims of genocide in Rwanda and Central Africa, and supporting development projects in Haiti and Vietnam. CRS is engaged in direct assistance to the victims of disasters and in self-help programs.

Campaign for Human Development, 1311 Fourth St., N.E., Washington, D.C., 20017; (202) 541-3210; Fax: (202) 541-3329.

The domestic development arm of the USCC, the Campaign for Human Development fosters local and national self-help projects for the poor in the United States.

The Interfaith Center on Corporate Responsibility (ICCR), 475 Riverside Drive, Rm. 566, New York, N.Y. 10115; (212) 870-2295; Fax: (212) 870-2023.

ICCR is a coalition of church investors—Protestant denominations and Catholic religious communities—concerned about corporate responsibility. ICCR researches the practices of corporations in light of justice and peace concerns and seeks to influence corporate policy through investment and proxy votes at annual corporate meetings. ICCR offers a variety of educational materials on corporate social responsibility.

Environment/Ecology

Greenpeace (USA), 1436 U Street, N.W., Washington, D.C. 20009; (202) 462-1177; Fax: (202) 462-4507.

Greenpeace educates, organizes, lobbies, and engages in nonviolent direct action on behalf of environmental and disarmament issues throughout the world. Greenpeace activists are renowned for trying to impose themselves between whaling ships and whales and for sailing the *Rainbow Warrior* into the danger zone in order to stop the atmospheric testing of nuclear weapons in the Pacific. Greenpeace publishes a magazine and provides a variety of educational materials.

The National Audubon Society, 700 Broadway, New York, N.Y. 10003; (212) 979-3000; Fax: (212) 353-0377.

The Audubon Society maintains seventy wildlife preserves in the United States. It has recently expanded its focus from wildlife to a host of environmental concerns. With local clubs acting as watchdogs and advocates, this organization can be a powerful force for conservation. The Society produces excellent wildlife films and other educational materials, including the *Audubon Activist*, a bimonthly to keep members informed on public policy developments regarding environmental issues.

Friends of the Earth, 1025 Vermont Ave., N.W., Suite 300, Washington, D.C. 20005; (202) 783-7400; Fax: (202) 783-0444.

This multinational environmental organization, founded in 1969, focuses on public policy advocacy on behalf of the environment and sustainable development. It publishes books, reports, and a bimonthly newsletter on environmental issues.

EarthAction, 30 Cottage Street, Amherst, MA 01002; (413) 549-8118; Fax: (413) 549-0544; E-mail: amherst@earthaction.org

EarthAction consists of a global network of 1,500 citizen groups in 142 countries. It has international offices in London and Santiago, Chile as well as in Amherst, Massachusetts. Its purpose is to enable thousands of organizations, journalists, citizens, and parliamentarians to act together around the world on global issues affecting the environment, social justice and peace. Eight or more times a year EarthAction sends an Action Kit to its members focusing on a particular global issue. The kit provides background information and suggestions for action. A recent Action Kit, for example, focused on the trade in toxic waste.

Human Rights

There are any number of organizations that work for the rights of various ethnic groups or minorities and for civil rights and the rights of women. This section will mention two organizations that defend human rights globally.

Amnesty International (AI), 322 Eighth Ave., New York, N.Y. 10001; (212) 807-8400; (800) AMNESTY; Fax: (212) 627-1451; http://www.organic.com.amnesty.

Amnesty International began in 1961 with a determination to work on behalf of "prisoners of conscience" throughout the world. Amnesty asks its members and affiliate groups to "adopt" a prisoner, to write to the prisoner letting them know that they are not forgotten, and to work for their release. AI investigates allegations of human rights abuses and of torture, and surveys the human rights situation of various countries. Amnesty International Reports are known for their accuracy and fairness. Amnesty was awarded the Nobel Peace Prize in 1977. Amnesty focuses on specific human rights violations and on patterns of abuse, but does not get directly involved in politics.

Human Rights Watch, 485 Fifth Ave., New York, N.Y. 10017-6104; (212) 972-8400; Fax: (212) 972-0905.

Human Rights Watch is a nongovernmental organization that monitors human rights abuses internationally and publishes an excellent quarterly newsletter. Like Amnesty, Human Rights Watch is known for accurate and unbiased reporting. It also publishes the *Human Rights Quarterly Newsletter*.

Peace and Disarmament

Pax Christi, 532 W. Eighth St., Erie, PA 16502; (814) 453-4955; Fax: (814) 452-4784; E-mail: paxchristi@igc.apc.org

This Catholic peace organization, affiliated with Pax Christi International based in Alkmaar, Holland, has been working for disarmament and against violence in the United States since 1972. Through publications, a newsletter, an annual conference, lobbying, and nonviolent direct action, Pax Christi (Peace of Christ) promotes nonviolence and opposes violence in all of its forms. There are regional, campus, parish, and community Pax Christi groups throughout the country. The Pax Christi group in Hartford, Connecticut, for example, sponsors a monthly peace Mass, regularly holds prayer vigils at Electric Boat where nuclear submarines are manufactured, and often serves at local soup kitchens.

Fellowship of Reconciliation (FOR), 523 N. Broadway (or P.O. Box 271), Nyack, N.Y. 10960; (914) 358-4601; Fax: (914) 358-4924; E-mail: fornatl@igc.org; http://www.nonviolence.org/~nvweb/for.

The FOR is an international and interfaith pacifist group begun in Europe during World War I. The FOR has been working courageously and creatively against war and for justice and human rights ever since. The nonviolent spirit of the civil rights movement in the United States in the 1960s was at least indirectly fostered by FOR, which was, of course, simultaneously working against the Vietnam War. The FOR publishes a magazine, *Fellowship*, eight times a year, and holds a biannual conference. It is also organized into local groups which educate and agitate for peace in their regions.

American Friends Service Committee, 1501 Cherry Street, Philadelphia, PA 19102; (215) 242-7000; (800) 226-9816; Fax: (215) 864-0104; E-mail: afscinfo@afsc.org; http://www.afsc.org

This Quaker-inspired pacifist organization has been in business about as long as FOR. AFSC covers the gamut of peace and justice work, from education, to lobbying, to relief assistance, to nonviolent direct action. Its regional offices throughout the country and the world give AFSC national and global reach. AFSC was the co-recipient of the Nobel Peace Prize in 1947.

Center for Defense Information, 1500 Massachusetts Ave. N.W., Washington, D.C. 20005; (202) 862-0700; Fax: (202) 862-0708; E-mail: cdi@igc.apc.org

This is primarily a research and educational center dedicated to keeping the public informed about weapons spending and disarmament. Their newsletter, *The Defense Monitor*, is an excellent resource on weapons and defense spending.

Catholic Social Teaching

Center of Concern, 3700 13th St., N.E., Washington, D.C. 20017; (202) 635-2757; Fax: (202) 832-9494; E-mail: coc@igc.apc.org

Founded in 1971, the Center of Concern is a sort of think tank providing resources that analyze global social problems and offer constructive responses from the perspective of Catholic social teaching. The Center publishes a bimonthly newsletter and educational materials, and its staff lecture and offer workshops on global justice and peace. The Center is an important educational resource that complements the *United States Catholic Conference*, 1312 Massachusetts Ave., N.W., Washington, D.C. 20005-4105; (202) 541-300; Fax: (202) 541-3322, the official educational arm on social issues of the National Conference of Catholic Bishops.

RESOURCES FOR FURTHER INFORMATION AND STUDY

The endnotes to the chapters can steer the reader toward books and articles related to the particular issues addressed in this book. The purpose of this section is to highlight journals and books that are dedicated in a general way to the themes of justice and peace.

The first section above mentioned that many organizations publish a periodical or newsletter to keep their members informed about issues, such as *Bread* (BFW), *Connection* (Network), *Fellowship* (FOR), *Greenpeace Quarterly*, and *Human Rights Quarterly*. There are other periodicals, such

as *Sojourners, Maryknoll, The National Catholic Reporter, The Catholic Worker, The Other Side, The Journal for Peace & Justice Studies, Cross Currents, America*, and *Commonweal* that regularly address social issues from a Christian perspective, and there are journals, such as *Current History, The Nation, Foreign Affairs, Foreign Policy*, and *Ethics and International Affairs*, that can provide background information and analysis on global issues. Most libraries carry these sources of information or can get articles for patrons through interlibrary loan. A daily newspaper that has good international coverage, such as the *New York Times* or *The Washington Post*, can provide a wealth of information, as can weekly news magazines such as *Time, Newsweek*, and *U.S. News and World Report*.
The following is an annotated list of books that are good general reference books on issues related to justice and peace:

Brown, Lester R., et al., *State of the World 1997*. New York: W.W. Norton, 1997. Every year the Worldwatch Institute publishes a progress report on the movement toward a sustainable society. These reports focus on environmental issues.

Corson-Finnerty, Adam Daniel, *World Citizen*. Maryknoll, New York: Orbis Books, 1982. Although this book is dated and out-of-print, it is included in the list because it serves as a model for this book. It is still worth reading.

Crocker, Chester A., Fen Osler Hampson, with Pamela Aall, eds., *Managing Global Chaos*. Washington, D.C.: United States Institute of Peace, 1996. This is a comprehensive collection of essays by respected researchers on global issues.

Goldstein, Joshua S., *International Relations*. Second Edition. New York: HarperCollins, 1996. This is perhaps the best of the texts in international relations. The book is clear, informative, and concerned about humanity.

Himes, Michael J. and Kenneth R. Himes, *Fullness of Faith: The Public Significance of Theology*. New York: Paulist Press, 1993. The Himes brothers have produced a creative theological reflection on public policy themes.

Kegley, Charles W. and Eugene R. Wittkopf, *World Politics: Trend and Transformation*. Sixth Edition. New York: St. Martin's Press, 1997. This is a clear and comprehensive text on international relations.

Kennedy, Paul, *Preparing for the Twenty-first Century*. New York: Random House, 1993. Kennedy, who is a historian and a best-selling author, has written a thoughtful, well-researched, and provocative overview of the global situation as humanity enters a new millennium.

Klare, Michael T. and Daniel C. Thomas, eds., *World Security: Challenges for a New Century*. Second Edition. New York: St. Martin's Press, 1994. This is an excellent collection of essays by top scholars in the field on global issues.

O'Brien, David J. and Thomas A. Shannon, eds., *Catholic Social Thought: The Documentary Heritage*. Maryknoll, New York: Orbis Books, 1992. This is a collection of the documents of the Catholic Church that comprise a hundred years of Catholic social teaching.

Powers, Gerard F., Drew Christiansen, and Robert T. Hennemeyer, eds., *Peacemaking: Moral and Policy Choices for a New World*. Washington, DC: United States Catholic Conference, 1994. This book includes the National Conference of Catholic Bishops statement *The Harvest of Justice Is Sown in Peace*, which reflects on international relations in the post-Cold War world, and scholarly but readable reflections on the various issues.

Russett, Bruce and Harvey Starr, *World Politics: The Menu for Choice*. Fifth Edition. New York: W. H. Freeman, 1996. This a clear textbook on international relations that offers some constructive proposals for social transformation.

Todaro, Michael P., *Economic Development*. Sixth Edition. Reading, MA: Addison-Wesley Publ. Co., 1997. This textbook on economic development is clear and comprehensive.

United Nations Development Programme, *Human Development Report 1996*. New York: Oxford University Press, 1996. This is a thoughtful and statistic-filled annual report on global progress toward human development.

World Resources Institute, *World Resources 1996–97*. New York: Oxford University Press, 1996. This is a regularly published comprehensive guide to the global environment. In 1996–97 the focus was on the urban environment, but global conditions are always monitored and discussed.

PROJECTS

There are many interesting research projects that can be undertaken in connection with this material. For example:

- A film festival related to a global issue. On colonialism, for example, such an event could include "Black Robe," "Mister Johnson," "The Mission," and "Gandhi." On Central America, "Romero," Under Fire," "El Norte," and "Choices of the Heart."
- Research a commodity, such as coffee or sugar, uncovering the justice questions involved in its production and marketing.
- Research a country, paying attention to questions of justice and peace.
- Follow an issue in the news related to justice and peace, keeping a file of clippings from newspapers and news magazines, and summarizing your thoughts on the issue.
- Offer your time and energy to a soup kitchen, shelter, prison, or community agency, and keep a journal of reflections on your experience.
- Identify an issue related to justice or conflict resolution at your school,

workplace, community, or household, and try to accomplish some constructive change.

- Do an internship with the legislature, or identify a piece of legislation related to justice and lobby for its passage.
- Start a justice and peace committee at your place of worship or in your local community.
- Organize a lecture series on justice and peace issues at your school or for your community.
- Start or join a discussion group on justice and peace issues. You might even use this book for group reading and study.

Characteristics of the Countries of the World

This Appendix contains three different tables listing information on the countries of the world. The World Resources Institute, which publishes *World Resources 1996–97* (New York: Oxford University Press, 1996), also makes available a database on computer disks. Much of the following data is from the World Resources Institute database diskettes, and it is used with permission.

Table A.1 contains historical and population information.
 Column 1: lists the countries of the world in alphabetical order based on *World Resources 1996–97* database.
 Column 2: gives the date of independence if it is after 1775. Sources: George Thomas Kurian, ed., *Encyclopedia of the Third World* Fourth Edition (New York: Facts on File, 1992), Volume 3, Appendix I, p. 2233 and Bruce Russett and Harvey Starr, *World Politics* (New York: W. H. Freeman, 1996), Appendix B, pp. 476–82.
 Column 3: lists the former colonial power(s) which exercised control over the country. Source: Kurian, *Encyclopedia of the Third World*, p. 2233.
 Column 4: gives the area of the country in square kilometers, based on the same sources as column 2.
 Column 5: gives the population of the country in thousands in 1995. Source: *World Resources 1996–97* database.
 Column 6: gives the percentage of the change in the population during the period 1990–1995. A positive number indicates the amount of annual increase in the population during the five year period. Zero would indicate zero population growth. Source: *World Resources 1996–97* database.
 Column 7: lists the population density of each country, that is, the average number of persons per square kilometer, in 1995. Source: *World Resources 1996–97* database.
 Columns 8 and 9: list the annual fertility rate of the countries during the periods 1970–75 and 1990–95. The fertility rate refers to the average number of children a woman would have in her lifetime based on the number of children born in a given year. When a country's fertility rate is about 2, it means that each couple is replacing itself without increasing the size of the future population. Source: *World Resources 1996–97* database.

Table A.2 contains economic and social indicators. All of the following information is from the *World Resources 1996–97* database.

Column 1: lists the countries of the world in alphabetical order.

Column 2: gives the Gross Domestic Product, based on the official exchange rate of currencies, in dollars for 1993. Zero indicates that accurate data were not available.

Columns 3 and 4: give the per capita Gross Domestic Product of each country, first calculated according to the official exchange rate of currencies (for 1993), and second calculated on the basis of purchasing power parity (how much of the local currency would be needed to purchase a market basket of goods) (for 1992), which is a generally more accurate and favorable calculation for developing countries. The figures are in U.S. dollars.

Column 5: gives the average life expectancy at birth for each country during the period 1990–95. For example, in 1995 the average American could expect to live 76 years.

Column 6: gives the infant mortality rate for each country during the period 1990–95, that is, the number of deaths of infants (under 1 year of age) per 1,000 live births.

Table A.3 contains the Human Development Index Rank and Value and the Gender Development Index Rank and Value. The source of this information is the United Nations Development Programme, *Human Development Report 1996* (New York: Oxford University Press, 1996), used with permission. The Human Development Index, explained in chapter 2, includes social indicators as well as economic ones to yield a more accurate picture of whether economic growth is resulting in human development. The Gender Development Index, referred to in chapter 4, uses social indicators specified by gender to point to the status of gender equality and the development of women in a country.

Column 1: lists the countries of the world according to their HDI rank.

Column 2: gives the HDI ranking of each country.

Column 3: gives the HDI value for each country, with 1 (one) being the best score.

Column 4: gives the GDI rank for each country.

Column 5: gives the GDI value with 1 (one) representing equality in the development and status of women and men.

Table A.1
Historical and Population Information

Country	Date of Independence	Former Colonial Power	Area (1,000 sq km)	Population (in thousands) 1995	Avg Annual Pop Change 1990–95	Population Density (per sq km) 1995	Fertility 1970–75	Fertility 1990–95
Afghanistan	1775		648	20141	5.83	31	7.14	6.90
Albania	1912		29	3441	0.90	120	4.66	2.85
Algeria	1962	France	2382	27939	2.27	12	7.38	3.85
Angola	1975	Portugal	1247	11072	3.72	9	6.60	7.20
Antigua and Barbuda	1981	U.K.	0.4	66	X	X	X	X
Argentina	1816	Spain	2767	34587	1.22	13	3.15	2.77
Armenia	1991		30	3599	1.43	121	3.04	2.60
Australia	1920	U.K.	7687	18088	1.37	2	2.53	1.87
Austria	1918		84	7968	0.67	95	2.02	1.53
Azerbaijan	1991		87	7558	1.20	87	4.29	2.50
Bahamas	1973	U.K.	14	276	1.51	20	2.99	2.00
Bahrain	1971	U.K.	1	564	2.80	831	5.94	3.75
Bangladesh	1971	U.K.	144	120433	2.16	836	7.02	4.35
Barbados	1966	U.K.	4	262	0.35	609	2.74	1.83
Belarus, Rep	1991		208	10141	-0.14	49	2.24	1.65
Belgium	1830		31	10113	0.32	331	1.94	1.64
Belgium/Luxembourg	1830		31	X	X	X	X	X
Belize	1981	U.K.	23	215	2.64	9	6.25	4.18
Benin	1960	France	113	5409	3.10	48	7.06	7.10

Table A.1 continued

Country	Date of Independence	Former Colonial Power	Area (1,000 sq km)	Population (in thousands) 1995	Avg Annual Pop Change 1990–95	Population Density (per sq km) 1995	Fertility 1970–75	Fertility 1990–95
Bhutan	1949		47	1638	1.18	35	5.92	5.86
Bolivia	1825	Spain	1099	7414	2.41	7	6.504.80	1.60
Bosnia and Herzegovina	1992		51	3459	-4.39	68	2.63	4.85
Botswana	1966	U.K.	600	1487	3.06	3	6.60	2.88
Brazil	1822	Portugal	8512	161790	1.72	19	4.70	3.07
Brunei	1984	U.K.	6	285	2.06	49	5.40	1.50
Bulgaria	1908		111	8769	-0.50	79	2.17	6.50
Burkina Faso	1960		274	10319	2.76	38	6.41	6.80
Burundi	1962	Belgium	28	6393	3.00	230	6.80	5.25
Cambodia	1953	France	181	10251	2.96	57	5.53	5.70
Cameroon	1960	France	475	13233	2.76	28	6.30	1.86
Canada	1920	U.K.	9976	29463	1.17	3	1.97	4.26
Cape Verde	1975	Portugal	4	392	2.77	97	7.00	5.69
Cent. African Republic	1960	France	623	3315	2.49	5	5.72	5.89
Chad	1960	France	1284	6361	2.72	5	5.99	2.54
Chile	1818	Spain	757	14262	1.62	19	3.63	1.95
China			9561	1221462	1.11	127	4.76	2.67
Colombia	1819	Spain	1139	35101	1.66	31	4.66	7.05
Comoros	1975	France	2	653	3.68	292	7.05	6.29
Congo	1960	France	342	2590	2.98	8	6.29	

Country	Year	Colonial Power						
Costa Rica	1821	Spain	51	3424	2.41	67	4.33	3.14
Côte d'Ivoire	1960	France		14253	3.48	44	7.41	7.41
Croatia, Rep	1991		56	4495	-0.10	80	1.96	1.65
Cuba	1902	Spain	115	11041	0.82	100	3.55	1.82
Cyprus	1960		9	742	1.11	80	2.48	2.48
Czech Republic	1993		128	10296	-0.02	131	2.21	1.83
Denmark			43	5181	0.16	120	1.97	1.70
Djibouti	1977	France	23	577	2.20	25	6.70	5.80
Dominica	1978	France & U.K.	1	71	X	X	X	X
Dominican Republic	1844	Spain	49	7823	1.91	161	5.63	3.09
Ecuador	1822	Spain	284	11460	2.20	40	6.00	3.52
Egypt	1922	U.K.	1001	62931	2.22	63	5.53	3.88
El Salvador	1841	Spain	21	5768	2.18	274	6.10	4.04
Equatorial Guinea	1968	Spain	2	400	2.55	14	5.68	5.89
Eritrea	1993		121	3531	2.72	30	6.20	5.80
Estonia, Rep	1991		45	1530	-0.57	34	2.15	1.61
Ethiopia			1222	55053	2.98	50	6.80	7.00
Fiji	1970	U.K.	18	784	1.52	43	4.20	2.98
Finland	1919		337	5107	0.48	15	1.62	1.85
France			547	57981	0.44	105	2.31	1.74
French Guiana				147	X	X	X	X
Gabon	1960	France	268	1320	2.83	5	4.26	5.34
Gambia	1965	U.K.	11	1118	3.83	99	6.50	5.60
Georgia, Rep	1991		69	5457	0.14	78	2.60	2.10

Table A.1 continued

Table A.1 continued

Country	Date of Independence	Former Colonial Power	Area (1,000 sq km)	Population (in thousands) 1995	Avg Annual Pop Change 1990–95	Population Density (per sq km) 1995	Fertility 1970–75	Fertility 1990–95
Germany	1871		357	81591	0.55	229	1.64	1.30
Ghana	1957	U.K.	239	17453	3.00	73	6.64	5.96
Greece	1828		132	10451	0.41	79	2.32	1.40
Greenland				58	X	X	X	X
Grenada	1974	U.K.	0.3	92	X	X	X	X
Guatemala	1821	Spain	109	10621	2.88	98	6.45	5.36
Guinea	1958	France	246	6700	3.04	27	7.00	7.00
Guinea-Bissau	1974	Portugal	37	1073	2.14	30	5.38	5.79
Guyana	1966	U.K.	215	835	0.94	4	4.90	2.55
Haiti	1804	France	28	7180	2.03	259	5.76	4.79
Honduras	1821	Spain	112	5654	2.95	50	7.05	4.92
Hong Kong	1997	U.K.		5865	0.55	5612	2.89	1.21
Hungary	1918		93	10115	-0.49	109	2.09	1.71
Iceland	1944		103	269	1.06	3	2.84	2.23
India	1947	U.K.	3288	935744	1.91	285	5.43	3.75
Indonesia	1945	Netherlands	2027	197588	1.55	104	5.10	2.90
Iran			1648	67283	2.65	41	6.54	5.00
Iraq	1932	U.K.	435	20449	2.47	47	7.11	5.70
Ireland	1922	U.K.	70	3553	0.28	51	3.80	2.10
Israel	1948		21	5629	3.78	267	3.77	2.88
Italy	1861		301	57187	0.06	190	2.28	1.27

Country	Year							
Japan			372	125095	0.25	331	2.07	1.50
Jordan	1946	U.K.	98	5439	4.89	56	7.79	5.57
Kazakhstan, Rep	1991		2717	17111	0.52	6	3.45	2.50
Kenya	1963	U.K.	583	28261	3.59	49	8.12	6.28
North Korea	1948	Japan	121	23917	1.88	198	5.70	2.37
South Korea	1948	Japan	98	44995	0.97	454	4.11	1.73
Kuwait	1961	U.K.	18	1547	-6.52	87	6.90	3.10
Kyrgyz Rep	1991		199	4745	1.68	24	4.73	3.70
Lao People's Dem Rep	1953	France		4882	3.00	21	6.15	6.69
Latvia, Rep	1991		64	2557	-0.87	40	2.00	1.64
Lebanon	1946	France	10	3009	3.27	289	4.92	3.09
Lesotho	1966	U.K.	30	2050	2.69	68	5.74	5.20
Liberia	1822		111	3039	3.32	27	6.80	6.80
Libya	1951	Italy	1760	5407	3.47	3	7.58	6.39
Lithuania, Rep	1991		65	3700	-0.06	57	2.31	1.83
Luxembourg			0.3	406	1.26	157	1.96	1.65
Macedonia	1991		25	2163	1.11	84	2.95	1.97
Madagascar	1958	France	587	14763	3.22	25	6.60	6.10
Malawi	1964	U.K.	118	11129	3.45	94	7.40	7.20
Malaysia	1957	U.K.	330	20140	2.37	61	5.15	3.62
Maldives	1965	U.K.	0.3	254	3.31	854	7.00	6.80
Mali	1960	France	1240	10795	3.17	9	7.10	7.10
Malta	1964		0.3	366	0.67	1159	2.07	2.05
Martinique				379	1.00	344	4.08	1.95
Mauritania	1960	France	1031	2274	2.54	2	6.50	5.40

Table A.1 continued

Table A.1 continued

Country	Date of Independence	Former Colonial Power	Area (1,000 sq km)	Population (in thousands) 1995	Avg Annual Pop Change 1990–95	Population Density (per sq km) 1995	Fertility 1970–75	Fertility 1990–95
Mauritius	1968	France & U.K.	2	1117	1.10	547	3.25	2.35
Mexico	1821	Spain	1973	93674	2.06	48	6.37	3.21
Moldova, Rep	1991		34	4432	0.32	132	2.56	2.13
Mongolia	1921		1565	2410	2.03	2	5.80	3.56
Morocco	1956	France	447	27028	2.10	61	6.89	3.75
Mozambique	1975	Portugal	802	16004	2.41	20	6.50	6.50
Myanmar (Burma)	1948	U.K.	677	46527	2.14	69	5.75	4.16
Namibia	1990		824	1540	2.65	2	6.00	5.25
Nepal			141	21918	2.59	156	6.26	5.42
Netherlands			41	15503	0.73	380	1.97	1.61
Neth. Antilles & Aruba				199	0.89	X	2.65	2.10
New Zealand	1920	U.K.	269	3575	1.24	13	2.79	2.17
Nicaragua	1821	Spain	130	4433	3.74	34	6.79	5.04
Niger	1960	France	1267	9151	3.37	7	8.12	7.40
Nigeria	1960	U.K.	924	111721	3.00	121	6.45	6.45
Norway	1905		324	4337	0.45	13	2.25	1.93
Oman	1970		300	2163	4.23	10	7.20	7.20
Pakistan	1947	U.K.	804	140497	2.83	176	7.00	6.17
Panama	1819	Spain	77	2631	1.86	35	4.93	2.88
Papua New Guinea	1975	Australia	462	4302	2.27	9	6.08	5.05
Paraguay	1811	Spain	407	4960	2.78	12	5.65	4.21

			1285	23780	1.93	19	6.00	3.40
Peru	1821	Spain	1285	23780	1.93	19	6.00	3.40
Philippines	1946	Spain & U.S.	300	67581	2.12	225	5.50	3.93
Poland, Rep	1919		313	38388	0.14	119	2.25	1.88
Portugal			92	9823	-0.09	106	2.76	1.55
Puerto Rico				3674	0.80	413	3.00	2.18
Qatar	1971	U.K.	1	551	2.53	50	6.76	4.33
Reunion				653	1.55	260	3.93	2.32
Romania	1878		238	22835	-0.32	96	2.63	1.50
Russian Federation				147000	-0.12	9	1.98	1.53
Rwanda	1962	Belgium	26	7952	2.59	302	8.29	6.55
São Tomé and Principe	1975	Portugal	1	133	X	X	X	X
Saudi Arabia	1902		2150	17880	2.16	8	7.30	6.37
Senegal	1960	France	196	8312	2.52	42	7.00	6.06
Seychelles	1976	France & U.K.	0.4	73	X	X	X	X
Sierra Leone	1961	U.K.	72	4509	2.40	63	6.50	6.50
Singapore	1965	U.K.	1	2848	1.03	4608	2.62	1.73
Slovak Republic	1993		49	5353	0.37	109	2.51	1.92
Slovenia, Rep	1991		20	1946	0.29	96	2.19	1.45
Solomon Islands	1978	U.K.	30	378	3.32	13	7.23	5.39
Somalia	1960	U.K. & Italy	638	9250	1.28	15	7.00	7.00
South Africa	1920		1221	41465	2.24	34	5.49	4.09
Spain			505	39621	0.18	78	2.89	1.23
Sri Lanka	1948	U.K.	66	18354	1.27	280	4.00	2.48

Table A.1 continued   **223**

Table A.1 continued

Country	Date of Independence	Former Colonial Power	Area (1,000 sq km)	Population (in thousands) 1995	Avg Annual Pop Change 1990–95	Population Density (per sq km) 1995	Fertility 1970–75	Fertility 1990–95
St. Kitts and Nevis	1983	U.K.	0.3	41	X	X	X	X
St. Lucia	1979	France	1	X	X	X	X	X
St. Vincent	1979	U.K.	0.4	112	X	X	X	X
Sudan	1956	U.K.	2506	28098	2.67	11	6.67	5.74
Suriname	1975	Netherlands	163	423	1.10	3	5.29	2.68
Swaziland	1968	U.K.	17	855	2.78	49	6.50	4.86
Sweden			450	8780	0.51	20	1.89	2.10
Switzerland			41	7202	1.05	174	1.81	1.60
Syria	1946	France		14661	3.43	79	7.69	5.90
Taiwan	1949		36	X	X	X	X	X
Tajikistan, Rep	1991		143	6101	2.86	43	6.83	4.90
Tanzania	1964	U.K.	945	29685	2.96	31	6.80	5.90
Thailand			514	58791	1.12	115	5.01	2.10
Togo	1960	France	57	4138	3.18	73	6.58	6.58
Tonga	1970	U.K.	1	98	X	X	X	X
Trinidad and Tobago	1962	U.K.	5	1306	1.10	255	3.45	2.40
Tunisia	1956	France	164	8896	1.92	54	6.15	3.15
Turkey			781	61945	1.98	79	5.04	3.35
Turkmenistan, Rep	1991		488	4099	2.28	8	6.19	4.00
Tuvalu	1978	U.K.	0.03	10	X	X	X	X
Uganda	1962	U.K.	236	21297	3.42	90	6.90	7.30

Ukraine	1991		604	51380	-0.10	85	2.04	1.64
United Arab Emirates	1971		84	1904	2.62	23	6.35	4.24
United Kingdom			244	58258	0.29	239	2.04	1.81
United States	1776	U.K.	9363	263250	1.04	28	2.02	2.08
Uruguay	1825	Spain	176	3186	0.58	18	3.00	2.33
Uzbekistan, Rep	1991		447	22843	2.24	51	6.01	3.90
Vanuatu	1980	U.K. & France	12	169	2.49	14	6.50	4.68
Venezuela	1811	Spain	912	21844	2.27	24	4.94	3.29
Viet Nam	1945	France	330	74545	2.23	225	5.85	3.87
Western Samoa	1962	U.K.	3	171	1.07	61	7.10	4.50
Yemen	1990		528	14501	4.97	27	7.61	7.60
Yemen, Republic of				14501	4.97	X	X	X
Yugoslavia (Serbia)				10849	1.32	106	2.36	2.03
Zaire/Congo	1960	Belgium	2345	43901	3.19	19	6.30	6.70
Zambia	1964	U.K.	753	9456	2.97	13	6.90	5.98
Zimbabwe	1980	U.K.	391	11261	2.57	29	7.20	5.01
AFRICA				728074	2.81		6.55	5.80
ASIA				3457957	1.64		5.06	3.03
CENTRAL AMER/CARIB				126419	2.24		6.31	3.52
EUROPE				726999	0.15		2.14	1.58
NORTH AMERICA				292841	1.05		2.01	2.06
OCEANIA				28549	1.54		3.21	2.51
SOUTH AMERICA				319790	1.74		4.61	2.97
WORLD				5716426	1.57		4.46	3.10

Table A.2
Economic and Social Indicators

Country	Gross Domestic Product (Exchange Rate Based) 1993	GDP Per Capita (Exchange Rate Based) 1993	GDP Per Capita (Constant PPP) 1992	Life Expectancy at Birth 1990–95	Infant Mortality Rate 1990–95
Afghanistan	$0	X	X	43.5	163
Albania	$0	X	X	72	30
Algeria	$49,762,265,284	1862	2719	67.1	55
Angola	$0	X	X	46.5	124
Antigua and Barbuda	$457,111,127	7032	X	X	X
Argentina	$255,594,581,140	7567	X	72.1	24
Armenia	$2,189,941,105	587	X	72.6	21
Australia	$289,390,386,121	16444	14458	77.6	7
Austria	$182,067,018,051	23159	12955	76.2	7
Azerbaijan	$4,992,354,907	676	X	70.6	28
Bahamas	$3,064,999,936	11444	X	73.1	23
Bahrain	$4,547,606,624	8530	X	71.6	18
Bangladesh	$23,976,728,457	208	1510	55.6	108
Barbados	$1,631,034,568	6273	X	75.6	9
Belarus, Rep	$27,545,052,800	2704	X	69.8	16
Belgium	$210,576,329,241	20957	13484	76.4	6
Belize	$523,900,000	2568	4253	73.6	33
Benin	$2,125,300,784	418	X	47.6	86
Bhutan	$238,936,764	X	X	50.7	124
Bolivia	$5,382,274,299	762	1721	59.4	75
Bosnia and Herzegovina	$0	X	X	72.4	15
Botswana	$3,813,446,337	2722	X	64.9	43
Brazil	$507,352,835,801	3242	3882	66.3	58
Brunei	$0	X	X	74.2	8
Bulgaria	$10,369,432,129	1169	5208	71.2	14
Burkina Faso	$2,814,663,989	288	514	47.4	130
Burundi	$948,270,144	157	569	50.2	102
Cambodia	$1,995,683,413	206	X	51.6	116
Cameroon	$11,081,717,796	885	1029	56	63
Canada	$546,349,346,160	18982	16362	77.4	7
Cape Verde	$309,597,513	837	1085	64.7	50
Cent.Afri. Rep	$1,233,491,839	391	514	49.4	102
Chad	$1,196,849,488	199	408	47.5	122
Chile	$45,638,782,436	3302	4890	73.8	16
China	$425,610,959,831	361	1493	68.5	44
Colombia	$54,076,342,379	1516	3380	69.3	37
Comoros	$247,944,498	526	527	56	89

Congo	$2,385,056,012	976	2240	51.3	84
Costa Rica	$7,577,328,880	2317	3569	76.3	14
Côte d'Ivoire	$9,297,980,062	698	1104	51	92
Croatia, Rep	$11,688,286,891	2591	X	71.4	9
Cuba	$0	X	X	75.3	12
Cyprus	$6,480,901,126	8930	9203	77	9
Czech Rep	$31,613,012,461	3070	X	71.3	9
Denmark	$135,997,704,067	26333	14091	75.3	7
Djibouti	$464,829,884	835	X	48.3	115
Dominica	$196,185,111	2763	X	X	X
Dominican Rep	$9,509,583,031	1261	2250	69.6	42
Ecuador	$14,304,142,774	1303	2830	68.8	50
Egypt	$39,356,843,591	697	1869	63.6	67
El Salvador	$7,624,892,201	1382	1876	66.4	46
Equatorial Guinea	$156,561,707	413	X	48	117
Eritrea	$487,865,421	X	X	50.4	105
Estonia, Rep	$5,092,054,476	3281	X	69.3	16
Ethiopia	$0	X	X	47.5	119
Fiji	$1,684,176,292	2210	X	71.5	23
Finland	$83,794,068,579	16566	12000	75.7	5
France	$1,251,689,229,402	21779	13918	76.9	7
French Guiana	$0	X	X	X	X
Gabon	$5,420,258,907	5383	3622	53.5	94
Gambia	$360,900,342	346	X	45	132
Georgia, Rep	$2,994,376,399	550	X	72.8	19
Germany	$1,910,760,774,135	23679	14709	76	6
Ghana	$6,084,209,488	370	956	56	81
Greece	$73,182,115,565	7060	X	77.6	10
Greenland	$0	X	X	X	X
Grenada	$221,703,771	2410	X	X	X
Guatemala	$11,309,401,320	1128	2247	64.8	48
Guinea	$3,171,637,869	503	740	44.5	134
Guinea-Bissau	$241,426,401	235	634	43.5	140
Guyana	$326,361,497	400	X	65.2	48
Haiti	$1,454,814,853	211	X	56.6	86
Honduras	$3,343,078,541	627	1385	67.7	43
Hong Kong	$109,598,869,924	18895	16471	78.6	7
Hungary	$38,099,487,071	3732	4645	69	15
Iceland	$6,075,985,614	23075	12618	78.2	5
India	$250,966,034,854	279	1282	60.4	82
Indonesia	$144,706,523,813	773	2102	62.7	58
Iran	$0	X	3685	67.5	36
Iraq	$0	X	X	66	58
Ireland	$47,676,701,979	13495	9637	75.3	7
Israel	$69,738,878,647	13362	9843	76.5	9

Table A.2 continued   **227**

Country	Gross Domestic Product (Exchange Rate Based) 1993	GDP Per Capita (Exchange Rate Based) 1993	GDP Per Capita (Constant PPP) 1992	Life Expectancy at Birth 1990–95	Infant Mortality Rate 1990–95
Italy	$991,385,705,619	17356	12721	77.5	8
Jamaica	$3,825,484,287	1587	X	73.6	14
Japan	$4,214,203,537,793	33857	15105	79.5	4
Jordan	$5,190,004,586	1265	X	67.9	36
Kazakhstan	$24,727,544,123	1459	X	69.6	30
Kenya	$5,538,706,753	219	914	55.7	69
Kiribati	$0	X	X	X	X
North Korea	$0	X	X	71.1	24
South Korea	$330,830,477,323	7497	X	71.1	11
Kuwait	$22,402,311,807	12711	X	74.9	18
Kyrgyz Rep	$3,915,442,583	853	X	69	35
Lao People's Dem Rep	$1,333,575,405	290	X	51	97
Latvia, Rep	$4,601,475,497	1762	X	69.1	14
Lebanon	$7,535,489,337	1955	X	68.5	34
Lesotho	$758,579,226	390	952	60.5	79
Liberia	$0	X	X	55.4	126
Libya	$0	X	X	63.1	68
Lithuania, Rep	$4,335,001,780	1168	X	70.4	13
Luxembourg	$12,503,519,084	31590	16798	75.7	7
Macedonia	$1,704,347,403	821	X	71.8	27
Madagascar	$3,352,211,653	242	608	56.5	93
Malawi	$1,973,688,548	188	496	45.6	143
Malaysia	$64,449,707,454	3384	5746	70.8	13
Maldives	$226,669,710	952	X	62.1	60
Mali	$2,662,099,948	263	X	46	159
Malta	$2,443,455,837	6766	X	76.1	9
Martinique	$0	X	X	76.2	8
Mauritania	$947,386,703	438	837	51.5	101
Mauritius	$3,279,796,805	3006	6167	70.2	18
Mexico	$343,472,416,242	3815	6253	70.8	36
Moldova, Rep	$4,292,250,952	974	X	67.6	25
Mongolia	$1,092,925,970	471	X	63.7	60
Morocco	$26,635,445,978	1027	2173	63.3	68
Mozambique	$1,467,456,457	97	711	46.4	148
Myanmar	$55,223,604,650	1238	X	57.6	84
Namibia	$2,507,550,763	1716	2774	58.8	60
Nepal	$3,748,230,808	180	X	53.5	99
Netherlands	$309,226,834,736	20237	13281	77.4	7
Neth. Antilles & Aruba	$0	X	X	73.1	X

New Zealand	$43,698,764,892	12530	11363	75.5	9
Nicaragua	$1,799,779,422	437	X	66.7	52
Niger	$2,219,985,853	260	X	46.5	124
Nigeria	$31,593,020,285	300	978	50.4	84
Norway	$103,418,596,029	24060	15518	76.9	8
Oman	$11,685,828,172	5879	X	69.6	30
Pakistan	$51,824,673,329	422	1432	61.5	91
Panama	$6,564,900,864	2587	3332	72.8	25
Papua New Guinea	$5,090,595,153	1239	1606	55.8	68
Paraguay	$6,824,662,417	1452	2178	70	38
Peru	$41,060,712,493	1794	2092	66	64
Philippines	$54,067,990,945	834	1689	66.3	44
Poland, Rep	$85,852,848,668	2241	3826	71.1	15
Portugal	$85,665,423,161	8705	X	74.6	10
Puerto Rico	$35,833,602,048	9909	X	75.3	11
Qatar	$7,428,571,214	14188	X	70.5	20
Reunion	$0	X	X	73.5	8
Romania	$25,968,663,901	1141	X	69.9	23
Russian Federation	$329,232,565,456	2214	X	67.6	21
Rwanda	$1,494,072,804	198	762	47.3	110
São Tomé and Principe	$39,171,794	321	X	X	X
Saudi Arabia	$0	X	X	69.7	29
Senegal	$5,770,480,189	730	X	49.3	68
Seychelles	$444,272,922	6170	X	X	X
Sierra Leone	$731,956,046	164	734	39	166
Singapore	$55,153,468,293	19769	12653	74.8	6
Slovak Rep	$11,075,864,087	2085	X	70.9	12
Slovenia, Rep	$11,974,356,165	6182	X	72.6	8
Solomon Islands	$0	X	X	70.4	27
Somalia	$0	X	X	47	122
South Africa	$117,432,985,821	2961	3068	62.9	53
Spain	$478,581,646,814	12122	9802	77.6	7
Sri Lanka	$10,472,350,082	585	2215	71.9	18
St. Kitts and Nevis	$194,962,960	4642	4799	X	X
St. Lucia	$495,666,670	3491	X	X	X
St. Vincent	$234,740,689	2134	X	X	X
Sudan	$0	X	X	53	78
Suriname	$420,181,269	1015	X	70.3	28
Swaziland	$1,037,943,732	1179	X	57.5	75
Sweden	$185,288,619,961	21320	13986	78.2	5
Switzerland	$232,160,576,133	32919	15887	78	6

Table A.2 continued   **229**

Syria	$0	X	X	67.1	39
Taiwan	$0	X	X	X	163
Tajikistan, Rep	$2,519,840,999	437	X	70.2	48
Tanzania	$2,373,163,622	85	X	52.1	85
Thailand	$124,861,725,746	2150	3942	69	37
Togo	$1,249,470,636	322	530	55	85
Trinidad and Tobago	$4,670,448,771	3654	X	71.6	18
Tunisia	$14,634,253,384	1691	3075	67.8	43
Turkey	$174,166,563,364	2922	3807	66.5	65
Turkmenistan	$0	X	X	65	57
Tuvalu	$0	179	547	X	X
Uganda	$3,235,656,131	179	547	44.9	115
Ukraine	$109,078,413,984	2116	X	69.4	16
United Arab Emirates	$35,404,522,973	19592	X	73.8	19
United Kingdom	$941,423,939,535	16255	12724	76.2	7
United States	$6,259,899,105,280	24279	17945	76	9
Uruguay	$13,143,548,493	4174	5185	72.5	20
Uzbekistan, Rep	$20,424,814,048	934	X	69.2	41
Vanuatu	$0	X	X	65.2	47
Venezuela	$59,995,039,142	2869	7082	71.7	23
Viet Nam	$12,834,414,151	180	X	65.2	42
Western Samoa	$0	X	X	67.6	64
Yemen	$0	X	X	50.2	119
Yemen, Rep	$12,615,928,043	956	X	X	X
Yugoslavia, Fed Rep (Serbia)	$0	X	X	72	20
Zaire/Congo	$0	X	X	52	93
Zambia	$3,685,173,759	412	X	48.9	104
Zimbabwe	$5,635,230,799	525	X	53.7	67

Table A.3
Human Development Index/Gender Development Index: Rank and Value

Country	HDI Rank	HDI Value	GDI Rank	GDI Value
Canada	1	0.951	2	0.927
USA	2	0.940	4	0.923
Japan	3	0.938	12	0.897
Netherlands	4	0.938	11	0.898
Norway	5	0.937	3	0.926
Finland	6	0.935	5	0.921
France	7	0.935	8	0.913
Iceland	8	0.934	6	0.920
Sweden	9	0.933	1	0.929
Spain	10	0.933	20	0.866
Australia	11	0.929	9	0.912
Belgium	12	0.929	15	0.885
Austria	13	0.928	13	0.887
New Zealand	14	0.927	10	0.906
Switzerland	15	0.926	19	0.869
United Kingdom	16	0.924	14	0.886
Denmark	17	0.924	7	0.913
Germany	18	0.920	17	0.883
Ireland	19	0.919	27	0.835
Italy	20	0.914	21	0.856
Greece	21	0.909	22	0.853
Hong Kong	22	0.909	25	0.843
Cyprus	23	0.909		
Israel	24	0.908		
Barbados	25	0.906	16	0.884
Bahamas	26	0.895	18	0.879
Luxembourg	27	0.895		
Malta	28	0.886		
South Korea	29	0.886	31	0.816
Argentina	30	0.885	45	0.766
Costa Rica	31	0.884	32	0.813
Uruguay	32	0.883	26	0.837
Chile	33	0.882	44	0.767
Singapore	34	0.881	29	0.833
Portugal	35	0.878	30	0.833
Brunei Darussalam	36	0.872	35	0.808
Czech Rep	37	0.872	23	0.853
Trinidad and Tobago	38	0.872	34	0.809
Bahrain	39	0.866	52	0.726
Antigua and Barbuda	40	0.866		

Table A.3 continued **231**

Country	HDI Rank	HDI Value	GDI Rank	GDI Value
Slovakia	41	0.864	24	0.850
United Arab Emirates	42	0.864	56	0.710
Panama	43	0.859	39	0.792
Venezuela	44	0.859	41	0.784
Saint Kitts and Nevis	45	0.858		
Hungary	46	0.855	28	0.835
Fiji	47	0.853	50	0.734
Mexico	48	0.845	46	0.755
Colombia	49	0.84	38	0.797
Qatar	50	0.839	58	0.700
Kuwait	51	0.836	55	0.719
Thailand	52	0.832	33	0.811
Malaysia	53	0.826	43	0.772
Mauritius	54	0.825	47	0.740
Latvia	55	0.820	36	0.806
Poland	56	0.819	37	0.802
Russian Federation	57	0.804	40	0.790
Brazil	58	0.796	49	0.739
Libya	59	0.792	73	0.633
Seychelles	60	0.792		
Belarus	61	0.787	42	0.778
Bulgaria	62	0.773		
Saudi Arabia	63	0.772	85	0.551
Ecuador	64	0.764	66	0.661
Dominica	65	0.764		
Iran	66	0.755	75	0.618
Belize	67	0.754		
Estonia	68	0.749	48	0.740
Algeria	69	0.746	81	0.596
Jordan	70	0.741		
Botswana	71	0.741	54	0.723
Kazakhstan	72	0.740	51	0.732
Saint Vincent	73	0.738		
Romania	74	0.738	53	0.726
Suriname	75	0.737		
Saint Lucia	76	0.733		
Grenada	77	0.729		
Tunisia	78	0.727	68	0.647
Cuba	79	0.726	59	0.699
Ukraine	80	0.719		
Lithuania	81	0.719	57	0.709
Oman	82	0.716		
North Korea	83	0.714		
Turkey	84	0.711	61	0.680

Paraguay	85	0.704	67	0.649
Jamaica	86	0.702	60	0.693
Dominican Rep.	87	0.701	71	0.641
Samoa (Western)	88	0.700		
Sri Lanka	89	0.698	62	0.679
Turkmenistan	90	0.695		
Peru	91	0.694	72	0.634
Syrian Arab Rep.	92	0.690	82	0.591
Armenia	93	0.680	63	0.677
Uzbekistan	94	0.679		
Philippines	95	0.666	70	0.644
Azerbaijan	96	0.665	65	0.661
Lebanon	97	0.664	77	0.615
Moldova, Rep. of	98	0.663		
Kyrgyzstan	99	0.663	64	0.661
South Africa	100	0.649	74	0.622
Georgia	101	0.645	69	0.646
Indonesia	102	0.641	76	0.616
Guyana	103	0.634	78	0.604
Albania	104	0.633	.	
Tajikistan	105	0.616		
Egypt	106	0.611	87	0.545
Maldives	107	0.61	80	0.599
China	108	0.609	79	0.601
Iraq	109	0.599	96	0.486
Swaziland	110	0.586	84	0.566
Bolivia	111	0.584	86	0.549
Guatemala	112	0.580	94	0.506
Mongolia	113	0.578	83	0.572
Honduras	114	0.577	90	0.542
El Salvador	115	0.576	88	0.544
Namibia	116	0.573		
Nicaragua	117	0.569	89	0.544
Solomon Islands	118	0.563		
Vanuatu	119	0.562		
Gabon	120	0.557		
Viet Nam	121	0.540	91	0.539
Cape Verde	122	0.539	93	0.517
Morocco	123	0.534	97	0.486
Zimbabwe	124	0.534	92	0.525
Congo	125	0.517		
Papua New Guinea	126	0.504	95	0.490
Cameroon	127	0.482	100	0.455
Kenya	128	0.473	98	0.469
Ghana	129	0.467	99	0.459
Lesotho	130	0.464	101	0.454
Equatorial Guinea	131	0.461		

Table A.3 continued   **233**

São Tomé and Principe	132	0.459		
Myanimar	133	0.451	102	0.447
Pakistan	134	0.442	107	0.383
India	135	0.436	103	0.410
Zambia	136	0.411	104	0.405
Nigeria	137	0.401	108	0.380
Lao People's Dem. Rep.	138	0.340	106	0.387
Comoros	139	0.399	105	0.391
Togo	140	0.385	110	0.364
Zaire/Congo	141	0.371	109	0.364
Yemen	142	0.366	122	0.311
Bangladesh	143	0.365	116	0.336
Tanzania	144	0.364	111	0.359
Haiti	145	0.360	112	0.354
Sudan	146	0.359	118	0.327
Côte d'Ivoire	147	0.357	117	0.328
Central African Rep.	148	0.355	113	0.346
Mauritania	149	0.353	115	0.338
Madagascar	150	0.349	114	0.346
Nepal	151	0.332	124	0.308
Rwanda	152	0.332		
Senegal	153	0.331	120	0.314
Benin	154	0.327	123	0.311
Uganda	155	0.327	119	0.318
Cambodia	156	0.325		
Malawi	157	0.321	121	0.312
Liberia	158	0.311		
Bhutan	159	0.307		
Guinea	160	0.307	125	0.286
Guinea-Bissau	161	0.297	126	0.281
Gambia	162	0.292	127	0.275
Chad	163	0.291	128	0.275
Djibouti	164	0.287		
Angola	165	0.283	130	0.270
Burundi	166	0.282	129	0.271
Mozambique	167	0.261	131	0.245
Ethiopia	168	0.237	132	0.227
Afghanistan	169	0.229	135	0.196
Burkina Faso	170	0.225	134	0.211
Mali	171	0.223	133	0.215
Somalia	172	0.221		·
Sierra Leone	173	0.219	136	0.196
Niger	174	0.204	137	0.192

Source: *Human Development Report 1996*, pp. 28–29, 138–139

Notes

INTRODUCTION

1. National Conference of Catholic Bishops (NCCB), *The Challenge of Peace: God's Promise and Our Response* (1983) in David J. O'Brien and Thomas A. Shannon, eds., *Catholic Social Thought: The Documentary Heritage* (Maryknoll, NY: Orbis Books, 1992), #68. References to official documents of the Catholic Church will use the paragraph or section numbers, rather than page numbers.
2. NCCB, *Economic Justice for All* (1986) in O'Brien and Shannon, eds., *Catholic Social Thought*, #8 in the introductory message. These two opening quotes indicate at least a description (rather than a definition) of peace and justice from a Christian perspective. Peace is not merely the absence of war, but the presence of justice and community. A society is just when every person has his or her basic needs met and the opportunity to realize his or her human potential, to flourish. The litmus test of the justice of a society is the condition of the poor and the marginalized people (#38, #123). The U.S. bishops present a fuller description of justice in *Economic Justice for All*, #68–95. See also Daniel C. Maguire, "The Primacy of Justice in Moral Theology," *Horizons* 10 (Spring, 1983), pp. 72–85.
3. The idea of a "starter" and "getting started" book comes from Adam Daniel Corson-Finnerty, *World Citizen: Action for Global Justice*, (Maryknoll, NY: Orbis Books, 1982). For several years, Corson-Finnerty's book informed and transformed my students in a course on "Christianity and Social Justice" in the way I hope this book can.
4. These sentences paraphrase ideas found in NCCB, *Economic Justice for All*, passim.
5. Daniel C. Maguire, *The Moral Choice* (Minneapolis, MN: Winston Press, 1978), ch. 5.
6. Quoted in Michael True, *Justice Seekers and Peace Makers: 32 Portraits in Courage* (Mystic, CT: Twenty-Third Publications, 1985), p. 96.
7. Fred Kammer, *Doing Faithjustice: An Introduction to Catholic Social Thought* (New York: Paulist Press, 1991), p. 73.
8. In analyzing the obstacles to justice and peace in the current world situation, this book takes up the task of developing a theology of peace as described by the U.S. bishops in *The Challenge of Peace*: "A theology of peace should ground the task of peacemaking solidly in the biblical vision of the kingdom of God, then place it centrally in the ministry of the Church. It should specify the obstacles in the way of peace, as these are understood theologically and in the social and political sciences. It should both identify the specific contributions a community of faith can make to the work of peace and relate these to the wider work of peace pursued by other groups and institutions in society. Finally, a theology of peace must include a message of hope" (#25).

235

1. THE POST-COLD WAR WORLD: HOW DID WE GET HERE?

1. National Conference of Catholic Bishops (NCCB), *The Harvest of Justice Is Sown in Peace*, (November 17, 1993) in Gerard F. Powers, et al., eds., *Peacemaking: Moral and Policy Challenges for a New World* (Washington, DC: United States Catholic Conference, 1994), p. 345.
2. In David S. Reynolds, "American Heritages," a book review of Edward Countryman's, *Americans: A Collision of Histories* (New York: Hill & Wang, 1996), *New York Times Book Review* (June 30, 1996), p. 31, quoting Mr. Countryman.
3. A few others could be added to this list, such as Ethiopia, which defeated Italian invaders, and Liberia, which had close ties to the United States, and some of the countries in the Persian Gulf. See George Thomas Kurian, ed., *Encyclopedia of the Third World*, 4th ed. (New York: Facts on File, 1992), Volume 3, Appendix I, p. 2233.
4. Adam Daniel Corson-Finnerty, *World Citizen* (Maryknoll, NY: Orbis Books, 1982), p. 9.
5. Ibid., p. 10. Corson-Finnerty is relying on D.K. Fieldhouse, *The Colonial Empires* (New York: Delacorte Press, 1967), p. 178.
6. This account relies on the summaries in Corson-Finnerty, *World Citizen*, ch. 1, and Paul Vallely, *Bad Samaritans: First World Ethics and Third World Debt* (Maryknoll, NY: Orbis Books, 1990), pp. 85–105.
7. Ross Gandy, *A Short History of Mexico: From the Olmecs to the PRI* (Cuernavaca, Mex.: The Center for Bilingual Multicultural Studies, 1987), p. 5. This account relies on Gandy and on Corson-Finnerty.
8. Corson-Finnerty, *World Citizen*, p. 12. See Gandy, *Short History*, pp. 6–7. Gandy counts the population of Mexico and Guatemala as 30 million when Cortéz arrived, and agrees that it was reduced to 1 million by the end of the sixteenth century.
9. Gandy, *Short History*, p. 7.
10. Joseph Collins, "World Hunger: A Scarcity of Food or a Scarcity of Democracy," in Michael T. Klare and Daniel C. Thomas, eds., *World Security: Challenges for a New Century*, 2d ed. (New York: St. Martin's Press, 1994), p. 360. Collins cites World Bank, *Assault on Poverty* (Washington, DC: World Bank, 1975), p. 244, and refers to Milton J. Esman, *Landlessness and Near Landlessness in Developing Countries* (Ithaca, NY: Cornell University, Center for International Studies, 1978). Jessica Tuchman Matthews says that, "In 1975, 7 percent of landowners in Latin America possessed 93 percent of all the arable land in this vast region. . . . These large holdings generally include the most desirable land and are often inefficiently used or not used at all." "The Environment and International Security," in Klare and Thomas, eds., *World Security*, p. 278.
11. Gandy, *Short History*, pp. 8–9.
12. Corson-Finnerty, *World Citizen*, p. 11.
13. Vallely, *Bad Samaritans*, p. 88, quoting Paul Harrison, *Inside the Third World* (London: Penguin, 1979).
14. Corson-Finnerty, *World Citizen*, p. 17. Cf. Vallely, *Bad Samaritans*, p. 91.
15. Elizabeth Morgan, *Global Poverty and Personal Responsibility* (New York: Paulist Press, 1989), pp. 70–71.
16. Vallely, *Bad Samaritans*, p. 91; Corson-Finnerty, *World Citizen*, p. 16.
17. Corson-Finnerty, *World Citizen*, p. 14; Vallely, *Bad Samaritans*, p. 96. Chapter

5 examines the ethnic conflict in Rwanda in some detail as an example of ethnic conflict in Africa.

18. Corson-Finnerty, *World Citizen*, p. 16. Corson-Finnerty relies on Richard D. Wolff, *The Economics of Colonialism—Britain and Kenya, 1870–1930* (New Haven, CT: Yale University Press, 1974). The films "Out of Africa" (dir. by Sydney Pollack, starring Meryl Streep and Robert Redford, 1985), and "Mister Johnson" (dir. by Bruce Beresford, 1991) dramatize British colonization in Africa. "Mister Johnson" is especially recommended.

19. Vallely, *Bad Samaritans*, p. 96.

20. Corson-Finnerty, *World Citizen*, p. 17; Vallely, *Bad Samaritans*, pp. 93–94.

21. The film "Black Robe" (dir. by Bruce Beresford, 1991) addresses this issue very well. It is set in French Canada. There are some violent scenes in the film.

22. Vallely, *Bad Samaritans*, p. 99.

23. Ibid., p. 97.

24. The film "Mister Johnson" illustrates this point well.

25. Louis Fischer, *Gandhi: His Life and Message to the World* (New York: New American Library, 1954), pp. 65–67. This massacre is also depicted in the film "Gandhi" (dir. by Richard Attenborough, starring Ben Kingsley, 1982). General Dyer's Indian troops fired 1,650 bullets at unarmed civilians who were trapped in an enclosed area, causing 1,516 casualties and 379 deaths.

26. See Stanley Karnow, *In Our Image: America's Empire in the Philippines* (New York: Ballantine Books, 1989), chs. 4–7, for a detailed account of this war and its political background.

27. Charles S. Olcott, *The Life of William McKinley*, Vol. 2 (Boston: Houghton Mifflin, 1916), p. 110.

28. Karnow, *In Our Image*, p. 198. William Howard Taft, the first American Governor of the Philippines, condescendingly referred to Filipinos as "little brown brothers" (p. 174). The term captures some of the air of superiority, racism, and self-deceptive benevolence that white Americans brought to their control of the Philippines.

29. Larry Rohter, "Remembering the Past; Repeating It Anyway," *New York Times* (July 24, 1994), pp. A1, A3. Mr. Rohter refers to the study of American intervention in the Caribbean basin from 1898–1989 by Ivan Musicant titled, *The Banana Wars* (New York: Macmillan, 1990).

30. Ibid.

31. Arthur Simon, *Bread for the World* (New York: Paulist Press, 1975), pp. 74–75, 90.

32. My memory of this cultural exhibit might be fuzzy on the details, but the overall impression is correct.

33. *Rerum Novarum* can be found in *Catholic Social Thought: The Documentary Heritage*, ed. by David J. O'Brien and Thomas A. Shannon, (Maryknoll, NY: Orbis Books, 1992), pp. 14–39.

34. Paul Kennedy, *Preparing for the Twenty-First Century* (New York: Random House, 1993), pp. 4–5. My account of Malthus and population is drawn from Kennedy, pp. 3–13.

35. Kennedy, *Preparing*, p. 8. The three escape hatches are discussed on pages 6–10.

36. Ibid., p. 9.

37. Ibid., pp. 10–11.

38. Quoted in Alvin Toffler, *Future Shock* (New York: Bantam Books, 1970), p. 13.

39. Toffler, *Future Shock*, chs. 1 & 2. See also Richard McBrien, *Catholicism* (San

Francisco: HarperCollins, 1994), pp. 80–85.

40. This history is common knowledge, but see Joshua S. Goldstein, *International Relations* (New York: HarperCollins, 1996), pp. 26–39, for a lucid summary.

41. Barbara Crossette, "Globally, Majority Rules," *New York Times* (August 4, 1996), pp. E1, E6. It is also worth noting that by January, 1997, the world was at relative peace. "There are civil wars, drug wars, gang wars and trade wars. But riproaring, sound-the-trumpet, bang-the-drum wars of national aggression seem to have gone out of fashion." Simon Jenkins, "At Long Last, Peace in Our Time." *Times of London* (January 1, 1997), op-ed, p. 14.

42. See Raymond Bonner, *Waltzing With a Dictator* (New York: Times Books, 1987) for an insightful account of these events.

2. POVERTY AND DEVELOPMENT

1. National Conference of Catholic Bishops, *Economic Justice for All* (1986) in David J. O'Brien and Thomas A. Shannon, eds. *Catholic Social Thought: The Documentary Heritage* (Maryknoll, NY: Orbis Books, 1992), #38, #123.

2. Negros is a relatively large island in the Visayas, a group of islands that make up the middle section of the Philippines. Bacolod is the capital city. Fr. Niall O'Brien, an Irish missionary to the Philippines, has written the moving story of Negros during this period in *Revolution from the Heart* (New York: Oxford University Press, 1987) and in *Island of Tears, Island of Hope* (Maryknoll, NY: Orbis Books, 1993). Gerald and Janice Vanderhaar have written a briefer account in *The Philippines: Agony and Hope* (Erie, PA: Pax Christi USA, 1989).

3. "20% of World's People Live on Dollar a Day," *New York Times*, June 24, 1996, p. A3. The article highlights a World Bank report on poverty.

4. Joshua Goldstein, *International Relations* (New York: HarperCollins, 1996), p. 467.

5. Michael P. Todaro, *Economic Development*, 6th ed. (Reading, MA: Addison-Wesley, 1997), p. 16. Todaro indicates that three-fourths of the Earth's nearly 6 billion people experience poverty (p. 3). For an integral concept of human development see also Pope Paul VI, *On the Development of Peoples (Populorum Progessio)* (1967) in O'Brien and Shannon, eds., *Catholic Social Thought*, #6, #14–21.

6. Goldstein, *International Relations*, pp. 18–22.

7. The World Resources Institute et al., *World Resources: 1996–97* (New York: Oxford University Press, 1996), p. 161.

8. High income countries had a Gross Domestic Product (GDP) per capita of $8,625 in 1993; middle income countries had a GDP per capita ranging from $696 to $8,625; low income below $696. These figures reflect a GDP per capita based on Purchasing Power Parity (PPP) rather than simply the exchange rate. See United Nations Development Program, *Human Development Report 1996* (New York: Oxford University Press, 1996), p. 226; and *World Resources: 1996–97*, p. 162. In 1997, Russia participated extensively in the G7 meeting held in the United States, but was not formally admitted. These economic classifications and organizations are fluid, and they are changing rapidly.

9. Goldstein, *International Relations*, pp. 344–46; *World Resources: 1996–97*, pp. 166–67.

10. Martin Ravillion and Shaohua Chen, *What Can New Survey Data Tell Us about Recent Changes in Living Standards in Developing and Transitional Economies?*

(Washington, DC: The World Bank, 1996), pp. 1–8, passim.

11. Edward N. Wolff, *Top Heavy: The Increasing Inequality of Wealth in America and What Can Be Done About It* (New York: New Press and Twentieth Century Fund, 1996), p. 13. Wolff writes about the increasing inequality of wealth in the United States. He points out that between 1983 and 1989 the already high Gini coefficient for the United States increased from 0.80 to 0.84, an almost unprecedented increase in wealth inequality. According to the *Human Development Report 1996*, a similar increase in wealth inequality has occurred in the formerly communist countries of Eastern Europe and the Republics of the Soviet Union in the period from 1989 to 1994, but the Gini coefficient there rose from a low 0.25 to a still low 0.30 (p. 17). Todaro, *Economic Development*, notes that, in the 1980s, the Gini coefficient for Indonesia and Peru was 0.31, for Sri Lanka and the Philippines it was 0.45, and for Kenya and Brazil it was 0.55 and 0.57, respectively (p. 149).

12. *World Resources: 1996–97*, pp. 159–67.

13. *Human Development Report 1996*, pp. 5, 28–29. Vincent Ferraro and Melissa Rosser, "Global Debt and Third World Development," in Michael T. Klare and Daniel C. Thomas, *World Security: Challenges for a New Century*, 2d ed. (New York: St. Martin's Press, 1994), pp. 335–36.

14. *Human Development Report 1996*, p. 2.

15. Ibid. It is not surprising that the gap between the rich and the poor is increasing. Indeed it would take phenomenal growth in the developing countries and a radical redistribution of wealth to make it otherwise. "These trends stem from the already large gaps in per capita GDP and the relatively low average incomes in many developing countries, such that even rapid per capita GDP growth in poor countries cannot add annual increments of per capita income as large as those in rich countries." *World Resources: 1996–97*, p. 162. In other words, if your annual income is $1000, and you experience a 1% increase, you receive $1010. If my annual income is $100, and I experience a 2% increase, twice your increase, I have $102. My economic growth is double yours, yet the gap between us has widened, not lessened. If the comparison is between countries instead of individuals, then population growth also has to be factored in. If a country has a 2% economic growth, but a 3% population growth, its per capita GDP decreases.

16. Goldstein, *International Relations*, pp. 509–10; *Human Development Report 1996*, p. 1.

17. *Human Development Report 1996*, p. 5.

18. Cf. Goldstein, *International Relations*, pp. 511–14.

19. Arthur Simon, *Bread for the World* (New York: Paulist Press, 1975), pp. 76–77.

20. John F. Burns, "Economic Surge in Bangladesh Undercut by Political Turmoil," *New York Times* (January 27, 1996), p. A1. "New Hope for Bangladesh," *New York Times* (July 23, 1996), editorial. The latter article was written shortly after the successful democratic election in Bangladesh.

21. See Robert Kaplan, "The Coming Anarchy," *Atlantic Monthly* 273 (February, 1994), pp. 44–54 for a stark description of West Africa. I do not share Kaplan's sense of despair, but his account justifies pessimism.

Todaro, in *Economic Development*, identifies the economic crisis in Sub-Saharan Africa as one of the critical issues of the twenty-first century: "Between 1980 and 1990, per capita output fell by 42.5%, per capita consumption (a more significant measure of human well-being) fell by 40%, domestic investment declined by 29.7%, exports fell by 34.5%, per capita food production dropped by 12.2%, and the total external debt rose by 162% to a level as large as the region's GNP! Debt service in 1990 was equal to 19% of total export earnings. Africa's poverty rate rose during the 1980s to 62%, or 325 million people; over the same period, real wages declined by over 30% (in some countries, the drop was in excess of 70%) (p. 655)." Nicholas D. Kristof, "Why Africa Can Thrive Like Asia," *New York Times* (May 25, 1997), pp. E1, E4 paints a slightly more optimistic picture of Africa, noting that four countries—Uganda, Angola, Lesotho, and Malawi—have experienced economic growth.

22. Ferraro and Rosser, "Global Debt," p. 334.
23. Ibid., pp. 337–339; Joseph Collins, "World Hunger: A Scarcity of Food or a Scarcity of Democracy?" in Klare and Thomas, eds., *World Security*, p. 363.
24. Collins, "World Hunger," p. 364.
25. Serge Schmemann, "In Jordan, Bread-Price Protests Signal Deep Anger," *New York Times* (August 21, 1996), p. A3.
26. Collins, "World Hunger," p. 364; Cf. Ferraro and Rosser, "Global Debt," pp. 339–49; Goldstein, *International Relations*, pp. 536–37. It is interesting to note that the deficit spending and external debt of the United States would technically make it ineligible for IMF assistance. Developing countries are being asked to impose an economic austerity on their people that Americans have consistently been unwilling to impose on themselves.
27. Ferraro and Rosser, "Global Debt," pp. 349–52. In the spring of 1997, the World Bank and the IMF initiated a program to forgive some of the loans to qualifying developing countries, beginning with Uganda. See Richard W. Stevenson, "Global Banks Offer a First: Forgiveness on Some Debt," *New York Times* (March 12, 1997), p. A5; and "Debt Relief for Model Countries," Ibid. (May 1, 1997), editorial.
28. Ferraro and Rosser, "Global Debt," p. 352.
29. National Conference of Catholic Bishops, *Economic Justice for All* (1986) in O'Brien and Shannon, eds. *Catholic Social Thought*, #1, 5, passim.
30. Bob Herbert, "Nike's Pyramid Scheme," *New York Times* (June 10, 1996), op-ed page.
31. Kathy McAfee, "Why the Third World Goes Hungry: Selling Cheap, Buying Dear," *Commonweal* 117 (June 15, 1990), p. 380.
32. James B. McGinnis, *Bread and Justice: Toward a New International Economic Order* (New York: Paulist Press, 1979), chs. 8–12; E. F. Schumacher, *Small Is Beautiful: Economics As If People Mattered* (New York: Harper & Row, 1973); Todaro, *Economic Development*, pp. 537–43.
33. Nancy Gibbs, "Cause Celeb," *Time* 147 (June 17, 1996), pp. 28–30. *New York Times* columnist Bob Herbert has repeatedly addressed this issue and has been especially critical of Michael Jordan and Nike. See his op-ed page columns June 10, June 14, June 24, July 12, and November 1, 1996, and March 28, March 31, and April 14, 1997. See also Seth Mydans, "For Indonesian Workers at Nike Plant: Just Do It," *New York Times* (August 9, 1996), p. A4; and Cynthia Enloe, "The Globetrotting Sneaker," *Ms.* 5 (March/April, 1995), pp. 10–15.
34. David Schilling, "Maquiladora Workers Deserve a Sustainable Living Wage," *Interfaith Center on Corporate Responsibility Brief* 23 (#10, 1995), p. 3B. Schilling is drawing on the research of Ruth Rosenbaum, *Market Basket Survey: A Comparison of the Buying Power of Maquiladora Workers in Mexico and UAW Assembly Workers in GM Plants in the U.S.* (F.L. Putnam Securities, Sept., 1994). Sam Dillon, "At U.S. Door, Huddled Masses Yearn for Better Pay," *New*

York Times (December 4, 1995), p. A4.

35. Bob Herbert, "Nike's Boot Camps," *New York Times* (March 31, 1997), op-ed page.

36. Andrew Julien, "Garment Workers Allege Exploitation," *Hartford Courant* (July 12, 1995), p. F1. Seth Mydans, "For Indonesian Workers," p. A4.

37. Schilling, "Maquiladora Workers," p. 3C. Schilling relies on Sarah Anderson, et al., *Workers Lose, CEOs Win II*, Institute for Policies Study, April 29, 1995.

38. Philip Knight, "Nike Pays Good Wages to Foreign Workers," *New York Times* (June 24, 1996), letter to the editor.

39. Enloe, "The Globetrotting Sneaker," pp. 10, 12, 13. For a sneaker that retails for $70, less than $1.70 goes for the labor that produced the shoes.

40. Larry Rohter, "To U.S. Critics, a Sweatshop; To Hondurans, a Better Life," *New York Times* (July 18, 1996), p. A1, A14.

41. Abigail McCarthy, "By the Sweat of Kid's Brows," *Commonweal* 123 (June 1, 1996), p. 8. See Bob Herbert, "A Sweatshop Victory," *New York Times* (December 22, 1995), op-ed page.

42. Carolyn Henson, "Child Labor Figures Climb," *Hartford Courant* (November 12, 1996), pp. F1, F2.

43. Abigail McCarthy, "By the Sweat of Kid's Brows," pp. 7–8. Steven Greenhouse, "Sporting Goods Concerns Agree to Combat Sale of Soccer Balls Made by Children," *New York Times* (February 14, 1997), p. A12.

44. Larry Rohter, "To U.S. Critics," p. A14. Kaushik Basu, "The Poor Need Child Labor," *New York Times* (November 29, 1994), op-ed page.

45. Steven Greenhouse, "Voluntary Rules on Apparel Labor Proving Elusive," *New York Times* (February 1, 1997), pp. A1, A7; Steven Greenhouse, "Accord to Combat Sweatshop Labor Faces Obstacles," Ibid. (April 13, 1997), pp. A1, A20; Bob Herbert, "A Good Start," Ibid. (April 14, 1997), op-ed page; "A Modest Start on Sweatshops," Ibid. (April 16, 1997), editorial; Abigail McCarthy, "Kinder, Gentler Sweatshops," *Commonweal* 124 (June 6, 1997), pp. 6–7; Robert A. Senser, "To End Sweatshops: Workers Rights in a Global Economy," *Commonweal* 124 (July 18, 1997), pp. 14–17.

46. Steven Greenhouse, "Foreign Aid: Under Siege in the Budget Wars," *New York Times* (April 30, 1995), p. E4. Don Noel, "Foreign Aid: Less Costly, More Effective Than Most Think," *Hartford Courant* (June 12, 1995), op-ed page. The poll was conducted by the Program on International Policy Attitudes at the University of Maryland.

47. "U.S. Drops to 4th in Aid to Developing Countries," *Hartford Courant* (June 18, 1996), reporting on an OECD report.

48. Simon, *Bread for the World*, pp. 136–37.

49. Greenhouse, "Foreign Aid," p. E4.

50. Blaine Harden, *Africa: Dispatches from a Fragile Continent* (New York: W.W. Norton, 1990), ch. 5, pp. 177–81. It should be noted that the Scandinavian countries are not only more generous with foreign aid, but generally target it on genuine development of the poor.

51. See Jeffrey D. Sachs, "When Foreign Aid Makes a Difference," *New York Times* (February 3, 1997), op-ed page. A current problem regarding development assistance is the tension between the needs of developing countries, especially the least developed ones, and the needs of the transition economies of the former Soviet empire. See Todaro, *Economic Development*, p. 658.

52. Todaro, *Economic Development*, ch. 13.

53. Ibid., p. 481.

54. Ibid., pp. 480, 489–90.

55. Based on Todaro, *Economic Development*, pp. 480–90.

56. McGinnis, *Bread and Justice*, pp. 89–91; Jay Mandle, "The Good Side of Going Global," *Commonweal* 124 (July 18, 1997), pp. 11–13.

57. Anthony DePalma, "Income Gulf in Mexico Grows and So Do Protests," *New York Times* (July 20, 1996), p. A3.

58. Sam Dillon, "Free Trade? Don't Sell Us That," *New York Times* (August 4, 1996), p. E6. "Depending on the View, NAFTA Glass Half Full or Half Empty," *Hartford Courant* (March 9, 1997), p. A13.

59. James Sterngold, "NAFTA Trade-Off: Some Jobs Lost, Others Gained," *New York Times* (October 9, 1995) p. A1, A13. Anthony DePalma, "For Mexico, NAFTA's Promise of Jobs Is Still Just a Promise," *New York Times* (October 10, 1995), p. A1, A10.

60. Peter Morici, "Grasping the Benefits of NAFTA," *Current History* 92 (February, 1993), p. 52; Mandle, "The Good Side of Going Global," p. 12.

61. Dillon, "Free Trade?" p. E6; "Depending on the View," p. A13.

62. *Human Development Report* 1996, p. 5. "Short-term advances in human development are possible—but they will not be sustainable without further growth. Conversely, economic growth is not sustainable without human development." See Peter Passell, "Asia's Path to More Equality and More Money for All," *New York Times* (August 25, 1996), p. E5.

63. *Human Development Report* 1996, p. 11.

64. This quote from Gandhi is found on an Oxfam poster on the environment. I have not been able to find the exact quote in Gandhi's extensive writings, but it is certainly true to his spirit. He says, for example, "The rich have a superfluous store of things which they do not need, and which are therefore neglected and wasted; while millions are starved to death for want of sustenance. If each retained possession only of what he needed, no one would be in want, and all would live in contentment. As it is the rich are discontented no less than the poor." M.K. Gandhi, *Non-Violent Resistance* (New York: Schocken Books, 1951), p. 46.

65. Diana Jean Schemo, "Brazil's Chief Acts to Take Land to Give to the Poor," *New York Times* (November 13, 1995), p. A9. Although the land reform hinted at by this article's title is a good idea, the article also suggests that this is a small, even a token, step in the right direction.

66. Nathaniel C. Nash, "Latin Economic Speedup Leaves the Poor in the Dust," *New York Times* (September 7, 1994), pp. A1, A14.

67. Anthony DePalma, "Income Gulf in Mexico Grows and So Do Protests," *New York Times* (July 20, 1996), p. A3.

68. Seth Mydans, "How Country Air Took the Sweat Out of One Shop," *New York Times* (January 10, 1997), p. A4.

69. *Human Development Report* 1996, p. 13.

70. Ibid., p. 16.

71. Based on *Human Development Report* 1996, pp. 6–8.

72. Ibid., p. 80. Paul Kennedy, *Preparing for the Twenty-First Century* (New York: Random House, 1993), pp. 197–98.

73. *Human Development Report* 1996, p. 8.

74. Patrick E. Tyler, "Star at Conference on Women: Banker Who Lends to the Poor," *New York Times* (September 14, 1995), p. A6; Paul Lewis, "Small Loans May Be Key to Helping Third World," Ibid. (January 26, 1997), p. 4; "Micro-Loans

for the Very Poor," Ibid. (January 16, 1997), editorial.

75. Goldstein, *International Relations*, p. 493–94. *Human Development Report 1996*, pp. 32–36, discussing the "gender-related development index" and the "gender empowerment measure."

76. Corruption is a serious obstacle to development. An organization called Transparency International has developed a corruption index that ranks countries on a scale of 0 to 10. See Barbara Crossette, "A Global Gauge of Greased Palms," *New York Times* (August 20, 1995), p. E3; and Raymond Bonner, "The Worldly Business of Bribes: Quiet Battle Is Joined," *New York Times* (July 8, 1996), p. A3. Recently the 26 members of the OECD committed themselves to re-write tax laws so that bribes will not be tax deductible. See Marlise Simons, "U.S. Enlists Rich Nations in Move to End Business Bribes," *New York Times* (April 12, 1996), p. A10. See also Goldstein, *International Relations*, 525–27, on the problem in general.

77. John Kenneth Galbraith, *The Good Society: The Humane Agenda* (Boston: Houghton Mifflin Company, 1996), ch. 17.

78. Keith Bradsher, "Gap in Wealth in U.S. Called Widest in the West," *New York Times* (April 17, 1995), pp. A1, D4. Mr. Bradsher is relying on Wolff, *Top Heavy*. See also Kevin Phillips, *The Politics of Rich and Poor* (New York: Random House, 1990), especially ch. 6; and Garry Wills, "It's His Party [Ronald Reagan's Legacy]," *New York Times Magazine* (August 11, 1996), pp. 30–37ff, at 36, on the increase in economic inequality in America during the Reagan administrations.

79. Paul Krugman, "The Wealth Gap Is Real and It's Growing," *New York Times* (August 21, 1995), op-ed page.

80. David E. Rosenbaum and Steve Lohr, "With a Stable Economy, Clinton Hopes for Credit," *New York Times* (August 3, 1996), p. A8.

81. Wolff, *Top Heavy*, p. 72.

82. National Conference of Catholic Bishops, "A Decade After 'Economic Justice for All': Continuing Principles, Changing Context, New Challenges," *Origins* 25 (November, 1995), p. 391.

83. Jack Nelson-Pallmeyer, *Brave New World Order* (Maryknoll, NY: Orbis Books, 1992), pp. 19–20. "Land of Haves and Have-Nots," *Hartford Courant* (April 25, 1995), editorial.

84. Rosenbaum and Lohr, "With a Stable Economy," p. A8–9.

85. See Goldstein, *International Relations*, pp. 368–71. Kennedy, *Preparing*, pp. 290–302.

86. Crime rates are actually down across the United States, but fear of crime is not. See Richard Lacayo, "Law and Order" *Time* 147 (January 15, 1996), pp. 48–56.

87. See Joseph Califano, "It's Drugs, Stupid," *New York Times Magazine* (January 29, 1995), pp. 40–41, for an argument about the centrality of drugs to American social problems.

88. Kennedy, *Preparing*, pp. 302–11. The Scholastic Aptitude Test (S.A.T.) scores for 1996, however, continued the upward trend that began in 1990. Karen W. Arenson, "Students Continue to Improve, College Board Says," *New York Times* (August 23, 1996), p. A16.

89. *New York Times Magazine* had a cover story (December 8, 1996) on both of these issues, "The Ellwoods and the Price of Reform." Paul Ellwood has been a key figure in health care reform and is the subject of Lisa Belkin's, "Health Care: The Quality Half." His son David Ellwood has been deeply involved in welfare reform and is the subject of Jason DeParle's, "Welfare: Progress Hijacked."

90. See Philip S. Keane, *Health Care Reform* (New York: Paulist Press, 1993), chs. 1 and 2 for a good overview of the problem.

91. Craig Whitney, "Rising Health Costs Threaten Generous Benefits in Europe," *New York Times* (August 6, 1996), pp. A1, A4.

92. Michael Wines and Robert Pear, "President Finds He Has Gained Even If He Lost on Health Care," *New York Times* (July 30, 1996), pp. A1, B8.

93. John Greenwald, "The Coverage That Travels," *Time* 148 (August 12, 1996), p. 22.

94. Quoted in George J. Church, "Ripping Up Welfare," *Time* 148 (August 12, 1996), p. 20.

95. Richard Lacayo, "Unraveling the Safety Net," *Time* 146 (January 10, 1994), p. 26. Another source suggests that the total costs of these programs in 1993 was $92 billion. Susan Mayer and Christopher Jencks, "War on Poverty: No Apologies, Please," *New York Times* (November 9, 1995), op-ed page. I do not know the reason for the discrepancy.

96. Jason DeParle, "Welfare As We Know It," *New York Times* (June 19, 1994), p. E4; Larry Williams and John A. MacDonald, "Welfare As We Know It," *Hartford Courant* (February 12, 1995), p. A14; Mayer and Jencks, "War on Poverty."

97. Mayer and Jencks, "War on Poverty."

98. Isabel Wilkerson, "An Intimate Look at Welfare: Women Who've Been There," *New York Times* (February 17, 1995), p. A18. DeParle, "Welfare As We Know It," p. E4. Thirty-eight percent of *children* on welfare are black, 33 percent are white, 21 percent are Hispanic, and 8 percent are Asian, Indian, or other, according to Jodie Allen, "Working Out Welfare," *Time* 148 (July 29, 1996), p. 53. In 1995 nearly 15 million children in the United States, or 1 out of 5, were poor, but only about 10 million were on welfare. Of children who are poor, whites outnumber blacks nearly 2 to 1, according to Peter T. Kilborn, "Shrinking Safety Net Cradles Hearts and Hopes of Children," *New York Times* (November 30, 1996), pp. A1, A10.

99. George F. Will, "Welfare Reform's Victims: Children," *Hartford Courant* (September 14, 1995), op-ed page. Christopher Jencks, "Welfare Reform: Time Limits on Welfare?" *Current* 350 (February, 1993), p. 10.

100. Wilkerson, "An Intimate Look at Welfare," p. A18. There have been a number of articles in the *New York Times* that focus on the story of families who receive welfare. See, for example, Melinda Henneberger, "Welfare Bashing Finds Its Mark," (March 5, 1995), p. E5; Michael Janofsky, "Kool-Aid, Not Soda: Living on Food Stamps," (April 5, 1995), pp. A1, A16; Celia W. Dugger, "Iowa Plan Tries to Cut Off Cash," (April 7, 1995), pp. A1, B6; Melinda Henneberger, "State Aid Is Capped, But to What Effect?" (April 11, 1995), pp. A1, A18; Mireya Navarro, "Threat of Benefits Cutoff: Will It Deter Pregnancies?" (April 17, 1995), pp. A1, B7; Jason DeParle, "Better Work Than Welfare, But What If There's Neither?" *New York Times Magazine* (December 18, 1994), pp. 42–49f.

101. William Julius Wilson, "Work," *New York Times Magazine* (August 18, 1996), pp. 26–31ff. Michael D. Weiss, "Reducing Poverty: Alternative Approaches," *Current* (December, 1992), p. 15. See also William Julius Wilson, *The Truly Disadvantaged: The Inner City, the Underclass, and Public Policy* (Chicago: University of Chicago Press, 1990); and *When Work Disappears: The World of the New Urban Poor* (New York: Alfred A. Knopf, 1996).

102. Nancy Gibbs, "The Vicious Cycle," *Time* 146 (June 20, 1994), p. 27.

103. William J. Bennett and Peter Wehner, "Pull the Plug on Aid for Unwed Mothers," *Hartford Courant* (February 6, 1994), op-ed page. In 1995, for the first time in nearly two decades there was a slight decline in the out-of-wedlock birth rate, and the teenage birth rate continued to decline. Both trends are seen as part of a general decline in the nation's birth rate. Steven A. Holmes, "U.S. Reports Drop in Rate of Births to Unwed Women," *New York Times* (October 5, 1996), p. A1. Although this is good news, it hardly resolves the problem.

104. Charles Murray is the author of *Losing Ground: American Social Policy, 1950–1980* (New York: Basic Books, 1984). David Ellwood served as a specialist on welfare reform in the first two years of the Clinton administration and is the author of *Poor Support: Poverty in the American Family* (New York: Basic Books, 1988) and editor, with Phoebe Cottingham, of *Welfare Policy for the 1990s* (Cambridge, MA: Harvard University Press, 1989).

105. Bennett and Wehner, "Pull the Plug."

106. See Kai Erickson, "Scandal or Scapegoating?" A review of *Dubious Conceptions: The Politics of Teenage Pregnancy* (Cambridge, MA: Harvard University Press, 1996), by Kristin Luker, *New York Times Book Review* (September 1, 1996), pp. 12–13. According to Erickson, Ms. Luker convincingly demonstrates that it is not so much teenage pregnancy, but out-of-wedlock pregnancy and single parenting that is increasing and that correlates with poverty. Ms. Luker does not think that welfare is an incentive for teenagers to have a baby.

107. Will, "Welfare Reform's Victims: Children."

108. Glen Stassen, *Just Peacemaking: Transforming Initiatives for Justice and Peace* (Louisville, KY: Westminster/John Knox Press, 1992), p. 172. Stassen depends on the research of the Children's Defense Fund and Marian Wright Edelman.

109. Ibid., p. 173.

110. Peter Edelman, "The Worst Thing Bill Clinton Has Done," *The Atlantic Monthly* 279 (March, 1997), pp. 43–58; Katherine S. Newman, "What Inner-City Jobs for Welfare Moms?" *New York Times* (May 20, 1995), op-ed page; Peter T. Kilborn, "Up from Welfare: It's Harder and Harder," *New York Times* (April 16, 1995), pp. E1, E4; Jim Wallis, "The Church Steps Forward," and "The Issue Is Poverty," *Sojourners* 26 (March–April, 1997), pp. 7–9, and 18–24.

111. Jason DeParle, "Learning Poverty Firsthand," *New York Times Magazine* (April 27, 1997), p. 34. This article reports on the research of Kathryn Edin and Laura Lein, *Making Ends Meet* (Russell Sage Foundation, 1997). See also Dirk Johnson, "Uncertain Future on Their Own Awaits," *New York Times* (March 16, 1997), pp. A1, A38, which profiles six welfare lives affected by the new legislation.

112. For a more in-depth discussion of welfare reform from a Christian perspective see Stanley W. Carlson-Thies and James W. Skillen, eds., *Welfare in America: Christian Perspectives on a Policy in Crisis* (Grand Rapids, MI: Wm. B. Eerdmans Publishing Co., 1996).

113. *Human Development Report 1996*, p. 26. Goldstein, *International Relations*, pp. 494–505.

114. Helder Camara, *Spiral of Violence* (London: Sheed and Ward, 1971).

115. Eileen Egan, "The Beatitudes, the Works of Mercy, and Pacifism," in Thomas Shannon, ed., *War or Peace?* (Maryknoll, NY: Orbis Books, 1980), pp. 173–75.

3. POPULATION EXPLOSION, RESOURCE DEPLETION, AND ENVIRONMENTAL DESTRUCTION

1. John Paul II, "Peace with God the Creator, Peace with All of Creation," *Origins* 19 (January 1, 1990), p. 467.
2. United Nations Development Programme, *Human Development Report 1996* (New York: Oxford University Press, 1996), pp. 5–6, passim.
3. Jim MacNeil, "Strategies for Sustainable Economic Development," *Scientific American* 261 (September, 1989), p. 155. This issue of *Scientific American* is devoted to environmental issues.
4. Lynn White, "The Historical Roots of the Ecological Crisis," *Science* 155 (March 10, 1967), pp. 1203–07.
5. Genesis 1:28. See also Genesis 9:1–7, where God repeats the admonition to subdue the earth and gives humanity the animals to eat as well.
6. See, for example, Mary Evelyn Jegen and Bruno V. Manno, eds., *The Earth Is the Lord's: Essays on Stewardship* (New York: Paulist Press, 1978); and Carolyn Thomas, *Gift and Response: A Biblical Spirituality for Contemporary Christians* (New York: Paulist Press, 1994), pp. 10–12.
7. Michael J. Himes and Kenneth R. Himes, *Fullness of Faith: The Public Significance of Theology* (New York: Paulist Press, 1993), ch. 5.
8. See James A. Nash, *Loving Nature: Ecological Integrity and Christian Responsibility* (Nashville: Abingdon Press, 1991), ch. 3, for a discussion of the claim against Christianity; see chs. 4 and 5 for a constructive theological response. H. Paul Santmire, *The Travail of Nature: The Ambiguous Ecological Promise of Christian Theology* (Minneapolis: Fortress, 1985); Sean McDonagh, *To Care for the Earth: A Call to a New Theology* (Santa Fe, NM: Bear & Co., 1986), and Larry L. Rasmussen, *Earth Community Earth Ethics* (Maryknoll, NY: Orbis Books, 1996), among others, also offer constructive theological responses.
9. Thomas Berry, *The Dream of the Earth* (San Francisco: Sierra Club Books, 1988).
10. See Bill Devall and George Sessions, *Deep Ecology: Living As If Nature Mattered* (Salt Lake City: G.M. Smith, 1985); and Arne Naess, "Sustained Development and Deep Ecology," in J. Ronald Engel and Joan Gibb Engel, eds. *Ethics of Environment and Development: Global Challenge, International Response* (University of Arizona Press, 1990). The "Deep Ecology" perspective rejects an anthropocentric approach that wishes to reform human behavior toward the environment, for a more radical view that recognizes the unity of humans, plants, animals, and the Earth. It calls for a new ecological consciousness, a change in human understanding of the relationship of humans and the ecosystem. The ecosystem itself becomes the primary value.
11. See Drew Christiansen, "Ecology, Justice, and Development," *Theological Studies* 51 (March, 1990), pp. 76–79.
12. This statement of values and perspective depends on Himes and Himes, *Fullness of Faith*, ch. 5.
13. Joshua Goldstein, *International Relations* (New York: HarperCollins, 1996), p. 451.
14. Paul Kennedy, *Preparing for the Twenty-First Century* (New York: Random House, 1993), p. 22; Dennis Pirages, "Demographic Change and Ecological Security," in Michael T. Klare and Daniel C. Thomas, *World Security: Challenges for a New Century*, 2d ed. (New York: St. Martin's Press, 1994), p. 316. Amartya Sen, "Population: Delusion and Reality," *The New York Review of Books*

(September 22, 1994), p. 62, describes the growth of population this way: "It took the world population millions of years to reach the first billion, then 123 years to get to the second, 33 years to the third, 14 years to the fourth, 13 years to the fifth billion, with the sixth billion to come, according to one U.N. projection, in another 11 years."

15. Joel E. Cohen, "Ten Myths of Population," *Discover* 17 (April, 1996), p. 42.
16. Barbara Crossette, "U.N. Is Facing Angry Debate on Population," *New York Times* (September 4, 1994), pp. A1, A16.
17. Bruce Russett and Harvey Starr, *World Politics: The Menu for Choice*, 5th ed. (New York: W.H. Freedman and Co., 1996), p. 437.
18. Barbara Crossette, "World Is Less Crowded Than Expected, the U.N. Reports," *New York Times* (November 17, 1996), p. A3; Russett and Starr, *World Politics*, p. 440; and Crossette, "U.N. Is Facing," p. 16.
19. Nathan Keyfitz, "The Growing Human Population," *Scientific American* 261 (September, 1989), p. 122.
20. The World Resources Institute, et al., *World Resources 1996–97* (New York: Oxford University Press, 1996), p. 173–74.
21. Ibid., p. 174.
22. Ibid.
23. Crossette, "U.N. Is Facing," p. 16.
24. *World Resources 1996–97*, p. 175. Richard W. Mansbach, *The Global Puzzle: Issues and Actors in World Politics* (Boston: Houghton Mifflin, 1994), p. 514. "More people live in Asia than in the rest of the world combined."
25. Sen, "Population: Delusion and Reality," p. 62.
26. Kennedy, *Preparing*, p. 24.
27. Sen, "Population: Delusion and Reality," p. 63.
28. *World Resources 1996–97*, p. 175. Lester R. Brown, "The Acceleration of History," in Lester R. Brown, et al., *State of the World 1996* (New York: W.W. Norton, 1996), pp. 12–13. Brown lists the 30 countries that have reached a stable population.
29. Kennedy, *Preparing*, pp. 32–33.
30. Russett and Starr, *World Politics*, pp. 450–51.
31. Mansbach, *The Global Puzzle*, p. 514.
32. John F. Burns, "Bangladesh, Still Poor, Cuts Birth Rate Sharply," *New York Times* (September 13, 1994), p. A10.
33. Mansbach, *The Global Puzzle*, p. 515.
34. *Pirages, "Demographic Change,"* p. 320.
35. Ibid., pp. 318–22.
36. *World Resources 1996–97*, chs. 1–6.
37. Pirages, "Demographic Change," pp. 319, 322.
38. Sen, "Population: Delusion and Reality," pp. 62–63.
39. Tas Papathanasis, "Population Debate Misses the Real Issue," *Hartford Courant* (September 30, 1994), op-ed page.
40. Russett and Starr, *World Politics*, p. 450.
41. Paul Erlich and Anne Erlich, "Population, Plenty, and Poverty," *National Geographic* 174 (December, 1988), p. 916.
42. Goldstein, *International Relations*, pp. 452–53.
43. Ibid., p. 453.
44. William K. Stevens, "Poor Lands' Success in Cutting Birth Rate Upsets Old Theories," *New York Times* (January 2, 1994), pp. A1, A8.

45. Anastasia Toufexis, "Too Many Mouths," *Time* (January 2, 1989), p. 50. This issue of *Time* is devoted to the ecological crisis by recognizing the earth as planet of the year.

46. John F. Burns, "Bangladesh, Still Poor, Cuts Birth Rate Sharply," p. A10. Sen, "Population: Delusion and Reality," p. 71, wonders if economic and social development will not be necessary for Bangladesh to lower its fertility rate to around 2, which would begin to stabilize its population.

47. Bill Keller, "Zimbabwe Taking a Lead in Promoting Birth Control," *New York Times* (September 4, 1994), p. 16.

48. Goldstein, *International Relations*, pp. 454–55.

49. Sen, "Population: Delusion and Reality," pp. 63–64. Sen suggests that the dire predictions of eco-pessimists such as Paul Erlich, *The Population Bomb* (New York: Ballantine, 1968), in the tradition of Malthus, leave them open to supporting coercive measures to limit population growth. He argues against coercion, and for the proven effectiveness of a collaborative approach that focuses on economic development and empowering women. For a succinct debate on this issue see Charles F. Westoff, "Finally, Control Population," and Ellen Chesler, "Stop Coercing Women," in *New York Times Magazine* (February 6, 1994), pp. 30–33.

50. See Charles E. Curran, "Population Control: Methods and Morality," in his *Issues in Sexual and Medical Ethics* (University of Notre Dame Press, 1978), pp. 168–197; and Charles E. Curran, ed., *Contraception: Authority and Dissent* (New York: Herder and Herder, 1969). In general, the Christian Churches in the Protestant or Reformed traditions do not oppose contraception or birth control, although most do oppose abortion.

51. Neil MacFarquhar, "With Iran Population Boom, Vasectomy Receives Blessing," *New York Times* (September 8, 1996), pp. A1, A14. See Burns, "Bangladesh, Still Poor, Cuts Birth Rate Sharply," p. A10.

52. Toufexis, "Too Many Mouths," p. 50. See Goldstein, *International Relations*, pp. 455–56.

53. See Julian Simon, *The Ultimate Resource* (Princeton University Press, 1981).

54. See Paul R. Erlich and Anne H. Erlich, *The Population Explosion* (New York: Simon and Schuster, 1990).

55. John Tierney, "Betting the Planet," *New York Times Magazine* (December 2, 1990), p. 81. This description is based on Tierney's article.

56. Ibid.

57. Russett and Starr, *World Politics*, p. 450.

58. Goldstein, *International Relations*, p. 443.

59. John H. Gibbons, Peter D. Blair, and Holly L. Gwin, "Strategies for Energy Use," *Scientific American* 261 (September, 1989), p. 136. This article says that fossil fuels account for 88 percent of energy consumption.

60. *World Resources 1996–97*, p. 273.

61. Russett and Starr, *World Politics*, p. 449.

62. *World Resources 1996–97*, p. 275.

63. William C. Clark, "Managing Planet Earth," *Scientific American* 261 (September, 1989), p. 47. *World Resources 1996–97*, p. 274.

64. Keyfitz, "The Growing Human Population," p. 121. The special issue of *Scientific American* 262 (September, 1990) was devoted to "Energy for Planet Earth."

65. *World Resources 1996–97*, pp. 274–78.

66. Goldstein, *International Relations*, pp. 445–46.

67. Paula Gonzalez, "Facing the Challenge of Global Warming," *Network* (July/August, 1996), pp.10–11. Gibbons, et al., "Strategies for Energy Use," p. 142.
68. Agis Salpukas, "Suburbia Can't Kick the Nozzle," *New York Times* (July 23, 1996), pp. D1, D5. See Keith Bradsher, "What Not to Drive to the Recycling Center," *New York Times* (July 28, 1996), p. E2 on the U.S. fascination with the environmentally harmful utility vehicle which gets about 15 miles to the gallon.
69. Brown, "The Acceleration of History," pp. 14–16. "What the U.S. Should Do," *Time* (January 2, 1989). p. 65.
70. Russett and Starr, *World Politics*, p. 449. See Donella H. Meadows, et al., *The Limits to Growth: A Report for the Club of Rome's Project on the Predicament of Mankind* (New York: New American Library, 1972), for similar sorts of projections made a decade earlier. The message of the Club of Rome was quite controversial, but, like that of other environmental prophets, it deserves critical attention.
71. Jessica Tuchman Matthews, "The Environment and International Security," in Klare and Thomas, eds., *World Security* , p. 276.
72. Eugene Linden, "The Death of Birth," *Time* (January 2, 1989), p. 32.
73. Edward O. Wilson, "Threats to Biodiversity," *Scientific American* 261 (September, 1989), p. 111.
74. *World Resources 1996–97*, pp. 201, 205. This source relies on a 1995 report by the Food and Agriculture Organization of the United Nations titled, "Forest Resources Assessment 1990: Global Synthesis," (Rome: FAO, 1995).
75. See Linden, "The Death of Birth," p. 32.
76. Wilson, "Threats to Biodiversity," p. 113.
77. *World Resources 1996–97*, p. 201.
78. Linden, "The Death of Birth," p. 32.
79. Wilson, "Threats to Biodiversity," p. 108.
80. *World Resources 1996–97*, p. 247.
81. Wilson, "Threats to Biodiversity," p. 112; Linden, "The Death of Birth," p. 32.
82. Linden, "The Death of Birth," p. 33. This phenomenon is dramatized in two films: "Medicine Man," (1992), and "The Emerald Forest," (1985). The latter focuses on the plight of indigenous people who live in tropical forests.
83. Wilson, "Threats to Biodiversity," p. 114.
84. Samuel Taylor Coleridge, "The Rime of the Ancient Mariner," in *The Complete Poetical Works of Samuel Taylor Coleridge*, ed. by Ernest Hartley Coleridge, Volume I (Oxford: Clarendon Press, 1912, 1957), line 120, p. 191. This is a paraphrase of the line from Coleridge's poem.
85. Russett and Starr, *World Politics*, p. 450. J.W. Maurits la Riviere, "Threats to the World's Water," *Scientific American* 261 (September, 1989), p. 80, puts the figure at .01 percent.
86. Sandra Postel, "Forging a Sustainable Water Strategy," in Brown, et al., *State of the World 1996* (New York: W.W. Norton, 1996), p. 41.
87. Russett and Starr, *World Politics*, p. 450.
88. Maurits la Riviere, "Threats to the World's Water," p. 80.
89. Postel, "Forging a Sustainable Water Strategy," pp. 42–47. Aquifers can be irreparably damaged because the pores and spaces that hold water can collapse when they are empty.
90. Ibid., p. 40.
91. Barry Commoner, *The Closing Circle* (New York: Bantam Books, 1971), ch. 6.

92. "The Rebirth of a River," *New York Times* (June 16, 1996), editorial. This editorial summed up a two-part series written by the *Times*' William Stevens and Andrew Revkin, published the previous week.

93. James C. McKinley, Jr., "An Amazon Weed Clogs an African Lake," *New York Times* (August 5, 1996), p. A5.

94. See Chris Bright, "Understanding the Threat of Bioinvasions," in Brown, et al., *State of the World 1996*, pp. 95–113, for many examples of this phenomenon and its economic and health cost; Gina Maranto, "In Nature vs. Nature, Nature May Not Win," *New York Times* (April 27, 1997), p. E6; and Mireya Navarro, "U.S. Dispatches an Army of Tree-Hungry Beetles to Fight Everglades Menace," Ibid. (May 4, 1997), p. A22.

95. Postel, "Forging a Sustainable Water Strategy," pp. 49–51; Peter Theroux, "The Imperiled Nile Delta," *National Geographic* 191 (January, 1997), pp. 2–35.

96. Postel, "Forging a Sustainable Water Strategy," pp. 55–59. *World Resources 1996–97*, p. 303.

97. *World Resources 1996–97*, p. 301–02.

98. Ibid., pp. 295–96.

99. Ibid., pp. 296–97.

100. Brown, "The Acceleration of History," p. 9.

101. *World Resources 1996–97*, pp. 297–98.

102. Goldstein, *International Relations*, pp. 437–40.

103. Joel E. Cohen has reflected and written extensively on the complex question of the carrying capacity of Earth. See *How Many People Can Earth Support?* (New York: W.W. Norton & Co., 1995); an article by the same title in *The Sciences* (November/December, 1995), pp. 18–23; and "Population Growth and Earth's Human Carrying Capacity," *Science* 296 (July 21, 1995), pp. 341–46. Cohen's book was reviewed by William D. Nordhaus, "Elbow Room," *New York Times Book Review* (January 14, 1996), pp. 12–13.

104. Brown, "The Acceleration of History," pp. 7–11, 16–17; Lester R. Brown, "Facing the Prospect of Food Scarcity," in *State of the World 1997* (New York: W.W. Norton & Co., 1997), pp. 23–41; and *Tough Choices: Facing the Challenge of Food Scarcity* (New York: W.W. Norton & Co., 1996); and *World Resources 1996–97*, p. 228–29.

105. Brown, "The Acceleration of History," p. 8.

106. *World Resources 1996–97*, p. 225.

107. Kennedy, *Preparing*, pp. 67.

108. *World Resources 1996–97*, pp. 226–27.

109. Brown, "The Acceleration of History," p. 9.

110. Matthews, "The Environment and International Security," p. 277.

111. *World Resources 1996–97*, pp. 230–33.

112. Kennedy, *Preparing*, pp. 70–81. Sen, "Population: Delusions and Reality," pp. 66–67, argues that food production is likely to keep up with population growth, despite the predictions of doomsayers; that Asia, in particular, has made dramatic advances in food production recently; but that Africa may be an exception.

113. *World Resources 1996–97*, pp. 235–36.

114. Michael D. Lemonick, "Deadly Danger in a Spray Can," *Time* (January 2, 1989), p. 42.

115. Ibid.; Goldstein, *International Relations*, pp. 432–33; Matthews, "The Environment and International Security," p. 283.

116. *World Resources 1996–97*, p. 316.

117. Ibid.; Russett and Starr, *World Politics*, p. 454.

118. Goldstein, *International Relations*, pp. 433–34.

119. Michael D. Lemonick, "Feeling the Heat," *Time* (January 2, 1989), p. 38. Thomas E. Graedel and Paul J. Crutzen, "The Changing Atmosphere," *Scientific American* 261 (September, 1989), pp. 58–68.

120. Trees absorb carbon dioxide, and when a tree dies, it releases the carbon dioxide whether it rots or burns. Lemonick, "Feeling the Heat," p. 38.

121. Christopher Flavin, "Facing Up to the Risks of Climate Change," in Brown, et al., *State of the World 1996*, p. 29. Carbon dioxide is about 4 times heavier than carbon. Thus, "In 1992, global emissions of carbon dioxide . . . amounted to 26.4 billion metric tons per year, of which 84 percent (22.3 billion metric tons) was from industrial activity." *World Resources 1996*, p. 316. As one who is not a scientist, I am amazed at these figures of *billions* of metric tons of carbon released into the atmosphere. Forests and oceans absorb about 3 billion tons of carbon per year. Any amount over that adds to the carbon accumulating in the atmosphere.

122. Lemonick, "Feeling the Heat," p. 38. *World Resources 1996–97*, p. 320.

123. Bill McKibben, "Not So Fast," *New York Times Magazine* (July 23, 1995), p. 24.

124. *World Resources 1996–97*, p. 316–18. The U.S. per capita emission of carbon is 5.26 tons per year. Flavin, "Facing Up," p. 29.

125. Russett and Starr, *World Politics*, p. 454. Stephen H. Schneider, "The Changing Climate," *Scientific American* 261 (September, 1989), pp. 70–79. Estimates vary on how much and how fast global temperature may rise.

126. Flavin, "Facing Up," pp. 22–23; Bill McKibben, "The Earth Does a Slow Burn," *New York Times* (May 3, 1997), op-ed page.

127. *World Resources 1996–97*, p. 322. See David Wirth, "Catastrophic Climate Change," in Klare and Thomas, eds., *World Security: Trends and Challenges at Century's End* (New York: St. Martin's Press, 1991), pp. 386–390.

128. Kennedy, *Preparing*, pp. 108–13. Michael D. Lemonick, "Heading for Apocalypse?" *Time* (October 2, 1995), pp. 54–55.

129. Flavin, "Facing Up," pp. 29–31.

130. McKibben, "Not So Fast," p. 25. On strategies for reducing carbon emissions, see also Flavin, "Facing Up," pp. 31–33; *World Resources 1996–97*, p. 324; Brown, "The Acceleration of History," pp. 15–16; Wirth, "Catastrophic Climate Change," pp. 390–96; Lemonick, "Heading for Apocalypse?", p. 55.

131. Flavin, "Facing Up," p. 33. It is also a moral and spiritual challenge.

132. Goldstein, *International Relations*, pp. 432; Flavin, "Facing Up," p. 21; Wirth, "Catastrophic Climate Change," pp. 395–96.

133. Flavin, "Facing Up," pp. 33–39; *World Resources 1996–97*, pp. 322–23.

134. Lemonick, "Heading for Apocalypse?" expresses skepticism that the developed countries will be willing to undergo such a radical transformation of their societies and lifestyles and be willing to subsidize the transformation of poorer countries. He thinks the world will have to adapt to global warming, rather than be able to prevent it.

135. Helen Caldicott, *Nuclear Madness* (Brookline, MA: Autumn Press, 1978), p. 65 and passim. Russett and Starr, *World Politics*, p. 453.

136. Eric Pooley, "Nuclear Warriors," *Time* (March 4, 1996), p. 50.

137. Ibid., pp. 47–54. This account of a whistle blower's concern about safety and the resistance of both Northeast Utilities and the NRC is worth reading. It is

an unsettling story, especially if you live near a nuclear power plant.

138. Ibid., p. 49.
139. John Langone, "A Stinking Mess," *Time* (January, 1989), p. 44; Goldstein, *International Relations*, p. 441.
140. Amal Kumar Naj, "Private Industry Could Clean Up Toxic Waste," in Neal Bernards, ed., *The Environmental Crisis: Opposing Viewpoints* (San Diego: Greenhaven Press, 1991), p. 173. Reprinted from *The Wall Street Journal* (September 15, 1988). Chapter 4 debates toxic waste disposal.
141. Langone, "A Stinking Mess," p. 45.
142. Goldstein, *International Relations*, p. 441.
143. National Solid Wastes Management Association (NSWMA), "New Landfills Can Solve the Garbage Crisis," in Bernards, ed., *The Environmental Crisis*, p. 123; Langone, "A Stinking Mess," p. 45.
144. NSWMA, "New Landfills," p. 123.
145. John Tierney, "Recycling Is Garbage," *New York Times Magazine* (June 10, 1996), pp. 28, 51.
146. Brent Staples, "Life in the Toxic Zone: Environmental Justice in Chester, Pa.," *New York Times* (September 15, 1996), editorial page.
147. Tierney, "Recycling Is Garbage," pp. 26–27.
148. "Recycling without Tears," *New York Times* (July 29, 1996), editorial.
149. Ibid.; Barry Commoner, "Recycling More, Spending Less," *New York Times* (July 6, 1996), op-ed page; Tierney, "Recycling Is Garbage," pp. 29, 41.
150. Tierney, "Recycling Is Garbage," pp. 48, 51; Langone, "A Stinking Mess," p. 45.
151. Thomas F. Homer-Dixon, Jeffrey H. Boutwell, and George W. Rathjens, "Environmental Change and Violent Conflict," *Scientific American* 268 (February, 1993), p. 38. These three co-authors are also co-directors of the "Environmental Change and Acute Conflict" research project, which is jointly sponsored by the University of Toronto and the American Academy of Arts and Sciences. Thomas Homer-Dixon has published the following related articles on this topic: "On the Threshold: Environmental Changes as Causes of Acute Conflict," *International Security* 16 (Fall, 1991), pp. 76–116; "Destruction and Death," *New York Times* (January 31, 1993), op-ed page; and "Environmental Security and Intergroup Conflict," in Klare and Thomas, eds., *World Security: Challenges for a New Century*, pp. 290–313. This section is based primarily on the latter, most recent article, although there is a great deal of overlap among these articles.
152. Goldstein, *International Relations*, 461; Pirages, "Demographic Change and Ecological Insecurity," pp. 325–26.
153. Steven Greenhouse, "The Greening of U.S. Diplomacy: Focus on Ecology," *New York Times* (October 9, 1996), p. A6; Matthews, "The Environment and International Security," pp. 288–89.
154. Goldstein, *International Relations*, pp. 449–50.
155. See Anne R. Platt, "Confronting Infectious Diseases," in Brown, et al., *State of the World 1996*, pp. 114–132; Eugene Linden, "Global Fever," *Time* (July 8, 1996), pp. 56–57; Gregg Easterbrook, "Forget PCB's. Radon. Alar.: The World's Greatest Environmental Dangers Are Dung Smoke and Dirty Water," *New York Times Magazine* (September 11, 1994), pp. 60–63; Pirages, "Demographic Change and Ecological Insecurity," p. 322.
156. Commoner, *The Closing Circle*, pp. 29–42.

157. *Human Development Report 1996*, pp. 5–6, and passim.
158. Goldstein, *International Relations*, p. 428; Clark, "Managing Planet Earth," p. 47.
159. Russett and Starr, *World Politics*, p. 460. This section depends on Russett and Starr.
160. Ibid.
161. Ibid., p. 462.
162. Nash, *Loving Nature*, pp. 200–02; Goldstein, *International Relations*, pp. 428–29.
163. Bill McKibben, "Buzzless Buzzword," *New York Times* (April 10, 1996), op-ed page. McKibben argues that "sustainability," while it is a word that is tossed around often, has not effectively stabilized economic growth. He wonders if "maturity" might not be a better buzzword, since it implies inner development rather than outer growth, and requires restraint, self-discipline, and other-directedness.

4. HUMAN RIGHTS

1. Pope John XXIII, *Peace on Earth (Pacem in Terris)* (1963), in David J. O'Brien and Thomas A. Shannon, eds., *Catholic Social Thought: The Documentary Heritage* (Maryknoll, NY: Orbis Books, 1992), #9.
2. *I, Rigoberta Menchú: An Indian Woman in Guatemala*, her autobiography, edited and introduced by Elizabeth Bungos-Debray, and trans. by Ann Wright; (London: Verso, 1984); and "Things Have Happened to Me as in a Movie," *New York Times* (October 17, 1992), op-ed page. Happily, the resistance leaders and the government of Guatemala signed an accord to end the decades old civil war there in September, 1996. See, Julia Preston, "Guatemala and Guerrillas Sign Accord to End 35-Year-Old War," *New York Times* (September 20, 1996), pp. A1, A16; Rachel M. Cleary, "Guatemala: Expectations For Peace," *Current History* 95 (February, 1996), pp. 88–92.
3. Jack Donnelly, *International Human Rights* (Boulder, CO: Westview Press, 1993), p. 177, endnote 2.
4. Originally these were envisioned to be one document, but the United States insisted that they be divided into two. Although ready by 1953, they were tabled until 1966, when they were finally issued. As with any treaty, governments first sign the treaty, then formally ratify it according to their constitutions. Because of concerns about sovereignty, the United States has only ratified the Covenant on Civil and Political Rights and that in 1992. Although the United States generally abides by the provisions of these Covenants, it refuses to subject itself to outside scrutiny. See Donnelly, *International Human Rights*, pp. 10, 100–103, 182.
5. See Stephen P. Marks, "Promoting Human Rights," in Michael T. Klare and Daniel C. Thomas, eds. *World Security: Trends and Challenges at Century's End* (New York: St Martin's Press, 1991), pp. 297–99, for a comparable list.
6. Donnelly, *International Human Rights*, pp. 57–82.
7. Jack Donnelly, "International Human Rights after the Cold War," in Michael T. Klare and Daniel C. Thomas, eds. *World Security: Challenges for a New Century*, 2d ed. (New York: St. Martin's Press, 1994), p. 237.
8. Barbara Crossette, "U.N. Reports Latin America Suffers Fewer 'Disappeared'," *New York Times* (May 25, 1997), p. A4.

9. Donnelly, *International Human Rights*, p. 150.
10. Donnelly, "International Human Rights after the Cold War," p. 241.
11. Donnelly, *International Human Rights*, p. 101. Donnelly calls this an attitude of "American exceptionalism."
12. Ibid., p. 238.
13. David Hollenbach, "Global Human Rights: An Interpretation of the Contemporary Catholic Understanding," in his *Justice, Peace, and Human Rights: American Catholic Social Ethics in a Pluralistic World* (New York: Crossroad, 1988), p.91. Originally in Alfred T. Hennelly and John Langan, eds., *Human Rights in the Americas* (Washington, DC: Georgetown University Press, 1982).
14. Michael J. Himes and Kenneth R. Himes, *Fullness of Faith: The Public Significance of Theology* (New York: Paulist Press, 1993), p. 64.
15. Donnelly, *International Human Rights*, pp. 19–28. Natural Law and Kantian philosophies would logically provide stronger bases for human rights than utilitarian or Marxist philosophies.
16. National Conference of Catholic Bishops (NCCB), *Economic Justice for All* in O'Brien and Shannon, eds., *Catholic Social Thought*, #25 and passim. "This tradition [of Catholic social thought] insists that human dignity, realized in community with others and with the whole of God's creation, is the norm against which every social institution must be measured."
17. Himes and Himes, *Fullness of Faith*, ch. 3, "The Trinity and Human Rights," pp. 55–73.
18. Richard W. Mansbach, *The Global Puzzle: Issues and Actors in World Politics* (Boston: Houghton Mifflin, 1994), p. 539.
19. David Hollenbach, *Claims in Conflict: Retrieving and Renewing the Catholic Human Rights Tradition* (New York: Paulist Press, 1979), p. 95. This section depends on Hollenbach, pp. 89–100.
20. Ibid., p. 97.
21. Ibid., p. 203. See pp. 195–207.
22. Ibid., p. 204.
23. Donnelly, *International Human Rights*, pp. 37–38. This section depends on Donnelly.
24. The whole idea of human rights is inimical to a strong conception of cultural relativism. This is, however, a much debated philosophical issue. It should be noted that Catholic theology has little difficulty with the idea of universal moral norms and principles, but there is much discussion of their interpretation and implementation.
25. "Prostituted Children," *New York Times* (August 26, 1996), editorial; and Barbara Crossette, "U.N. Is Urged To Combat Sex Abuse of Children," *New York Times* (September 25, 1996), p. A7.
26. Donnelly, *International Human Rights*, p. 38. "The New Attack on Human Rights," *New York Times* (December 10, 1995), editorial, which concludes, "On Human Rights Day, let it be affirmed again that some truths are globally self-evident, and that a society deserves to be judged by its treatment of those least able to defend themselves, and by the degree to which rulers govern by consent and persuasion, rather than by terror."
27. United Nations Development Programme, *Human Development Report 1996* (New York: Oxford University Press, 1996), pp. 138–40, the gender-related development index table. The GDI was introduced in 1995.
28. Ibid., pp. 32–34.

29. Ibid., pp. 141–43, Gender Empowerment Measure Table.
30. Ibid., p. 35.
31. Adam Daniel Corson-Finnerty, *World Citizen* (Maryknoll, NY: Orbis Books, 1982), p. 76–77.
32. Owen R. Jackson, *Dignity and Solidarity: An Introduction to Peace and Justice Education* (Chicago: Loyola University Press, 1990), p. 178. NCCB, *Economic Justice For All*, #178–80.
33. Saint Joseph College, the women's college where I teach, was founded in 1932 by the Sisters of Mercy because there was no opportunity for women to acquire a college education in the area at that time.
34. Women hold less than 3 percent of the seats in these countries' parliaments. *Human Development Report 1996*, pp. 141–43.
35. Paul Lewis, "In the World's Parliaments, Women Are Still a Small Minority," *New York Times* (March 16, 1997), p. A10.
36. Carole J. Sheffield, "Sexual Terrorism," in Jo Freeman, ed., *Woman: A Feminist Perspective* (Mountain View, CA: Mayfield, 1989), pp. 3–19; Charlotte Bunch and Roxanna Carrillo, "Global Violence Against Women: The Challenge to Human Rights and Development," in Klare and Thomas, eds. *World Security: Challenges for a New Century*, p. 261; Marie M. Fortune, *Sexual Violence: The Unmentionable Sin* (New York: Pilgrim Press, 1983).
37. Celia W. Dugger, "African Ritual Pain: Genital Cutting," *New York Times* (October 5, 1996), pp. A1, A6, A7.
38. Neil MacFarquhar, "Mutilation of Egyptian Girls: Despite Ban, It Goes On," *New York Times* (August 8, 1996), p. A3.
39. Dugger, "African Ritual Pain," p. 6; Corson-Finnerty, *World Citizen*, p. 79.
40. "Egyptian Girl Dies After Genital Mutilation," *New York Times* (August 25, 1996), p. A18. This girl was the second known to have bled to death after the procedure in Egypt in two months. See also Howard W. French, "The Ritual: Disfiguring, Hurtful, Wildly Festive," Ibid. (January 31, 1997), p. A4.; and "Africa's Culture War: Old Customs, New Values," Ibid. (February 2, 1997), p. E1.
41. Dugger, "African Ritual Pain," p. A6.
42. MacFarquhar, "Mutilation of Egyptian Girls," p. A3.
43. Celia W. Dugger, "A Refugee's Body Is Intact but Her Family Is Torn," *New York Times* (September 11, 1996), pp. A1, B6–7.
44. Corson-Finnerty, *World Citizen*, p. 78; Howard W. French, "The Ritual Slaves of Ghana," *New York Times* (January 20, 1997), pp. A1, A5.
45. Ellen Goodman, "Outlaw Female Genital Mutilation Before Girls Are Harmed," *Hartford Courant* (October 20, 1995), op-ed page; Barbara Crossette, "Female Genital Mutilation by Immigrants Is Becoming Cause for Concern in the U.S.," *New York Times* (December 10, 1995), p. A18.
46. Celia W. Dugger, "New Law Bans Genital Cutting in United States," *New York Times* (October 12, 1996), pp. A1, A28.
47. Bunch and Carrillo, "Global Violence Against Women," p. 256.
48. For example, women often suffer from harsh discrimination in Islamic societies, but many scholars of Islam argue that the Koran can be interpreted to support the equality of women. See Elaine Sciolino, "The Many Faces of Islamic Law," *New York Times* (October 13, 1996), p. E4.
    The Catholic Church affirms the equality of women and men and condemns discrimination against women. See Pope John XXIII, *Pacem in Terris*, #41, and the National Conference of Catholic Bishops, *To Live in Christ Jesus: A Pastoral*

Reflection on the Moral Life (Washington, DC: United States Catholic Conference, 1976), pp. 24–25. Many Catholic theologians disagree with the Catholic Church's prohibition on the ordination of women, in part, precisely on human rights grounds. See Jackson, *Dignity and Solidarity*, p. 177.

49. Jackson, *Dignity and Solidarity*, p. 187.

50. Corson-Finnerty, *World Citizen*, p. 67.

51. Dee Brown, *Bury My Heart at Wounded Knee: An Indian History if the American West* (New York: Bantam Books, 1970).

52. Ibid., pp. 86–89. Some recent films dramatize this tragic history, for example, "Little Big Man," directed by Arthur Penn and starring Dustin Hoffman (1970), and "Dances with Wolves," directed by and starring Kevin Costner (1990).

53. Jackson, *Dignity and Solidarity*, pp. 188–89. See Alex Haley, *Roots* (Garden City, NY: Doubleday, 1976), and the made-for-TV movie based on this book for a good insight into the reality of slavery in the southern United States.

54. See John Howard Griffin, *Black Like Me* (New York: New American Library, 1961), for a moving account of the daily life of blacks in the segregated South.

55. See Taylor Branch, *Parting the Waters: America in the King Years 1954–63* (New York: Simon & Schuster, 1988), for a thorough account of the early Civil Rights movement, or David J. Garrow, *Bearing the Cross: Martin Luther King, Jr. and the Southern Christian Leadership Conference* (New York: William Morrow, 1986). Both books won the Pulitzer Prize. The PBS series "Eyes on the Prize," (1986) and "Eyes on the Prize II," (1989) (Boston: Blackside, Inc.) are excellent video documentaries of the Civil Rights movement.

56. For example, over 100 churches with predominantly black congregations, mainly in the South, were burned between January 1995 and the end of summer, 1996. About 20 percent of these arsons appear to be racially motivated. Officials of the U.S. Commission on Civil Rights, which held community forums on the church arsons, have discovered evidence of deep racial divisions in Southern states. See "Church Fire Probe Finds Rise in Racial Tensions," *Hartford Courant* (October 10, 1996), p. A4.
Gordon Witkin and Jeannye Thornton, "Pride and Prejudice," *U.S. News and World Report* (July 15/22, 1996), pp. 74–76, discuss the rise of hate crimes and the resurgence of racism in the United States.

57. Corson-Finnerty, *World Citizen*, pp. 68–69; Donnelly, *International Human Rights*, pp. 70–75, 121–25; H. Paul Santmire, *South African Testament* (Grand Rapids, MI: Wm. B. Eerdmans, 1987), pp. 6–11, passim; and Oliver Williams, *The Apartheid Crisis* (San Francisco: Harper & Row, 1986), especially chs. 1 & 2. There are several good films that dramatize apartheid in South Africa: "A Dry White Season," (1989) directed by Euzhan Palcy; "A World Apart," (1988) directed by Chris Menges; "Mandela," (1987) directed by Philip Saville; "Master Harold and the Boys," (1986) directed by Michael Lindsay-Hogg.

58. See Ted Robert Gurr and Barbara Harff, *Ethnic Conflict in World Politics* (Boulder, CO: Westview Press, 1994), pp. 65–75; Marlise Simons, "Tangier a Magnet for Africans Slipping into Spain," *New York Times* (August 26, 1996), p. A2.
Judy Mayotte, *Disposable People? The Plight of Refugees* (Maryknoll, NY: Orbis Books, 1992) discusses the situation of refugees in Cambodia, Afghanistan, Eritrea, and Sudan.

59. There is a voluminous literature on the Holocaust. See Jackson, *Dignity and Solidarity*, ch. 17; and Elie Wiesel, *Night* (New York: Bantam Books, 1960). The

movie "Schindler's List," directed by Steven Spielberg and starring Liam Neeson (1993), conveys the horror well.

60. Corson-Finnerty, *World Citizen*, p. 66.
61. Calvin Sims, "For Blacks in Peru, There's No Room at the Top," *New York Times* (August 17, 1996), p. A2.
62. Corson-Finnerty, *World Citizen*, p. 67.
63. Ibid., p. 69–70.
64. Anthony P. Maingot, "Haiti and Aristide: The Legacy of History," *Current History* 91 (February, 1992), p. 65.
65. Gaddis Smith, "Haiti: From Intervention to Intervasion," *Current History* 94 (February, 1995), pp. 54–55; Maingot, "Haiti and Aristide," p. 66.
66. Smith, "Haiti: From Intervention to Intervasion," p. 56.
67. Anthony P. Maingot, "Haiti: The Political Rot Within," *Current History* 94 (February, 1995), pp. 60–61.
68. Pamela Constable, "Haiti: A Nation in Despair, A Policy Adrift," *Current History* 93 (March, 1994), pp. 109–10; Michael S. Serrill, "Haiti: Rising from Ruin," *Time* 146 (October 16, 1995), p. 88.
69. Anthony T. Bryan, "Haiti: Kick Starting the Economy," *Current History* 94 (February, 1995), p. 66.
70. Constable, "Haiti: A Nation in Despair," pp. 108–09, 112.
71. Smith, "Haiti: From Intervention to Intervasion," p. 58.
72. Johanna McGeary, "Did the American Mission Matter?" *Time* 147 (February 19, 1996), p. 38; Serrill, "Haiti: Rising from Ruin," p. 88.
73. McGeary, "Did the American Mission Matter?" pp. 37–38.
74. Ibid., p. 38.
75. "Danger Signs in Haiti," *New York Times* (September 9, 1996), editorial.
76. Bryan, "Haiti: Kick Starting the Economy," p. 65.
77. Serrill, "Haiti: Rising from Ruin," pp. 87–88.
78. Patrick Jordan, "The State of Haiti," *Commonweal* 123 (May 3, 1996), pp. 10–11; McGeary, "Did the American Mission Matter?" p. 38; Larry Rohter, "Freeze in U.S. Aid Hampers New Haitian President's Recovery Effort," *New York Times* (April 29, 1996), p. A12.
79. McGeary, "Did the American Mission Matter?" p. 39.
80. See Bryan, "Haiti: Kick Starting the Economy," pp. 68–69.
81. Constable, "Haiti: A Nation in Despair," p. 110.
82. Smith, "Haiti: From Intervention to Intervasion," p. 58.
83. McGeary, "Did the American Mission Matter?" p. 36.
84. See Pamela Constable, "A Fresh Start for Haiti?" *Current History* 95 (February, 1996), pp. 65–69.
85. Elizabeth Rubin, "Haiti Takes Policing 101," *New York Times Magazine* (May 25, 1997), pp. 42–45, discusses the difficulties of accomplishing this task.

5. ETHNO-NATIONALIST CONFLICT

1. National Conference of Catholic Bishops (NCCB), "The Harvest of Justice Is Sown in Peace," in Gerard F. Powers, et al., eds., *Peacemaking: Moral and Policy Challenges for a New World* (Washington, DC: United States Catholic Conference, 1994), pp. 329, 331.
2. Alex De Waal and Rakiya Omaar, "The Genocide in Rwanda and the International Response," *Current History* 94 (April 1995), p. 156.

3. Lenard J. Cohen, "Bosnia and Herzegovina: Fragile Peace in a Segmented State," *Current History* 95 (March, 1996), pp. 103, 111–12.

4. Marsha A. Hewitt, "Neither Bread nor Roses: Women, War, & Intervention in the Balkans," *The Ecumenist* (May/June, 1994), p. 57.

5. Michael Specter, "In War-Ravaged Cechnya, Russia's Presence Is Fading," *New York Times* (November 1, 1996), pp. A1, A16. See also Vera Tolz, "The War in Cechnya," *Current History* 95 (October 1996), pp. 316–21.

6. Kalpana Isaac, "Sri Lanka's Ethnic Divide," *Current History* 95 (April, 1996), pp. 177, 179.

7. "The London Bombing," *New York Times* (February 11, 1996), editorial. The IRA re-established a cease-fire in Northern Ireland on July 20, 1997.

8. Ted Robert Gurr and Barbara Harff, *Ethnic Conflict in World Politics* (Boulder, CO: Westview Press, 1994), p. xiii.

9. Francis Fukuyama, "The End of History," *The National Interest* (Summer, 1989), pp. 3–18.

10. Rodolfo Stavenhagen, "Ethnic Conflicts and Their Impact on International Society," *International Social Science Journal* 43 (February, 1991), pp. 118–19; James Lee Ray, *Global Politics* (Boston: Houghton Mifflin, 1995), pp. 112–14.

11. Gurr and Harff, *Ethnic Conflict in World Politics*, p. 5.

12. Ibid., p. 144, see also pp. 18–26; Gidon Gottlieb, *Nation Against State: A New Approach to Ethnic Conflicts and the Decline of Sovereignty* (New York: Council on Foreign Relations, 1993), p. xii. Most often the nation lives in the territory it claims as its homeland, as with the Slovenes and Croats in the former Yugoslavia, or the Kurds in parts of Turkey, Iraq, Iran, and Syria. But the claim can also be primarily historical as with the Jews toward Israel prior to 1948.

13. Walker Connor, "From Tribe to Nation?" *History of European Ideas* 13 (1991), p. 6. Walker Connor, "The Specter of Ethno-Nationalist Movements Today," *PAWSS Perspectives* 1 (April, 1991), p. 2.

14. Connor, "From Tribe to Nation," p. 9.

15. Walker Connor, "Beyond Reason: The Nature of the Ethnonational Bond," *Ethnic and Racial Studies* 16 (July, 1993), p. 382.

16. Walker Connor, "When Is a Nation?" *Ethnic and Racial Studies* 13 (January, 1990), pp. 97–98.

17. Connor, "The Specter," p. 4.

18. Michael Ignatieff, *Blood and Belonging: Journeys into the New Nationalism* (New York: Farrar, Straus and Giroux, 1993), pp. 37–38.

19. Bruce Russett and Harvey Starr, *World Politics* (New York: W.H. Freeman and Company, 1996), p. 54; Ray, *Global Politics*, p. 168.

20. Connor, "Beyond Reason," pp. 374–75; Connor, "The Specter," p. 3.

21. Gurr and Harff, *Ethnic Conflict in World Politics*, p. 5.

22. Gottlieb, *Nation Against State*, p. 78, referring to the Genocide Convention of 1948.

23. Joshua S. Goldstein, *International Relations* (New York: Harper-Collins, 1996), pp. 201–02.

24. Gottlieb, *Nation Against State*, p. 35.

25. Ted Robert Gurr, "Communal Conflicts and Global Security," *Current History* 94 (May, 1995), pp. 212–14. This article is a revision of chapter 11 of Ted Robert Gurr, *Minorities at Risk: A Global View of Ethnopolitical Conflicts* (Washington, DC: United States Institute of Peace Press, 1993), where Gurr counted 233 minorities at risk. Thus I have used the more recent figures. See also the appen-

dix in Gurr and Harff, *Ethnic Conflict in World Politics*, pp. 159–65, for a list by region of "Serious and Emerging Ethnopolitical Conflicts in 1993."

26. Gurr and Harff, *Ethnic Conflict in World Politics*, p. 17.

27. This section depends on Michael J. Himes and Kenneth R. Himes, *Fullness of Faith: The Public Significance of Theology* (Mahwah, NJ: Paulist Press, 1993), Chapter 6, "Incarnation and Patriotism," pp. 125–56, and Chapter 7, "The Communion of Saints and an Ethic of Solidarity," pp. 157–83.

28. Ibid., p. 130.

29. John Paul II, *On Social Concern (Sollicitudo Rei Socialis)* (December 30, 1987) in David J. O'Brien and Thomas A. Shannon, *Catholic Social Thought: The Documentary Heritage* (Maryknoll, NY: Orbis Books, 1992), #38, p. 421.

30. Himes and Himes, *Fullness of Faith*, p. 146.

31. Ignatieff, *Blood and Belonging*, pp. 6–8.

32. Jean Bethke Elshtain, "Identity, Sovereignty, and Self-Determination," in Powers, et al., eds., *Peacemaking*, pp. 101–104.

33. Gurr and Harff, *Ethnic Conflict in World Politics*, pp. 139–44; Gottlieb, *Nation Against State*, p. 31, passim.

34. Goldstein, *International Relations*, p. 204; David Little, "Religious Nationalism and Human Rights," in Powers, et al., eds., *Peacemaking*, pp. 88–89.

35. David Little, *Sri Lanka: The Invention of Enmity* (Washington, DC: United States Institute of Peace Press, 1994), pp. 103–07; Mark Juergensmeyer, "Religious Nationalism: A Global Threat?" *Current History* 95 (November, 1996), pp. 372–76.

36. Gurr, "Communal Conflicts and Global Security," p. 214; Douglas M. Johnston, "Religion and Conflict Resolution," *The Fletcher Forum of World Affairs* 20 (Winter, 1996), p. 53.

37. NCCB, "The Harvest of Justice Is Sown in Peace," in Powers, et al., eds., *Peacemaking*, p. 329. Quote is from John Paul II, "To Build Peace, Respect Minorities," 1989 World Day of Peace Message, *Origins* 18 (December 29, 1988), p. 469. On p. 330 the American Catholic bishops say that authentic religion is the proper response to religiously authorized ethnic hatred. See Gerard F. Powers, "Conclusion: The Power of Virtue and the Virtue of Belief in Foreign Policy," in Powers, et al., eds., *Peacemaking*, pp. 301–04; Gregory Baum and Harold Wells, eds., *The Reconciliation of Peoples: Challenge to the Churches* (Maryknoll, NY: Orbis Books, 1997); and Johnston, "Religion and Conflict Resolution," pp. 53–60.

38. Daniel Patrick Moynihan, *Pandaemonium: Ethnicity in International Politics* (New York: Oxford University Press, 1993), p. 15. See Ignatieff, *Blood and Belonging*, pp. 21–22.

39. This history is based primarily on Bill Weinberg and Dorie Wilsnak, *War at the Crossroads: An Historical Guide Through the Balkan Labyrinth* (New York: War Resister's League pamphlet, 1993).

40. Ignatieff, *Blood and Belonging*, p. 22–23.

41. Josef Joffe, "Bosnia: The Return of History," *Commentary* 94 (October, 1992), p. 25.

42. Ignatieff, *Blood and Belonging*, p. 21. See also Jim Forest, "A Dialogue on Reconciliation in Belgrade," in Baum and Wells, eds., *The Reconciliation of Peoples*, pp. 112–14.

43. This account is based on the following sources: Sabrina Petra Ramet, "The Bosnian War and the Diplomacy of Accommodation," *Current History* 93

(November, 1994), pp. 380–85. Misha Glenny, "Yugoslavia: The Great Fall," *The New York Review of Books* (March 23, 1995), pp. 56–65. Warren Zimmerman, "The Last Ambassador," *Foreign Affairs* 74 (March/April, 1995), pp. 2–21. Charles G. Boyd, "Making Peace with the Guilty: The Truth about Bosnia," *Foreign Affairs* 74 (September/October, 1995), pp. 22–38. Lenard J. Cohen, "Bosnia and Herzegovina: Fragile Peace in a Segmented State," *Current History* 95 (March, 1996), pp. 103–12. Ignatieff, *Blood and Belonging*, Chapter 1, pp. 19–55.

44. Cohen, "Bosnia and Herzegovina," p. 106.
45. Ibid., p. 108.
46. Boyd, "Making Peace with the Guilty," p. 96. See also Ignatieff, *Blood and Belonging*, pp. 24–27.
47. Zimmerman, "The Last Ambassador," p. 16.
48. Glenny, "Yugoslavia: The Great Fall," p. 63.
49. This section primarily relies on: Little, *Sri Lanka: The Invention of Enmity*; Isaac, "Sri Lanka's Ethnic Divide;" and Lucinda Kaye, "Chances for Peace in Sri Lanka," *Peacework* #260 (February, 1996), pp. 7–11. See also Priit J. Vesilind, "Sri Lanka," *National Geographic* 191 (January, 1997), pp. 111–133.
50. Little, *Sri Lanka*, ch. 2.
51. Ibid., p. 36.
52. Ibid., p. 37.
53. Kaye, "Chances for Peace in Sri Lanka," p. 10.
54. See the following articles by John F. Burns in the *New York Times*: "A Corner of Sri Lanka Tires of Living Under Siege" (October 16, 1994); "After the Sri Lanka Violence: A Sense of Despair" (October 30, 1994); "Sri Lankans Hear Details of Decade of Slaughter" (May 21, 1995); "Torn by War, Sri Lanka Faces Deepening Despair" (January 19, 1997).
55. Isaac, "Sri Lanka's Ethnic Divide," pp. 177, 179.
56. Little, *Sri Lanka*, ch. 7.
57. The number of Tutsi killed is disputed. *New York Times* now consistently reports that at least 500,000 Tutsi were killed during this period. See, for example, James C. McKinley, Jr., "Old Revolutionary Is New Power to Be Reckoned with in Central Africa," *New York Times* (November 27, 1996), p. A12. De Waal and Omaar ("The Genocide in Rwanda," p. 156) put the number at 750,000 people slaughtered. Ann Rall, "Genocide in Rwanda—A Western-Made Massacre," *Peacework* Issue 260 (February, 1996), p. 2, says as many as one million were killed, including 300,000 children. Whether the number is 500,000 or twice that, the massacre is an act of genocide. The number of refugees resulting from this event (mostly Hutu) likewise varies from one million to two million.
58. Kevin Fedarko, "Death Cries of a Nation," *Time* 148 (November 11, 1996), pp. 46–47.
59. Ian Linden, "The Church and Genocide," in Baum and Wells, eds., *The Reconciliation of Peoples*, p. 51.
60. Rall, "Genocide in Rwanda," pp. 2–3; James Murray, "Rwanda's Bloody Roots, *New York Times* (September 3, 1994), op-ed page; Raymond Bonner, "A Once Peaceful Village Shows the Roots of Rwanda's Violence," *New York Times* (July 11, 1994), pp. A1, A8; James C. McKinley, Jr., "Rwanda's Past Again Vies to Be Prologue," *New York Times* (November 24, 1996), p. E6; Frederick Ehrenreich, "Causes of Conflict in Rwanda," *Geographic and Global Issues Quarterly* 4 (Summer, 1994), pp. 9–10.

61. Rall, "The Genocide in Rwanda," p. 3; Murray, "Rwanda's Bloody Roots;" Ehrenreich, "Causes of Conflict in Rwanda," p. 10.
62. Peter Uvin, "Tragedy in Rwanda: The Political Ecology of Conflict," *Environment* 38 (April, 1996), pp. 8–9.
63. Rall, "Genocide in Rwanda," p. 3.
64. De Waal and Omaar, "The Genocide in Rwanda," p. 156; Uvin, "The Tragedy in Rwanda," pp. 11–12; Ehrenreich, "Causes of Conflict in Rwanda," pp. 10–11.
65. See Jane Perlez, "Under the Bougainvillea, Hutu Litany on the Tutsi," *New York Times* (August 15, 1994), p. A6 for an interview with a highly-placed Hutu government administrator in exile, to get a taste of Hutu bigotry against the Tutsi.
66. Rall, "Genocide in Rwanda," pp. 3–4; Uvin, "Tragedy in Rwanda," pp. 12–13; De Waal and Omaar, "The Genocide in Rwanda," pp. 156–57.
67. De Waal and Omaar, "The Genocide in Rwanda," pp. 156–57.
68. Raymond Bonner, "Rwandans in Death Squad Say Choice Was Kill or Die," *New York Times* (August 14, 1994), pp. A1, A16.
69. James C. McKinley, Jr., "Legacy of Rwanda Violence: The Thousands Born of Rape," *New York Times* (September 23, 1996), pp. A1, A9.
70. Shawn H. McCormick, "The Lessons of Intervention in Africa," *Current History* 94 (April, 1995), pp. 163–64; Rall, "The Genocide in Rwanda," p. 4; De Waal and Omaar, "The Genocide in Rwanda," p. 157.
71. James C. McKinley, Jr., "In Pastoral Western Rwanda, Ethnic Foes Engage in Murderous Tit for Tat," *New York Times* (October 6, 1996), p. A16.
72. De Waal and Omaar, "The Genocide in Rwanda," pp. 157–61.
73. Uvin, "The Tragedy of Rwanda," p. 15.
74. James C. McKinley, Jr., "Old Revolutionary," p. A12; James C. McKinley, Jr., "Arriving Rwandans Find Home Not So Sweet," *New York Times* (November 18, 1996), pp. A1, A6.
75. Suzanne Daley, "For Rwandans, the Time to Heal Confronts a Passion for Revenge," *New York Times* (December 3, 1996), pp. A1, A6.
76. Philip Gourevitch, "Justice in Exile," *New York Times* (June 24, 1996), op-ed page; Nancy Landon Kassebaum, "First, Train Prosecutors in Rwanda So Justice Can Be Restored," *Hartford Courant* (December 4, 1996), op-ed page.
77. Uvin, "The Tragedy in Rwanda," p. 11.
78. Todd Salzman, "Catholics and Colonialism: the Church's Failure in Rwanda," *Commonweal* 124 (May 23, 1997), pp. 17–19; Linden, "The Church and Genocide," pp. 49–54.
79. Jean-Pierre Chretien, "Burundi: The Obsession with Genocide," *Current History* 95 (May, 1996), pp. 206–10.
80. Howard W. French, "The Anatomy of Autocracy: Mobutuism's Three Decades," *New York Times* (May 17, 1997), pp. A1, A7; and Nicholas D. Kristof, "In Congo, a New Era with Old Burdens," *New York Times* (May 29, 1997), pp. A1, A10.
81. Tim Pat Coogan, *The Troubles: Ireland's Ordeal 1966–1996 and the Search for Peace* (Boulder, CO: Roberts Rinehart Publishers, 1996), pp. 3–5.
82. Michael MacDonald, *Children of Wrath: Political Violence in Northern Ireland* (Cambridge, UK: Polity Press, 1986), p. 54.
83. See Ignatieff, *Blood and Belonging*, ch. 6. Although Ulster is commonly used to designate Northern Ireland, actually only six of its nine counties comprise Northern Ireland.
84. MacDonald, *Children of Wrath*, p. 25.
85. Coogan, *The Troubles*, pp. 6–12.

86. Ibid., pp. 12–25. The film "Michael Collins," (1996) directed by Neil Jordan and with Liam Neeson in the title role, depicts the period from 1916–1922 in Irish history, but there is scant attention paid to Ulster. The neglect of Ulster at the time of the establishment of the Republic of Ireland seems to be historically accurate.

87. Ibid., pp. 26–34; Ronnie Munck, "The Making of the Troubles in Northern Ireland," *Journal of Contemporary History* 27 (April, 1992), pp. 211–15. MacDonald, *The Children of Wrath*, ch. 6 reflects on the comparison between the Protestants of Ulster and the Boers of South Africa.

88. MacDonald, *Children of Wrath*, pp. 75–79; Munck, "The Making of the Troubles," pp. 215–28; Sabine Wichert, "The Role of Nationalism in the Northern Ireland Conflict," *History of European Ideas* 16 (January, 1993), pp. 110–14.

89. Coogan, *The Troubles*, p. 20.

90. MacDonald, *Children of Wrath*, pp. 85–90.

91. Wichert, "The Role of Nationalism," p. 112.

92. James F. Clarity, "In What Passes for Peace in Ulster, Anxiety Still," *New York Times* (September 1, 1995), p. A3. Note that this is about the same proportion of the population as the 50,000 deaths in Sri Lanka.

93. John Darnton, "After a Massacre in Ulster, Another Season of Fear," *New York Times* (November 1, 1993), pp. A1, A12.

94. Ibid.

95. Joseph O'Grady, "An Irish Policy Born in the U.S.A.," *Foreign Affairs* 75 (May/June, 1996), pp. 2–7.

96. Coogan, *The Troubles*, the Preface and the Epilogue; Kevin Toolis, "Why the IRA Stopped Talking," *New York Times* (February 21, 1996), op-ed page.

97. James F. Clarity, "I.R.A. Wing and British Hold Meeting," *New York Times* (May 22, 1997), p. A9; Ibid. "Blair's Undaunted Envoy to Ulster: Devil or Angel?" *New York Times* (May 25, 1997), p. 12; Ibid. "I.R.A. Announce A New Cease-Fire Beginning Today." *New York Times* (July 28, 1997), pp. A1, A9.

98. MacDonald, *Children of Wrath*, p. 95; Wichert, "The Role of Nationalism," pp. 112–14.

99. Scott Anderson, "Making a Killing," *Harper's Magazine* (February, 1994), pp. 45–54; Richard W. Stevenson, "Peace on Irish Horizon Doesn't Spell Prosperity," *New York Times* (September 4, 1994), p. E3.

100. MacDonald, *Children of Wrath*, p. 150; Ignatieff, *Blood and Belonging*, pp. 218–19; Michael Hurley, "Reconciliation and the Churches in Northern Ireland," in Baum and Wells, eds., *The Reconciliation of Peoples*, pp. 120–21.

101. Coogan, *The Troubles*, pp. 12–13.

102. Darnton, "After a Massacre," p. A12; Hurley, "Reconciliation and the Churches in Northern Ireland," p. 127.

103. Hurley, "Reconciliation and the Churches in Northern Ireland," pp. 120–26.

104. Gurr and Harff, *Ethnic Conflict in World Politics*, p. 30.

105. Ibid., p. 31; Ignatieff, *Blood and Belonging*, p. 179.

106. Marvin Zonis, "The Dispossessed: A Review of *A Modern History of the Kurds* by David McDowall (New York: I.B. Tauris/St Martin's Press, 1996)," *New York Times Book Review* (March 10, 1996), p. 15.

107. Celestine Bohlen, "War on Rebel Kurds Puts Turkey's Ideals to Test," *New York Times* (July 16, 1995), p. A3; Celestine Bohlen, "In Turkey, Open Discussion of Kurds Is Casualty of Effort to Confront War," *New York Times* (October

29, 1995), p. A20; Ignatieff, *Blood and Belonging*, pp. 199–212; Zonis, "The Dispossessed," p. 14.

108. Ignatieff, *Blood and Belonging*, pp. 194–98; Zonis, "The Dispossessed," p. 15.
109. Ignatieff, *Blood and Belonging*, p. 182.
110. Ibid., p. 184.
111. Zonis, "The Dispossessed," p. 15.
112. Ibid.
113. Gottlieb, *Nation Against State*, suggests new ideas and institutions.

6. WEAPONS AND DISARMAMENT

1. National Conference of Catholic Bishops, *The Challenge of Peace* (1986) in David J. O'Brien and Thomas A. Shannon, eds., *Catholic Social Thought: The Documentary Heritage* (Maryknoll, NY: Orbis Books, 1992), #219. Quote from John Paul II, "Homily at Bagington Airport," Coventry, England, #2, *Origins* 12 (1982), p. 55.
2. Michael T. Klare, "Deadly Convergence: The Arms Trade, Nuclear/ Chemical/Missile Proliferation, and Regional Conflict in the 1990s," in Michael T. Klare and Daniel C. Thomas, eds., *World Security: Trends and Challenges at Century's End*, (New York: St. Martin's Press, 1991), pp. 170–196.
3. Rakiya Omaar, "Somalia: At War with Itself," *Current History* 91 (October, 1991), p. 231.
4. It needs to be remembered that nuclear terrorism was a way for the West to stand against the terrorism represented by the totalitarian communist system. Thus, with the end of the Cold War, the people of the West could shed their fear of an attack from the East and of imminent nuclear holocaust, and the people of the East could shed their fear of a midnight knock on the door and of imminent nuclear holocaust.
5. This description is based on Ronald Sider and Richard Taylor, *Nuclear Holocaust & Christian Hope* (Downers Grove, IL: Intervarsity Press, 1982), ch. 1; Richard McSorley, *Kill? For Peace?* (Georgetown University: Center for Peace Studies, 1977), ch 1; John Hershey, *Hiroshima* (New York: Bantam, 1956); and informational material from Physicians for Social Responsibility, including the film "The Last Epidemic: Medical Consequences of Nuclear Weapons and Nuclear War."
6. Jonathan Schell, *The Fate of the Earth* (New York: Alfred A. Knopf, 1982), pp. 181–82. Originally in *The New Yorker* (February 15, 1982), p. 45.
7. The film "Crimson Tide" (1995) (directed by Tony Scott, starring Denzel Washington and Gene Hackman), dramatizes both the possibility of a change for the worse in Russia and the power of the captain of a nuclear submarine.
8. Paul Walker, *Seizing the Initiative: First Steps to Disarmament* (Philadelphia: American Friends Service Committee, 1983), pp. 8–16; Joshua Goldstein, *International Relations*, 2d ed. (New York: HarperCollins, 1996), pp. 259–62.
9. Allan S. Krass, "Death and Transfiguration: Nuclear Arms Control in the 1980s and 1990s," in Klare and Thomas, eds. *World Security: Trends and Challenges At Century's End*, pp. 75–79.
   Strategic nuclear weapons are those which can be delivered from one superpower to the other. *Intermediate* nuclear forces have a shorter, yet significant range. They could be fired from France to Russia, for example, or from Russia

to China. *Tactical* nuclear weapons are designed for battlefield use. Their range is shorter and they have less power, although there is no such thing as a nuclear weapon that is genuinely limited in its blast effect, or truly discriminate in its target or effect.

10. Krass, "The Second Nuclear Era: Nuclear Weapons in a Transformed World," pp. 92–3.

11. Peter Gray, *Briefing Book on U.S. Leadership and the Future of Nuclear Arsenals* (Washington, DC: Council for a Livable World Education Fund, 1996), p. 12; Steven Erlanger, "After 3-Year Wait, START II Wins Senate Approval but Still Faces Russian Opposition," *New York Times* (January 27, 1996), p. A5; Mikhail Gorbachev, "NATO's Plans Threaten START II," *New York Times* (February 10, 1996), op-ed page; David Hoffman, "Future of Arms Limitations Cloudy in Wake of Helsinki Summit," *New York Times* (March 23, 1997), p. A15; Thomas L. Friedman, "It's Unclear," *New York Times* (June 2, 1997), op-ed page.

12. "Russia, Iran and the Bomb," *New York Times* (February 26, 1995) editorial. In 1996 Russia was also selling weapons-grade material to France and Germany, despite a U.S.-imposed embargo on such sales. Paul Leventhal, "The Nuclear End Run," *New York Times* (June 5, 1996), op-ed page.

13. Michael R. Gordon, "Russia Struggles in Long Race to Prevent an Atomic Theft," *New York Times* (April 20, 1996), pp. A1, A4; Philip Shenon, "Ex-Soviet A-Bomb Fuel an Easy Target for Terrorists, U.S. Says," *New York Times* (March 13, 1996), p. A5; Tim Zimmerman and Alan Cooperman, "The Russian Connection," *U.S. News & World Report* 119 (October 23, 1995), pp. 56–67; Jane Perlez, "Tracing a Nuclear Risk: Stolen Enriched Uranium," *New York Times* (February 15, 1995), p. A3; Craig R. Whitney, "Germans Seize 3rd Atom Sample, Smuggled by Plane from Russia," *New York Times* (August 14, 1994), p. A1; Michael R. Gordon and Matthew L. Wald, "Russian Controls on Bomb Material Are Leaky," *New York Times* (August 18, 1994), p. A1; and Matthew L. Wald and Michael R. Gordon, "Russia Treasures Plutonium, But U.S. Wants to Destroy It," *New York Times* (August 19, 1994), p. A1; Bruce W. Nelan, "Formula for Terror," *Time* (August 29, 1994), pp. 47–51.

14. Russia is clearly the cause of most concern in this regard. Yet when the United States made public the records of all the plutonium that ever passed through Federal hands, Washington disclosed that it had shipped three-quarters of a ton of plutonium to 39 countries under the Atoms for Peace program. All of these transfers were legal; many of them involved small amounts; and none of the plutonium was of bomb-grade quality. Nevertheless, experts say that these peaceful transfers undoubtedly aided the development of nuclear arms in some cases. William J. Broad, "U.S. Sent Ton of Plutonium to 39 Countries," *New York Times* (February 6, 1996), p. A10. China provokes anxiety on this matter as well. Patrick E. Tyler, "China Raises Nuclear Stakes on the Subcontinent," *New York Times* (August 27, 1996), p. A6; A.M. Rosenthal, "The Nuclear Gamble," *New York Times* (October 11, 1996), op-ed page.

15. Matthew L. Wald, "Nuclear Lapses Raise Questions of Safety," *New York Times* (June 26, 1996), pp. A1, A16.

16. Peter Passell, "Profit Motive Clouding Effort to Buy Up A-Bomb Material," *New York Times* (August 28, 1996), p. A1, D3; William J. Broad, "Deal for U.S. to Buy Bomb Fuel from Russia Said to Be in Peril," *New York Times* (June 12, 1995), p. A1.

17. On the above problems see Krass, "The Second Nuclear Era," pp. 85–105;

Matthew L. Wald, "Agency to Pursue 2 Plans to Shrink Plutonium Supply," *New York Times* (December 10, 1996), pp. A1, B8; Peter Passell, "U.S. Set to Allow Reactors to Use Plutonium from Disarmed Bombs," *New York Times* (November 22, 1996), pp. A1, D18; Matthew L. Wald, "Factory Set to Process Dangerous Nuclear Waste," *New York Times* (March 13, 1996), p. A16; Matthew L. Wald, "Plan for Managing Nuclear Arms Leaves a Tough Issue Unresolved," *New York Times* (February 29, 1996), p. A18; Matthew L. Wald, "Today's Drama: The Twilight of the Nukes," *New York Times* (July 16, 1995), p. E5.

18. Matthew L. Wald, "Big Price Tag for A-Bombs, Study Finds: 50 Year Cost to U.S. Is Almost $4 Trillion," *New York Times* (July 13, 1995), p. A19; Stephen I. Schwartz, "Atomic Audit: What the U.S. Nuclear Arsenal Has Cost," *The Brookings Review* (Fall, 1995), pp. 14–17.

19. "The Pastoral Constitution on the Church in the Modern World," in *The Documents of Vatican II*, edited by Walter Abbott and translated by Joseph Gallagher (Geoffrey Chapman, 1966), # 81.

20. Matthew L. Wald, "Study Finds Destruction in the Making of A-Bombs," *New York Times* (July 26, 1995), p. A12, reports on a study produced over six years by the International Physicians for the Prevention of Nuclear War, winners of the Nobel Peace Prize in 1985, on the environmental damage from the nuclear weapons program. See Arjun Makhijani and Katherine Yih, eds., *Nuclear Wastelands: A Global Guide to Nuclear Weapons Production and its Health and Environmental Effects* (Cambridge, MA: MIT Press, 1995).

21. Goldstein, *International Relations*, pp. 245–47.

22. These Church documents are available from the United States Catholic Conference (USCC) in Washington, DC. *The Challenge of Peace* and *Peace on Earth* can also be found in *Catholic Social Thought: The Documentary Heritage*, David O'Brien and Thomas Shannon, eds. (Maryknoll, NY: Orbis Books, 1992), and *The Harvest of Justice Is Sown in Peace* is included in *Peacemaking: Moral and Policy Challenges for a New World*, Gerard F. Powers, et al., eds. (Washington, DC: USCC, 1994), reference at p. 333.

23. Joseph Cirincione, "The Non-Proliferation Treaty and the Nuclear Balance," *Current History* 94 (May, 1995), p. 205. See Selig S. Harrison, "Zero Nuclear Weapons. Zero." *New York Times* (February 15, 1995), op-ed; Gray, *Briefing Book on U.S. Leadership and the Future of Nuclear Arsenals*, which presents the debate about deterrence or disarmament and argues for the latter. See Richard N. Haass, "It's Dangerous to Disarm," *New York Times* (December 11, 1996), op-ed page, for a dissenting view.

24. Cirincione, "The Non-Proliferation Treaty," p. 205; "General Suggests U.S. Get Rid of Nuclear Arms," *The Hartford Courant* (July 16, 1994).

25. On the controversy about using the atomic bomb see Guy Alperovitz, "Use of the Atomic Bomb Was Not Inevitable," *The Hartford Courant* (October 23, 1994), pp. C1, C4; Ronald Takaki, *Hiroshima: Why America Dropped the Atomic Bomb* (Boston: Little, Brown and Company, 1995).

26. "Belarus Gives Up Last Nuclear Missile," *The Hartford Courant* (November, 1996), p. A7; Jane Perlez, "Sunflower Seeds Replace Ukraine's Old Missile Sites," *New York Times* (June 5, 1996), p. A5.

27. "Nuclear Breakthrough in Korea," *New York Times* (October 19, 1994), editorial; "North Korea Nuclear Plan Gains," *New York Times* (September 30, 1996), p. A8.

28. Cirincione, "The Non-Proliferation Treaty," pp. 201–06; Barbara Crossette,

"Discord over Renewing Pact on Spread of Nuclear Arms," *New York Times* (April 17, 1995), p. A1; Zachary S. Davis, "Nuclear Proliferation and Nonproliferation Policy in the 1990s," in Michael T. Klare and Daniel C. Thomas, eds., *World Security: Challenges for a New Century*, 2d ed., (New York, NY: St. Martin's Press, 1994), pp. 106–133; "A Nuclear Milestone," *New York Times*, (May 12, 1995), editorial.

29. "Nuclear Commitments," *New York Times* (June 12, 1995), editorial.

30. Barbara Crossette, "U.N. Endorses a Treaty to Halt All Nuclear Testing," *New York Times* (September 11, 1996), p. A4; Alison Mitchell, "Clinton at U.N., Signs Treaty Banning All Nuclear Testing," *New York Times* (September 25, 1996), pp. A1, A6. The United States has honored a moratorium (now a ban) on nuclear testing since October 1992. Now scientists are trying to devise a way to study whether aging plutonium in the U.S. nuclear arsenal will still detonate. Critics contend these experiments, which do not involve a nuclear explosion, may still violate the CBT and may provide data needed to design new nuclear weapons without having to test them. See Matthew L. Wald, "Lab's Task: Assuring Bombs' Quality Without Pulling Nuclear Trigger," New York Times (June 3, 1997), p. A16.

31. George F. Will, "The ABM Treaty Is Outdated," *The Hartford Courant* (September 21, 1995), op-ed page; William Safire, "Defenseless America," *New York Times* (May 9, 1996), op-ed page; and "Anti-Missile Issue," Ibid., (August 22, 1996), op-ed page.

32. Jessica Stern, "Preventing Portable Nukes," *New York Times* (April 10, 1996), op-ed page.

33. Joseph Cirincione, "No Defense," *New York Times* (May 8, 1996), op-ed page; Spurgeon M. Kenny, Jr., "The Arms Race Is On," Ibid., (September 12, 1995), op-ed page; "Star Wars Just Won't Die," Ibid., (June 13, 1996), editorial; Steven Erlanger, "Russia Will Put Off Signing Agreement on Missile Systems," Ibid., (October 31, 1996), p. A8, regarding amending the ABM treaty.

34. Goldstein, *International Relations*, pp. 250–51.

35. Barbara Crossette, "Treaty Banning Chemical Arms Worldwide Is Set for Spring," *New York Times* (November 3, 1996), p. A20.

36. "Mr. Dole Bumps a Good Treaty," *New York Times* (September 15, 1996), editorial.

37. Jon Kyl, "A Treaty That Deserved to Die," *New York Times* (September 13, 1996), op-ed page; George F. Will, "A Piece of Paper Won't Stop Evildoers," *The Hartford Courant* (September 9, 1996), op-ed page; and "A Flawed Pact That Won't Limit Chemical Weapons," Ibid. (May 1, 1997), op-ed page.

38. See "Chemical Arms Treaty: The Fine Print," *New York Times* (April 24, 1997), p. A6; "Russians Fail to Ratify Chemical Weapons Pact," *Hartford Courant* (April 26, 1997), p. A3.

39. Tim Weiner, "Huge Chemical Arms Plant Near Completion in Libya, U.S. Says," *New York Times* (February 25, 1996), p. A8; A. M. Rosenthal, "Shall We Wait and See?" Ibid., (February 27, 1996), op-ed page.

40. James Brooke, "At Utah Plant, Safety Debate Rages," *New York Times* (November 28, 1996), p. A4. See Jill Smolowe, "Chemical Time Bombs," *Time* 147 (February 12, 1996), pp. 42–43.

41. Barbara Crossette, "A Russian Scientist Cautions Chemical Arms Safety Is Lax," *New York Times* (October 1, 1995), p. A12.

42. Goldstein, *International Relations*, pp. 251–52.

43. Anne Goldfield and Holly Nyers, "Declare a Moratorium on the Use of Land Mines," *The Hartford Courant* (July 21, 1995), op-ed page.
44. Kevin Fedarko, "Land Mines: Cheap, Deadly and Cruel," *Time* 147 (May 13, 1996), p. 54.
45. Christopher S. Wren, "Everywhere, Weapons That Keep on Killing," *New York Times* (October 8, 1995), p. E3.
46. Goldfield and Nyers, "Declare a Moratorium."
47. Bernard E. Trainor, "Land Mines Saved My Life," *New York Times* (March 27, 1996), op-ed page.
48. Barbara Crossette, "Pact on Land Mines Stops Short of Total Ban," *New York Times* (May 4, 1996), p. A4.
49. Ibid.; see Philip Shenon, "Rights Group Presses Drive on U.S. Makers of Land-Mine Parts," *New York Times* (April 18, 1997), p. A10, for a consumer approach to curbing the production of land mines.
50. "U.S. Offers a U.N. Resolution to Ban Land Mines," *New York Times* (November 9, 1996), p. A4; "Lagging on Land Mines," *New York Times* (June 13, 1997), editorial; Steven Lee Myers, "Why Washington Likes Land Mines," *New York Times* (August 24, 1997), p. E5.
51. Michael T. Klare, "Adding Fuel to the Fire: The Conventional Arms Trade in the 1990s," in Klare and Thomas, eds. *World Security: Challenges for a New Century*, pp. 134–54, at 147.
52. Klare, "Adding Fuel to the Fire," pp. 147–48; Klare, "Deadly Convergences," pp. 186–87.
53. Mark R. Amstutz, *International Conflict and Cooperation: An Introduction to World Politics* (Madison, WI: Brown & Benchmark, 1995), p. 383.
54. Charles M. Sennott, "Armed for Profit: The Selling of U.S. Weapons," *The Boston Globe* (February 11, 1996), a Special Report, p. B2.
55. Klare, "Adding Fuel to the Fire," pp. 134, 139.
56. Ibid., pp. 139–42; Tim Weiner, "China Is Top Supplier to Nations Seeking Powerful, Banned Arms," *New York Times* (July 3, 1997), p. A10.
57. Sennott, "Armed for Profit," pp. B6, B8.
58. Ibid., p. B6.
59. Philip Shenon, "Russia Outstrips U.S. as Chief Arms Seller to Developing Nations," *New York Times* (August 20, 1996), p. A3.
60. Klare, "Adding Fuel to the Fire," pp. 134–36.
61. Shenon, "Russia Outstrips," p. A3.
62. Sennott, "Armed for Profit," p. B2.
63. Ibid., p. B11, also B7; See James Sterngold, "A Swift Transformation," *New York Times* (December 16, 1996), pp. A1, D14.
64. Sennott, "Armed for Profit," p. B12. The salaries of the next four highest paid CEOs ranged from $1.6 to $4.6 million.
65. Klare, "Adding Fuel to the Fire," pp. 135–36.
66. Ibid., p. 138.
67. Ibid., pp. 148–51.
68. Jonathan Rauch, "Tooth Fairy Defense Budgets," *New York Times* (September 25, 1996), op-ed page; Sennott, "Armed for Profit," pp. B2, B4.
69. Frank Dworak, "Economic Justice and the U.S. Budget: How Much of Our Spending Is Military?" *Catholic Peace Voice* (Spring, 1996), p. 10.
70. Sennott, "Armed for Profit," p. B4.
71. Figures drawn from Sennott, "Armed for Profit," p. B4; and a chart developed

by the Council for a Livable World Education Fund, 110 Maryland Ave., N.E. Suite 211, Washington, DC 20002, based on *The Military Balance 1995/96*, published by the International Institute for Strategic Studies.

72. Goldstein, *International Relations*, pp. 224–26; Bruce Russett and Harvey Starr, *World Politics: The Menu For Choice* (New York: W.H. Freeman, 1996), pp. 295–96.

7. PEACE AND SECURITY IN THE POST-COLD WAR WORLD

1. National Conference of Catholic Bishops (NCCB), *The Harvest of Justice is Sown in Peace* (November 17, 1993), in Gerard F. Powers, et al., eds., *Peacemaking: Moral and Policy Challenges for a New World* (Washington, DC: United States Catholic Conference, 1994), pp. 340–41.
2. Leslie H. Gelb, "Fresh Faces," *New York Times Magazine* (December 8, 1991), pp. 50–54. Gelb suggests that the new thinking needed in foreign policy requires "fresh faces" making policy and decisions.
3. George Weigel, "Back to Basics: Moral Reasoning and Foreign Policy 'After Containment,'" in Powers, et al., eds., *Peacemaking*, pp. 57–60.
4. Joshua S. Goldstein, *International Relations* 2d ed., (New York: HarperCollins, 1996), pp. 52–53; Pierre de Senarclens, "The 'Realist' Paradigm and International Conflicts," *International Social Science Journal* 43 (February, 1991), pp. 5–6; Richard Falk, "Theory, Realism, and World Security," in Michael T. Klare and Daniel C. Thomas, eds., *World Security: Trends and Challenges at Century's End* (New York: St. Martin's Press, 1991), pp. 10–17.
5. Besides the sources in the previous endnote see Michael T. Klare and Daniel C. Thomas, "Introduction: Thinking about World Security," in their *World Security: Challenges for a New Century*, 2d ed., (New York: St. Martin's Press, 1994), p. 2; Seyom Brown, "World Interests and the Changing Dimensions of Security," ibid., pp. 10–12; and Charles W. Kegley, Jr. and Eugene R. Wittkopf, *World Politics: Trend and Transformation* 6th ed., (New York: St. Martin's Press, 1997), pp. 22–25.
6. De Senarclens, "The 'Realist' Paradigm and International Conflicts," p. 9.
7. Ibid., p. 17.
8. Brown, "World Interests and the Changing Dimensions of Power," pp. 10–26; Falk, "Theory, Realism, and World Security," pp. 19–21; Goldstein, *International Relations*, p. 96.
9. Klare and Thomas, "Introduction: Thinking about World Security," pp. 2–3.
10. See Robert C. Johansen, "Building World Security: The Need for Strengthened International Institutions," in Klare and Thomas, eds., *World Security: Challenges for a New Century* (1994), pp. 374–76; Charles W. Kegley, Jr., "The New Global Order: The Power of Principle in a Pluralistic World," in Joel H. Rosenthal, ed., *Ethics and International Affairs: A Reader* (Washington, DC: Georgetown University Press, 1995), p. 123; Gerard F. Powers, "Conclusion: The Power of Virtue, the Virtue of Belief in Foreign Policy," in Powers, et al., eds., *Peacemaking*, p. 305; Goldstein, *International Relations*, pp. 104–08.
11. Goldstein, *International Relations*, pp. 104–06. See David C. Hendrickson, "The Ethics of Collective Security," in Rosenthal, ed., *Ethics and International Affairs*, pp. 197–212, for a critical discussion of collective security.
12. Michael T. Klare, "Redefining Security: The New Global Schisms," *Current History* 95 (November, 1996), pp. 353–58, at 358.

13. Chester A. Crocker and Fen Osler Hampson with Pamela Aall, "Conclusion," in their *Managing Global Chaos: Sources of and Response to International Conflict* (Washington, DC: United States Institute of Peace, 1996), p. 624. Cf. Klare, "Redefining Security," pp. 353–58.

14. Crocker, Hampson, and Aall, "Conclusion," pp. 624–26.

15. Johansen, "Building World Security," p. 376.

16. This analysis is primarily drawn from Michael T. Klare, *Rogue States and Nuclear Outlaws: America's Search for a New Foreign Policy* (New York: Hill and Wang, 1995), ch. 7, "Beyond the Rogues: Military Doctrine in a World of Chaos"; and Johansen, "Building World Security," pp. 372–97.

17. See, for example, Mark Juergensmeyer, *Fighting Fair: A Nonviolent Strategy for Resolving Everyday Conflicts* (San Francisco: Harper & Row, 1986); Glen H. Stassen, *Just Peacemaking: Transforming Initiatives for Justice and Peace* (Louisville, KY: Westminster/John Knox Press, 1992); and Roger Fisher and William Ury, with Bruce Patton, *Getting to Yes: Negotiating Agreement Without Giving In* (New York: Penguin Books, 1983).

18. Kegley, "The New Global Order," p. 121. Although Kegley emphasizes reciprocity, toward the end of his article he seems to reduce the Golden Rule to "Let's leave one another alone." Reciprocity might be more effective when it is more active and more interventionist.

19. Johansen, "Building World Security," p. 377.

20. Klare, *Rogue States*, pp. 214–15.

21. Ibid., p. 215; NCCB, *The Harvest of Justice Is Sown in Peace*, p. 325; Johansen, "Building World Security," pp. 378, 389–91; Charles William Maynes, "Containing Ethnic Conflict," *Foreign Policy* (Spring, 1993), pp. 6–11; Brian Hall, "Blue Helmets, Empty Guns," *New York Times Magazine* (January 2, 1994), pp. 19–28ff; Paul Lewis, "U.N. Panel Proposes Expanding Security Council to 24 Members," *New York Times* (March 21, 1997), p. A13.

22. See Margaret P. Karns and Karen A. Mingst, "Maintaining International Peace and Security: U.N. Peacekeeping and Peacemaking," in Klare and Thomas, eds., *World Security: Challenges for a New Century*, pp. 188–215; and Alvaro de Soto, "Strengthening Global Institutions," in Powers, et al., eds., *Peacemaking*, pp. 149–64.

23. Klare, *Rogue States*, p. 215; NCCB, *The Harvest of Justice Is Sown in Peace*, p. 325.

24. NCCB, *The Harvest of Justice Is Sown in Peace*, p. 327.

25. Johansen, "Building World Security," pp. 379–81. Johansen analyzes separately the principles of "equity" and "sustainability." See Klare, *Rogue States*, p. 217.

26. Johansen, "Building World Security," pp. 379–82.

27. Johansen, "Building World Security," pp. 385–86; NCCB, *The Harvest of Justice Is Sown in Peace*, p. 326.

28. Bruce Russett, "Peace and the Moral Imperative of Democracy," in Powers, et al., eds., *Peacemaking*, pp. 105–15, at 107.

29. Ibid.

30. Johansen, "Building World Security," p. 384.

31. Ibid., p. 387.

32. Klare, *Rogue States*, p. 217. Chapter six above outlines a regime for reducing the arms trade.

33. The following is a summary of the elegant argument in Klare, *Rogue States and Nuclear Outlaws*.

34. Klare, *Rogue States*, p. 228. In May of 1997 the Pentagon published the results of its "Quadrennial Defense Review." It called for some trimming of the military, but no basic changes either in the strategy of being prepared to fight two regional wars simultaneously, or in force strength and weapons programs. See Philip Shenon, "Pentagon Urges Trims in Military and New Round of Base Closings," *New York Times* (May 20, 1997), pp. A1, A18. For a point/counterpoint response to the Pentagon review see George F. Will, "There's Always a Need for Adequate Funding of Armed Forces," *The Hartford Courant* (May 22, 1997), op-ed page; and Lawrence J. Korb, "The Pentagon's War on Thrift," *New York Times* (May 22, 1997), op-ed page.

35. See Chris Hedges "Studying Bosnia's U.S. 'Prisoners of Peace'," *New York Times* (March 30, 1997), p. A11 for a discussion of the morale and psychological problems that arise when troops trained for combat are used for peacekeeping missions, such as in Bosnia.

36. "School of Dictators," *New York Times* (September 28, 1996), editorial; "Be All You Can Be: Your Future as an Extortionist," Ibid., (October 6, 1996), p. E9; Dana Priest, "U.S. Instructed Latins on Executions, Torture," *Washington Post* (September 21, 1996), pp. A1, A9; and Jack Nelson-Pallmeyer, *School of Assassins* (Maryknoll, NY: Orbis Books, 1997). Fr. Roy Bourgeois, a Maryknoll priest who lived and worked with the poor in Bolivia, has established "School of the Americas (SOA) Watch" (1719 Irving Street, N.W., Washington, DC 20010; (202) 234-3440) to educate Americans about the SOA and to lobby congress to close it. An educational film titled "School of Assassins" is available from Maryknoll, New York 10545.

37. NCCB, *The Harvest of Justice Is Sown in Peace*, p. 336.

38. J. Bryan Hehir, "Intervention: From Theories to Cases," *Ethics and International Affairs* 9 (1995), pp. 3–6; Kenneth R. Himes, "The Morality of Humanitarian Intervention," *Theological Studies* 55 (1994), pp. 84–85, 92–93.

39. Hehir, "Intervention," p. 8; Himes, "The Morality of Humanitarian Intervention," p. 97.

40. Hehir, "Intervention," p. 13.

41. Himes, "The Morality of Humanitarian Intervention," p. 97.

42. Kenneth R. Himes, "Catholic Social Thought and Humanitarian Intervention," in Powers, et al., eds., *Peacemaking*, pp. 218–20; NCCB, *The Harvest of Justice Is Sown in Peace*, p. 337.

43. NCCB, *The Challenge of Peace* (1983) in David O'Brien and Thomas Shannon, eds., *Catholic Social Thought* (Maryknoll, NY: Orbis Books, 1992), #66–121.

44. See Richard B. Miller, "Casuistry, Pacifism, and the Just War Tradition in the Post-Cold War Era," in Powers, et al., eds., *Peacemaking*, pp. 205–09; Robert Phillips and Duane L. Cady, *Humanitarian Intervention: Just War vs. Pacifism* (Lanham, MD: Rowman & Littlefield, 1996). Cady explicates the position of a philosophical pacifist. Himes, "Catholic Social Thought and Humanitarian Intervention," pp. 224–35.

45. Hehir, "Intervention," pp. 7–8; Cady, *Humanitarian Intervention*, pp. 61–62; NCCB, *The Harvest of Justice Is Sown in Peace*, p. 337.

46. Hehir, "Intervention," p. 8.

47. See Hehir, "Intervention," pp. 9, 11–13; Himes, "The Morality of Humanitarian Intervention," pp. 100–01.

48. Hehir, "Intervention," p. 9; Himes, "The Morality of Humanitarian Intervention," pp. 98–100.

49. This is the argument of Robert Phillips in *Humanitarian Intervention*.

50. Himes, "Catholic Social Teaching and Humanitarian Intervention," p. 227.

51. Himes, "The Morality of Humanitarian Intervention," pp. 101–04; Hehir, "Intervention," p. 13.

52. Hehir, "Intervention," pp. 10–11; Himes, "The Morality of Humanitarian Intervention," pp. 101–02.

8. JESUS, CATHOLIC SOCIAL TEACHING, AND CHRISTIAN CITIZENSHIP

1. National Conference of Catholic Bishops (NCCB), *The Challenge of Peace: God's Promise and Our Response* (1983) in David J. O'Brien & Thomas A. Shannon, eds., *Catholic Social Thought: The Documentary Heritage* (Maryknoll, NY: Orbis Books, 1992), #276, p. 551–52.

2. See chapter 5 of the Song of Solomon in the Hebrew Scriptures where the female lover wearies her friends with talk of her beloved.

3. Marcus J. Borg, *Meeting Jesus Again for the First Time* (HarperSanFrancisco, 1994), pp. 31–32. This section on Jesus as a spirit person relies on Borg, pp. 30–39.

4. All three synoptic gospels—Matthew, Mark, and Luke—have accounts of these visions by Jesus.

5. Borg, *Meeting Jesus*, p. 46. This section depends on Chapter 3 "Jesus, Compassion, and Politics," in Borg and on Donald P. McNeill, Douglas A. Morrison, and Henri J. M. Nouwen, *Compassion: A Reflection on the Christian Life* (Garden City, New York: Doubleday Image Book, 1982), Part One.

6. The New Revised Standard Version of the Bible uses the term merciful instead of compassionate, which is found in the Jerusalem Bible and the New English Bible. Borg argues persuasively that compassion is a better translation, pp. 47–48.

7. Richard Gula, *Reason Informed by Faith*, (New York: Paulist Press, 1989), p. 185. By this expression Gula means to indicate that Jesus is God's fullest revelation of the invitation of divine love to us and the fullest human response to God.

8. McNeill, et al., *Compassion*, pp. 15–16.

9. Borg, *Meeting Jesus*, pp. 47–49; McNeill, et al., *Compassion*, pp. 15–17. See John Shea, *Stories of Faith* (Chicago: Thomas More Press, 1980), chapter 6 for a poetic account of Jesus, the "Son Who Must Die."

10. Borg, *Meeting Jesus*, p. 49. This section on the politics of compassion versus the politics of purity depends on Borg, pp. 49–61.

11. Borg, *Meeting Jesus*, pp. 51–52.

12. Mt 23:23; Lk 11:42. Borg, *Meeting Jesus*, p. 54.

13. See also Isaiah 1:10-15. Ronald J. Sider, *Rich Christians in an Age of Hunger: A Biblical Study* (New York: Paulist Press, 1977), pp. 80–81, makes this point well.

14. Borg, *Meeting Jesus*, pp. 55–57.

15. See also Acts 4:32-37.

16. Sider, *Rich Christians*, p. 101.

17. Ibid., pp. 101–10, quote at p. 106.

18. See Jack Nelson-Pallmeyer, *Brave New World Order* (Maryknoll, NY: Orbis Books, 1992), chapter 8, "Mark, Jesus, and the Kingdom: Confronting World Orders, Old and New"; and Ched Myers, *Binding the Strong Man: A Political Reading of Mark's Story of Jesus* (Maryknoll, NY: Orbis Books, 1988).

19. The Zealots emerge clearly only at the time of the 70 A.D. revolt against the

Romans that led to the destruction of the Temple by the Romans, but their brand of militant nationalism was surely around in Jesus' time. They are mentioned indirectly in the gospels. The Essenes were a sort of monastic community that retreated to the desert to lead a holy and pure and faithful religious life. The Pharisees, who are prominent in the Gospels, become Jesus' adversaries. See Donald Senior, *Jesus: A Gospel Portrait* (Cincinnati: Pflaum Standard, 1975), chapter 2, "The World of Jesus."

20. Ibid., pp. 47–48.
21. Ms. Egan said this in a personal conversation. For a sense of what she had in mind see her "The Beatitudes, the Works of Mercy, and Pacifism," in Thomas A. Shannon, ed., *War or Peace?* (Maryknoll, NY: Orbis Books, 1980), pp. 169–87.
22. Walter Wink, *Violence and Nonviolence in South Africa: Jesus' Third Way* (Philadelphia: New Society Publishers, 1987), chapter 2.
23. Ibid, p. 15.
24. Two of the early scenes in the movie "Gandhi" (directed by Richard Attenborough, starring Ben Kingsley, 1982) illustrate this point well. Both take place in South Africa. In the first, Gandhi is beaten by a police officer while taking part in a protest where Indians burn their passbooks. Gandhi's defiant, but nonviolent resistance both provokes and puzzles the police officer. In the second, Gandhi meets an American minister and is challenged by some young white thugs as they walk to Gandhi's office. The minister wants to walk around the Sermon on the Mount, but Gandhi decides to walk through it.
25. Wink, *Violence and Nonviolence*, p. 17.
26. Luke's slightly different version of this saying ends with "Be compassionate as your Father is compassionate," the verse that Borg finds so central to the message of Jesus.
27. Jesus' rejection of dominating love is a key to understanding Jesus and discipleship according to Richard Gula, *Reason Informed By Faith*, pp. 189–97.
28. See Roland Bainton, *Christian Attitudes Toward War and Peace* (Nashville: Abingdon Press, 1960), chapter 5; and John Helgeland, Robert J. Daly, and J. Patout Burns, *Christians and the Military: The Early Experience* (Philadelphia: Fortress Press, 1985).
29. Mk 1:14-15; Mt 4:17.
30. For a theological discussion of the notion of transformation that is rooted in H. Richard Niebuhr's classic work, *Christ and Culture* (New York: Harper, 1951) see Glen H. Stassen, D. M. Yeager, and John Howard Yoder, *Authentic Transformation* (Nashville: Abingdon Press, 1996).
31. Charles E. Curran, "Conversion: The Central Moral Message of Jesus," in his *A New Look at Christian Morality* (Notre Dame, IN: Fides, 1968), p. 65. See also James P. Hanigan, "Conversion and Christian Ethics," *Theology Today* 40 (April, 1983), pp. 33–34.
32. See Suzanne Toton, *World Hunger* (Maryknoll, NY: Orbis Books, 1982), pp. 115–21; and Donal Dorr, *The Social Justice Agenda* (Maryknoll, NY: Orbis Books, 1991).
33. There is no official canon for Catholic social teaching. In Catholic ecclesiastical polity, the official teachings of Councils of the whole Church (Vatican II), of the popes (social encyclicals), and of Vatican Synods carry more weight and authority than that of National Conferences of bishops or of individual bishops, yet all of these documents could be considered official Catholic teaching that in some degree should bind or guide a Catholic. For a listing of the papal, conciliar, and

synod documents see Charles Curran, "A Century of Catholic Social Teaching," *Theology Today* 48 (July, 1991), p. 154, ftnt. 2. David J. O'Brien and Thomas A. Shannon have produced two very helpful collections of documents associated with Catholic social teaching: *Renewing the Earth: Catholic Documents on Peace, Justice, and Liberation* (Garden City, NY: Image Books, Doubleday & Co., 1977); and *Catholic Social Thought: The Documentary Heritage* (Maryknoll, NY: Orbis Books, 1992).

34. Peter J. Henriot, Edward P. DeBerri, and Michael J. Schultheis, *Catholic Social Teaching: Our Best Kept Secret* (Maryknoll, NY: Orbis Books, 1988).
35. See for example: Philip S. Land, *Catholic Social Teaching: As I Have Lived, Loathed, and Loved It* (Chicago: Loyola University Press, 1996); John A. Coleman, ed., *One Hundred Years of Catholic Social Thought: Celebration and Challenge* (Maryknoll, NY: Orbis Books, 1991); Fred Kammer, *Doing Faithjustice: An Introduction to Catholic Social Thought* (New York: Paulist Press, 1991); Gregory Baum, *Compassion and Solidarity: The Church for Others* (New York: Paulist Press, 1990); Charles E. Curran and Richard A. McCormick, eds., *Readings in Moral Theology No. 5: Official Catholic Social Teaching* (New York: Paulist Press, 1986); Donal Dorr, *Option for the Poor: A Hundred Years of Vatican Social Teaching* (Maryknoll, NY: Orbis Books, 1983); and John C. Haughey, ed., *The Faith That Does Justice* (New York: Paulist Press, 1977).
36. In O'Brien and Shannon, eds., *Catholic Social Thought*, p. 289.
37. National Conference of Catholic Bishops (NCCB), *Economic Justice for All*, (1986) in O'Brien and Shannon, eds., *Catholic Social Thought*, Introduction, #25.
38. Ibid., #35–36.
39. Ibid., #36; See Kammer, *Doing Faithjustice*, pp. 22–24; and Sider, *Rich Christians*, pp. 88–93.
40. Sider, *Rich Christians*, pp. 60–65. On the biblical concept of justice, see Daniel A. Maguire, "The Primacy of Justice in Moral Theology," *Horizons* 10 (Spring, 1983), pp. 72–85; Stephen Charles Mott, *Biblical Ethics and Social Change* (New York: Oxford University Press, 1982); and John R. Donahue, "Biblical Perspectives on Justice," in Haughey, ed., *The Faith That Does Justice*, pp. 68–112. On the spiritual consciousness and experience of the prophets see Abraham Heschel, *The Prophets* (New York: Harper & Row, 1962), pp. 12–37, 223–31, 307–19, 483–86.
41. I have chosen to consistently quote from the prophet Micah in this section, but similar quotes could be taken from any of the prophetic books, such as Amos, Hosea, Isaiah, Jeremiah, or Ezekiel.
42. See NCCB, *Economic Justice for All*, #123.
43. Pope John XXIII, *Peace on Earth (Pacem in Terris)*, in O'Brien and Shannon, eds., *Catholic Social Thought*, pp. 131–62. See also Pope John Paul II, *On the Hundredth Anniversary of "Rerum Novarum" (Centesimus Annus)*, ibid., #47, for a sort of summary statement of human rights.
44. See NCCB, *Economic Justice for All*, #79–85; David Hollenbach, "Global Human Rights: An Interpretation of Contemporary Catholic Understanding," in Curran and McCormick, eds., *Readings in Moral Theology No. 5*, pp. 366–83; and John Langan, "Human Rights in Roman Catholicism," ibid., pp. 110–29.
45. Pope John Paul II, *On Social Concern (Sollicitudo Rei Socialis)*, (1987), in O'Brien and Shannon, eds., *Catholic Social Thought*, #36.
46. Ibid., #37.

47. See Synod of Bishops, *Justice in the World*, in O'Brien and Shannon, eds., *Catholic Social Thought*, pp. 290–91, passim; Pope Paul VI, *Evangelization in the Modern World (Evangelii Nuntiandi)*, Ibid., #31, 36; Kammer, *Doing Faithjustice*, chapter 5.

48. Pope John Paul II, *On Social Concern*, #38. See Jacques Delcourt, "The New Status of Solidarity in the Social Teaching of the Catholic Church," in Samuel M. Natale and Francis P. McHugh, eds., *Proceedings of the First International Conference on Social Values*, held at St. Edmond's College, University of Cambridge, Volume I (New Rochelle, NY: Iona College, 1991), pp. 189–96.

49. Pope John Paul II, *On Social Concern*, #39; NCCB, *Economic Justice for All*, #66, and chapter 4, "A New American Experiment: Partnership for the Public Good."

50. The principle of participation is developed in Paul VI, *A Call to Action (Octagesima Adveniens)* (1971), #22, 24; Synod of Bishops, *Justice in the World*, pp. 291, 298–99; John Paul II, *On the Hundredth Anniversary*, #43, 46–48; and throughout NCCB, *Economic Justice for All*. Theological reflection on participation would include: John Donaghy, "Justice as Participation: An Emerging Understanding," in Natale and McHugh, eds., *Proceedings of the First International Conference on Social Values*, Volume II, pp. 61–79; George Weigel, "Catholicism and Democracy," *Washington Quarterly* 12 (Autumn, 1989), pp. 5–28; and David Hollenbach, *Justice, Peace, and Human Rights: American Catholic Social Ethics in a Pluralistic Context* (New York: Crossroad, 1988).

51. NCCB, *Economic Justice for All*, #71.

52. John Paul II, *On the Hundredth Anniversary*, #46–48; NCCB, *Economic Justice for All*, #77, passim; and Canadian Conference of Catholic Bishops, *Ethical Choices and Political Challenges: Ethical Reflections on the Future of Canada's Socio-economic Order* in David M. Byers, ed., *Justice in the Marketplace: Collected Statements of the Vatican and the U.S. Catholic Bishops on Economic Policy, 1891–1984* (Washington, DC: United States Catholic Conference, 1985), p. 485.

53. Synod of Bishops, *Justice in the World*, pp. 298–99.

54. The principle of subsidiarity was first articulated by Pope Pius XI, *After Forty Years (Quadragesimo Anno)*, (1931), in O'Brien and Shannon, eds., *Catholic Social Thought*, #79–80. See also John Paul II, *On the Hundredth Anniversary*, #48; and NCCB, *Economic Justice for All*, #99, 124.

55. Pope John XXIII, *Christianity and Social Progress (Mater et Magistra)*, (1961) in O'Brien and Shannon, eds., *Catholic Social Thought*, #51–67; NCCB, *Economic Justice for All*, #124. See Kammer, *Doing Faithjustice*, pp. 80, 83.

56. NCCB, *Economic Justice for All*, 52, 85–91, passim.

57. Ibid., #24.

58. Second Vatican Council, "Pastoral Constitution on the Church in the Modern World," (1965) in O'Brien and Shannon, eds., *Catholic Social Thought*, #4.

59. The pertinent *Medellín Conference Documents* can be found in O'Brien and Shannon, eds., *Renewing the Earth*, pp. 549–84. The Puebla Conference Documents can be found in John Eagleson and Philip Sharper, eds., *Puebla and Beyond: Documentation and Commentary*. Translated by John Drury. (Maryknoll, NY: Orbis Books, 1979).

60. These documents are in O'Brien and Shannon, eds., *Catholic Social Thought*. Pope John Paul II returns to the question of development and the "social mortgage" on private property in his encyclical, *On the Hundredth Anniversary*,

#30–46. See also Pope Paul VI, *A Call to Action (Octogesima Adveniens)*, #23.

61. Peter J. Henriot, *Opting for the Poor: A Challenge for North Americans* (Washington, DC: Center for Concern, 1990), p. 24.

62. NCCB, *Economic Justice for All*, #86. Henriot, *Opting for the Poor*, p. 25, distinguishes between the "needy" and the poor. The needy, of course, should not be neglected, but the poor require our committed attention and action.

63. Henriot, *Opting for the Poor*, p. 26.

64. This is the description of this principle preferred by Kammer, *Doing Faithjustice*, chapter 4.

65. This is the critical question in the title of Ronald Sider's book *Rich Christians in a Hungry World*. It is based primarily on the parable of the rich man who overlooked a poor beggar at his gate in Lk 16:19-31 and secondarily on the parable of the rich fool in Lk 12:13-21. In chapter 5 Sider explores a "Biblical attitude toward property and wealth." He concludes that, according to Scripture, possessions, although not innately evil, are "positively dangerous because they often encourage unconcern for the poor, because they lead to strife and war, and because they seduce people into forsaking God" (122).

66. NCCB, *The Challenge of Peace*, in O'Brien and Shannon, eds., *Catholic Social Thought*, #71-78, 111-21. See NCCB, *The Harvest of Justice Is Sown in Peace* in Gerard F. Powers, et al., eds., *Peacemaking: Moral and Policy Challenges for a New World* (Washington, DC: United States Catholic Conference, 1994), pp. 317-19.

67. Paul VI, *On the Development of Peoples*, #87, 76-77. John Paul II, *On Social Concern*, #39, and *On the Hundredth Anniversary*, #52.

68. See Vatican II, "The Pastoral Constitution on the Church in the Modern World," #85; and NCCB, *The Harvest of Justice Is Sown in Peace*, pp. 316-17.

69. Vatican II, "The Pastoral Constitution on the Church in the Modern World," #80.

70. NCCB, *The Challenge of Peace*, #160-61, 188, passim.

71. Ibid., #186, 188.

72. This is not to conclude, however, that the Persian Gulf War was morally justified nor that it was conducted justly. See, for example, Thomas C. Fox, *Iraq: Military Victory, Moral Defeat* (Kansas City, MO: Sheed and Ward, 1991); and Kenneth L. Vaux, *Ethics and the Gulf War* (Boulder, CO: Westview Press, 1992). The U.S. bishops themselves differed on these questions.

73. See, for example, *On the Hundredth Anniversary*, #52. This has been a constant theme of his World Day of Peace statements and of his talks and homilies on his various journeys. In my opinion, however, the Pope missed an important opportunity in not highlighting violence and war, along with capital punishment, abortion, and euthanasia, in his encyclical *The Gospel of Life*, in *Origins* 24 (April 6, 1995), pp. 690-727.

74. Vatican II, "The Pastoral Constitution on the Church in the Modern World," #81. See also John Paul II, *On Social Concern*, #23-24.

75. See Vatican II, "The Pastoral Constitution on the Church in the Modern World," #82; NCCB, *The Challenge of Peace*, #235-244; John Paul II, *On Social Concern*, #41-45; NCCB, *The Harvest of Justice Is Sown in Peace*, p. 325, passim.

76. See John Paul II, *On Social Concern*, #25, 26, 34; *On the Hundredth Anniversary*, #37; "Peace with All Creation," *Origins* 19 (1990), pp. 465-68. Drew Christiansen, "Ecology, Justice, and Development," *Theological Studies* 51 (1990), pp. 68-71, indicates that the Pope's treatment of the issue in *On Social*

Concern is significant. While it is certainly good that the Pope is aware of the issue and addresses it in the context of development, I do not think the Pope gives the issue the attention it deserves. The Philippine Bishops Conference has issued a very thoughtful Pastoral Letter on ecology titled, "What Is Happening to Our Beautiful Land?" (1988) but it is not widely available.

77. See, for example, Pax Christi's Peacemaker Pamphlet Series and Mary Ann Luke, ed., *Pilgrims and Seekers: Saints without Pedestals* (Erie, PA: Pax Christi USA, 1995); and Michael True, *Justice Seekers, Peace Makers: 32 Portraits in Courage* (Mystic, CT: Twenty-Third Publications, 1985) and *To Construct Peace: 30 More Justice Seekers and Peace Makers*, (Ibid., 1992).

78. See James W. Douglass, *Resistance and Contemplation: The Way of Liberation* (New York: Dell Publishing Co., 1972).

79. See I Kings 3:3-15 where Solomon asks God for the gift of wisdom.

80. Curran, "Conversion: The Central Moral Message of Jesus," pp. 50–52.

81. See John F. Kavanaugh, *Following Christ in a Consumer Society: The Spirituality of Cultural Resistance*, Revised Edition. (Maryknoll, NY: Orbis Books, 1991).

82. Adam Daniel Finnerty, *No More Plastic Jesus: Global Justice and Christian Lifestyle* (Maryknoll, NY: Orbis Books, 1977), p. 97.

83. Sider, *Rich Christians*, pp. 92–93.

84. NCCB, *Economic Justice for All*, #97–98; John Paul II, *On Human Work (Laborens Exercens)* in O'Brien and Shannon, eds., *Catholic Social Thought*, #6, 9, 10.

85. NCCB, *Economic Justice for All*, #92.

86. See Joseph A. Grassi, *Broken Bread and Broken Bodies: The Lord's Supper and World Hunger* (Maryknoll, NY: Orbis Books, 1985); and Monica K. Hellwig, *The Eucharist and the Hunger of the World* (New York: Paulist Press, 1976).

87. "While the Church is bound to give witness to justice, she recognizes that everyone who ventures to speak to people about justice must first be just in their eyes. Hence we must undertake an examination of the modes of acting and of the possessions and lifestyle found within the Church herself." Synod of Bishops, *Justice in the World*, p. 295.

88. Arthur Simon, *Christian Faith and Public Policy: No Grounds for Divorce* (Grand Rapids, MI: Wm. B. Eerdmans Publishing Co., 1987), p. 12 and chapter 5.

89. See J. Milburn Thompson, "A Theological Perspective on Church and Politics in the United States," in Natale and McHugh, eds., *Proceedings of the First International Conference on Social Values* Volume II, pp. 37–44, at 39–41.

90. See Arthur Simon, *Christian Faith and Public Policy*, pp. 104–13. Arthur Simon is a founding member and past Executive Director of Bread for the World.

91. The following letter is based upon "Jesse Helms Mocks the Senate," *New York Times* (February 10, 1997), editorial.

92. See Gene Sharp, *The Politics of Nonviolent Action* Three Volumes, especially Volume II, *The Methods of Nonviolent Action* (Boston: Porter Sargent Publishers, 1973); and Elizabeth Morgan, *Global Poverty and Personal Responsibility* (New York: Paulist Press, 1989), pp. 148–53.